Prentice Hall
in International

D1463091

Enduring Questions in Changing Times

Charles W. Kegley, Jr., *Series Editor*

In the era of globalization in the twenty-first century, people cannot afford to ignore the impact of international relations on their future. From the value of one's investments to the quality of the air one breathes, international relations matter. The instantaneous spread of communications throughout the world is making for the internationalization of all phenomena, while the distinction between the domestic and the foreign, the public and the private, and the national and the international is vanishing. Globalization is an accelerating trend that is transforming how virtually every field of study in the social sciences is being investigated and taught.

Contemporary scholarship has made bold advances in understanding the many facets of international relations. It has also laid a firm foundation for interpreting the major forces and factors that are shaping the global future.

To introduce the latest research findings and theoretical commentary, a new publication series has been launched. *Prentice Hall Studies in International Relations: Enduring Questions in Changing Times* presents books that focus on the issues, controversies, and trends that are defining the central topics dominating discussion about international relations.

Exorcising the Ghost of Westphalia

Building World Order in the New Millennium

Charles W. Kegley, Jr.

University of South Carolina

Gregory A. Raymond

Boise State University

Prentice
Hall

Upper Saddle River, New Jersey 07458

Library of Congress Cataloging-in-Publication Data

Kegley, Charles W.
    Exorcising the ghost of Westphalia : building world order in the new millennium /
Charles W. Kegley, Jr., Gregory A. Raymond.—1st ed.
        p. cm. — (Prentice Hall Studies in international relations. Enduring questions in
    changing times)
    Includes bibliographical references and index.
    ISBN 0-13-016302-3 (pbk.)
        1. Thirty Years' War, 1618–1648—History. 2. Peace of Westphalia (1648)—History. 3.
International relations—Sources. I. Raymond, Gregory A. II. Title. III. Series.
JZ1330 .K44 2002
940.2'41—dc21
                                                        00-069884

VP, Editorial Director: Laura Pearson
Senior Acquisitions Editor: Heather Shelstad
Assistant Editor: Brian Prybella
Editorial/production supervision and interior design: Mary Araneo
Director of Marketing: Beth Gillett Mejia
Editorial Assistant: Jessica Drew
Prepress and Manufacturing Buyer: Ben Smith
Cover Art Director: Jayne Conte
Cover Designer: Bruce Kenselaar
Interior Image Specialist: Beth Boyd
Manager, Rights and Permissions: Kay Dellosa
Director, Image Resource Center: Melinda Reo
Photo Researcher: Teri Stratford

This book was set in 10/12 New Baskerville by A & A Publishing Services, Inc.,
and was printed and bound by Courier Companies, Inc. The cover was
printed by Phoenix Color Corp.

© 2002 by Pearson Education, Inc.
Upper Saddle River, New Jersey 07458

Printed in the United States of America

10 9 8 7 6 5 4 3 2 1

ISBN   0-13-016302-3

PRENTICE-HALL INTERNATIONAL (UK) LIMITED, *London*
PRENTICE-HALL OF AUSTRALIA PTY. LIMITED, *Sydney*
PRENTICE-HALL CANADA INC., *Toronto*
PRENTICE-HALL HISPANOAMERICANA, S.A., *Mexico*
PRENTICE-HALL OF INDIA PRIVATE LIMITED, *New Delhi*
PRENTICE-HALL OF JAPAN, INC., *Tokyo*
PEARSON EDUCATION ASIA PTE. LTD., *Singapore*
EDITORA PRENTICE-HALL DO BRASIL, LTDA., *Rio de Janeiro*

In loving expectations for my daughter:
Suzanne Mitchell Douglas (1969–   )

CWK

In loving memory of my maternal grandmother:
Julia Franko Skalicky (1889–1966)

GAR

Contents

About the Authors

Charles W. Kegley, Jr., (Ph.D., Syracuse University) is Pearce Professor of International Relations at the University of South Carolina. A past president of the International Studies Association (1993–1994), he has held appointments at Georgetown University, the University of Texas, and Rutgers University. With Eugene R. Wittkopf, his books include *World Politics: Trend and Transformation, Eighth Edition,* (2001); *The Global Agenda: Issues and Perspectives, Sixth Edition* (2001); *American Foreign Policy: Pattern and Process, Fifth Edition* (1996); and *The Nuclear Reader: Strategy, Weapons, War, Second Edition* (1989). He was also the editor, with Wittkopf, of the first editions of *The Future of American Foreign Policy* (1992) and *The Domestic Source of American Foreign Policy* (1988). Kegley also published *The Long Postwar Peace: Contending Explanations and Projections* (1991) and *International Terrorism: Characteristics, Causes, and Controls* (1990) as well as many articles in a wide range of scholarly journals.

Gregory A. Raymond (Ph.D., University of South Carolina) is director of the Honors College at Boise State University. Selected as the Idaho Professor of the Year (1994) by the Carnegie Foundation for the Advancement of Teaching, his books include *The Other Western Europe: A Comparative Analysis of the Smaller Democracies, Second Edition* (1983); *Third World Policies of Industrialized Nations* (1982); and *Conflict Resolution and the Structure of the State System* (1980). He has also published many articles on foreign policy and world politics in various scholarly journals. Raymond has spoken on international issues at numerous professional conferences throughout Europe, the United States, and Latin America.

Together Kegley and Raymond have previously coauthored *From War to Peace* (2002), *How Nations Make Peace* (1999), *A Multipolar Peace? Great-Power Politics in the Twenty-First Century* (1994); *When Trust Breaks Down: Alliance Norms and World Politics* (1990); and *International Events and the Comparative Analysis of Foreign Policy* (1975). They have also coauthored over two dozen articles in a diverse range of periodicals, including *International Studies Quarterly,* the *Journal of Conflict Resolution,* the *Journal of Peace Research, International Interactions,* and the *Harvard International Review.* Both Kegley and Raymond were Pew Faculty Fellows at the John F. Kennedy School of Government at Harvard University.

Preface

The dawn of the twenty-first century has prompted scholars and policy makers alike to ask whether the new age will be more peaceful than its predecessor. Changing conditions always entice thoughtful people to reevaluate the conventional wisdom of their age. As the first years of the new millennium are etched into history, several competing visions of how to build a new world order are emerging from sober reflections on the turbulent twentieth century. Our book frames the debate over the ideals and institutions most capable of protecting humankind from the curse of armed conflict.

To illuminate the options for maintaining peace, we take as a point of departure the precedent-setting agreements established by the Peace of Westphalia that ended the Thirty Years' War in 1648. Considered the most important peace settlement of the last millennium,[1] the treaties crafted at Münster and Osnabrück have charted the course of international politics for the next 350 years. They deserve close scrutiny because they serve as a model against which all subsequent peace settlements have been judged. As one scholar observes, "The Congresses of Münster and Osnabrück, which produced the Treaties of Westphalia, were the first of their kind. Europe had not previously witnessed a multilateral diplomatic gathering that was designed both to terminate a Pan-European War and to build some sort of order out of the chaos into which Europe had increasingly fallen since the late fifteenth century.[2]

Readers familiar with our previous scholarly endeavors may be somewhat puzzled to discover that we have selected a single case—The Thirty Years' War and the Peace of Westphalia—as the springboard for analyzing alternative architectures for world order in the twenty-first century. Our careers have been dedicated to the comparative study of foreign policy and of the relationship of transnational norms to international security, for the purpose of deriving insights and nomothetic generalizations about behavioral patterns in world history, using primarily quantitative methods to analyze cross-national and longitudinal aggregate data. Our prior collaborative books, *International Events and the Comparative Analysis of Foreign Policy* (1975), *When Trust Breaks Down: Alliance Norms and World Politics* (1990), *A Multipolar Peace* (1994), *How Nations Make Peace* (1999), and *From War to Peace* (2002) have drawn from either comparative case studies or, more commonly, from statistical analyses of macro-quantitative indicators. So why, now, do we concentrate on a single case from the distant past in order to think theoretically about the preconditions for international security in the future?

The answer stems from our conviction, buttressed by our experiences as Pew Faculty Fellows in International Relations at Harvard University, that a carefully selected single case study is a powerful *educational* tool, or heuristic, to generate propositions about the general properties of stable world orders, and without a doubt the case we select meets the criteria of salience, permanence, and impact that stimulates critical thinking about causal inferences and policy prescriptions to be drawn. Moreover, we are persuaded by the argument that the most useful pedagogy is to instruct by beginning with a treatment of a key historical period or event in order to tease out the theoretical insights and policy dilemmas that that case study offers, rather than beginning with theory and then applying it to practice. Introducing theory by first providing history permits an instructor to raise awareness about the important controversies embedded in the narrative so that they later can be systematically and rigorously examined by reference to the more formal models and theoretical traditions available in the scholarly study of international relations. Rather than "subjecting students to staid theoretical and disciplinary debates," our objective is to illuminate the value of historical interpretation for building theory inductively from a heuristic case that provokes questions about the linkages "between history and theory, and between theory and practice."[3]

What makes the Thirty Years' War and the Peace of Westphalia so valuable for more intensive study is that the details surrounding the anarchy prevailing in the mid-seventeenth century bear an uncanny resemblance to today's international conditions when, as one recent headline in the *International Herald Tribune* proclaimed, "Globalization Sparks Another Anarchist Revival."[4] Still other parallels between the code of diplomatic conduct in 1648 and today are evident. Consider, as an example, Robert Kaplan's prediction of *The Coming Anarchy*[5] at the very time when a global culture is crystallizing and serious attention is being directed toward creating institutions for meaningful global governance. The Westphalian Peace stands out as critical, even today. As Fareed Zakaria, the editor of *Foreign Affairs*, summarizes, we need to pay careful attention to Westphalia because this settlement "ushered in the modern state system that governs the world—the very state system that is now, 350 years later, being undermined by transnational forces like the euro, the Internet and Amnesty International."[6] Hence, we purposely have chosen to use a rather detailed account of the origins of that system-transforming peace settlement to base our conclusions about its effects in the future.

We posit that it is time to jettison many of the problematic tenets on which the Westphalian approach to international order has precariously rested and suggest how a new architecture might be built that combines the positive elements of the Westphalian legacy with new pillars to enhance global security in the twenty-first century. If our endeavors provoke scholars, students and policy makers to question old diplomatic formulas and to join us in thinking about new approaches for new realities, this book will have served its primary educational goal.

Many people have contributed to the development of this book, and their assistance is appreciated. We are especially indebted to the professional staff at the archives, libraries, and museums in Austria, Denmark, France, Italy, Germany, The Netherlands, Spain, and Sweden who helped sharpen our understanding of the Thirty Years' War and the Peace of Westphalia. In addition, we are grateful for the two referees who provided blind critical reviews of the first draft of our manuscript and whose constructive suggestions gave us confidence in the merits of this intellectual endeavor and helped us improve the presentation; we have learned since that Robert A. Denemark of the University of Delaware, Richard A. Falk of Princeton University, and John Vasquez of Vanderbilt University are the experts for whom we are indebted for their valuable advice. Moreover, special thanks must go to Tahir Cevik, Ruth Cooper, Gerhard Sagic, Holly Gastineau-Grimes, Min Ye, and Fehrettin Súmer for their assistance in the preparation of this manuscript.

Finally, Gregory Raymond would like to express his gratitude for the constant encouragement and cheerful support of his wife, Christine, and Charles Kegley wishes to thank Debbie, his soul-mate, for her loving support for this project.

Exorcising the Ghost
of Westphalia

Introduction

The end of the Thirty Years' War can be seen as one of the major turning points in modern history.[1] The wars of religion in Europe ended, the Holy Roman Empire no longer threatened to establish hegemony over the continent, and the modern state system based on sovereignty came into being. The Peace of Westphalia not only brought the Thirty Years' War to a conclusion; it ushered in a new diplomatic era whose influence still colors a considerable swath of contemporary world politics. Indeed, the rules for statecraft drafted in the mid-seventeenth century still define the basic norms governing relations between nations, and the diplomatic vocabulary used to discuss international affairs today was born from the crucible of this system-transforming treaty.

The Peace of Westphalia illustrates the fateful consequences of hard choices about the means to lasting peace. Some regard the Westphalian system as an innovative response to chronic European crises, a source of stability for successive generations at a time when conditions were not hospitable to that achievement. For example, Charles Giraud depicts the peace settlement as the source of "a community of destinies and of interests...born of facts but consecrated by law."[2] Not everyone agrees with his assessment, however; others critique the Westphalian system as devoid of substance, exhibiting "not the shadow of a constructive idea" for international order.[3] Given this controversy, a fresh evaluation of the Westphalian design for modern international relations is needed to sharpen current thinking about how to build a new world order. At issue is whether such an enduring set of principles for international politics is, on the whole, capable of meeting the needs for order with justice in the present epoch of international history.

Thus, our objective is not to provide yet another history of the Thirty Years' War and Westphalian Peace; nor do we purport to provide an original account based on newly discovered primary sources or a revisionist interpretation of the diplomatic record. Rather, *Exorcising the Ghost of Westphalia* looks to the norm-defining precedents of the distant past for the purpose of visualizing the future. It examines events and decisions at a critical juncture in the early seventeenth century that created Westphalia's skeletal blueprint for future international relations, in order to evaluate how we might best respond to the international dilemmas facing the global community at the start of the twenty-first century in a world in which the Westphalian "ghost" remains the primary scheme for organizing the conduct of international relations.

By taking seriously the questions of the historical origins of the modern state system, our book provides the important historical background on the Westphalian Peace so as to expand awareness of the foundations for the contemporary international politics and the reasons why it has the characteristics it does. We believe that this sort of historical analysis is what is often missing in the contemporary debate about the Westphalian system. In particular, by reexamining the Thirty Years' War we have a basis for understanding the nature of the contemporary international system. In addition, by looking at trends which are unfolding today we have a basis for evaluating the extent to which the Westphalia system is currently undergoing challenge and is deteriorating under pressure from profound changes in world politics. From this historical point of departure, our aim is to show how a very old subject becomes a subject about the present and the future. At Westphalia in 1648, a set of general rules for the conduct of international relations was concretized in the peace treaties. As we show, those rules make it difficult for the world to deal with many kinds of contemporary problems, and our critique of the Westphalian settlement rests on the belief that these kinds of global problems for which Westphalia is dysfunctional have grown most dramatically over the years and are therefore in the most dire need of attention. Westphalia, which we metaphorically label a "ghost," is best envisioned as a imperfect solution to a set of problems in the distant past which has a long shadow, shading the present and future in ways that inhibit the maintenance of peaceful international relations. In advancing the argument about the need to exorcize the Westphalian ghost, we aver that the time has come to revise those Westphalian rules to allow for different kinds of interactions to occur on the global stage. The rationale for our approach is grounded in the striking parallels between the seventeenth century and the early twenty-first century, which, we submit, renders the former instructive for evaluating the latter. Consider the following similarities:

- both the mid-seventeenth and twenty-first centuries were turning points in history, critical junctures during which one pattern of international relations was in the process of ending and a new pattern was forming;
- both weathered sweeping changes that created enormous confusion, and

both periods experienced a growing number of issues on the political agendas of the day, creating further uncertainty about the true character of international relations and its core challenges;

- both were fraught with a "clash of civilizations," a "clash of moral values," and a "clash of vision" between advocates of international unity through global governance and proponents of national autonomy through sovereign independence;
- both were times when some failing nations were subdividing into smaller units while others were uniting to become great powers;
- both were periods when the relationship of religion to politics and church to state were contested, and when authority and sovereignty were topics of much controversy;
- both were periods when the status of the core concept of the sovereign territorial state was much in doubt;
- both were times of extreme crisis for millions of civilians seeking sanctuary from the ravages of war, creating a mass exodus that produced an international refugee crisis;
- both were periods when the topic of humanitarian intervention received serious consideration;
- in both periods, channels of contact among distant peoples were growing exponentially, owing to an unprecedented revolution in information technology, with the printing press then and the computer now;
- in both periods, goods, money, and ideas began to cross borders with increasing ease, thereby reducing the capacity of governments to manage their domestic affairs and external relations.

Given the pace of change, it is not a coincidence that neither epoch had yet to acquire a name or label to describe itself. For the mid-1600s there was a vague sense that what was to become later known as the Middle Ages was disappearing, and something known as "modern" was coming into being, but at the time people did not have an intellectual title for their age.[4] Likewise, at the start of the new millennium, people have not agreed on the name for their period, referring to it only by the unsatisfactory term of "post-Cold War." Neither period enjoyed a consensus about its primary properties. Because of these and other similarities, we submit that our examination of the policy dilemmas facing peacemakers in 1648 at the Congresses of Westphalia can illuminate the choices, practical and ethical, that confront those seeking lasting peace today, when certainties about the most stable institutional architecture for world order are as elusive as they were 350 years ago.

The philosopher and mathematician Gottfried Wilhelm Leibniz once commented that "the present is big with the future, the future might be read in the past." In expressing this sentiment, he highlighted the underlying principle that informs our study: the Peace of Westphalia is instructive for studying world order issues because there is a propensity for habitual foreign policy practices to crystallize as new rules *for* behavior. What is the norm in a purely descriptive, model sense tends, over time, to change into a norm in a prescriptive, deontological sense. To put it another way, the "is" of international life has a striking tendency to evolve into an "ought." Behavior that becomes customary is one of the primary authors of the ideas that eventually reign, and our constructivist interpretation of the origins of Westphalian conceptions is based upon this analytic principle.

The Thirty Years' War and the Peace Congresses of Westphalia, we shall argue, exemplify this process. The former was an imprinting experience that shaped the consensus about rules for statecraft which emerged in the latter. The competition and sharp practices that became entrenched between 1618 and 1648 had a direct bearing on the code of foreign-policy conduct that was crafted at Münster and Osnabrück and would guide state behavior for the next three and a half centuries. Our premise is that we can better understand the implications of the choices we make today on how to build a stable, just world order by deconstructing the normative consensus about international politics that emerged from Westphalia in the aftermath of diplomatic practices that arose during the Thirty Years' War.

As we shall argue, there are many reasons to question the suitability of the Westphalian approach to the preservation of peace under prevailing circumstances. *Exorcising the Ghost of Westphalia: Building World Order in the New Millennium* does more than merely frame the debate over what ideals and institutions ought to shape the next century. It advances a thesis. After evaluating the peace treaties signed in Münster and Osnabrück that brought the Thirty Years' War to a close, we conclude that the Westphalian settlement was flawed then and that it remains dangerous today. Simply put, in its effort to create a stable international order, Westphalia went too far in liberating states from moral restraints. Expediency overshadowed justice. By legitimating the drive for military power and the use of force, and by placing international stability on the precarious foundation of the successful operation of the balance of power, Westphalia enabled anarchy and amorality to take root in international affairs. The first task of a security regime is to create order; its second is to create justice: "only an order which implicates justice can achieve a stable peace."[5] The Westphalian blueprint failed to accomplish either goal.

If the Westphalian rudimentary architectural skeleton was deficient for the conditions that existed more than three centuries ago, it appears even less suitable for the conditions of complex interdependence that now prevail. The once impermeable, hard-shell boundaries separating states have become porous. The Westphalian rules for statecraft have lost their capacity to speak to and address the principal security and welfare needs of humanity. Westphalia is anachronistic and ineffectual. And yet, the ghost of Westphalia still walks, haunting the relations among nations and weakening the prospects for a twenty-first century peace.

As we demonstrate in our concluding chapters, a number of trends have taken root and converged which are transforming before our eyes the environment in which international relations is now being conducted. We agree with John Steinbruner that "Although the full implications are still obscure, it is increasingly apparent that contemporary societies are encountering a major deflection in the course of their development," and that these global changes make imperative new principles of global security.[6] Collectively, these trends have created a condition known as globalization that has rendered the Westphalian conception of international diplomacy increasingly impractical and dysfunctional. "Both critics and proponents of globalization argue that the increasing integration of national societies has led to a decrease in the economic, political, and cultural autonomy of nation-states, or the end of their national sovereignty."[7] The retreat of the sovereign state and the advent of an interdependent era of globalization presages the coming end of the Westphalian conception as a useful blueprint for international security. We argue that it is time to exorcise this ghost, to expel a troublesome and menacing structure that is for contemporary realities more a curse than a cure. In its place, we propose an approach to world order that emphasizes the advantages of global governance guided by a moral consensus, one that involves a complex, interlocking mix of supranational, national, and private subnational actors. Our aim is to develop this argument and set the stage for investigating alternative pathways to peace and prosperity.

PART I

The Thirty Years' War and the Genesis of the Modern International System: A Prologue to the Future

To see the future, the first step is to look back to the past immediately prior to the birth of modernism—the wars in medieval Europe.

—Robert D. Kaplan

Throughout history, war has been a potent force for change. In its wake lie destruction, despair, and devastated lives. Understandably, much of history has been the story of humankind's quest to avoid war by constructing a stable international order. Paradoxically, the horrors of war have often stimulated creative innovation and change. "War," writes Jim Hoagland, "is the formative experience for most important nations and many governing institutions. After doing their worst, humans frequently find in the ashes they have produced reasons to think differently about themselves and their neighbors."[1] As Benjamin Franklin once observed, "the things that hurt, instruct." Wars provoke change in part because they painfully remind people what is important in life and force them "to make moral choices."[2]

When wars end, the peacemakers are inclined to build from such painful learning experiences by thinking afresh about the principles and practices that can preserve peace so as to prevent a resumption of the terrifying events they just experienced. Indeed, it is through the deliberations at post-war peace congresses that most changes in the international society's "diplomatic culture," the "common stock of ideas and values possessed by official representatives,"[3] have been born. New norms emerge as reigning ideas fade away. "The spread of new norms or ideas and the discrediting of old ones are related [because] when one set of norms are exhausted or lose their legitimacy, opportunities for the spread of new norms open up."[4]

This is especially true of history's major wars—the largest, deadliest, and longest wars that involve the most participants. These clashes are the most powerful catalysts of historical change, ushering in transformations in belief and behavior that profoundly alter international relations. It is this characteristic of warfare on a grand scale that leads us to conduct a case study of the Thirty Years' War and the Peace of Westphalia.

The reasons for concentrating on this war and peace settlement should be self-evident to the student of international affairs. Without fear of exaggeration, it can be said that the events of 1618–1648 shattered one pattern of international affairs and introduced a new one—a pattern which even today, like a ghost, haunts contemporary international politics. The Thirty Years' War and Westphalian Peace are the bridge between the old world and the new, between the medieval and the modern. This period truly revolutionized the conduct of diplomacy, jettisoning one set of agents and structures for another, and leaving behind a new body of rules in place of an older code of conduct. Westphalia, born of a brutal war lasting three decades, produced a scheme for international security that has endured for more than three and one-half centuries. As Richard Falk puts it, it was through "the Peace of Westphalia in 1648 that ended the Thirty Years' War that the modern system of states was formally established as the dominant world order framework, and it was not for another century or so that it seemed possible to appreciate that indeed Westphalia had provided a definitive threshold—of course, overgeneralized and simplified, but yet a convenient shorthand by which to situate the transition from the medieval to the modern. This transition has been generally treated as one of global scope."[5]

As important as the Peace of Westphalia is as the basis for the contemporary system of international relations, it would, of course, be hyperbole to assert that the entire edifice from which the modern rules of interstate interaction originate began exclusively with the Peace of Westphalia. That claim would certainly be an exaggeration, for, to be sure, from a long-term historical perspective many of the ideas and rules embedded in the Westphalian treaties originated in ideas, ideals, and institutions that predated the Thirty Years' War and the Westphalian settlement. Indeed, all the architecture for the modern international system did not originate in Westphalia, and, for that matter, much of what we witness today derives from practices and innovations that occurred much earlier in history and outside of the European context.

In highlighting the unassailable fact that the basic structure of international relations is a product of the Peace of Westphalia that codified evolving practices in Europe in the seventeenth century and then spread throughout the globe, we need to acknowledge the potential danger of introducing a Eurocentric bias. For example, sovereignty was not an exclusively European concept; it existed and was acknowledged in texts in China and India in the first millennium B.C.E., and Hsun Tzu (a student of Lao Tzu) discussed the anarchy problematique, the role of alliances in the balance of international power, the conditions requiring humanitarian intervention, and the ways that free trade might help to mitigate violence among sovereign entities by binding their commercial interests together. Likewise, Indian scholars wrote in Sanskrit text as far back as 200 B.C.E. about the ceaseless competition among aggressor states and how their violence could be controlled by alliance structures and norms supporting the sanctity of treaties.[6]

Thus in concentrating on Westphalia in order to trace the historical origins of the contemporary international system and to identify the characteristics that still define the basic rules for the conduct of international relations, we ask our readers to keep in mind that the long history of international relations includes elements that predated the seventeenth century and that were rooted in cultures and experiences outside the European cauldron from which today's rules for international relations emanated. Hence, although much of what was codified in the Peace of Westphalia was not new and had abundant precedents both within the European system and beyond it, we still concentrate on that general peace settlement which, in the final analysis, was the last great set of European organizing agreements before Europe began to take over much of the rest of the planet; it was that Westphalian blueprint for international relations that enabled Europe to spread the Westphalian diplomatic code of conduct throughout the world, and it is the Westphalian ghost which most influences thinking about international relations today.[7]

The three chapters in Part I focus on the Thirty Years' War, from which the existing architecture for twenty-first century international order still derives much of its inspiration and texture. This war made states, and these newly made states became the basic building blocks in the Westphalian Peace settlement which transformed international relations. Ironically, the war itself "proved fruitless in the end. More significant, indeed momentous, were the treaty concluded at mid-century and the cultural consequences of the war."[8] Simply put, "Westphalia signals the consolidation, not the creation *ex nihilo,* of the modern system. It was not an instant metamorphosis, as elements of sovereign statehood had indeed been accumulating for three centuries. Even modernity's victory after Westphalia must be qualified, for some medieval anomalies persisted. But consummate fissures in history are rare, and Westphalia is as clean as historical faults come."[9]

Chapter 1, "The Causes of the Thirty Years' War," develops the thesis that the origins of major wars shape their character as well as the conclusions diplomats reach at the peace talks about the rules needed for a new world order. If the eminent historian Will Durant is correct in saying that "moral codes adjust themselves to environmental conditions,"[10] then the social, economic, and political conditions existing prior to the war's outbreak had much to do with the code of conduct that guided the belligerents. The cultural climate in Europe in 1648—heavily influenced by the Renaissance and Reformation, along with burgeoning prosperity fueled by trade and colonialism—had much to do with the temper of the war. Those conditions, we contend, were the genesis of the amoral conduct that followed.

Chapter 2, "The Evolutionary Course of the Thirty Years' War," extends this interpretation of the influence of environmental conditions on the emergent consensus about the rules for statecraft. We document how evolving practices during the fighting led to an increasingly ruthless philosophy as the various contestants escalated their brutality in a series of moves that made "holy wars" and battles of annihilation increasingly acceptable. Fueled by a revolution in military technology and tactics, the war encouraged the growth of absolute monarchs, privateer armies, military intervention into civil wars, the acceptance of deceit and betrayal of allies, and the expedient use of third parties for self-advantage. Moreover, how the belligerents acted ultimately altered their perceptions of how they ought to act. What the warriors practiced, they later, at the peace conferences, began to preach. The views that "might makes right," that "the end justifies the means," and that "necessity knows no laws," took root. Why the war lasted so long is investigated in the context of the hypothesis that as practices in warfare become widespread they tend to become accepted. As ruthless self-interested behavior became prevalent, even more belligerents assumed that this was how states ought to act. The more savage warfare to defeat the enemy became, the more obligatory those practices were perceived.

In Chapter 3, "The Costs of the Thirty Years' War," we evaluate the immediate and long-term consequences that resulted from the war. The impact of the Thirty Years' War on the countries and principalities that waged it was enormous. Many were converted into highly centralized military monarchies organized for fighting one another, which enabled kings and aristocrats to rule over their subjects with few constraints. Not only politically, but economically, morally, and spiritually, European civic culture collapsed; in its place arose a Hobbesian "war of all against all," where a set of warlord states recognizing no authority above them wielded armed force as a personal tool. True, thirty years of perpetual warfare removed militant religious competition from the landscape, but at a significant cost—amorality became a way of diplomatic life, armed conflict was now considered normal, and cosmopolitan unity and supranational governance were condemned as treason to one's state. In short, the war gave birth to a culture of mistrust.

The Thirty Years' War is distinguished by its complexity. It involved multiple actors, mixed motives, changing ideologies, and crosscutting issues. Fateful decisions were made during the war that crystallized in a new age. The climate of intellectual opinion radically shifted, preparing the way for a new international system founded on a new set of rules. When the participants convened in Westphalia to construct a peace settlement, they took to the bargaining tables the lessons they had extracted from the battlefield. "The deplorable customs of the territorial princes thus received judicial sanction."[11] The complexities and difficulties experienced through the tumult of three decades of fighting bequeathed a revolutionary new regime for governing international affairs.

The story of Westphalia is thus the story of how a prolonged war contributed to the rise of the modern national state controlled by absolute centralized governments, wielding power of unprecedented proportions, and recognizing no superior authority to regulate their relations with one another. "The danger of anarchy prevailing among these separate and equal sovereignties was so evident that it stimulated thought about law and order through some overarching rule."[12] The three chapters in Part I illuminate how the causes, character, and consequences of the Thirty Years' War influenced the design for the rules of statecraft to which the peacemakers agreed at Westphalia in 1648.

In charting the origins of the Westphalian design for international relations, we proceed from the belief that today, for all the optimism about the prospects for peace with prosperity in the twenty-first century, we need to confront the reality that the international community still faces the same questions and dilemmas about the preconditions for world order that faced people in the seventeenth century. The relationship of a system of autonomous, sovereign independent territorial states to global order was crucial in 1648 and remains critical now. Ideas, culture, and norms structure international politics, and the long shadow of the Westphalian normative order continues to be cast across the future. What will be the ultimate consequences? Will rules for relations between states forged in the seventeenth century meet the needs of the new millennium? The inquiry that motivates our focus on the Thirty Years' War and the Peace of Westphalia centers on these questions because "It is widely recognized that the notion of international order that European modernity continually proposed and reproposed, at least since the Peace of Westphalia, is now in crisis."[13] Despite this, "the basic postulates of the Westphalian conception continue to hold."[14] By probing the genesis and nature of that set of principles for state-to-state interaction, "we may," in the words of Hersh Lauterpacht, "not only fathom the secret of its influence upon generations of scholars and men of affairs. We may [also], and that is no less important, obtain an insight into the persistent problems of international [relations] in the past, in the present, and, probably for some long time to come in the future."[15] It is on this journey to the future that we begin in Part I, with an account of the conditions from which the Westphalian ghost originates.

CHAPTER 1

The Causes of the Thirty Years' War

Thrice is he arm'd
that hath his quarrel just.
—Shakespeare, *Henry VI*

Every peace settlement is influenced by the origins, conduct, and outcome of military hostilities. The Peace of Westphalia was no exception. The treaties negotiated at Osnabrück and Münster that ended the Thirty Years' War in 1648 were shaped by the war's multiple causes, the bitter memories of the fighting, and the conditions surrounding the negotiations. "Making peace is about making choices," observes Joel Rosenthal, "and nearly all choices are based on competing underlying principles."[1] The Thirty Years' War was a wrenching experience for the belligerents, and when they gathered in Westphalia, they made choices based on contending moral principles suggested by their wartime experiences. This introductory chapter examines the background to these choices by tracing the origins of the Thirty Years' War.

An investigation of the Thirty Years' War of 1618–1648 may seem puzzling. Why concentrate on a war that occurred in the distant past, more than 350 years ago? The rationale stems from three noncontroversial assumptions: (1) Major wars are the crucible from which new approaches to international security are forged, and the Thirty Years' War perhaps more than any other laid the foundations for the rules that continue to shape international relations today; (2) the underlying causes of widely destructive, system-shattering wars such as the Thirty Years' War strongly influence the manner in which they are fought and the philosophies the participants take to the peace negotiations when the war ends; and (3) this particular case illuminates better than most how wartime experiences affect the climate of moral opinion that emerges about the necessary and sufficient conditions required to preserve peace—after the cannons have been silenced and the warring parties take on the challenge of designing a future international order stable enough to prevent another catastrophic war. A fourth assumption can be added: The Thirty Years' War is an ideal case study because its origins and outcome provide insight into the core theoretical, policy, and ethical questions regarding war and peace. In looking at the multiple causes of the Thirty Years' War, therefore, we can begin, through a reading of the historical background to its outbreak, to search for lessons about the relationship of the origins of this war to the ultimate origins of the international system's essential character. This episode forces us to think theoretically about the roots of war and global change, because the Thirty Years' War provided the fuel for "epochal change—the kinetic energy of ideas"[2] that led to the death of the medieval age and the corresponding birth of the modern system of contemporary international relations.

In looking at the determinants of this system-transforming war, we undertake an intellectual journey. To help us find our way, we need a roadmap, a set of guidelines for inspecting the combination of factors that led to the war's outbreak. These guidelines are provided by the impact that past decisions and practices made as conditioning influences on the beliefs and actions that contributed to the outbreak of this war. We ask you to explore the origins of the Thirty Years' War by examining the potential impact of previously evolving developments on the images of European leaders in the early seventeenth century. What conditions prevailed prior to the war, accepted as widely acknowledged features of international life in Europe, that produced the war's onset? How did emerging practices influence future actions? Let us look for clues in the coverage that follows, guided by the premise that the Thirty Years' War started in 1618 owing to certain causes;

> . . . but it went on so long that by the time the original causes were ready to be settled other vital interests had become involved, so that every year seemed to add to the difficulty of [preventing] it. So widespread and so conflicting were these interests that people almost gave up hope of a solution; and, as always happens during prolonged hostilities, [European] society began to adapt itself to war-conditions as if war, not peace, was to be the normal condition of mankind henceforward. . . . Thus the conditions—mental, moral, social, military and even economic—were not favorable to the efforts of diplomacy [to reach compromises through negotiation to prevent the war's outbreak].[3]

To begin our intellectual journey through the Thirty Years' War, we must start with some definitional preliminaries.

What was the "Thirty Years' War"? The very name is ambiguous because historians do not agree about how it should be described. "History [has] found no more appropriate name," notes Henry Kissinger,[4] "than its duration—the Thirty Years' War." Yet even this dating is problematic (see Table 1.1). Some historians refer to the "Thirty Years' War" as a way of identifying the most intense and destructive period of a series of wars that swept across Europe in the century between 1559, when the war between Spain and the Netherlands began, and 1659, when France and Spain signed the Treaty of the Pyrenees.[5] Other historians see the "Thirty Years' War" as an extension of the Spanish Hapsburgs's so-called imperialistic "Eighty Years' War" in the Low Countries to conquer the Netherlands and to prevent Dutch independence. Still other historians fix the onset of the Thirty Years' War with the 1598 Treaty of Nervin between France and Spain, while many others believe it began with the March 1609 War of the Jülich Succession. Depending on the starting and ending dates accepted, the "Thirty Years' War" might just as accurately be termed a war of thirty-nine, fifty, sixty-one, eighty, or one hundred years, even if by convention it refers to the series of wars, fought primarily in Germany and Bohemia, that began in 1618 and ended three decades later in 1648.

TABLE 1.1   A Chronology of Events Leading to Europe's First General War

---

1517	Publication of Martin Luther's Ninety-Five Theses engenders Protestant Reformation.
1520	The pope formally excommunicates Martin Luther.
1521	Martin Luther defends himself before the Imperial Diet.
1522	Knight's War is repressed.
1524	Peasants and citizens revolt in towns across Germany.
1530	Peace of Augsburg seeks to reconcile religious disputes.
1531	Lutheran princes create the Schmalkaldic League.
1534	Society of Jesus is founded, and the Jesuits begin a campaign to combat forces hostile to the Catholic Church.
1546–1555	Civil wars break out in the Holy Roman Empire.
1545–1563	The pope convenes the Council of Trent.
1555	The Peace of Augsburg puts an end to thirty years of sporadic confessional warfare in Germany between Catholics and Protestants, giving secular rulers the right (known as *cuius regio, eius religio*) to dictate whether their subjects' religion was to be Lutheran or Catholic.
1556	Charles V abdicates from Holy Roman Empire.
1559	War breaks out between the Netherlands and Spain.
1559	Treaty of Comtesis is signed.
1562–1581	War between Spain and the Netherlands continues.
1567	The Dutch revolt against King Philip II.
1572	St. Bartholomew's Day Massacre occurs in France.
1581	Union of Utrecht is created in the Netherlands.
1588	English defeat the Spanish Armada.
1589	Henry IV becomes King of France.
1593	Henry IV abandons Protestantism and converts to Roman Catholicism.
1598	France and Spain sign Treaty of Nervin.
1608	On 14 May, the Evangelical, or Protestant Union, is formed as an association for self-defense.

1609	In March, a new crisis begins with the death of John William, the childless Duke of Cleves-Jülich.
1609	On 9 July, the *Letter of Majesty (Majestätsbrief)* signed by Emperor Rudolf II grants full toleration to Protestants and creates a standing committee of the Estates, known as "the Defensors," to ensure that the settlement will be respected.
1609	On 10 July, Duke Maximilian of Bavaria forges the Catholic League alliance with its neighbors.
1609	Albert succeeds in bringing the war between Spain and the Dutch Republic to a temporary close with the *Twelve Years' Truce.*
1610	Henry IV of France is killed; Louis XIII becomes King of France.
1611	Emperor Rudolph tries to revoke the *Letter of Majesty* and to depose the Defensors by sending a small Hapsburg army into Prague, but a force of superior strength mobilizes against the invaders and the Estates resolve to depose Rudolph and offer the crown to Matthias.
1612	Emperor Rudolph dies.
1613	The Protestant Union signs a defensive treaty with the Dutch Republic.
1613	Spanish forces in Lombardy engage in combat with troops of the Duke of Savoy over the succession to the childless Duke of Mantua; the intervention lasts until 1617 and prevents Spain from militarily supporting the Holy Roman Emperor.
1617	Papal diplomats secure a temporary settlement of the Mantuan question, as Spanish troops aid Archduke Ferdinand.
1617	The Estates of both Bohemia and Hungary recognize Archduke Ferdinand unconditionally as designated King of Bohemia.
1618	Ferdinand initiates a protracted campaign to halt the concessions made to Protestants, and creates a Council of Regency for Bohemia that is overwhelmingly Catholic and that soon begins to censor works printed in Prague and to prevent non-Catholics from holding government office.
1618	The Defenestration of Prague signals the beginning of the Thirty Years' War.
1618	In May the Defensors created by the Letter of Majesty summon the Estates of the realm to convene.

Regardless of how the Thirty Years' War is dated, it has a lasting reputation as one of the most violent and revolutionary periods of European history. It occurred in an era historians have variously called "the Age of Power, the Crisis of the Seventeenth Century, the Transformation of Europe, the Age of Religious Wars, [and] the Era of the Military Revolution."[6] The Thirty Years' War was a bridge between the medieval and the modern worlds. To interpret its ultimate impact on the Westphalian Peace, a deeper examination of the war's causes is required, inasmuch as the causes of the Thirty Years' War were the conduit to the system-transforming rules for statecraft institutionalized after the war's termination. To make sense of the present, we must go back in time and contemplate how the origins of the Thirty Years' War were rooted in forces that continue to exert a powerful influence in the twenty-first century. [7] We can only understand how these influences affected the Westphalian settlement and, by extension, contemporary international politics, by examining how they shaped the decisions to start the Thirty Years' War.

THE CONTROVERSIAL ROOTS OF THE THIRTY YEARS' WAR

Historians often disagree about the causes of wars—and rarely has any war stemmed from a single precipitating event. This lack of consensus certainly applies to the Thirty Years' War, which was ignited by a multitude of causes. How to weigh their relative contribution has eluded scholarship. We possess rival hypotheses, not a definitive answer.

Despite the unresolved debates among diplomatic historians about the roots of the Thirty Years' War, they generally concur on at least one analytic principle: The Thirty Years' War is best interpreted by viewing it as a product of the profound long-term changes that were sweeping Europe in the twilight of the medieval period. The war emerged from multiple issues that were festering during the sixteenth century. The Renaissance and Reformation that ushered in the modern age provoked intense controversies about ideas, institutions, religious beliefs, and the distribution of political and religious authority. It is our premise that the causes, evolution, and impact of the Thirty Years' War require factoring into the account the mixed motives in play as the actors in this human tragedy tried to balance their concerns about security, reputation, liberties, and many other ideals and interests.

In tracing the mix of motives that led to decisions to wage war, many issues must be considered: What were the participants' objectives? Was there a hierarchy to their values that set priorities? If so, which preferences and ideals took precedence? Did the warring parties care most about religion, nationality, or wealth? How did the participants reconcile these values when they collided? By asking these questions, we hope to explore a wider set of issues. The documentary evidence about the participants' values illuminates the general properties of international decision making under conditions of crisis and uncertainty.

In observing the words and deeds of the participants, we should also entertain questions about the impact of the Thirty Years' War on the beliefs and behaviors of the people suffering under its yoke. This constructivist inquiry is necessary because it is probable that the war altered the values and motives of the participants as it evolved, making them at times conciliatory and compromising and at other historical turning points vindictive and violent. The trade-offs between competing visions and values in times of cataclysmic changes and challenges are characteristic of pivotal events in the evolution of the international system. This was apparent on the eve of the seventeenth century, and it is equally apparent today when, as in 1618, profound changes were forcing leaders to confront their ideals and interests, as they set priorities.

As circumstances changed to alter the character of the war, the belligerents' motives underwent equally profound changes. Consider the thesis that shall be advanced: that like a chameleon that changes color as its environment changes, what began primarily as a theological struggle, exacerbated by religious intolerance over confessional doctrines, eventually became a larger hegemonical contest fought by great powers for political supremacy in the European balance of power. Conversely, we shall also entertain the antithesis; the Thirty Years' War originated from dynastic competition for financial profit and political hegemony and only later was dominated by disputes over confessional jurisdiction within Christendom.

Historical analysis necessitates thinking in terms of rival hypotheses about causes, characteristics, and consequences. We shall try in Chapter 1 to separate the multiple roots of this protracted war—a war that ended only when the belligerents' hopes for conquest vanished as the resources needed for them to continue the fighting became depleted.

FAITH, FATHERLAND, OR FINANCE? PRECONDITIONS FOR WAR IN SIXTEENTH-CENTURY EUROPE

A clash of cultures occurred in the sixteenth century that set the stage for the cataclysm which erupted in 1618. Although it is difficult to disentangle the various interacting causal forces, our major focus will be on the primary linkage between religion and power politics as these were modified by other background influences. To place our account into a broader historical context, we shall position the underlying contestation between church and state within three more deeply embedded controversies that arose in the twilight of the Medieval Ages: (1) the intellectual impact of the Renaissance, (2) the escalating struggle over temporal authority, and (3) the economic influence of gyrating cycles of growth and decline. Let us begin with a brief overview of the first of these controversies by examining the European environment prior to the onset of the Thirty Years' War.

The Intellectual Origins of International Conflict

At one level, the Thirty Years' War can be seen as stemming from a new faith in reason as a means of improving the human condition. Rationalism engendered rising expectations that had profound social and political implications. This is not to claim that European culture was bursting with pride and self-confidence. Except when dealing with the indigenous people of Africa and the Americas, Europeans during the fifteenth century did not think of themselves as the center of the political universe which all other peoples turned to for ideas and institutions to emulate. One historian has described the prevailing mood in the following terms:

> What we today call "Europeans" thought of themselves as part of Christendom, and a Christendom . . . that desperately needed to return to some of its founding truths. Similarly, they did not regard themselves as the bearers of the highest culture. Ancient Greece and Rome, they knew, had lived at a higher level, which is why the Renaissance felt the need to recover and imitate classical models. The

fabled wealth of the distant Orient and the clearly superior civilization of nearby Islam did not allow Christendom to think itself culturally advanced or, more significantly, to turn in on itself, as self-satisfied empires of the time such as China did. Contemporary European maps—the ones all the early mariners consulted in the Age of Discovery—bear witness to their central belief: Jerusalem, not Europe, was the center of the world.

But this very sense of threat and inferiority, combined with the unsettled social diversity of Europe at the time, gave Europeans a rich and dynamic restlessness. Not surprisingly, the rise towards a renewed Europe began in the places least affected by the population implosion and, therefore, more prosperous: what we today call the Low Countries and, above all, Northern Italy.[8]

Still, ideas have consequences, and the rebirth of learning led to an exuberance and excitement that unleashed forces with which the world still wrestles today. The scientific philosophy of the Renaissance in the fifteenth century produced the likes of Michelangelo, Leonardo da Vinci, and Galileo. Their discoveries and insights opened the door to the age of Renaissance diplomacy and, with it, to the age of modern diplomacy whose precedents still define most of the major practices and procedures for the conduct of international relations.

During the sixteenth century, remarkable achievements in natural science led to wide acceptance of the belief that the universe was governed by inexorable natural laws that reason could discover, and that the discovery of these laws could usher in a new era of human progress. The emergence of an independent-minded commercial and merchant middle class was made possible by technological advances in this "age of discovery," generating a culture ripe for revolt against the stagnant feudal hierarchy of the Dark Ages. The light of reason, people began to believe, could dispel much of the evil in the world and pave the way to perpetual peace and prosperity. Indeed, the Enlightenment spawned a growing socially constructed view that perceived reality, based on objective truths, could be divided into two separate categories—sacred and secular spheres.

This frame of mind undermined traditional religious dogmas and ideologies such as the idea of the divine right of kings to rule their subjects. In this sense the Thirty Years' War might be interpreted as emanating from the seeds sown by the belief in material progress and a rebellion against the status quo by people dissatisfied with perceived barriers to their acquisition of wealth, power, and freedom. Although the new faith rejected religious absolutism, vested interests had powerful incentives to resist the currents of intellectual change. Indeed, their opposition to new ideas and new forms of governance explains why "the sixteenth century was an age of intolerance."[9]

There was an understandable need for many to seek emancipation from the confines of this age; however, also underway was a mounting search to construct a new consensus about the basis for order, in the absence of agreements about the line between absolute truth and tolerance for different beliefs. Without the anchor of a moral consensus about the normative principles and rules that could provide for domestic and international order, the overriding "postmodern" question was whether, as "postmodernism" might argue today, *all* beliefs should be tolerated. The growing nihilistic sentiment, that nothing can really be known and that all faith in faith should be suspended, was a portent for the coming secular age. The older, pre-Renaissance order gradually gave way to another, creating a breeding ground for war: "European man's new sense of dynamism had about it a strange quality of fear and foreboding, almost as if they had opened a door on terrors that in the centuries before had been locked up. The wars and insurrections, the violence, destruction, and hard times of the first six decades of the seventeenth century justified this fear and foreboding."[10]

A Struggle between Authority and Anarchy

At a second, connected level, the Thirty Years' War can be interpreted as fundamentally a contest growing from competing ideas about political institutions for governance, with the struggle centering on the ageless debate about the need for a central authority to maintain order versus a decentralized system of separated power that allowed independent states to pursue their own chosen goals. In this respect the Thirty Years' War can be seen as the result of a macro-transformation between the hierarchial or pyramidal structure of the medieval feudal system with the king and/or the pope at the apex of power, and the modern era "which witnessed the discovery of the individual and the growth of democracy."[11]

From this perspective, the onset of armed conflict in 1618 was the logical culmination of an intellectual controversy, brewing since the early sixteenth century, about the pillars for international order. The Thirty Years' War might be accounted for as the outcome of a grand contest throughout Europe between competing visions about the ascribed advantages of unity and disunity, centralization and decentralization, and vertical versus horizontal organizational structures for the global community. In this sense, the Thirty Years' War was a product of dissension—a war that pitted one value, supranational global management under hierarchical control, against another value, autonomous freedom of action without a supreme authority to make and enforce rules for statecraft. That perennial conflict in turn forced European culture to wrestle with the ageless potential conflict between self-interested behavior and the collective good.

Within the setting of European affairs during the sixteenth century, the struggle between hierarchy and decentralization was becoming even more salient in political thought and moral discourse. There was increasing confusion about the primary units of the international community, as well as their relationships to one another and to the society of which they were a part. The territorial state became "the cornerstone of the modern state system" after the Treaty of Westphalia in 1648 when the rules of international law were conceived.[12] However, the birth of the state was a prolonged evolutionary process that commenced much earlier, and the Thirty Years' War signifies only the ratification of the process that led to the modern state system. Scholars generally date the origins of the modern world at the close of the fifteenth century in Europe (see Figure 1.1). This was a time when a group of so-called "New Monarchs" in Europe expanded their armed forces, curbed civil strife, increased state revenues through taxation, and limited the influence of feudal nobles. Leaders such as Henry VII (1485–1509) of the Tudor line in England and Louis XI (1461–1483) of the Valois line in France exemplified these trends. By defining themselves as sovereigns who possessed the authority to enact and enforce law over everyone residing within their territorial boundaries, they departed from the medieval conception of suzerainty or of local landlords and laid the foundation for national states.

FIGURE 1.1   Renaissance Europe at the End of the Fifteenth Century

On the eve of the sixteenth century, Europe was composed of myriad quasi-independent polities, many of which were strategically allied through dynastic intermarriages but (as today) most of whom were fierce competitors in commerce and trade. At the center stood the Holy Roman Empire, led by Emperor Maximilian I, who reigned between 1493 and 1519 and exerted imperial control over seven major German Electoral Princes who, in turn, collectively represented more than 300 confederated principalities and towns. The modern territorial state as we know it was not to become a legal sovereign entity for another century and a half.[13]

Concurrent with the internal consolidation of power across Europe was the emergence of a new system of kingdom. Throughout the Middle Ages, Europeans thought of themselves as part of an all-pervading Christian commonwealth, despite living in a galaxy of separate political jurisdictions. To be sure, strong local ties accompanied this sense of belonging to Christendom, but a broad-based sense of national loyalty to country was absent. Even royal families, like the Hohenstaufen and the Plantagenets, did not think of themselves as being limited to a particular nation; they intermarried in strategic alliances to expand the size of their domains, but saw themselves as members of a separate aristocratic class, disconnected from the common people who resided in their realm. With the rise of strong, centralized governments, however, the transnational structure of medieval Christendom was gradually replaced by a national structure of competitive, independent states.

Far-reaching changes accompanied the rise of these states. New methods in mining and metallurgy, new means of finance, and new techniques of warfare added to the strength of the various emerging territorial states. Improvements in navigation and shipbuilding facilitated transoceanic expansion, which ultimately led to the globalization of international politics. The beginning of the sixteenth century thus marked the dawn of the modern international system.

Born in the vortex of European state building and stimulated by a dramatic upsurge in economic growth, the system of fledging states and multiple principalities gradually grew far beyond its European core. This transformation has been called as dramatic as "the crystallization of a liquid" or "the changing of a gear."[14] While the processes behind it may have taken centuries to develop, they matured at "a quite definite moment," in much the same way that "water gathers in the basin of a fountain until, at a particular moment, the basin is filled and the water overflows into a second, surrounding basin."[15]

The origins of this process can be traced to a struggle over Italy between France and the Spanish throne under Charles V of the Hapsburg dynasty, which put the "proto-state system" to a severe test. With no states yet formed in central Europe, had the Hapsburgs "gained mastery of the area south of the Alps and added it to their lands in the north of them, they could have assembled a gigantic family domain which, coupled with Spain, could [have functioned] as the solid base of an imperial hegemony."[16] However, the bid to forcefully unite most of the continent in the so-called Italian wars between 1494 and 1516 was successfully resisted. As a result, movement toward a nascent system of states continued on its long-term path to development that was to reach its ultimate destiny 150 years later, when the Westphalian treaties at the end of the Thirty Years' War in 1648 ratified the modern system of sovereign states which survives today.

Along the way, numerous questions had to be answered. What was to be most prized: the individual, the group, or the commands of God? Should the emerging social ethic put the wider European community ahead of rulers and ruled, or prize the autonomy of the individual and the state? Should states be seen as an outcropping of divine sanction, rulers as selected by God and therefore beyond the boundaries of moral judgment? Or should states, rulers, and citizens be obligated to obey higher divine moral commands, and therefore be held accountable to ethical standards? Was a Christian "duty-bound to support the state as the maintainer of law and order as long as the state does not require him to disobey God,"[17] or was the state perceived as so indispensable to security that it was to be worshiped and its power increased by every means possible? These were the questions about statecraft that first arose in public discourse in the early sixteenth century, and later defined the issues that would dominate in the seventeenth century (see Box 1.1.).

BOX 1.1
The Emerging Consensus about States and Statecraft in the Early Sixteenth Century

Contested ideas about the nature of the state and the relationship of the state to war were routine, of course. They trace back to antiquity. And even as the Middle Ages were ending, philosophers such as Dante Alighieri critiqued claims of papal supremacy over secular affairs by arguing that a universal monarch is indispensable for the peace of the world, advocating "Submission to a single Prince [because] Monarchy is necessary to the world for its well-being."[18] The crucible for the emergence of this doctrine was the growth and rivalry among the three new post-feudal monarchies of western Europe in the late fifteenth century: England in 1485 with the coronation of Henry VII and concomitant reduction of the power of parliament; France in 1453 with the end of the Hundred Years' War and the reign of Louis XI (nicknamed "The Spider King" for his cunning practice of manipulation and intrigue); and Spain in 1469 with the marriage of Ferdinand of Aragon and Isabella of Castile. These monarchies planted the seeds for the philosophies of power politics that were to blossom 150 years later in the Thirty Years' War, producing dreams of strong rulers leading mighty armies, protected by the prayers of a deferential clergy, and supported by an obedient subject population willing to assign its rulers unlimited temporal authority to prevent foreign invasion.

The single most influential expression of this growing consensus about states and statecraft was authored by Niccolò Machiavelli (1469–1527), whose *The Prince* (1513) and *The Art of War* (1521) circulated widely and captured the imagination of future rulers. Machiavelli observed the wars of his time and advanced a set of conclusions about human nature, the sovereign power of the state, and the conduct of diplomacy. He maintained that human nature is the least changeable factor in politics, and that it is driven by an innate and insatiable lust for power. Accordingly, the purpose of rulership is to practice the art of political manipulation to control rivals. Rejecting Christian charity, humility, and other-worldliness, Machiavelli extolled the virtues of courage, assertiveness, and determination. Arguing that a successful ruler must use all means necessary, including fear and deception, Machiavelli paved the road to the modern doctrine of military necessity.[19] He justified the exercise of power by a stern and ruthless sovereign ruler by his perception of the need for a strong absolute state to preserve itself, by any means necessary, for the higher ideal of maintaining order. "But he is not opposed to warfare. A state must, in his view, expand or decay."[20] Therefore from this aspiration derives Machiavelli's revival of the classical principle of *raison d'état* (reason of state) and his "glorification of warfare."[21] Machiavelli accepted as normal the practices he observed, and elevated them to a governing philosophy predicated on interest, power, prudence, and expediency. His message defined the ethos of the coming seventeenth century. It instructs "a prince how to secure and retain power, by seeming virtuous while not being so, by distributing favors himself, and leaving the dirty work of punishment to subordinates, . . . by inflicting injuries as rapidly as possible, by supporting weak allies rather than great ones, by inspiring fear rather than love. . . ."[22]

This vision of politics as an amoral power struggle portrayed the practices that were occurring in the early sixteenth century, although others advanced alternative approaches to peace. Among those resisting the cruel and calculating culture of the time were Thomas More, whose *Utopia* (1516) advocated tolerance for religious and political diversity within a commonwealth holding property in common. Even more expressive was Desiderius Erasmus who sought to restore the pacifism of The Gospels by challenging, in *The Education of a Christian Prince* (1516) and *The Complaint of Peace* (1517), the growing acceptance of war. Arguing that "the whole philosophy of Christ teaches against it,"[23] Erasmus maintained that war causes "the shipwreck of all that is good" and asked the Prince to see how evil war inherently is by questioning "if there is any war which can be called 'just.' "[24] However, these views ran against the intellectual currents that were gathering speed in the early sixteenth century.

Machiavelli: Forerunner of the Modern Realist School of Power Politics

Niccolò Machiavelli voiced opinions about statecraft during the Renaissance that dominated thinking and practice during the Thirty Years' War and the negotiations that produced the Peace of Westphalia. He accepted the amoral struggle for power as a permanent condition and concluded that the insatiable hunger for domination meant that "War is not to be avoided."[25] Exposed in his lifetime to constant military struggle, Machiavelli argued that "A man striving in every way to be good will meet his ruin among the great number who are not good. Hence it is necessary for a prince . . . to learn how not to be good and to use his knowledge or refrain from using it as he may need."[26] He "justified the practice of bad faith" in statecraft, concluding that "anything is permissible where freedom is at stake."[27]

"Politics is first and foremost about the relationship of individuals to group," a "public phenomenon of the entire society . . . about how resources are allocated, how justice is both defined and served . . . in short, it is about who gets what, and why."[28] The sixteenth century became highly politicized, and compelled Europeans to make a choice between rival models, one based on an all-powerful hegemon to keep peace, and the other on a *laissez faire*, autonomous freedom of choice. European society descended into a maelstrom of bitter political battles as the medieval world view disintegrated. As we shall see, the Westphalian settlement of this issue rejected the view that "the Christian passes beyond nationalism to internationalism precisely because he believes that God—no less!—is the source of love, justice, and law, so that any given state should be the servant, not the lord of justice."[29] Instead, the rise of the secular state became the focal point of loyalty. This development was to have far-reaching, long-lasting consequences whose impact survives today. The birth of the modern state signified the coming merger of the state with religion, and the subordination of the latter to the sovereign power of the former. In considering why and how the Thirty Years' War erupted, therefore, we must keep in mind the importance of the marriage of organized religion with the nation-state. "In the sixteenth century, in the midst of the Reformation and that violent battle among the forces of modernity, the patrimony monarchy was still presented as the guarantee of peace and social life. It was still granted control over social development in such a way that it could absorb that process within its machine of domination, '*Cujus regio, ejus religio*'—or, really, religion, had to be subordinated to the territorial control of the sovereign. There was nothing diplomatic about this adage; on the contrary, it confided entirely to the power of the patrimonial sovereign in the management of the passage to the new order. Even religion was the sovereign's property."[30] The revolutionary but gradual ascendance of the absolute monarch exercising complete control over religious and political practices in the secular state's territory did not directly cause the Thirty Years' War; but that war could not have occurred had not the feudal bases of power not withered away prior to the early seventeenth century.

A War Produced by Pursuit of Profit and Prosperity

Economic factors are a third background ingredient in the causal equation explaining the outbreak of the Thirty Years' War. When economic fortunes and fates rise, the consequence is not always satisfaction. Prosperity can generate greed and envy, especially when economic growth is uneven. It can also lead to the stratification of society into classes increasingly divided between rich and poor. In short, rapid growth can breed resentment. Because it redistributes wealth from some at the expense of others, it provokes those left behind who have nothing to lose but their chains of impoverishment.

All these divergent trends and disruptive developments were underway during the sixteenth century, when European society underwent an unprecedented economic growth fueled by technological innovations in an age of exploration and mercantilist imperial expansion. At the same time, Europe underwent a demographic surge that expanded its population from about 60 million to 100 million between 1500 and 1600.[31] These disruptions swept political and religious institutions into turbulent, uncharted waters. Personal ambition accelerated in a feverish mood of rising expectations for new opportunities, and these changes shook the foundations of dynasties and empires. The economic agents of change eventually became catalysts to political and religious change.

The optimistic beliefs and rebellious attitudes of the sixteenth century culminated in frustration and warfare during the early seventeenth century when economic expansion was followed by contraction. As rivalries between kingdoms and princedoms intensified, civil unrest began to dissolve the old feudal order. From this perspective, "the Thirty Years' War should itself be seen as an economic phenomenon intimately linked with the cycle of economic expansion and contraction: 'The Thirty Years' War was a social occurrence, Heiner Haan argues, resulting from the long-term economic growth of the sixteenth century; it lived off the wealth produced in this expansion, and in the end destroyed that very wealth.'"[32]

To be sure, a host of other explanations could be introduced in an effort to trace the roots of the Thirty Years' War. But an inventory is not our purpose in evaluating how the background forces provided a climate conducive to a systemwide European war. Instead, in the remainder of our account, we shall concentrate on the issue on which nearly all historians rivet their attention regarding the origins of Thirty Years' War and the Peace of Westphalia; that is, we will look at the extent to which politics mixed with religion to produce the tragic spectacle of Europeans slaughtering Europeans on a horrifying, inhumane scale.

POLITICS AND RELIGION IN THE SIXTEENTH AND SEVENTEENTH CENTURIES

In the new millennium, it is customary to conceive of religion and of politics as residing in separate realms, distinct and therefore different. That conceptualization would have been strange to the average European in the 1500s and early 1600s. The idea of separation of church and state was alien. Religion and politics, church and state, were co-mingled in a complex web of legal and institutional interdependence. Monasteries were state supported; centers of theology at universities were subsidized by princes serving as patrons for their faith; monks often became knights; kings were customarily counseled by members of religious orders such as the Jesuits and Dominicans in Spain; the papacy maintained armies and some popes, such as the "warrior pope" Julius II, personally led the troops of the Papal States in battle. In many respects, church and state were one and the same: the church sought to expand its temporal power, and the state controlled church policy and property with the consent of subordinate clergy and their institutional superiors.

Modern historians are divided over the role of religion and politics in the Thirty Years' War. Whereas some refer to it as "a war of religion,"others see it as "a hegemonic war" between national rivals for political control of European affairs. In the former construction, the Thirty Years' War was caused by the confessional division of Christianity between Catholics and Protestants following the Reformation. In the latter construction, the Thirty Years' War was caused by the contest between the Spanish and Austrian thrones of the House of Hapsburg on the one hand, and the Danish, Swedish, Dutch, and French thrones, on the other, who resisted the Hapsburg attempt to subjugate them.

There are many elements of truth in both these contending interpretations, which is why they are woven into virtually every historical account of the war. Let us evaluate the claims of these two interpretations individually before we consider how both religion and state politics interacted with each other, at varying degrees of influence during each phase of the Thirty Years' War and at the 1648 peace conferences in Westphalia.

A War between Religious Confessions?

In the first image, the Thirty Years' War is seen as an outgrowth of the religious wars between Catholic and Protestant forces *within* Christendom during the sixteenth and seventeenth centuries. Many historians call the Thirty Years' War a "war of religion" among Christian sects for sound reasons, arguing that "allowing for the role of political and economic factors, the fact remains that the Reformation was first and foremost a religious upheaval [for which] men with enthusiasm would cut each other's throat because they differed."[33]

Yet, it is in the abstract curious to view the Thirty Years' War as a religious conflict. After all, Christianity is a religion that teaches to "love your enemies," to "turn the other cheek" against aggressors, and to "beat swords into plowshares." Indeed, despite some basic theological disagreements about the meaning of Biblical Scripture, the beliefs of the Catholics, Lutherans, and Calvinists had much more in common than issues that divided them. All Christians— Catholic and Protestants alike—accepted the incarnate Jesus Christ and believed that faith in Him and adherence to Jesus' message allowed for the forgiveness of sins on earth and the rewards of eternal life after death. All Christians recognized the authority of Biblical Scripture and saw the Eucharist as the bridge between believers and God. All rejected the view that reason and self-reliance were paths to salvation. There were not many, if any, princes participating in the slaughter of the Thirty Years' War "who wished to slay their neighbors for heresy," observes W. F. Reddaway, and there were "few princes, if any, in that age who were callous hypocrites, masking their greed and ambition with a religious zeal of which they felt nothing."[34] Given the substantial confessional consensus among all Christians, why, then, did the Thirty Years' War gain the reputation as a war of religion?

The Roots of Political Revolt During the Reformation.   In an epoch united by a consensus about major religious doctrines, why did the princes and kings of the age raise mass armies and order them into combat to kill other Christians—Christians whose commandments included a strict pacifist principle derived from the Jewish roots of its theology, "Thou shall not kill"? Why did Christianity divide, and the fragmented sects compete with one another, to the point of taking up arms?

The answers are unclear, and it is easy to exaggerate the religious discord of the sixteenth century and overlook the fact that intrafaith militance had been as pervasive in other times alongside interfaith rivalry and warfare. Almost from the very beginnings, Christianity as an institution had experienced internecine grievances and theological controversies. Confessional disputes were almost invariably interwoven with political and constitutional controversies. For example, during the Babylonian captivity from 1305 to 1378, seven popes resided in Avignon as clients of the French king; and during the Great Schism from 1378 to 1417, three popes claimed to be pontiff holding the true keys to the kingdom of Heaven, each of whom was the pawn of a particular monarch who made the papacy an instrument for his political ambitions. Sectarian schisms thus had occurred prior to the Thirty Years' War among Christians emphasizing different aspects of the meaning of Scripture. Christianity's severe splintering in the 1500s did not cause a rupture; division and denominationalism within Christendom had started centuries earlier. The 1500s merely witnessed the widening of preexisting divisions within Christendom.

Hostility toward the Catholic Church in Rome escalated following the Reformation—a multifaceted phenomenon stemming from many perceived abuses by the Church hierarchy. Acceptance of the Roman Catholic Church, its authority, and the unifying principle of centralized administration, had deteriorated in the late Middle Ages. People had steadily drifted away from the pope's proclaimed right to speak exclusively and infallibly for Christianity on behalf of the princes, towns, knights, bourgeois, and peasants throughout Europe. To a growing segment of all classes of European society, Rome was viewed as having long ago abandoned Christian doctrine because it had steadily sought political power and wealth by methods that disregarded the principles for moral conduct that Scripture advocated for people of faith. Many Europeans believed that a series of self-interested, aggrandizing popes had corrupted the true faith, and sacrificed the papacy's claim to moral and secular authority.

By the end of the fifteenth century, a diminishing proportion of the European population freely accepted papal rule in religious or secular matters, although many rulers found it expedient to provide financial support for their Catholic bishops in exchange for their bishops' cooperation in repressing revolts by the antiaristocratic landowners, merchants, and exploited peasants. Guten-berg's invention of the printing press in the mid-fifteenth century made pos-sible the wide distribution of books and propaganda pamphlets,[35] which exacerbated the Roman Church's problems by disseminating reports of papal corruption. In this increasingly hostile environment, movements for church reform were perhaps inevitable.

The so-called Protestant Reformation that swept across Europe in the 1500s was part of a long-term transformation that had been underway for some time. Beginning in the second half of the fifteenth century, formerly impotent territories governed by princes ruling over more than 1,000 principalities in central Europe began to accumulate the political power to challenge the pre-viously dominant central authority of the papacy. Strong kings emerged in France, England, and Spain and were able to increase central governmental control over their subjects in a development that presaged the birth of what was to become the modern national territorial state.

These thrones monopolized political and religious power in ways that reduced the papacy's political control of secular affairs. For example, the 1516 Concordat of Bologna gave King Francis I of France the sovereign right to appoint bishops and abbots, and Pope Leo X had no recourse but to recog-nize this agreement that legalized the nationalization of the French clergy and church property in exchange for the renunciation of the doctrine that the pope should be accountable to a supreme council. Similarly, in Spain the union of church and state became complete. Ferdinand and Isabella built a united Spanish nation-state through control of the church, under the claim that as devout Christians the two "Catholic Sovereigns" (as they titled themselves) were saving Catholicism by securing the "right to appoint prelates, tax the churches, rid it of abuses and curtail the right of ecclesiastical appeal to Rome."[36] The fall of papal authority and concomitant rise of secular authority were revolu-tionary in their impact. They became the soil from which grew the rejection of a unified Christianity under supranational hegemonic control in Rome (see Box 1.2). The seeds of the growing contest between religious and secular polit-ical authority were sown and from them grew the continuing conflict between church and state—an issue that still haunts world politics.[37]

BOX 1.2
What Were the Protestants Protesting? The Confessional and Political Origins of the Reformation

By the early sixteenth century, the roots of revolt against the papacy were broad and deep. As Barbara Tuchman notes,

> Since the beginning of the [sixteenth] century, dissatisfaction with the Church had grown and widened, expressing itself clerically in synods and sermons, popularly in tracts and satires, letters, poems, songs and the apocalyptic prophecies of preachers. To

everyone but the government of the Church, it was plain that an outbreak of dissent was approaching. In 1513, an Italian preaching friar felt it close at hand, predicting the downfall of Rome and of all priests and friars in a holocaust that would leave no unworthy clergy alive and no Mass said for three years. The respectable middle class was made indignant by the reckless extravagance and debts of the papacy, and every class and group in every nation resented the insatiable papal taxation.[38]

Intense hostility to the church was dircted not exclusively at the material excesses of the papacy, but at the decline of spirituality within the monastic orders that had previously been the vanguard of devout worship, charitable work, and civic education. The sporadic reform efforts of several friars were of little avail. For example, when the friar Girolamo Savonarola in Florence was burned at the stake in 1498, Pope Alexander VI celebrated the silencing of Savonarola's campaign to purify the Church. The disdain for the Church and growing attacks on the temporal power of the clergy were fueled by the widespread perception that corruption permeated the entire Catholic Church hierarchy:

> The deeds of Rodrigo Borgia, Alexander VI (1492–1503), made his name a byword for lust and cruelty. During his pontificate the immorality and venality of the papacy knew no bounds. Much of the money that poured into Rome from Catholic Christendom was spent on an attempt to create an Italian kingdom for his beloved son Cesare. Julius II (1503–1513) was the favorite nephew of Pope Sixtus IV. His doting uncle made him a cardinal at twenty-eight, endowing him with twelve bishoprics, one archbishop, and three abbeys. As pope, Julius made his chief task the expansion of the temporal power of the papacy. In pursuit of this ambition he engaged in a number of wars and sometimes personally led his troops into combat, thereby winning the nick-name, the Warrior Pope. Leo X (1513–1521), son of Lorenzo de' Medici, used the wealth of the Church for magnificent pageantry and patronage of the arts.
>
> The ever-increasing press of the popes for money, their worldliness, and their immorality had their counterparts down the ladder of the Church hierarchy. Bishops, whether or not they were princes in their own right—as were a number in Germany—were heavily involved in affairs of the secular state and were subsidized by the faithful to do the work of princes. Many laymen were jealous of the lucrative offices monopolized by clerics. A wider resentment grew from the arrogance of the higher clergy, the ostentatiousness of their wealth and power, their large jurisdiction in moral matters, and always their apparent greed. This resentment merged with contempt for a clergy that appeared to have lost its vocation, the cure of souls. By 1500 anti-clericalism was rife.[39]

The Impact of Martin Luther.   Although the lay intelligentsia were the most vocal in their criticism of Church abuse, ironically the revolt that led to Church reform came from *within* the contemptuous clergy. The Reformation emerged from many ecclesiastical complaints by Christian believers. The most vocal and visible was Martin Luther, an observant Augustinian friar. History records that the Reformation gathered speed when on October 31, 1517, All Saint's Eve, Martin Luther took a fateful step by nailing to the door of the castle church at Wittenberg his *95 Theses* that summarized arguments against corruptive church practices, especially the pope's commercialization of indulgences.

Luther's proclamation against Rome fell on receptive ears in northeastern Germany, where popular opposition to Rome was intense, in part because Rome extracted huge sums of money from these principalities. The Papal Nuncio Girolamo Alessandro warned the pope in 1516 that many pious German Christians were hoping to voice their complaints. But this warning fell on deaf ears in the Vatican.

> Within a year, the awaited moment came through the instrumentality of [the pope's] agent for the sale of papal indulgences in Germany, Johann Tetzel. Indulgences were not new, nor were they invented by Leo. Originally granted as a release from all or part of the good works required of a sinner to satisfy a penance imposed by his priest, indulgence gradually came to be considered a release from the guilt of the sin itself. This was a usage severely condemned by purists and protesters. More objectionable was the commercial sale of a spiritual grace. The grace once granted in return for pious donations for church repairs, hospitals, ransom of captives of the Turks and other good works had grown into a vast traffic of which a half or third of the receipts customarily went to Rome and the rest to the local domain, with various percentages to the agents and pardoners who held the concessions. The Church had become a machine for making money, declared John Colet in 1513, with the fee considered as the effective factor rather than repentance and good works. Employing charlatans, misleading the credulous, this traffic became one of the persistent evils of organized religion.
>
> When pardoners allowed the belief—though never explicitly stated by the popes—that indulgences could take care of future sins not yet committed, the Church had reached the point of virtually encouraging vice, as its critics did not fail to point out. To enlarge the market, Sixtus IV ruled in 1476 that indulgences applied to souls in Purgatory, causing the common people to believe that they must pay for the relief of departed relatives. The more prayers and masses and indulgences bought for the deceased, the shorter their terms in Purgatory, and since this arrangement favored the rich, it was naturally resented by the poor and made them readier when the moment came to reject all official sacraments.
>
> Tetzel, a Dominican monk, was a promoter who might have made Barnum blush. Upon arrival in a town, he would be greeted by a prearranged procession of clergy and commoners coming out to meet him with flags and lighted candles while church bells rang joyful tunes. Traveling with a brass-bound chest and a bag of printed receipts, and preceded by an assistant friar bearing the Bull of Indulgence on a velvet cushion, he would set up shop in the nave of the principal church in front of a huge cross raised for the occasion and draped with the papal banner. At his side an agent of the Fuggers kept careful count of the money that purchasers dropped into a bowl placed on top of the chest, as each received a printed indulgence from the bag.
>
> "I have here," Tetzel would call out, "the passports . . . to lead the human soul to the celestial joys of Paradise." For a mortal sin, seven years of penance were due. "Who then would hesitate for a quarter-florin to secure one of these letters of remission?" Warming up, he would say that if a Christian had slept with his mother and put money in the pope's bowl, "the Holy Father had the power in Heaven and earth to forgive the sin, and if he forgave it, God must do so also." In behalf of the deceased, he said that "as soon as the coin rang in the bowl, the soul

for whom it was paid would fly out of Purgatory straight to Heaven." The ring of these coins was the summons to Luther. [40]

Luther's goal was to reform the Catholic Church, not secede from it. In response to Tetzel's campaign, Luther nailed his *95 Theses* on the church door at Wittenberg, assailing the abuse of indulgence as sacrilegious, although without yet suggesting a break with Rome.[41]

For his defiance of papal authority, in June of 1520 the pope formally excommunicated Luther, who publicly protested by burning the *Exurge Domine*, the papal Bull of Excommunication. In 1521 Luther defended himself before the Imperial Diet at Worms with the ringing words that unleashed the Reformation: "I am overcome by the Scriptures I have quoted; my conscience is captive to God's World. I cannot and will not revoke anything, for to act against conscience is neither safe nor honest . . . *Hier stehe ich. Ich kann nicht anders.* ["Here I stand. I cannot do otherwise."]" In what was to become a widespread marriage between religion and politics, a prince favoring Luther's theological protest gave Luther sanctuary in the Wartburg Castle, where Luther allocated his time translating the Bible into German and writing numerous religious books advocating the education of women and other polemics running counter to the Roman Catholic doctrine at the time. Most defiant was Luther's radical position that any Christian had the right to interpret the Bible; his doctrine of "the priesthood of all believers" denied the Roman Church's final authority about Biblical interpretation.

The Saxon Elector Frederick the Wise chose to protect Luther's safety and freedom of speech and belief from papal persecution, but Frederick's motives were partly political. Like the other Electors in the Empire and many other princes and nobles, Frederick "saw in the religious confusions a chance to improve their economic position and increase their political importance."[42] The rulers of Germany immediately grasped that from religious revolt they could prevent the flow of gold to Rome and establish their independence. In taking a stance for Luther, Electors like Frederick the Wise were able to defy the pope's political authority and taxation, and the reform movement provided them a means of acquiring political liberties and economic gains including, potentially, claims on some of the Church's vast property and territory.

When the 1520 Papal ban against Luther could not be enforced, religious protest became a political revolt that spread like a wildfire across the central European landscape. Germany now split between proponents and opponents of Luther's confessional position. "The free cities of western Germany became Lutheran within a few months after Luther's appearance at the Diet of Worms in 1521, and soon a number of secular principalities followed their example."[43] "Christendom had fractured, and the continent now contained large numbers of individuals drawn into a transnational struggle over religious doctrine."[44]

Luther strongly believed that Scripture asked people to abide by morality in their interpersonal conduct, because Scripture held that one's relationship to others reveals one's relationship to God (*Isaiah 58:6–9; Luke 10:25–31*). But Luther's political reading of Scripture emphasized an interpretation of the moral responsibilities of people to civil government that had appeal to the German princes in the Empire. Luther took Jesus Christ's advice to "render under Caesar that which is Caesar's and unto God that which is God's" to heart, and insisted that it was a Christian's duty to obey civil authority while concentrating on the search for obedience to God's commands. Lutheranism voiced support for the supremacy of the state on secular affairs and the supremacy of Biblical Scripture about the teachings of Jesus Christ on religious principles, since God's sovereignty prevailed in the final analysis over popular sovereignty. "The world of God cannot be received and honored by any works, but by faith alone," Luther wrote in his tract *Christian Liberty*.

Theological revisions of doctrine always carry with them political implications. In the reform efforts of Martin Luther and other Protestants (especially John Calvin), criticism of the Roman Catholic Church's autocratic structure represented a clear populist assault against the medieval order. However, it would be a misreading of Luther's motives to see his emphasis on salvation by faith and on the primacy of Biblical Scripture through the independent interpretation by a "priesthood of all believers" as advocacy of dissent against authority. Protestants such as Luther "had been forced to define carefully what they meant by *sola scriptura* [and although] they found it an effective banner to unfurl when attacking Catholics [they quickly learned that this position] was always a bit troublesome when common people began to take the teaching seriously."[45]

Exploited people could easily seize this doctrine to justify civil disobedience, and thereby interpret in the theological message the divine right to revolt against any and all exploitative political power by the state. That possibility became a reality when a revolt spread across northwestern Germany by downtrodden peasants who saw in Lutheranism a basis for rebellion against a civil structure they perceived to be unjust. This crisis forced both Luther and the Catholic hierarchy to confront the political issues that the theological discourse had raised about the proper relationship between church and state. Luther reacted harshly to the threat of widespread violent grassroots rebellion by the masses, and defined the proper relationship between religion and politics in a way that sought to separate the two realms. "For the Reformers, popular translations of the Bible did not imply that people were to understand the Scriptures apart from ministerial guidance, and for Luther a populist reading of Scripture could not warrant, based on conclusions deduced from the Bible, a right to civil disobedience."[46]

At a time when the authority of the Church, feudal nobility, and other privileged princes were facing a threat to their predominance, and when trust in them had broken down, a creed emphasizing civil obedience could only provide them reassurance. In the name of domestic stability, Catholics and Lutherans aligned to repress the so-called Knights War of 1522, led by Franz von Sickingen and Ulrich von Hutton.

The true political meaning of Luther's Augustinian concept of "two realms" became even more apparent shortly thereafter when, in 1524, a revolt by peasants spread across Germany, seeing in Protestantism a justification to terminate serfdom where it still existed, limit payments to the Church, and lower rents paid to their overlords. However, Luther sided with the German princes and Catholic Church, based on his conviction that it was a Christian's duty to obey civil government and that violence against authority was never justified. His passionate condemnation of the revolt was all the princes needed to crush the uprising, and an estimated 100,000 rebels lost their lives.[47] Luther pleaded, without success, for the rebels to be treated with mercy after the revolt, but his cry for compassion was ignored. The result was a step toward the union of the German princes with religious authority and the severance of religious authority, either Lutheran or Catholic, from broad-based popular support. In the evolution of political-religious relationships, a fateful step had been taken toward the marriage of princely power with religious support to the exclusion of the mass of believers at the bottom rung of German society. The bridge between state and church was built in this cauldron, and from it principles placing governmental leadership over clerical authority developed that were, 150 years later, embedded in the Peace of Westphalia.

A number of new radical Christian sects arose from disappointed followers of Luther who had wished to advance political and religious reforms at a much faster pace. These included the Anabaptists ("re-baptizers") pursuing piety and spiritual regeneration while advocating the termination of state power over Christianity. To deter this kind of independence that threatened their interests, Protestant and Catholic governments joined together to disarm independent-minded separatists, and in 1535 deployed brute force to besiege and decimate the Anabaptist stronghold of Münster and, from there, conducted a campaign to destroy the remnants of radical resistance to established civil and religious authority.[48] The result of these developments was the institutionalization of both Catholicism and of Orthodox Protestantism as extensions of the power of particular states with whom princes chose to align.

Luther's doctrine of "justification by faith" liberated German princes from the authority of the pope. "Protestant dissenters," writes Nathan Hatch, "challenged forces of religious orthodoxy occupying the most culturally sanctioned command posts," and their challenge led to the "withering of establishments" and their replacement by new, more autonomous political architectures.[49] "Secular rulers welcomed Luther's teaching because it freed them from the interference of a foreign pope."[50] Many rulers quickly took advantage of the opportunity they saw in Luther's proclamation of the right for people of faith to think for themselves as a justification for their separation from Catholicism. The push to restore a Biblical Christianity independent of human political authority, reliant on *sola scripture* as interpreted apart from higher Church dogma, provided a rationale for casting off papal control. For example, in Prussia, Albert von Hohenzollern, the Grand Master of the Order of the Teutonic

Knights, converted to Lutheranism and declared himself Duke of a secularized Prussian state. Similarly, King Gustavus Vasa and the Swedish National Assembly declared Lutheranism as the state religion and acquired all Catholic Church property in one stroke, setting a precedent for Frederick I, the King of Denmark, Norway, and Iceland to follow when he made Lutheranism his state's official religion. Thus, religious rebellion led to political rebellion. "By the time Luther died in 1546, most of northern Germany had become Lutheran,"[51] and the growing separation of states from the political jurisdiction of the papacy expanded exponentially.

The prospects for a united Germany were further reduced when the Holy Roman Emperor made it his goal to destroy Lutheranism. Charles V, the Holy Roman Emperor between 1519 and 1556, was deeply hostile to the rise of Lutheranism, Calvinism, and other Protestant sects because he foresaw in these religious reform movements a direct threat to the stability of his empire. When the Emperor ordered Luther to appear before him in 1530, the meeting, known as the Confession of Augsburg, "made the division between Catholics and Lutherans [in the Holy Roman Empire] obvious and irreparable."[52]

In prior years, converts to the Lutheran faith had already acquired Catholic church lands from princes, and sought to retain title to these lands. The newly independent princes fought vigorously to defend Lutheranism in their principalities, so they could also assert their independence from the Empire and the pope. For this, several German Lutheran cities and princes formed the Schmalkaldic League in 1531—a direct challenge to the Catholic Hapsburgs.

The Catholic Counter-Reformation.   Under pressure, the Roman Catholic Church began to experiment with innovative institutional approaches to restore the Christian unity under papal authority. One response was to permit devout Catholics to organize religious orders that could attract followers without compromising the pope's authority. The plan allowed the orders to prepare seminaries for training a new generation of clergy who, imbued with a reinvigorated spiritual commitment and cleansed of corruption through vows of chastity, poverty, and charitable works, could offer a viable alternative to the relatively pious Protestant pastors that had attracted a wide popular following. The Order of Theatines formed in 1524 was the first of these Catholic orders created in reaction to the Protestant Reformation; it was a "secular" order designed to train the sons of noble families and prepare them for service to the Catholic Church and their states.

As Protestantism continued to gain ground in Catholic principalities, the Church undertook a more vigorous strategy. It founded the Society of Jesus in 1534, which under the direction of a Spanish soldier, Ignatius Loyola, equipped zealously committed Catholics to act as a papal army. The Theatines and other orders such as the Capuchins and the Ursuline nuns had made an impact inhibiting the growth of Protestantism, but

Only with the foundation of the Society of Jesus in 1534 did the Counter-Reformation truly begin. It was in a sense the last of the military orders and the greatest; in its ultimate development a hierarchy of highly trained men bounded by an oath of unquestioning obedience to their superiors and controlled by the General, its organization was essentially that of an army. When the Catholic Church arose at length from the Council of Trent armed for conflict, it had a fighting force in the Jesuits who were prepared to carry the faith by any means and at any personal cost into any land of the globe. Under their influence the Inquisition, native in Spain, had been re-established at Rome as the effective instrument for the discovery and extirpation of heresy.[53]

The Jesuits perceived themselves as "soldiers of Christ," and dedicated themselves to the Roman Catholic Church and the pope, who was defined as God's representative on earth. It was said of the Jesuit creed: "To attain the truth in all things, we ought always to hold what we believe that seems white to be black, if the Hierarchical Church so defines it."[54] The Jesuits "taught that liberty of belief endangers the state" as a means of pursuing "the real aim [of] subordinating the Catholic monarchies to papal tutelage."[55]

The Jesuit-led Counter-Reformation brought into European affairs a new element: the complete politicization of religion and the use by militant religious interests of military means to win converts and to control independent states. Religion intervened in secular affairs, just as states intervened in religious affairs. It was a practice that would have long-lasting consequences, extending all the way to the early twenty-first century.[56]

> The Counter-Reformation's primary enemy was not Lutheranism but Calvinism. Moreover the Jesuits were a picked force, chosen for their vocation. The Calvinists, as their religion spread, became a heterogeneous mass of scattered communities without a central government. Besides which, although they were the most active and efficient of the new heresies, they could not fulfil the part of defenders and missionaries of the Protestant faith as the Jesuits did for the Church of Rome. They formed the militant left wing of the Protestants as the Jesuits formed the militant right wing of the Catholics, but with this difference, that the Jesuits championed a comparatively united cause, but the Calvinists hated their fellow-Protestants, the Lutherans in particular, almost more than the Papists themselves.[57]

The Counter-Reformation's ruthless campaign against all alleged heretics took the heated political contest to new heights of militancy.[58] The Jesuits were tightly organized on a disciplined military model to wage battle against other faiths and confessions; their diplomatic conduct was cloaked in the *realpolitik* language of Machiavelli. "The first principle of the Society was the complete subordination of the individual will."[59] The second principle was to service the pope and to pursue whatever orders the pope might identify for the Jesuits to perform. The third principal was a tight chain of command, with each "soldier" offering blind obedience to his superior (with the Company of Jesus managed by a chief commander, beginning with Loyola). The fourth principle was expedience: employing a calculating *realpolitik* philosophy that accepted otherwise immoral practices and policies for the just cause of carrying out God's work on earth. The Jesuit doctrine, for instance, "that faith need not be kept with heretics"[60] was a *raison d'religion* stratagem that coincided with the emerging political doctrine in diplomacy of *raison d'état*. Together, these motives, principles and policies were to be emulated by the enemies of the Catholic popes leading the Counter-Reformation, especially after 1540 when Pope Paul III officially endorsed the establishment of the Society of Jesus pledging to win back converts and territorial possessions to Catholicism under the Vatican's jurisdiction. Militant Catholicism was to later breed militant Protestantism as the Counter-Reformation and Reformation collided, with both sets of Christendom reciprocally taking on the characteristics and tactics of the other.

Inevitably, the clash of religions was driven to center on the geopolitics of international relations. The religious preferences of princes was to be a decisive factor in determining the political-ecclesiastic balance of power.

The Catholic-Calvinist Cold War.   In 1533, following the conversion of John Calvin to Protestantism and his pronouncement of a theology that differed in important respects from Lutheran doctrine, Catholicism began to lose influence in many important towns and bishoprics. Equally threatening to Catholics was Calvin's rejection of the supremacy of the state in secular affairs and his emphasis on popular governance over church administration, both of which challenged the papal claim for absolute religious authority and the doctrine of the divine right of kings. In an atmosphere of mutual disdain and distrust, the pope convened the Council of Trent between 1545 and 1563 and directed Catholic bishops and religious orders to concentrate their warfare on the perceived greater threat posed by Calvinism rather than on Lutheranism.

> Roman Catholicism refurbished, rigidified, and armed by the Council of Trent conceived its prime enemy to be Calvinism. As early as 1542, Cardinal Caraffa (later Pope Paul IV) instructed the Roman Inquisition that "none is to lower himself by showing toleration towards any sort of heretic, least of all a Calvinist." The confrontation of the two disciplined and ideologically zealous antagonists merged with the dynastic and political ambitions of princes and nationalist loyalties to keep Europe in turmoil for a century in a seemingly endless series of international wars and civil conflicts.[61]

Although tensions were high between Protestant and Catholic principalities, war did not break out in the Empire until 1546, the year of Martin Luther's death, when the Schmalkaldic League, backed by France, created a defensive alliance and pledged to use force if necessary against the Catholic Holy Roman Emperor. Blood then spilled. Charles V won several initial battles, including an important one at Muhlberg in April 1547. The tide turned, though, and in 1552 Charles V lost control of the Tyrol in Austria and fled across the Alps to find sanctuary. The civil and religious wars ended in 1555 with the signing of the Peace of Augsburg.

The Peace of Augsburg.   Some historians claim that the Augsburg peace settlement was a complete victory for Lutheranism and the small states of the German Empire.[62] In one sense, it was, for the Peace of Augsburg established a new principle that permitted the prince in each region to determine its own religion, under the rule *cujus regio ejus religio,* "whose the region, his the religion." The treaty was a compromise settlement between the Lutheran and Catholic Estates in the Empire. Like all compromises, it entailed both costs and benefits for both sides. The treaty did not provide true religious liberty. "No individual freedom of religion was permitted; if a ruler or a free city decided for Lutheranism, then all persons had to be Lutheran. Similarly, in Catholic states all had to be Catholic."[63] Moreover, dissidents of both religions had to convert or leave the territory. True, a sovereign prince was now free to change his religion and that of his subjects, but the Peace of Augsburg redistributed the religious balance of power by freezing the religious boundaries to those that had existed in 1552 when Protestant allegiances had fallen to their lowest level, and the retributive settlement prohibited any Catholic bishopric or city from switching to the Lutheran confessional creed. Thus, the spirit of the age began to drift toward acceptance of wheeling and dealing in political bargaining that elevated the political power of ruling princes to expediently control their subjects—all in the name of preserving order by repressing individual freedom over such human rights as freedom of religion.

Division and discord were the by-products of this precedent-setting settlement. Indeed, it might even be claimed that the deficiencies of the Augsburg Peace sowed the seeds for the Thirty Years' War because it represented "the success of localism against central power."[64] Regionalism overruled universalism, and separatism overshadowed supranationalism. The Peace of Augsburg was a significant step toward the permanent division of Christianity: Catholicism henceforth prevailed mainly in the south, except for certain cities in the Rhine Valley and the family possessions controlled by the Hapsburgs in Northern Europe; Lutheranism prevailed mainly in the north, except for the Duchy of Württemberg and a few other free cities in the south. By accepting the principle of *cujus regio ejus religio,* the Augsburg treaty weakened the authority of the Holy Roman Emperor by permitting each prince, not the emperor, to decide which religion held sway. The Holy Roman Empire was thus almost evenly divided after 1555 between the conflicting religions and was on the verge of disintegrating into an increasing number of separate, more sovereign states. Indeed, fragmentation prevailed over integration, just as it does today in an age of failed states, separatist revolts, and devolution (see Chapter 6).

Attempts at peaceful religious coexistence after 1555 were undermined by major defects of the Augsburg Peace. Rather than restore trust, it generated additional conflict by limiting the right of religious choice to only Lutheranism or Catholicism. Further undermining inter-faith trust was the fact that the Ecclesiastical Reservation clause to the Augsburg Treaty stipulated that any Catholic prince who converted to Lutheranism would lose his political authority and a Catholic successor must be appointed in his place. Moreover, the language of the treaty was left ambiguous in order to gain ratification, but in the absence of explicit criteria for interpreting its application the door was opened to an elastic reading for political gain. In short, religious differences went unresolved, and precedents were set for writing treaties in vague, ambiguous language to reach compromise and to postpone fighting over the resolution of critical issues for another day.

To sum up, the Peace of Augsburg ultimately proved itself deficient because it guaranteed that religious conflict would be perpetuated. After 1555, Lutherans enjoyed considerable gains in territory which meant a loss of influence and revenue that was deeply resented by the Catholic Church. Another weakness of the Augsburg settlement not to be underestimated in its ultimate political consequences was that, although it recognized Lutheranism and Catholicism, the treaty ignored Calvinism. Separate, exclusionary peace settlements harbor dangers. Thus denied recognition, Calvinism reacted defensively, as a persecuted sect; bound together by outside opposition, Calvinism rapidly became a more militant form of Protestantism, and thereafter spread quickly throughout Germany, becoming the primary threat to Catholicism.[65] Although Calvinists had no rights in the Empire, several states had become Calvinist in faith. One such place was the Palatinate, where its Calvinist ruler was one of the seven Electors of the Holy Roman Emperor. It was in this region of the Empire that events would most rapidly accelerate toward armed hostilities.

The Decline of Catholicism.   In the last half of the sixteenth century several trends took root that were to undermine further the prospects for peace. The most explosive was the waning influence of the Roman Catholic Church and the two halves of the House of Hapsburg, one in Austria and the other in Spain. The Roman Catholic Church and the Holy Roman Empire were equally threatened by the collapse of popular adherence to centralized Church authority. The erosion of the Church's position was most severe in the German principalities, especially lower Austria and Bavaria. According to one study:

> By 1580, some 90 percent of the nobles of Lower Austria were Protestant (almost all of them Lutherans), and the situation was similar in Upper Austria (except that several nobles became Calvinists). The Roman Catholic church in both duchies was moribund: parishes remained almost permanently vacant, congregations were abandoned, and the surviving establishments languished in an unedifying condition. Lower Austria in 1563 could boast 122 monasteries, with a total of only 463 monks and 160 nuns, but 199 concubines, 55 wives and 443 children.[66]

This situation was even more difficult in the Palatinate, where the staunchly Calvinist ruler, the youthful, Imperial Elector Frederick, helped form a Protestant Union of German princes to protect the gains which permitted Protestant services to be conducted with Protestant pastors in regions ruled by their Hapsburg overlords. The alliance required political support to survive against pressure from the powerful Hapsburg family, so "the Protestants negotiated with the Dutch, with the English, and with Henry IV of France."[67] The Protestants were highly vulnerable, however. To protect and exploit their weakness, the Bavarian Catholic states backed by Spain also reorganized the Catholic League alliance in 1609.

From this conflict between contending faiths emerges the hypothesis that religion is intimately connected to politics and warfare. At the extreme, it arouses the argument that, through its internecine conflicts and appeals to religious warrant and identity, Christianity and other major religions cause war.[68] Suspicions about the political impact of religion arose during the Enlightenment, when critics observed the militant attitudes that tend to develop because people of intense religious conviction, readily convinced of the certainty of their faith, become intolerant "toward persons informed by rival, often equally certain commitments."[69] To be sure, this dynamic was evident in the mores of the sixteenth and seventeenth centuries, when conflicts between rival Christian sects began to justify holy wars against one another to resolve their debate.

This simple explanation of the origins of the Thirty Years' War as profoundly rooted in religion, to the exclusion of other causes, is patently too narrow. As James Turner Johnson observes, even though religious opposition undoubtedly fueled the flames of conflict during the Reformation and Counter-Reformation "any conflict has a diversity of causes of which Christian religion could be at most one."[70] The fact of the matter is that in this atmosphere what made warfare so probable was precisely that the Christian religion was being, in a step-by-step evolutionary process, divorced from the politics of international relations; this liberation then enabled the contestant states, empires, and principalities to wage wars unrestrained by the moral code of Christian doctrine, as defined by either Catholicism or Protestantism. Princes used religion as an excuse for military action, rather than religion deterring princes from taking up arms against one another for reasons of power more than over questions of theological doctrine. The pacification of international politics that might have occurred in a culture restrained by religious prohibition against warfare was sacrificed. Christianity preaches the means for reconciling disputes peacefully and transcending them; its theology does not justify exacerbating political differences. But this message for Christian conflict resolution was ignored, which suggests that in the final analysis "The upshot is that the argument that Christianity causes war has the matter exactly backwards. Where Christianity is highly differentiated and pluralistic in relation to the public sphere, as it is in voluntary forms of Christian religion, the contribution of religion has been almost entirely directed to peaceful reconciliation internally and peace in foreign affairs."[71] Thus, it was largely the use made by kings and princes of religious cleavages within Christianity, and not their fervent adherence to Christian principles in the statecraft of the day, which converted a war of words into a military war between rulers. Religion was less a cause of strife than was the uses to which states in Europe put religion to justify their wars for power against one another.[72]

The Instability of a Bipolar Religious World.   The formation of these two religious unions of allied states revealed the degree to which Europe was anticipating another war. The Austrian Hapsburgs were preparing to erase all traces of Protestantism from the Empire, and France, in order to combat Hapsburg domination, put itself in the role of chief protector of Protestant faith. Thus in the early part of the seventeenth century Europe stood divided into rival blocs poised for armed conflict.

The religious roots of the Thirty Years' War are difficult to deny. As described by Henry Kissinger, this was "an age still dominated by religious zeal and ideological fanaticism" when "the Hapsburg Holy Roman Emperor Ferdinand II was attempting to revive Catholic universality," and "the Emperor came to be perceived in Protestant lands less an agent of God than as a Viennese warlord tied to a decadent pope."[73] To be sure, calling the Thirty Years' War a "religious war" is apt because much of the bloodletting was precipitated by the alacrity with which princes exploited, for their parochial political purposes, the intra-Christian sectarian conflicts that dominated European politics during the Reformation and Counter-Reformation.

A rival interpretation, equally popular among historians, must also be considered. Many analysts see the Thirty Years' War as originating from a great-power clash for geostrategic dominance. According to this explanation, a hegemonical struggle intensified and, almost exactly a century after Martin Luther's 1517 act of defiance of papal abuses, ignited the Thirty Years' War largely because "the Hapsburg dynasty attempted to turn back the Reformation in Bohemia"[74] as a means to establish its political suzerainty over the continent.

A War between Rivals for Hegemony?   As a challenge to the thesis that the Thirty Years' War was a religious war in origin, some historians claim that the war erupted less over religion than political issues. To this school of thought, the Thirty Years' War was a classic hegemonic struggle for supremacy. Richard Cavendish neatly sums up these two contending opinions about the causes of the Thirty Years' War when he avers that it originated from the Hapsburgs's search for domination—that, as a by-product, "pitted Protestant against Catholic, the Holy Roman Empire against France, the German Princes and princelings against the Emperor and each other, and France against the Hapsburgs of Spain. The Swedes, the Danes, the Poles, the Russians, the Dutch, and the Swiss were all dragged in or dived in." Thus, while "commercial interests and rivalries played a part, as did religion and power politics,"[75] a compelling explanation of the seeds of the Thirty Years' War posits that it would not have happened had there not existed a clash between the Bourbons centered in France and the Hapsburgs who, after Charles V's 1519 election as Holy Roman Emperor, consolidated the Spanish and Austrian territories. From this vantage point, great-power politics transcended religious conflict. In the words of Geoffrey Parker:

> The diplomatic system created in the century after 1450, first in Renaissance Italy and later elsewhere, permitted the construction of elaborate and sophisticated networks of alliances aimed primarily at preserving the status quo. Larger states found security in weakening their neighbors, rather than in dominating them; threatened states sought to divert their more powerful enemies by creating difficulties for them elsewhere. But the success of the Reformation cut clean across these recently established political affiliations. The traditional amity between England and Castile, for example, was fatally undermined when the Tudor dynasty embraced Protestantism; and the 'auld alliance' between Scotland and France was likewise wrecked by the progress of the Reformation in Scotland after 1560. But these new orientations in international affairs did not discourage diplomatic intercourse; on the contrary, they intensified the creation of alliances, the exchange of ambassadors, and the signature of mutual defense pacts. Periods of relative peace, such as the decade before 1618, saw frenzied attempts to create international alignments which would guarantee support in case of attack. . . . But on what criteria were these 'friends and allies' to be chosen? It was here that the polarization of Europe into separate religious camps between the 1520s and the 1640s proved so unsettling, for confessional and political advantage seldom totally coincided.[76]

The era of balance-of-power politics was coming into its own as the preferred approach driving international competition, with war and shifting alliances increasingly seen as instruments to prevent the military domination by a hegemon of the continent divorced from ideological considerations.[77]

The Rise of an Empire.   At the core of European politics since the late 1400s stood the Holy Roman Empire, a territory composed of many small principalities all united through marriages under the rule of the Catholic Hapsburgs. This family dynasty built more through marital than through martial strategies had unlimited territorial ambitions. The Empire at first consisted mainly of Germans centered in Vienna, but the family holdings had radiated out over time to include the Czechs of Bohemia and a sizeable French-speaking population in the areas that are now Belgium, Lorraine, eastern Burgundy, and western Switzerland, until the Empire stretched from France on the west to Poland and Hungary on the east.

What gave the monarchy in Vienna enormous stature and supremacy was the Empire's consolidation with Spain in 1519 following Charles V of Spain's election as Holy Roman Emperor. Charles led the most powerful navy and army that Europe had to that time; he was ruler of the first empire over which the sun never set.

The origins of military and economic power within a single empire had started from a modest base, but beginning in 1500 the Hapsburg Empire had expanded in a series of marital allegiances (see Figure 1.1). It was to eventually encompass an ever-widening area that spread from Gibraltar to Hungary and from Sicily to Amsterdam, exceeding in size any feudal holding by a single dynasty since the time of Charlemagne. "About one quarter of the peoples of early modern Europe were living in Hapsburg-ruled territory"—or approximately 25 million out of a total population of 105 million in 1600.[78]

It is important to view the Holy Roman Empire as a sum of its major parts. First, consider the family center of power in Vienna. The Austrian Hapsburg Empire was composed of an Emperor who served in a similar role as did the King of England, and an Imperial Diet which served as a general assembly. Below the King and Diet were a number of princes and bishops who ruled over particular regions within the Empire. The princes were neither exclusively secular nor religious: there were numerous Catholic bishops who also served as princes, and bishops who did not serve as princes but also had significant power.

After the Protestant Reformation, as the number of Lutheran and Calvinist Protestants expanded in central Europe, the Vatican sought and often succeeded in influencing the policies of the Austrian rulers (who opposed the spread of these new Protestant faiths becoming increasingly popular among the Germanic people), though most governments professed loyalty to the pope. As religious differences intensified, they fomented political differences.

The Holy Roman Empire did not rule supreme, and in the 1500s faced challenges to its control on several fronts. Two major centers of political rebellion within the Empire were the revolt by the Netherlands from the Spanish Hapsburg throne and the uprisings in Bohemia from the Austrian throne. The Dutch revolt began in 1567 against King Philip II's attempts to raise taxes and to enforce Catholicism; the Bohemian resistance stemmed from an earlier time when the followers of the Czech religious reformer Jan Huss and others protesting against the pope were burned at the stake for their defiance of papal authority.[79]

The Spanish Factor.   The German Empire was not the only territory facing opposition in the sixteenth century. King Philip II, the son of the Hapsburg Holy Roman Emperor Charles V, obtained possession of the Spanish throne when in a strategic maneuver he married the only surviving descendant of the Spanish King, Catherine "the Loco." Charles V had abdicated his throne in 1556, a year after the Peace of Augsburg. His brother Ferdinand (who was soon to become Holy Roman Emperor) inherited Austria, Bohemia, and Hungary. Philip, his son, received all of Charles's other possessions.

The Hapsburg dynasty then combined two separate branches, the Spanish and the Austrian, which cooperated with one another to dominate European affairs. Their political agenda for hegemonic control was interwoven with an ideological agenda aimed at expanding Catholic influence. The Hapsburgs pledged to propagate the Catholic religion (following the crusade of Isabella, "the Catholic," who in 1492, "on the very day Columbus set sail,"[80] suspended religious tolerance in Spain and unleashed the Inquisition to force all who would not conform to Catholic orthodoxy to either convert, emigrate, or be killed). After Philip inherited territories from other relatives, the Spanish empire grew rapidly through vigorous pursuit of a grand strategy of "messianic imperialism"[81] dedicated to defend the Catholic Church against all enemies and to gain control of Europe and the New World. Philip was fanatically loyal to his version of Catholicism, even though his understanding of what Catholicism stood for put him in frequent conflict with a whole series of popes. Philip's world view precluded religious tolerance, because in his mind freedom of worship was a recipe for sedition that would weaken his frail, delusory empire composed of diverse subjects. Civil peace, he believed, required the unity of religion and politics, and this outlook helped to prepare the way for the wars of religion in his century and the next one.[82] Under Philip's guidance, Spain became the world's strongest military and naval power, controlling not only Iberia and the Spanish colonial empire in the New World, but also the seventeen provinces of the Netherlands, the free county of Burgundy, the Kingdom of Two Sicilies, Sardinia, and the Balearic Islands.

The tentacles of Hapsburg family possessions spread by a policy of strategic marriages. Philip's four wives illustrate the Hapsburg plan of expansion through family intermarriages and marriages to other dynasties. Philip married Maria of Portugal, Mary Tudor of England, Elizabeth of Valois and his own niece, Anna of Austria. The policy of strategic marriage succeeded, but the price of inbreeding was high. Fed by the Hapsburgs's obsession with dynastic succession, as seen by the fact that Philip's retarded son Don Carlos had only four as opposed to eight great-grandparents, the mental capabilities of the Hapsburg genetic line deteriorated badly and eventually diminished the dynasty's capacity to rule and exercise global leadership.

In the on-going struggle for religious dominance on the European continent it was of great importance which religion the leader of the world's largest power espoused. Thrown into the Counter-Reformation's ideological and religious struggle, Philip II of Spain followed in his Austrian father's footsteps in the crusade against non-Catholics, especially Protestants and Muslims. Said to have been "before all else a Catholic, fervid and fanatical, committed to upholding the sway of the universal church," Philip "took upon himself the leadership of the far-flung Catholic counteroffensive, into which he poured with grim persistence the blood and treasure of all his kingdoms."[83] This otherwise reticent and somber Hapsburg perceived few limits to his ambitions. A symbol of his pride and megalomania was his order in 1563 to build *El Escorial*, a massive palace and fortress monastery on a mountaintop outside Madrid. Modeled after the way his Spanish architects imagined King Solomon's Temple in Jerusalem to have looked, *El Escorial* became the largest building in Europe and a symbol of the grandiloquent self-image of the Spanish Hapsburg monarchy.

At the time Calvinism was gaining considerable influence in the Spanish

Netherlands. Control of the Low Countries was given in 1559 to Philip's half sister Margaret as regent. A devout Catholic, Margaret introduced the Inquisition into the Netherlands to extirpate all opposition to the Roman Catholic Church. This policy led to the deterioration of economic and social conditions in the Netherlands. High taxes and a series of inflationary grain prices provoked a destructive uprising by the Calvinist commercial and professional classes, and the revolt spread from Antwerp to Brussels, Ghent, and Zeeland in Holland,[84] and in the course of the rampage more than thirty churches were destroyed and numerous libraries burned. Philip II responded by sending over twenty thousand troops from Madrid under the command of the Duke of Alva, who interpreted his order of "pacification to mean the ruthless extermination of religious and political dissidents. On top of the Inquisition he opened his own tribunal, soon called the 'Council of Blood.' The rationale for its name can be seen in the gruesome events March 3, 1568, when fifteen hundred men were executed."[85]

This ruthless campaign to enforce peace by the sword did not end the struggle between Spain and the Netherlands. The rebellion continued for ten more years. In 1578 Philip assigned his nephew Alexander Farnese the task of crushing the rebellion, and Farnese laid siege to Maastricht, Tournai, Bruges, Ghent, and finally Antwerp. When the campaign concluded, the Spanish imposed a vindictive peace plan that prohibited Calvinist worship and forced all dissenters from the Catholic Church to either flee or convert.[86]

However, this phase of Spanish imperialism in the Netherlands did not terminate Dutch opposition to Spanish colonial rule. Resistance continued, and the United Provinces repeatedly sought external assistance from the most sympathetic foreign ally—Elizabeth, the Queen of England, who was a Protestant. Despite Elizabeth's efforts to isolate her country from these struggles, England was drawn into the continent's troubles because the English crown feared an invasion if Spain subdued the revolt in the Netherlands. After England sent aid to the United Provinces, relations between Spain and England soured, and each side prepared to use force to redress the balance of power at the other's expense.

Philip oversaw building of *La Felicissima Armada,* a huge fleet created to cross the English Channel and, with the 19,000 soldiers on board the Armada's 130 galleons, to invade, conquer, and re-Catholicize England. Philip's grand strategy combined both ideological and military motives in a messianic mission for both religious triumph and national aggrandizement.[87]

Philip's bold military venture failed miserably: The complete destruction of the Spanish Armada in July and August 1588 was one of the most decisive and influential battles in naval history, and signaled the rise of English political fortunes. Elizabeth gained considerable political clout as a result of the victory, and, after this "power transition" through a change in the international power hierarchy, England was positioned to compete as a global power. Although the Armada's defeat was a severe setback to Spanish goals, the war dragged on until

1604, when the borders that had been formerly created in the Netherlands in 1581 were reluctantly recognized by Philip III of Spain in a treaty that gave independence to the northern provinces.

Nevertheless, war for aggrandizement was to remain a core element of Spanish grand strategy. The Spanish were by no means removed from the top of the hierarchy of European powers after their defeat. Indeed, English sea power did not succeed in its effort to blockade Spain or to sever the flow of gold and silver from the Spanish colonies in the New World. With this treasure the Spanish rebuilt their navy and maintained military preponderance.[88] Still, the English victory encouraged resistance by other nations to Madrid's political ambitions. To retain its dominant position, Spain relied on intervention. For example, Philip sent troops to assist the Catholic League, and inserted himself into the religious wars in France, claiming to defend Catholicism from Protestantism. His plans proved abortive after Henry of Navarre converted to Catholicism, therein discrediting Philip's justification for sending an occupation army.

Enter the French.   In the waning of the sixteenth century, France also experienced civil wars between opposed religious groups. "Eight separate civil wars, the first beginning in 1562 and the last ending in 1593, can be viewed as one war that lasted for thirty years broken by short periods of truce."[89]

Although France was a predominately Catholic country, after the Reformation many Protestants found a religious home in Christian belief outside the control of the papacy. Approximately 1.2 million of the 16 million Frenchmen embraced the teachings of John Calvin, and because a large portion of these converts belonged to the nobility, the Calvinist influence was disproportionate to its modest numbers. Religion, however, was largely a surface issue; the deeper issue was a power struggle between the nobles and the monarchy: "Just as German princes in the Holy Roman Empire had adopted Lutheranism as a means of opposition to Emperor Charles V, so French nobles frequently adopted the 'reformed religion' as a religious cloak for their independence."[90]

Warfare broke out between the Catholics and the Huguenots (the French Calvinists) in the 1560s. In reaction to past persecution, the Huguenots destroyed Catholic Churches, icons, and sacred Eucharistic vessels. The Catholic Third Estate responded by attacking the Protestants in 1561, and hundreds of Huguenots were tortured, maimed, burned, and murdered. Queen Catherine de' Medici, the acting regent in France for her sons (Francis II, Charles IX, and Henry III, respectively), sought a compromise and, as a step toward peace building between Catholics and Protestants, pledged her daughter Margaret to marry Henry Bourbon, the Protestant King of Navarre. In March 1562 Catherine issued an edict granting Huguenots the right to worship. The concessions outraged the Catholics, some of whom sought revenge by massacring Protestants while they were worshiping.[91]

A bitter civil war unfolded in France for the next eight years, with the fortunes of both sides rising and falling as leaders constantly changed. The most climactic event of this period occurred on August 24, 1572, when, in the so-called St. Bartholomew's Day Massacre, Catherine de' Medici authorized Catholics to decapitate the Huguenot noble leadership who had congregated in Paris to attend the wedding of Henry of Navarre and her daughter Margaret. The killing was horrendous and widespread:

> Protestants were shot on the roof-tops; they were butchered in their beds, run to the earth in the Louvre, and even in the bedroom of Margaret of Navarre. For three days they were stabbed, drowned, hanged, and their bodies dragged along the streets. The massacre was soon followed by looting. Similar scenes took place at Orleans, Lyons, Rouen, Bordeaux and Toulouse.[92]

The massacre lasted until October 3, 1572, killing an estimated twelve thousand people.

These traumatic events were followed by the War of the Three Henrys. The ill-fated Henry III became King of France in 1574 after his brother Charles IX died. Like his brothers before him, Henry was a weak and ineffectual king under the thumb of his mother, Catherine de' Medici. Henry, Duke of Guise, became the leader of the all-powerful Catholic League and with the support of Spain was able to gain control of French public policy. Henry III perceived the Duke of Guise a threat to his power, and in 1588 ordered him assassinated.[93] An uprising soon followed in Paris provoking the King with help from Henry of Navarre to lay siege to Paris. This crisis was followed by another when Henry III, who was childless, was stabbed to death on August 1, 1589, by a Dominican monk, ending the Valois dynasty. The heir to the throne was Henry of Navarre, a Protestant who had led the Huguenots in the Calvinist Union.

Henry of Navarre was officially crowned Henry IV, the first French King of the Bourbon dynasty. To gain control of the lands his title conferred to him, Henry needed to win the support of the French people. The fact that he was a Protestant did not help him, a problem underscored by the appeal of the alarmed members of the Catholic League to Philip II of Spain for aid. Troops from Spain soon intervened, and France's religious civil war became internationalized.

To secure his position as the king, in 1593 Henry IV converted to Catholicism, proclaiming "Paris is worth a mass."[94] This boldly manipulative act pacified some of the opposition, but Spanish troops continued to fight against him in order to bring France within the House of Hapsburg's sphere of influence. In 1598 Henry drove the foreign troops from France and issued the *Edict of Nantes*, granting limited religious toleration to the Huguenots in France, and thereby enabled a fragile religious peace to develop within the country. "This regime of tolerance established in France after thirty-six years of civil war was, of course, incomplete and precarious; but it was the only one that Europe knew. In every other country, religious unity was being imposed by force."[95] In this sense, France set a precedent for religious reconciliation as a method of restoring internal order—a precedent that was later to become an accepted principle in future negotiations aimed at settling international religious conflict.

This is not to argue that France eschewed warfare as a policy in jockeying for position among European powers. Indeed, France geared its diplomacy to *realpolitik*, and in conformity with the mores of the age sought war with Spain to settle the mounting Franco-Spanish struggle for supremacy in Europe. But before he could wage war, Henry IV was assassinated in 1610 by a Catholic fanatic, highlighting the fact that in France, much like in England, religious tensions were still high.[96]

Following Henry IV's death, in 1624 Cardinal Richelieu (Armand Jean du Plessis) became the Chief Minister of France (see Box 2.2 for a profile of this pioneer of *realpolitik* grand strategy). The influential Cardinal Richelieu used his cunning diplomatic statecraft to build French power. He focused his attention on providing France with a natural barrier against attack from Vienna or Spain. For this goal he sought to acquire territory within the Hapsburg sphere of influence and at the same time to bargain manipulatively with opposed adversaries to entice those most useful to French security to become French allies. To Richelieu, an added advantage of French expansion was that it would splinter the Hapsburgs.[97]

The growing contest over political and religious control had now become an extension of the struggle brewing between the Holy Roman Empire and France. France under the Bourbon Kings Louis XIII and Louis XIV sought to reduce the growing Hapsburg sphere of influence in Germany and adjacent territories. Recall that in 1552 French armies had intervened in Germany to support Protestant states in order to resist Hapsburg hegemony, but the 1555 Peace of Augsburg and the 1559 Treaty of Comtesis had temporarily suspended both the religious and the Franco-Spanish rivalries. Those conflicts now resumed. France formed alliances with the Ottomans, England, and with some of the prosperous seventeen provinces that made up the Netherlands, and, in so doing, elevated strategic coalition-building to a guiding practice in statecraft; alliance formation to play one enemy off against another was becoming a prime feature of balance-of-power politics.

In the twilight of the sixteenth century the European continent split into opposed coalitions, each threatened by the other and fearful of subjugation. The European geopolitical chessboard was complex, with numerous crosscutting alliances and percolating national rivalries (such as the brewing Anglo-Spanish, Danish-Swedish, Austro-Turkish, and Russo-Polish confrontations). But on the eve of the Thirty Years' War, the center of competition was concentrated between two contending aspirants for hegemonic domination: the Austrian and Spanish branches of the House of Hapsburg at one pole and the aligned great powers nominally headed by France at the opposite pole.

The Instability of a Bipolar Political World.   The first confrontation between the contending blocs occurred in 1608 when the Catholic Duke of Bavaria put down a Protestant uprising. Angry Protestants joined forces to form the Evangelical Union under the Elector Frederick of the Palatine, the first

Calvinist prince in the Empire.[98] Maximilian I promptly responded in 1609 by creating the Catholic League. "It was a measure of political anarchy within the Empire that two armed camps, the Evangelical Union and the Catholic League, had come into existence by 1609, clearly anticipating the outbreak of civil war."[99]

We see in the emerging bipolar division of Europe the way religious differences overlaid the political-military conflict. The Protestant Union that had formed on May 14, 1608, under the leadership of Christian of Anhalt, incorporated in its network of allies princes and towns in the southern area of Austria. The alliance's purpose was explicitly stated: "In religious matters as well as in their civil rights the princes were engaged to assist each other mutually, and permit no individual oppression; that any member of the Union, when attacked, should be assisted by the rest; that his territories, towns, and castles should be opened to them; and that whatever conquests were made should be divided among the whole."[100] In addition to these defensive measures which embraced elements of collective-security calculations, Christian of Anhalt also asserted that the Union would pursue preemptive strategies for defense, proclaiming "he believed that the safety of Protestantism could not be secured without the overthrow of the German branch of the House of Austria."[101]

The creation of the Protestant Union prompted Maximilian, Duke of Bavaria, to form the Catholic League which proclaimed the same grand strategies for the same allegedly defensive purposes as those articulated by the Protestant Union. A security dilemma was created as measures to prepare for war by one coalition provoked the same countermeasures by the opposing coalition, with the result that both alliances' sense of security declined as their military preparations increased. These two opposed blocs symbolized the growing apprehension felt by Europeans throughout the first decade of the seventeenth century. The continent was a tinderbox awaiting a spark that would ignite a general war.

That spark came as the twelve-year armistice agreed to in the 1609 Truce of Antwerp by Spain and Holland was scheduled to end in 1621. Both sides began to mobilize troops in preparation for war, for Spain in a campaign to repress the rebellious Dutch "heretics" and recover Spain's wealthiest European province, and for the Dutch to formalize recognition of the independence of the United Provinces. The Holy Roman Emperor made a compact, agreeing to intensify the Austrian Hapsburgs' military efforts to control Germany while at the same time promising the Hapsburg rulers in Madrid Austrian military assistance in the Spanish effort to restore the Netherlands to the Empire.

> Spain was only awaiting the end of a twelve-year truce made in 1609 to renew its efforts to reconquer the rebellious provinces in the Netherlands. Because of Dutch naval strength, the Spanish would have to send their troops to the Netherlands by way of Italy, the Alpine passes, and the Rhine River Valley. A strong Emperor meant greater imperial authority in the Rhineland and with it more ease in mov-

ing troops. Indeed, Ferdinand had already promised Alsace to his Spanish cousins in return for supporting his candidacy to the imperial throne, and he was to promise more in return for military assistance.[102]

From the instabilities surrounding these counterpoised coalitions we can easily discern why it is so compelling for many historians to interpret the origins of the Thirty Years' War as an instance of a hegemonic rivalry. In many respects, the Thirty Years' War that began in 1618 was largely a struggle of polarized alliances nested within the longer and larger epic struggle between the French Bourbon monarchy against the Austrian and Spanish branches of the House of Hapsburg, with other dynastic kingdoms such as the Vasas in Sweden participating in the power struggle. The 1618–1648 segment saw the German Protestant princes ally with France, Sweden, Denmark, and the United Provinces against the power of the Hapsburgs, representing the Holy Roman Empire and allied with the Catholic princes of Germany. A systemwide war erupted because all the belligerents were motivated by their fear of subjugation. Together, religious strife and geopolitical struggle proved to be a deadly combination; it created a consensus that the competitive quest for self-preservation through war should be *the* most important foreign policy priority for all the great powers. The acceptance of the pursuit of national interest through military policy, and the indifference to ethical principle, created a mistrustful climate of opinion conducive to an explosive military contest for dominion. Seen in this perspective, the Thirty Years' War was the product of twin forces—the "last effort of the Roman Catholic Church and the House of Hapsburg to re-establish unity by the triumph of Catholicism over the Protestant heresies and the renewal of the Emperor's universal power,"[103] and the first effort of the Protestant princes aided by Bourbon France to liberate themselves from Hapsburg dominion and Catholic persecution by securing their sovereign independence.

MILITARY ANSWERS TO THEOLOGICAL AND POLITICAL QUESTIONS

The conflict originating in the territory of the Holy Roman Empire eventually engulfed almost all the continental powers. Each great power struggled not only with finding a solution to the widening split between Catholics and Protestants following the Reformation, but also to the protracted rivalry between an ascending Bourbon France and the Hapsburg dynasty. These intertwined motives suggest that the most meaningful interpretation of the origins of the Thirty Years' War is that it was a product of the twin forces of religious conflict and of political conflict. Neither conflict alone was a sufficient cause for the Thirty Years' War; it was their interaction that made a European-wide war possible.

To this conclusion must quickly be added a qualification: it was the presence of other background factors that made this "confrontation between governments, and between governments and governed, likely."[104] For example, Europe's division was exacerbated by the decay of the Holy Roman Empire as well as the division between the Spanish and Austrian Hapsburg courts. These wrenching changes produced a dangerous power vacuum when Spain, through mismanagement of the treasures it obtained from overseas colonies, began to relinquish the military supremacy it had enjoyed for over a century, and a gap in income began to develop between the increasingly prosperous Protestant principalities and the increasingly debt-ridden Catholic strongholds in many parts of the Holy Roman Empire. Imperial decay fed pervasive insecurities of all the rival factions in a divided Europe; "Almost all [the combatants]," wrote one of its most distinguished historians, "were actuated by fear rather than by lust of conquest or passion of faith. They wanted peace and they fought for thirty years to be sure of it."[105]

These various religious, political, and economic pressures exploded in Bohemia which had been ruled by the Hapsburgs since the sixteenth century. In the early 1600s Bohemia was in the midst of a national and religious revival under the leadership of a strongly Protestant and fiercely patriotic local nobility. The Bohemians refused to elect Ferdinand of Austria to the throne and offered it instead to the Calvinist Count Frederick of the Palatine. When the Hapsburgs in Austria and Spain responded with force, the European tinderbox was ignited in a war that would not be extinguished for decades.

From this foregoing historical summary in this chapter, we can see that the Thirty Years' War originated from a welter of crosscurrents: intellectual, territorial, dynastic, religious, economic, military, and political issues combined to generate a multifaceted armed conflict. To better grasp how these factors animated the belligerents and how their repeated behaviors became socially sanctioned customs, the next chapter traces the evolution of the Thirty Years' War between 1618 and 1648, a tragic period of transition, similar to today's, during which "there was no consensus among the political elite concerning the correct principles upon which foreign policy should be based."[106]

CHAPTER 2

The Evolutionary Course of the Thirty Years' War

It is difficult to fight often and always win.
—Armand Jean du Plessis
(Cardinal Richelieu)

How wars are fought shapes how peace settlements are crafted. The nearly continuous European armed struggle that raged between 1618 and 1648 exerted a profound impact upon the hopes and philosophical beliefs of those who labored to construct a durable peace settlement. Because what is called the "Thirty Years' War" was more accurately a collection of nearly a dozen interconnected wars fought in different parts of Europe which threw "all Europe . . . in a state of intermittent turmoil,"[1] the negotiators at the peace congresses in Westphalia faced an enormously complex task. The security architecture they constructed was bound together by a new set of principles and rules that would govern international affairs for the next three and one-half centuries.

The peace treaties signed in Münster and Osnabrück would not have been so revolutionary in their long-term effects had it not been for the new system of international norms that coalesced around the concept of state sovereignty. Diplomatic and military practices that became entrenched during three decades of brutal warfare shaped the socially constructed new code of state conduct ratified by the Peace of Westphalia. How the war was fought affected how the peace agreements were designed which, in turn, facilitated the growth of a normative order that countenanced amorality, appeals to expedience, and a reliance on forcible measures of self-help.

To illuminate the origins of these principles and rules, we need to follow the Thirty Years' War through its evolutionary course and chart how each step in the struggle influenced the views and visions of the peacemakers at West-phalia seeking to devise new rules for statecraft. The Thirty Years' War widened through a series of consecutive phases, beginning with the Bohemian rebel-lion against the Hapsburgs in 1618. Historians conventionally divide the war into sequential periods. We adhere to that practice, and separate the war into five stages: the Bohemian (1618–1620), the Palatinate (1620–1624), the Danish (1625–1629), the Swedish (1630–1635), and the Franco-Swedish (1635–1648). To assist in the interpretation of these stages, Table 2.1 provides a chronology that identifies the major events that ultimately led to the war's conclusion.

In tracing the path of the Thirty Years' War, it is necessary to recognize that the geographic boundaries of the fighting changed over time, with dif-ferent territories affected in each period. By following the ebb and flow of the war across the European landscape, we can see that the "religious and politi-cal passions which were to produce the Thirty Years' War did not in fact origi-nate in Germany, but in the lands that surrounded it, and above all in the states governed by Europe's foremost dynasty, the Spanish and Austrian Hapsburgs."[2] In addition, we can also better appreciate both the myriad motives of the bel-ligerents and why the war was "so much more than a simple dynastic conflict, reli-gious imbroglio, civil war, or uncontrolled form of adventurism, [why it] was a truly continental war fought for multiple objectives. . . [and why] in its very multiplicity of purposes and participants the war marked a break in the character of previous hostilities."[3]

TABLE 2.1   A Chronology of the Major Events, Battles, and Peace Treaties during the Thirty Years' War

---

1618–1625   The Bohemian Period of the War

1618   In May, Protestants revolt against suspension of their right to worship, and the event known as the Defenestration of Prague signals the beginning of the war.

1619   The Bohemians depose Ferdinand and offer the crown to Frederick V who, after entering Prague, is crowned King by the religious rebels.

1619   In May, the Protestant rebel army lays siege to Ferdinand's supporters in Vienna; within weeks the Protestants are forced to withdraw when a large Spanish army, partly financed by the pope, invades Bohemia.

1619   The Catholic League is recreated, and its leaders are authorized the levy of an army of 25,000 to be used as Maximilian of Bavaria orders. A crisis occurs as Phillip III and Archduke Albert each promise to send a new army into Germany to assist Ferdinand (who succeeds the late Matthias as Holy Roman Emperor).

1619   Bethlen Gabor and Bohemian forces lay siege to Vienna for the second time.

1620s   Gustavus II of Sweden organizes an army to intervene in Poland-Lithuania, seek-ing to acquire territory on the southern shore of the Baltic.

1620   The Spanish Imperial Army commanded by General Spinola crosses from the Netherlands and occupies the Rhine Palatinate.

1620   *On November 3, the first significant battle of the war takes place at the White Mountain on the outskirts of Prague, where the victorious Catholic Hapsburg Army ends the Bohemian rebellion and positions itself for conquest of the Palatinate.**

1620–1624	**The Palatinate Period of the War**
1621	War between Sweden and Poland-Lithuania begins; it lasts until 1629.
1621	War in the Netherlands begins.
1621	French Huguenot War breaks out.
1623	On February 25, the Hapsburg Empire transfers Palatine Elector to Maximilian.
1624	Cardinal Richelieu comes to power as Chief Minister to King Louis XIII and manages French foreign policy.
1625–1629	**The Danish Period of the War**
1625	King Christian of Denmark intervenes in the war.
1625	In March, Spain's war with England reignites, and lasts until 1630.
1625	In June, the Swedish army invades Prussia. Ferdinand authorizes Albrecht von Wallenstein to raise a new Imperial army of 25,000 men and move northward to meet the Danish threat.
1625	On December 9, the Hague Alliance is signed.
1626	*On August 26, the Danes are routed at the Battle of Lütter, compelling the withdrawal of Denmark from the war; the Imperial army advances northward.*
1626	Upper Austria rebels in response to the persecution of Protestants.
1627	In December, after the death of the last native ruler of the strategic states of Mantua and Montferrat, Spanish forces from Lombardy launch an invasion, but the garrisons of Mantua and Montferrat are declared for the late Duke's relative, the French-born Duke of Nevers.
1627	War erupts between France and England, and lasts until 1629.
1628	War of the Mantuan Succession breaks out.
1628	In May, Bavaria annexes the Upper Palatinate.
1629	On March 28, the Edict of Restitution is issued.
1629	Calvinist rebels are defeated in France, making it possible for the King and his chief minister to deploy troops in Italy to aid the Duke of Nevers. To meet this threat, Philip IV of Spain asks the Emperor to send his troops to Italy rather than to the Netherlands.
1629	King Christian of Denmark sues for peace, promising never again to intervene in the Holy Roman Empire.
1629	On July 7, the Peace Treaty of Lübeck ends Swedish war with Poland-Lithuania and Russia.
1629	On September 26, with the aid of French and British mediators, the Truce of Altmark is reached and Poland-Lithuania makes numerous concessions in return for a six-year truce.
1630–1635	**The Swedish Period of the War**
1630	Louis XIII launches a second invasion of Italy. Some 50,000 Imperial troops are brought south from Spain to oppose them, reducing the war for Mantua to a stalemate but delivering the Dutch republic from immediate danger and weakening the Emperor's hold on Germany.
1630	On July 6, Gustavus Adolphus leads a Swedish interventionary force ashore near Stralsund in Germany with the declared intention of saving the "liberties of the Empire" and preserving the security of the Baltic.
1630	On August 13, Emperor Ferdinand dismisses Wallenstein, his most capable commander.
1631	On May 20, Tilly's Imperial Army sacks Magdeburg in a brutal massacre which horrifies Europeans.
1631	On June 22, Brandenburg signs a mutual defense treaty with Sweden.
1631	In September, Saxony, Bremen and Hense-Kassel ally with Sweden.
1631	*On September 17, in a turning point in the war, Gustavus Adolphus defeats the Emperor's forces in the Battle of Breitenfeld, just outside Leipzig in Saxony, and Swedish forces begin to overrun most of central Germany and Bohemia.*

1631	On October 13, the Peace of Regensburg is signed.
1632	On April 13, Wallenstein is restored Imperial Commander-in-Chief.
1632	*On November 1, Wallenstein's Imperial Army fights Swedish forces at Lützen, Gustavus Adolphus dies in battle.*
1632	Russian invasion of Poland-Lithuania ties down the forces of both powers for almost two years.
1633	On April 19, the Franco-Swedish Treaty of Alliance is renewed.
1633	On April 23, the Heilbrun League of Protestant States' alliance solidifies.
1634	On February 25, Wallenstein is assassinated by his own officers by command of the Emperor.
1634	On June 4, Russia makes peace with Poland-Lithuania at Polyanov.
1634	*On September 6, Spain sends a large army across the Alps from Lombardy to join the Imperial forces at the Battle of Nördlingen; the Swedes are decisively beaten and obliged to withdraw their forces from most of southern Germany, and Sweden's capacity to lead the anti-Hapsburg coalition declines.*
1635	French troops begin to mass along the borders of Germany, preparing to enter the war on the side of the Protestants in order to prevent Hapsburg hegemony; France increases its subsidies to the Dutch fighting the Spanish Hapsburgs.
1635	France signs an offensive and defensive alliance with the Dutch Republic (February 8), with Sweden (April 28), and with Savoy (July 11).
1635	On May 19, France declares war on Spain.
1635	On May 30, the Peace of Prague is signed between the Catholic Emperor and the Lutheran Saxons; within a year most other German Lutherans, seeking self-preservation and fearing annihilation under the changed circumstances withdraw from their prior treaty agreements and shift their political allegiance from Stockholm to Vienna.
1635	On September 12, France mediates a twenty-year truce between Sweden and Poland-Lithuania.
1635–1648	**The Franco-Swedish Period of the War**
1636	In March, France declares war on the Hapsburg Emperor Ferdinand II; the Treaty of Wismar strengthens the Franco-Swedish alliance.
1636	On October 4, Swedes win victory at Wittstock; Ferdinand III is elected the next designate Holy Roman Emperor.
1636	On December 23, the ailing Ferdinand II meets the Electors of the Imperial Diet at Regensburg.
1637	On February 15, Ferdinand II dies; Ferdinand III becomes Holy Roman Emperor.
1637	In March, revolt of the Valtellina leads to Spanish occupation.
1638	French military forces make gains in Alsace and the middle Rhine.
1639	Swedish army invades Bohemia following the Treaty of Hamburg between France and Sweden.
1640	In February, Ferdinand III assembles the Imperial Diet at Nuremberg for the first time since 1613 in order to settle the outstanding German problems of the amnesty question and the restitution of church lands.
1640	Catalonia and Portugal revolt against Spain.
1641	On July 24, Brandenburg and Sweden sign a separate peace agreement.
1642	Brandenburg and Brunswick strike a separate agreement with Sweden.
1642	On November 2, the Hapsburg Imperial army is routed in Saxony at the Second Battle of Breitenfeld.
1643	War breaks out between Denmark and Sweden and lasts two years.
1644	Peace negotiations commence in the Westphalian towns of Münster and Osnabrück.
1645	On March 6, the Swedish armies reenter Bohemia, and at Jankov totally destroy another Imperial army prior to Denmark's final surrender.

1645	On June 1, France and Sweden bring propositions of peace, which are discussed by the Estates of the Empire from October 1645 to April 1646.
1645	On August 3, Maximilian's forces are decisively defeated at Allerheim.
1645	The Elector of Saxony makes a separate peace with Sweden and withdraws from the war.
1645	In November, the French attempt to sabotage the peace agreements previously made in the negotiations.
1646	French forces occupy Bavaria.
1646	With the aid of French and Swedish mediation, the territorial rulers are granted a large degree of sovereignty (*Landeshoheit*); a general amnesty is issued to all German princes, an eighth electorate is created for the son of Frederick V (so that both he and Maximilian can continue to possess that power); the Edict of Restitution is finally abandoned within the Empire, and Calvinism is granted official toleration. A pragmatic coalition of Protestants and Catholics secure acceptance of a formula that recognizes as Protestant all church lands in secular hands on January 1, 1624 (that is, those gains prior to the territorial acquisitions made by Wallenstein and Tilly).
1647	In June, the first phase of negotiations enables the chief Imperial negotiator, Maximilian, Count Trauttmannsdorf, to resolve most issues.
1647	Cardinal Mazarin of France, despite a preliminary agreement with the Emperor in September 1646 which conveyed parts of Alsace and Lorraine to France, starts a new military campaign in Germany to secure more territory.
1648	On January 30, Philip IV of Spain signs a peace treaty that recognizes the Dutch Republic as independent and agrees to liberalize trade between the Netherlands and the Iberian world.
1648	The "amicable composition" principle is finally accepted by all belligerents, thus resolving the last remaining issue in German affairs.
1648	On May 17, another Bavarian army is destroyed at Zusmarshausen, near Nördlingen, and the French forces occupy Maximilian's lands.
1648	Pressure of the war on French taxpayers creates tensions that erupt into the revolt known as the *Fronde*.
1648	On January 30, Spain and the Netherlands sign terms of the Westphalian Treaty.
1648	On August 6, Sweden makes a separate peace with the Emperor.
1648	On October 24, the terms of the Peace of Westphalia are accepted between the Holy Roman Emperor Ferdinand III, the other German princes, France, and Sweden.

* The five major battles that most altered the course of the war are highlighted in italics.

THE 1618–1620 BOHEMIAN PHASE

Bohemia was the wealthiest of the Austrian Hapsburg regions of the Holy Roman Empire. Despite competition among Utraquists, Lutherans, and Calvinists, and strife between the nobility and the peasants, the Czech-speaking Bohemian Kingdom had remained relatively stable until the 1547 Schmalkaldic War, when Hapsburg Catholic rule was more firmly established with Emperor Rudolph making Prague his Imperial capital. Czech nationalism combined with Bohemian Protestantism to oppose Emperor Rudolf II and his brother, Emperor Heinrich Matthias, and their intolerant and strictly Catholic policies.[4]

The immediate trigger of the revolt in Bohemia was the threat posed to the material interests of Protestant Czechs by the political and social repression under the Catholic rule of the Holy Roman Emperors. The Protestant Electors in the Imperial Diet sought to counterbalance the aspiration of the Catholic Hapsburgs to institutionalize absolute control over the entire Empire. "Tension increased until flash-point was reached over the candidature to the Bohemian crown. In 1617, the enthusiastic Catholic and pro-Jesuit Ferdinand, cousin to the aged Hapsburg Emperor, Matthias, succeeded to the Bohemian throne."[5] Matthias impetuously issued decrees withdrawing the charters of Protestant churches, ending appointments of non-Catholics, and banning Protestant meetings. In addition to issuing these unpopular decrees, he designated his cousin, Ferdinand of Styria, as the successor to the imperial Bohemian crown. Under Matthias's direction, the Bohemian Diet followed the Emperor's orders and elected Ferdinand, a member of the House of Hapsburg and a fervent Catholic, the new ruler of Bohemia (in 1619, Ferdinand was to become Holy Roman Emperor Ferdinand II). These actions were widely interpreted as an intolerant effort to impose a version of Catholic fundamentalism on the population by force. As is often the case today, intolerance of diversity then fathered a fractious dispute that ultimately turned violent. Religious differences divided what had been a united civic culture, sparking an outburst of civil strife that would eventually engulf much of Europe.

All of the major faiths in Bohemia—Catholic, Lutheran, Calvinist, and Hussite—had previously enjoyed a great amount of religious freedom. The reform-intentioned Protestants in Bohemia appealed to Emperor Ferdinand to stop abuses by the Catholic hierarchy in their country. Ferdinand ignored their pleas and continued closing down Protestant churches. His repressive tactics particularly alarmed the Calvinists who feared they would lose more religious rights under a leader whose goals were to establish absolute control and lead a Catholic Counter-Reformation. Seen in this light, what became "the Bohemian revolt . . . was primarily a nationalist and religious opposition to Hapsburg rule and an attempt to tighten up on the administration of Bohemia."[6]

The Defenestration of Prague

The revolt began in Prague on May 21, 1618, in a dramatic act of defiance that was to become known as the Defenestration of Prague. Imitating the steps that started an earlier religious revolt in Prague that had followed the burning at the stake of Jan Hus in 1415, the aroused delegates to the Prague Assembly, protesting anti-Protestant policies, threw two vocal Catholic Hapsburg governors and their secretary from a high window in the Hradschin Castle into a dungheap below.[7] While only minor injuries were sustained by the royal councilmen from their seventy-foot fall into the heap of manure, this dramatic act of rebellion formally signaled the beginning of a war that was to last thirty years.

The German Count Heinrich Matthias Thurn and Prince Christian of

Anhalt combined forces to quickly seize control of Bohemia and depose the King-elect, Archduke Ferdinand. The enigmatic Ferdinand had never been elected and his popularity vanished after he violated the 1609 *Majestätsbriefe* (the *Letter of Majesty* or the *Royal Charter of Toleration*) in an effort to drive Protestantism out of Bohemia. The rebellious Bohemian nobles did not have a strategic plan, however. At first, they considered the possibility of creating an independent republic, inspired by the hope that this would elicit the support of the Dutch, who shared their ideological interests in self-rule and religious freedom. Instead, they appointed a Directorate of thirty deputies and named Wenceslas Ruppa its president. The Protestant members of the Bohemian Diet saw the Defenestration of Prague revolt as a justifiable response to the attacks on Protestant churches and electoral political rights, and this perception of Imperial injustice provided the rationale for Frederick V to ascend to the Bohemian throne after Archduke Ferdinand had been deposed. The Directorate declared that it had formed, not to personally oppose the Emperor, but to rebel against the abrogation of Ferdinand's July 9, 1609 *Letter of Majesty* that had guaranteed religious freedom.

Besides expelling the Jesuits and arming self-defense corps in towns throughout Bohemia, the new Bohemian Directorate made what proved to be a poor decision: it elected as King the youthful staunch Calvinist Elector Frederick of the strategically critical Rhineland Palatinate. The decision killed any hopes of managing the crisis, for the twenty-one-year-old Frederick was ill-prepared to make and implement policy.[8] Innocently naive, he pictured himself as the defender of religious freedom in a Slavonic nation. His decision to accept the assignment ruptured any hope of conciliation with the Emperor.[9]

Frederick became his own worst enemy. He destroyed his legitimacy by accepting the Crown of Bohemia offered by the rebel nobility and by using military intervention to achieve his political aims. The act of intervention by the Elector from the Palatinate was

> . . . looked at askance by all the Protestant rulers, as it was directly opposed to the accepted political morality of the time [and Frederick's tyrannical policies] intensified the hatred of the Bohemian Lutherans for the Calvinists . . . Disillusionment soon followed, when Frederick showed that he was unfit to be a national leader, and soon the behavior of himself and his court deeply shocked a nation distinguished by its conviction that religion necessarily includes morality.[10]

It is important to interpret this crisis in the light of prior events. Recall that the contending factions in Germany had been divided into two alliances, the Protestant (or Evangelical) Union forged in 1608 and the Catholic League that had been built by Maximilian I of Bavaria in 1609 and renewed in 1617. Tensions between these counterpoised alliances increased because the authoritarian Frederick was the nominal head of the fragile alliance which labeled itself the Protestant Union.

The Empire Strikes Back

Amidst rising tension, it is easy to understand why the Catholic Hapsburgs reacted so extremely to the shocking news of the latest revolt in Bohemia against their rule, and why Ferdinand II, who had been elected the next Holy Roman Emperor at the August 1619 meetings of the Imperial Diet in Frankfurt following Emperor Matthias's death, had compelling reasons to see a serious threat if Frederick V were to succeed in consolidating his position in Bavaria by obtaining the expected assistance of England, the Dutch and Venetian Republics, the Calvinists from Transylvania in Hungary, and the diverse princedoms in the Protestant Union. The revolt against Austrian imperial authority was a direct threat to the Hapsburg dreams of total control over the German princes, as symbolized by the proud motto of Charles V in 1558: "*Austria est Imperare Urbi Universo.*" Indeed, Ferdinand II saw no choice but to regain Bohemia because it was the crown jewel in Hapsburg status and an important source of Imperial revenues, and its Elector held one of the seven Imperial electoral votes. Since three votes already belonged to Protestant princes, the loss of Bohemia would have assured the selection of a Protestant in an Imperial election. Ferdinand firmly believed that as Holy Roman Emperor he had a divine calling to preserve Christianity under Catholicism, following the script of one of his Hapsburg predecessors who as Emperor had pronounced himself "King of Kings" to ensure Catholic rule.[11] Ferdinand II was a practitioner of power politics whose lack of prudence in public affairs came from his blinding moral self-righteousness.

In May 1619, the Spanish dispatched an interventionary force from their army in Flanders to suppress the rebellion, and the reinforcements grew with additional financial subsidies provided by the papacy. To help save the Empire for the Catholics, Ferdinand II also won the support of Maximilian I of Bavaria, whose House of Wittelsbach in Munich was the leader of the Catholic League in both southern and northwest Germany (but challenged through dynastic rivalry by a Calvinist Wittelsbach family member holding power in Heidelberg at the center of the Palatinate). With Maximilian's external support, the rebel siege of Vienna was lifted.

No sooner than the threat against Vienna had been repelled, when another danger emerged. Bethlen Gabor, the King of Hungary, was intent to escape from Hapsburg suzerainty and saw in the Bohemian rebellion an opportunity to establish an independent state. Averring that he was a Calvinist, his forces defeated an Imperial army commanded by Ferdinand's brother Leopold in Hungary, and then allied with the Bohemians under General Matthias Thurn and invaded Austria, marching up the Danube to lay siege to Vienna for the second time in five months. Lacking organizational discipline, however, the rebel armies were unable to capitalize on their initial successes. The Hapsburgs were now confident of success. After Frederick V and his wife arrived in Prague for his coronation late in 1619 the Jesuits predicted "He will be a winter king. When summer comes he will be driven from the field."[12]

The first significant military encounter took place at the battle of White Mountain. Backed by the 25,000 soldiers of the Imperial army of the Catholic League commanded by Johan Tserclaes von Tilly (the Count of Brabout), Maximilian I's Imperial Army confronted the Bohemians near Prague on November 8, 1620. They were aided by John George of Saxony, the leading German Lutheran prince who perceived it expedient to back the Catholic Emperor in order to oppose the spread of Calvinism. When Frederick failed to receive hoped-for military assistance from the Dutch, the princes in the Protestant Union, or from his English father-in-law, King James I, his fate was sealed. Frederick's forces were crushed by an Imperial army commanded by Count Tilly.[13] The revolt by the Austrian Estates ended, and with it Frederick's brief rule.[14] The Jesuit prophecy had been fulfilled: the "Winter King" had to flee Bavaria and ignominiously take refuge in the Netherlands. When Ferdinand II's troops successfully recaptured Prague from the Protestant rebels, "a reign of terror began in Bohemia."[15]

> The Emperor's triumph was so complete that Bohemia lay at his mercy; speedily Ferdinand took advantage of his position. He did more than execute leading rebels, expel Protestant officials, or let his troops sack Prague; he confiscated the estates of Bohemian nobles and used the vast domains now in his gift to reward reliable servants and to found monasteries and convents. The [Catholic] Counter-Reformation triumphed in a mainly Protestant land through religious example, economic pressure, and physical compulsion.[16]

Other Hapsburg dominions such as Transylvania which had also revolted against the Hapsburgs similarly found themselves targets of extreme punishment; "the revenge massacre of several hundred Protestants in the Valtellina by the Spanish faction in 1620"[17] provides another illustration of the repressive Hapsburg reaction.

In the peace agreement, the Palatinate was given to the Emperor's son Maximilian who led the Catholic League, and Ferdinand was finally officially crowned King of Bohemia. The Hapsburg pieces now seemed to be in place for Ferdinand to lay "the foundations of despotic power unhampered by foreign intervention."[18] Bohemia's native nobility was ruthlessly suppressed so that the country could systematically be Catholicized and Germanized. Calvinists and Lutherans were expelled, and those "who tried to keep their Protestant faith had to pay special heavy taxes and have soldiers quartered in their homes. An estimated 150,000 people fled the country, among whom were most of Bohemia's leading intellectuals."[19]

Thus, the Bohemian period ended with a Hapsburg military victory, a punitive peace settlement, and a mass migration of refugees similar, proportionately, to the refugees crises the globe is experiencing today (see Chapter 6).

As is often the case, war fosters centralized governance and seldom provides a hospitable environment for civil liberties or the growth of democracy. Intoxicated with his military success, Ferdinand promptly abolished elective monarchy and pronounced that thereafter the Bohemian throne would be hereditary in the Hapsburg dynasty. The victory enabled the Emperor to restore the troubled area to its earlier status as a dependent region sending tax revenues to the Emperor in Vienna. The "punishment of Bohemia was to inaugurate a new policy, by which the Hapsburg lands were to be molded into one state united by religion and controlled from Vienna, the essential foundation for the rebuilding of Catholic Europe."[20]

When Ferdinand took Prague, "the intoxication of success . . . caused more dreadful consequences."[21] Ferdinand's victory over Frederick whetted his thirst to expand Hapsburg power elsewhere. The lands in the Palatinate formerly held by the "Winter King" were invaded from the Spanish Netherlands and seized by the Bavarians.[22]

Although the Calvinist revolt had been suppressed, the Hapsburg victory proved to be ephemeral. The invasion of the Palatinate led to the resumption of war as the Protestant princes grew determined to intervene before the Hapsburgs could consolidate their position. Other threatened principalities soon joined the conflict and organized a defense resulting in another twenty-eight years of fighting.[23] Thus, Germany became the battlefield on which the war would continue.

THE 1620–1624 PALATINATE PHASE

In May 1621 the vanquished Protestant Union agreed to disband in return for a pledge that its retreating forces would not be attacked by the Emperor's Imperial army on their way home. "German Protestantism was henceforth divided into the Lutheran faction headed by the Elector John George of Saxony and the discredited but still-warring and ambitious party represented by such [Calvinist] leaders as Frederick and Christian of Anhalt."[24] At the same time, the Spanish General Ambrosia Spinola resumed his campaigns to reconquer the United Provinces in the Netherlands while establishing Imperial control of the Palatinate. It appeared that the House of Hapsburg would now succeed in its goals of dominating Europe and securing the position of Catholicism as the single representation of Christianity.

Count Ernst von Mansfeld and Christian, the Duke of Brunswick, led the Protestant resistance to Hapsburg rule in the Palatinate. While in exile Frederick had expected substantial aid to be provided from his father-in-law, James I of England, but in an epoch of deep mistrust it is not surprising that Frederick received little assistance. Frederick's position and faith in allegiances was further weakened when Lutheran Saxony sided with the Emperor in exchange for the Emperor's transfer of Lusatia to Saxony. However, Frederick eventually found the support he desperately needed from the Dutch. Following the expiration of their Twelve-Year Truce with Spain in 1621, Dutch forces entered the Rhineland to counter Spanish Hapsburg occupation armies under General Spinola and also confronted Spanish forces under General Gonzale Fernádez de Córdoba in the Palatinate. Hapsburg hegemony was again contested, and the Dutch intervention re-ignited the war.

The infamous Imperial Austrian General Johann Tserclaes von Tilly (see Box 2.1 for a profile), Commander of the Catholic League army since 1610, joined the Spanish forces in 1622 and began a campaign to conquer lands in northern Germany. Together with Córdoba's forces, Tilly led the Imperialists to crushing victories on May 6, 1622 at Wimpfen and at the bridgehead of Höchst two miles west of Frankfurt a month later. On September 10, 1622, Tilly took Heidelberg by assault and laid siege to Frankenthal, therein consolidating the Emperor's control of the Rhineland.

Tilly relied on a campaign of terror to subjugate the lands his mercenary armies sought to subjugate and plunder. Lacking provisions, Tilly supplied his soldiers by stripping all food from the land. Unwilling to yield the lands Tilly's storm troops had militarily subjugated, the Emperor refused to negotiate a peace settlement at the Brussels peace conference organized by England. Tilly's Imperial victory at Stadtlohn on August 6, 1623 over Christian of Brunswick ended this phase of the war, with the Hapsburgs in ascendancy. The Emperor now controlled Austria and Bohemia, with Maximilian given the title of Elector to rule southern and northwestern Germany. The Spanish Hapsburgs gained control of the Rhenish Palatinate, and Frederick became a landless exile surviving in sanctuary on the welfare of Dutch supporters. Everywhere in Germany the situation now became more menacing for the Protestants.[25]

Two other developments complicated the geostrategic situation: (1) the contest for suzerainty over the Valtellina controlled by the Graubünden (Grisons), or Union of Grey Leagues aligned loosely with the Swiss cantons, and (2) the 1621 outbreak of the Swedish-Polish War.

The Valtellina contained the shortest and safest land route with which the Spanish Hapsburgs in the Duchy of Milan and their satellite the Republic of Genoa could supply their armies in the Netherlands and the Palatinate. Because the Valtellina was held by the Graubünden, the House of Hapsburg sought to gain control of this strategic passage so obviously indispensable to Hapsburg hegemonical ambitions since the 1588 sinking of the Spanish Armada had severed the northern sea route between Spain and the Spanish Netherlands.

To gain control of this overland passage from Italy to northern Europe, Spanish forces began a campaign to occupy the Valtellina, and they were supported in 1621 by Austrian troops from the north. France and Venice protested, but to little avail. Pope Urban VIII intervened with papal troops and negotiated the "deposit" of the Valtellina to the Vatican as a means of assuring Spanish control.[26]

Fearing Hapsburg encirclement, in 1624 France signed a defense treaty with the Netherlands and sent a force to expel the papal garrisons and occupy the Graubünden.[27] Spain relinquished its position "as the chief minister, the Count de Olivares, was not prepared to go to war for the sake of a remote Alpine valley. Accordingly, on February 14, 1623 he agreed that papal troops should take over the Valtellina for a transitional period of four months to allow Spanish forces to withdraw."[28]

The second geostratic development at this time was the rise on the European periphery of Sweden as an expansionist power. Beginning in 1611, the youthful Swedish King Gustavus Adolphus seized upon the so-called "Time of Troubles" in Russia to convert the Gulf of Finland into a "Swedish Lake" when, through the 1617 Peace of Stolbova, he acquired Karelia and Ingria and thereby established a territorial merger of Swedish Finland with Swedish Estonia. Four years later, Sweden attacked Poland-Lithuania and acquired the major Baltic port Riga and the Duchy of Prussia. Inspired by Sweden's military successes, Frederick's Palatinate court in exile pursued an alliance with the Swedish King aimed at Frederick's restoration to power in Bohemia and the installation of Gustavus Adolphus as a new Protestant Holy Roman Emperor.[29] These were ambitious aims, especially in the light of the military position of Denmark, whose stature at the time made Swedish aspirations appear premature.

THE 1625–1629 DANISH PHASE

Fearing the rise of Hapsburg control of northern Germany, in 1625 Christian IV, the King of Denmark and Norway, became the first Protestant neutral to intervene in the fighting. Anticipating subjugation if he remained on the sidelines, Christian sought to champion the beleaguered Lutherans in Germany, but his motives were not entirely religious because he recognized that military intervention could also serve his political goal of enlarging the German possessions to which he already held title.

Christian had maintained his loyalty to the Holy Roman Emperor until 1625, partly because as the Duke of Holstein, a German principality within the Empire, tradition required him to practice strict neutrality. However, at this critical juncture he decided to challenge the Emperor. His motives for taking military action were not purely religious; he "hoped by acquiring a few bishoprics in Germany to construct a kingdom for his younger son Frederick."[30] Christian also sought to challenge the expansion of Swedish power and secure Danish preponderance at the mouths of the Elbe and Weser rivers on the Baltic. This latter objective was strategically important, for Danish foreign policy was centered on maintaining military preponderance in Scandinavia. Since assuming the Danish throne in 1596, Christian had allocated large sums for defense, and as recently as 1611 had fought a two-year war with Sweden to reduce its influence in the Baltic.

The English and the Dutch, who had pledged substantial subsidies on behalf of Denmark's military intervention, did not fulfill their promises. The emerging mores of the age had begun to accept the expedient breaking of commitments when national interests were not served by faithful compliance with previous promises, and this betrayal accordingly did not generate substantial surprise or criticism. Because Christian had prudently built a sizeable war chest with the wise investment of Swedish reparation payments, Denmark was able unilaterally to enter the fray against the Holy Roman Empire with 20,000 mercenaries Christian had personally recruited. Emboldened by his election in the spring of 1625 to the position as Director of the Empire's Lower Saxon "Circle," Christian felt confident that his intervention ultimately would be supported by other Protestant enemies of the Hapsburgs. England, France, the United Provinces of the Netherlands, and the Hungarian Protestants from Transylvania ultimately formed the Hague Coalition and provided subsidies so that Christian could challenge the Imperial army commanded by General Tilly. What Christian did not anticipate was that the Emperor would choose to create a new army, assigning supreme command to an adventurous Czech nobleman, Albrecht Wenceslas von Waldstein (or, simply "Wallenstein"), whose managerial and strategic skills were to shift the tide of battle (see Box 2.1 for a profile of Wallenstein and the other colorful cast of military commanders in the Thirty Years' War arena).

BOX 2.1
Prime Military Players in the Thirty Years' War Drama

Gustavus Adolphus II, King of Sweden

Great and prolonged wars generate the need for creative military leaders, and the Thirty Years' War produced some of history's most innovative and famous commanders. Three stand out as especially noteworthy. The first is Gustavus Adolphus, or King Gustav II Adolf of Sweden (1594–1632). Gustavus is known as "the father of modern warfare" because he engineered a revolution in military strategy and tactics comparable to the so-called "revolution in military affairs" (RMA) occurring today that now seeks with high-tech weapons to make fighting without mass armies possible. Also nicknamed "the Lion of the North" for his championing of Protestantism, Gustavus demonstrated how well-disciplined, trained, and paid troops in uniform, reporting through a clear chain of command to professional officers, could use linear formations to defeat the massive *tercios* relied upon by the Imperial forces. Gustavus introduced platoons firing continuous salvos, the use of light cannon and artillery, and coordinated shock-action attacks by combat teams, and these organizational and strategic innovations of Gustavus' Swedish army set the standard for other national armies to emulate.

Johan Tserclaes, Count Tilly

Next is Johan Tserclaes (1559–1632), who was named a count by the Holy Roman Empire, and who as a Flemish soldier gained a reputation as a military terrorist when he skillfully commanded the mercenary forces of the Catholic League. Count Tilly's brutal tactics of mass annihilation relied on terror to subjugate and/or force the surrender of cities that stood in his line of attack—strategies which led to crushing victories at Lütter (1626) and Magdeburg (1631). Tilly broke down the preexisting limits in just war doctrine to the uses of aggression in ways that inaugurated acceptance of "total war" against civilian populations.

Third is Albrecht Wensel Eusebius Wallenstein (Waldstein) (1583–1634). An ambitious and entrepreneurial Bohemian general and Catholic convert, Wallenstein received a commission to become Hapsburg Commander of the Holy Roman Empire's Imperial Army, and his mercenary troops engaged in ruthless campaigns almost crushing the German Protestant forces; as a reward for his smashing victories, this so-called "war profiteer" was given the title of Duke of Mecklenburg and Friedland. Suspected of treasonous crypto-allegiance with the Emperor's enemies in a climate of growing mistrust, the opportunistic Wallenstein was dismissed in 1630 but promptly reinstated to use his military genius to defend the Empire against the Swedish advances. Wallenstein recovered Bohemia but was defeated by Gustavus's multinational army at Lützen in 1632. Out-maneuvered on the field of battle, Wallenstein's intrigues led to another

Albrecht Eusebius Wenzel von Wallenstein, Duke of Friedland and Mecklenburg

Imperial proclamation of treason that was followed by his assassination through the plot of a group of his own Irish mercenary officers.

Wallenstein's Long Shadow

As a convert from the Lutheranism to which he was exposed in his youth to Catholicism, Wallenstein was largely indifferent to religious dogma, embracing astrology rather than particular theological conviction. A product of the temper of his times, Wallenstein's motives were more practical than idealistic; like his contemporaries for whom the creed was mostly greed, Wallenstein was more interested in expanding his fortune and fame than fighting for a particular faith.[31] A Bohemian nobleman by birth, the audacious Wallenstein began military service under Emperor Ferdinand in 1606, and immediately grasped the potential rewards of serving as a war profiteer. During the Bohemian rebellion against the Emperor, Wallenstein had remained loyal to Ferdinand and lent the Emperor huge sums of money. In 1625 the Emperor was forced to repay his debt by rewarding Wallenstein with an appointment to head all Imperial troops.

Wallenstein offered to raise an army of fifty thousand troops at his own expense to fight for the Emperor, contingent upon the Emperor's acceptance of Wallenstein's many demands for large financial guarantees and total control of the Imperial army, including the experienced Catholic League troops commanded by the aging General Tilly. Emperor Ferdinand felt he could not refuse.[32] Named the Prince of Friedland as a reward, Wallenstein prepared his troops to support Tilly's army, which had already moved against the Protestants because of the old general's refusal to accept Wallenstein's management of military strategy.

The anti-Hapsburg coalition undertook what appeared to be a coordinated strategic plan: Christian IV of Denmark was to engage Tilly and conquer Lower Saxony; Christian of Brunswick was to take the Wittelsbach Bishoprics in Westphalia and the lower Rhineland; General Ernst von Mansfeld was to lead the alliance into Bohemia, passing through Silesia and Moravia; and Prince Bethlen Gabor was to march his Hungarian troops from Transylvania to join with Count von Mansfeld's army in Bohemia. The plan was coherent, but the means were insufficient. The coalition was deprived of external military assistance when the Anglo-French alliance dissolved, and King Gustavus Adolphus unexpectedly decided to concentrate Swedish forces on the conquest of Polish Prussia.

The Empire's Drive for Dominion

Tilly and Wallenstein had the geostrategic advantage of being positioned to fight from the interior, able to confront one enemy at a time. Drawing upon this advantage, Wallenstein won a battle on April 25, 1626, for the Bridge of Dessau on the Elbe River. But the Protestants rebounded and penetrated Germany elsewhere. Count von Mansfeld's troops pulled Wallenstein's forces away from the support of Tilly's army and, to compound the Empire's problems, a widespread peasant revolt in Upper Austria could only be repressed with the deployment of needed Imperial Bavarian forces. Perceiving a clear path to the Imperial nerve center in Vienna, Christian and "the Protestant adventurer from Savoy, Albert von Mansfeld"[33] advanced from different directions, forging ahead in an effort to carry out their strategy to link with their allies in the south commanded by Bethlen Gabor in Transylvania.

As the Protestant Union forces reached the Danube River through Silesia, Wallenstein's powerful Imperial army countered. His success was aided by a series of anti-Imperial miscalculations. Facing defeat from Wallenstein's forces at Dessau on April 25, 1626, von Mansfeld never took advantage of his preponderant position in Silesia or, later, of the May 1626 Austrian peasant revolt against the Hapsburgs. The Imperial cause was also assisted by fate: Bethlen Gabor was unexpectedly deprived of aid from the Ottomans when the Turkish siege of Baghdad failed. "I see I must make peace with the Emperor," who now demanded an awesome price for peace,[34] Bethlen Gabor lamented. Fate also helped the Hapsburg cause through a series of untimely deaths: Christian of Brunswick died on June 16, 1626; Albert von Mansfeld died five months later while traveling to Venice to obtain desperately needed additional subsidies; and Bethlen Gabor subsequently died in a remote Bosnian village during his retreat.

The anti-Imperialists never consummated their military plan. On August 27, 1626, Wallenstein's army decimated the core of Christian's Danish troops at Lütter, the remainder of which were pursued by both Wallenstein and Tilly into Jutland. Mecklenburg and its strategic ports on the Baltic then fell into the Empire's possession. The Imperial armies swept, without effective resistance, through most of the Protestant stronghold in northern Germany. The Empire's army crushed what little remained of its opposition, destroying in the process the morale of the Protestant princes such as the Duchy of Mecklenburg who began to advocate reconciliation with the Empire.

"The years 1625–1626," C. V. Wedgwood observes, "had seen the rise and fall of a remaining European movement against the Hapsburg dynasty."[35] The Imperial task that remained was to terminate all opposition to Hapsburg hegemony. Now with an opportunity to destroy the Protestant Union, Tilly secured the additional aid of the Spanish Hapsburgs, who joined the fighting under the motto "God is Spanish and fights for our nation these days."

The combined Imperial forces overran the Netherlands. By 1627, with Denmark out of the picture and France unwilling to fight the Spanish, the Catholic League appeared poised to reassert Hapsburg Imperial control over a unified German state and institutionalize the Empire's control as far north as the Baltic Sea. However, the Imperialists failed to defeat the Protestants in the 1628 Battle at Stralsund in a bid to add this valuable Baltic port to those gained at Wismar and Rostack.

By the provisions of the 1629 Treaty of Lübeck, Denmark was forced to withdraw from the war, surrendering its bishoprics in northern Germany. The Peace of Lübeck was lenient. In exchange for Christian IV's promise to refrain from further involvement in the Empire's internal affairs, Wallenstein offered recovery of all lost Danish territories, permission for Denmark to once again levy tolls on the Elbe River, and permission to let the defeated Danes withdraw from the war without the burden of reparation payments.

The Hapsburgs were at the peak of their power, reaching beyond the boundaries of the Empire's previous expansion in 1547 following Charles V's victory over the Lutheran Schmalkalden League. Despite the leniency of the Peace of Lübeck, the victorious Hapsburgs "left Europe in no doubt that they intended to exploit their successes to the full. After a century of standing on the defensive, the Catholics of Germany had many scores to settle."[36]

The Edict of Restitution

Intoxicated by military triumph, "the war was diverted . . . into an enterprise for making the Hapsburgs absolute in Germany."[37] On March 6, 1629, Ferdinand II unilaterally issued the Edict of Restitution in an attempt to enforce the ecclesiastical reservation of the 1555 Peace of Augsburg that had granted rulers the right to control their region's religion. The triumphant Emperor declared void previous Protestant titles to lands secularized after 1551, when Protestantism had gained many new followers. The Edict was issued by a Hapsburg dynasty that equated universal Catholicism with the salvation of Imperial Dominion and of their souls. It also communicated in no uncertain terms that Ferdinand II regarded his Imperial power absolute. The philosophy leading to the Edict of Restitution was to become known as one of the last efforts to retain the marriage between church and state. The Hapsburg vision saw what was good for the Roman Catholic Church to be automatically good for the Empire (and for most periods, the papacy held a mirror image of this mutually beneficial relationship). The promulgation of Catholicism was considered critical to the expansion of the Empire, and anything that threatened the domination of either Roman Catholicism or the House of Hapsburg was to be fought.

Church and State Relations in the Tumult of War

Inasmuch as religion and politics, church and state, were seen as inseparable, the Hapsburgs saw a war against the Protestant heretics as inherently just. The House of Hapsburg was, in its self-image, the direct descendant of the early Christians in Rome, and the Holy Roman Empire's quest to combat heresy and expand the dominion of the Empire were expressions of their attempt to create confessional absolutism and theological uniformity throughout Europe, even against the protestations of Catholics as well as Protestants who were alienated by the Hapsburg's radical equation of Imperial rule with religious orthodoxy.

It is instructive that the Hapsburg world view did not even find consistent favor with the Roman Church, which the Hapsburg wars of expansion claimed to benefit. True, Pope Gregory XV welcomed the advantages for the Roman

Catholic Church derived by the Empire's victories under Ferdinand, and in 1625 established the *Congregation for the Propagation of Faith* to assist Ferdinand's efforts to recatholicize Europe. However,

> Urban VIII, who had been elected Pope in 1623, did not share the pro-Hapsburg stance of his predecessors. He ended the subsidies sent by Rome to Ferdinand and the League, preferring to concentrate on what he perceived as the interests of the papal states in Italy—a task which he believed required the neutralization of Hapsburg influence in the peninsula. The alienation between Ferdinand and Pope Urban VIII became a major international factor during the 1620s and 1630s.[38]

The Edict of Restitution enlarged the gap between religion and politics, and became an inflection point in the trend toward the separation of church and state that was to culminate at the conclusion of the Thirty Years' War in 1648. Through the Peace of Westphalia, religion and politics were decoupled within and between sovereign states. That outcome was the opposite, of course, of the intentions of the Empire when the Edict of Restitution was issued in 1629.

The Edict of Restitution backfired; it worked against the objectives of the Emperor by reenergizing the Protestant cause and enraging formerly neutral German princes. They correctly recognized that the Edict signaled the Hapsburg intention to eradicate both Protestantism and the independence of princes (including Catholic powers, whose anxiety was raised when the Emperor appointed his relatives to head the recovered bishoprics and assigned his Jesuit advisors to control a number of strategically important monasteries). From the perspective of many, the Edict was an attempt to revise the Empire's constitution, in order to provide the Emperor with control over religious *and* political policy. Those fears were compounded by the Imperial army's targeting of the Electoral of Cologne's bishoprics of Münster and Osnabrück for forced conversion from Lutheranism to Catholicism, following the Emperor's July 1630 decision to enforce the *autonomia* constitutional right of a Catholic ruler to make his subjects practice his faith.

A revolt against the Emperor's imposition of absolute rule ensued at the 1630 Electoral Diet of Regensburg, led by Lutheran Saxony and Catholic Bavaria. "Filled with suspicions, leading Catholic princes refused to name Ferdinand's son 'King of the Romans' (the traditional title of the heir-apparent)."[39] When Wallenstein sought to mediate the conflict, Ferdinand ill-advisedly consented to the Catholic princes' demands to dismiss Wallenstein, his best general, and dissolve his army. This decision left the Empire seriously weakened.

Hapsburg weakness began to appear when the Duke of Mantua and Montferrant, Vincenzo II Gonzaga, died and the 1628–1631 War of the Mantuan Succession began. This conflict pitted France against Emperor Ferdinand and the Spanish Hapsburgs, who were seeking to depose the legitimate Gonzaga heir (Charles, duc de Nevers) in order to consolidate the Empire's Imperial control of Italy. The clash ended when Cardinal Richelieu masterminded the forced Hapsburg withdrawal from Casale in October 1630 and squashed the so-called "Day of Dupes" organized by the Catholic extremists within France to support the Spanish Hapsburgs.

The crisis had altered the diplomatic chessboard composed of a cross-cutting clash of competing loyalties and interests. New pieces and allegiances appeared after the French chose to become directly involved. The June 1631 Treaty of Cherasco splintered the Austrian-Spanish stranglehold on Italy, and Pope Urban VIII chipped away further at Hapsburg hegemony by acquiring the vacant Imperial fiefdom Urbino in Italy. The pope was later to complain that the Mantuan War led to the downfall of the Catholic cause by destroying the political unity of the Hapsburgs, the French, and all the other Catholic princes.[40]

What was becoming clear as the war unfolded was that expediency was being elevated from a fact of political and military life to an international norm, under which loyalty to allies or to religious causes was disregarded when opportunities for individual gain presented themselves. The next stage of the war would further dramatize the extent to which raw power politics, driven by myopic self-interest, was becoming an expectation about the primal motives underlying international actors' behavior.

THE 1630–1635 SWEDISH PHASE

The Swedish entry into the Thirty Years' War was precipitated largely by Emperor Ferdinand's signing of the Edict of Restitution in 1629. Not only had the Edict forced Protestants to give up territories acquired since 1555, Ferdinand also had explicitly stated his intent to use Wallenstein and the Imperial army to put down any resistance to his policy. The loss of rights and the threat of further repression aroused the Protestant states and provoked hitherto neutral princes to renew their efforts to oppose Hapsburg imperialism. In response to the unbending Edict of Restitution, the Protestant princes convened in Leipzig and then met in Frankfurt with Catholic princes, who felt the Edict undermined the Empire as well as the Catholic faith because it destroyed all trust among Christians. The result was the creation of a defensive coalition backed by the *Leipziger Bund* army. In response, the May 1631 Treaty of Fontaine forged a secret pact between Maximilian and Cardinal Richelieu that committed Bavaria and France to nonaggression against each other and to nonalignment with one another's adversaries. Thus, "although the likelihood of a Hapsburg triumph appeared strong, the Protestant powers and secretly Cardinal Richelieu of France were determined to avert such a possibility."[41]

Gustavus Adolphus Enters the War

At this juncture the formerly neutral Protestant ruler Gustavus Adolphus of Sweden, "the only real strategist in the Thirty Years' War,"[42] stepped forward as the champion of Protestant interests. A pious Lutheran tolerant of Calvinism and opposed to forced religious conversion, Gustavus's main interests in entering the war were to gain greater control of the Baltic, to expand into northern Germany, and to establish Swedish influence over northern Germany. The fearless, self-confident king (pictured in Box 2.1), known as the "Lion of the North," felt compelled to enter the war when General Tilly defeated Denmark, and Wallenstein's forces arrived on the Baltic coast, threatening Swedish trade. Gustavus had even more ambitious plans for a reorganized Germany. In his *Norma Futurarum Actionum* of 1631 he laid out ideas to create a new Protestant Union to defy Catholicism within a Swedish-controlled confederation.[43]

The soldierly Swedish King was heralded as the military leader who would finally defeat the Roman Catholics and save the Protestant faith in Europe. Trained from childhood for his kingly duties, Gustavus Adolphus took the throne at age seventeen in 1611 as Gustavus II. His army was not large, but it was well trained by Dutch officers and strictly disciplined. Before he was twenty years old Gustavus had won a war against Denmark, and by 1630 he had extended his kingdom around the whole eastern shore of the Baltic as a result of military victories over Russia and Poland. When the 1629 Swedish-Polish Treaty of Altmark was signed, Gustavus was able to concentrate his efforts on intervention in Germany.

Success followed the Swedish King into battle for the Protestant cause. Gustavus organized a well-trained, highly mobile mass army of conscripts. Unlike his enemy's "polyglot herds of mercenaries," while enlisting soldiers of all religions, Lutheranism was the army's official creed, and Gustavus's "army had a collective knowledge of its purpose [because] he exacted loyalty . . . to the ideals for which he fought and for which he was prepared to die."[44] The army was highly efficient, but restrained by a military code of conduct that prohibited attacks on civilians, churches, and schools. Inspired by a sense of fighting for justice to liberate the oppressed, Gustavus's army also had the advantage of many innovations in tactics, such as "the use of mobile infantry, light artillery, and soldiers dressed in blue and yellow uniforms to differentiate themselves from the enemy that revolutionized the whole art of warfare."[45]

Swedish intervention transformed the conflict by giving the remnants of the unorganized and leaderless Protestant coalition military discipline and renewed hope. When Wallenstein laid siege to the port of Stralsund in May 1628, Gustavus became convinced that he had to intervene.[46] His army of 30,000 men captured several ports on the Baltic in Poland and Polish Prussia, in what he claimed was a preemptive strike. In June 1630 he occupied Pomerania and retook Wallenstein's Duchy of Mecklinburg. But the Polish-Imperial Army stopped Gustavus's advance there, and the Swedish king needed allies to support a move into Germany. The Lutheran German princes were reluctant to break their neutrality, and the financial burden of pursuing the campaign with insufficient resources created a crisis. Then the Swedish king found assistance from an unlikely source—France.

Cardinal Richelieu Orchestrates French Involvement

French foreign policy by now was under the calculating *realpolitic* leadership of Jean du Plessis, Cardinal de Richelieu (see Box 2.2). Italian by birth and not highly fluent in French, Cardinal Richelieu was thoroughly dedicated to the regeneration of France as a means of preventing the House of Hapsburg from subjecting Christendom to political and religious tyranny.[47] Although France was a predominately Catholic state, the Catholic Cardinal saw his goal of halting the growing Hapsburg power as best served by forging strategic alliances with all powers hostile to Hapsburg hegemony, whether they were Protestant or Catholic. "If Germany is lost," Richelieu reasoned, "France cannot exist."[48] Thus what mattered to him was not how a potential ally stood on religious matters, but its ability to contribute to French security.

"Richelieu did not intend to confine the war to north Germany. The House of Hapsburg was his enemy, but he most feared Spain rather than Austria, and his object was to hold Austria in check in Germany while the main onslaught was [later taken] upon Spain on the Rhine and in north Italy."[49] On January 23, 1631, Cardinal Richelieu signed the Treaty of Bärwalde to carry out his strategy, promising French financial support for Sweden to resist the Hapsburgs. The French pledge of annual subsidies of 1 million livres (the equivalent of 40,000 Imperial thalers) were provided to fight for "liberty" against the Emperor's "oppression," and the monetary assistance enabled Swedish troops, which had swelled to over 42,000 soldiers by 1630, to double over the next year and march into Germany.[50] Gustavus opened negotiations with the dissatisfied German princes, thereby sowing discord and further alienating Emperor Ferdinand II. At first, Gustavus's effort failed because of opposition by the influential Lutheran leader John George of Saxony, who sided with the German Emperor against the Swedish King whom he rejected as a foreign invader. To the Saxon Elector, fatherland mattered more than faith.

BOX 2.2
Richelieu and the Realist Rationale for National Expansion

The consolidation of political authority in the hands of powerful secular states had been a long-term process, but its pace escalated during the Thirty Years' War when the needs for centralized management of political and military affairs intensified. Armand Jean du Plessis was a force in the philosophical transition to the new age of statecraft that was born in 1648, three years after his death. A Catholic, born in 1585 in Richelieu, France, he was a protégé of the French queen, Marie de' Medici, and became Minister of State in 1624, which positioned him to rule France on behalf of the Bourbon monarchy. In that capacity, Cardinal Richelieu propounded a calculating realist approach to the practice of statecraft that reflected and extended the ruthless spirit of the times.

Armand Jean du Plessis, Cardinal Richelieu

At the center of Richelieu's *realpolitik* philosophy was his core conviction that the primary purpose of foreign and domestic policy was to increase the power and international prestige of the French throne. In his hierarchy of values, the first duty of statecraft was to maneuver the state into a position of preeminence in the world. All other values, such as adherence to a religious code of ethical conduct, were secondary in importance and, as such, were to be sacrificed when they stood in the way of successfully promoting the state's interests. Cardinal Richelieu put his philosophy into practice when he played the role of "the worldly ecclesiastic and soldier-statesman who masterminded France's exploitation of the Thirty Years' War and centralized the power of the Bourbon monarchy"[51] at a time when such ambitions for national aggrandizement were accepted practice, and pacifism and Christian charity were looked upon as naïve sentiments. Richelieu's *realpolitik* outlook cemented the mores of power politics. He made *raison d'état,* or reason of state, a guide to prudent policy, arguing that

> Among various types of political units claiming autonomy, the centralized state deserved to be bestowed with supreme power because it had unique duties to carry out, such as defense of the realm. Under Cardinal Richelieu in France what could be termed the cult of the state reached its climax. To this day the term is capitalized in French as *Etat* as if to wrap the state in a cloak of mystery.[52]

Richelieu's rationale for the military expansion of state power rested on his belief—consistent with his age—that this goal was a natural right; the need for self-preservation and self-promotion made it obligatory to *not* let morality interfere with the attainment of military supremacy. "In matters of state," Richelieu argued in his *Political Testament,* "he who has the power often has the right, and he who is weak can only with difficulty keep from being wrong in the opinion of the majority of the world."[53] International politics, in Richelieu's view, was a struggle cut off from the tether of moral precepts. It followed that, to meet the threat of Catholic Hapsburg encirclement, Catholic France was required to play balance-of-power politics by supporting Sweden and the other Protestant powers that fought Hapsburg domination and its ambition to reconvert all of Europe to Catholicism. Embracing the doctrine of military necessity as a principle for action, Richelieu acted on the tenet that "the end justified the means," which provoked Hugo Grotius to condemn both "the means used by the Cardinal" [through] imposition of a virtual dictatorship" and "Richelieu's purpose: the establishment of France as the preponderant power within the framework of a Western state system since it was at variance with . . . Christendom,"[54]

Henry Kissinger summarizes the importance of Cardinal Richelieu in the revision of the rules by which states would thereafter compete against one another to obtain national security, just as they had in the Thirty Years' War:

> Few statesmen can claim a greater impact on history. Richelieu was the father of the modern state system. He promulgated the concept of *raison d'etat* and practiced it relentlessly. . . . Under his auspices, *raison d'état* replaced the medieval concept of universal moral values as the operating principle. . . . A balance of power emerged, first as a fact of life, then as a system for organizing international relations. . . . Richelieu left behind him a world radically different from the one he had found. . . .[55]

After 1630, "the choice between Catholic and Protestant had lost its meaning," C. V. Wedgwood observes. "Hapsburg aggression had driven the papacy and Catholic France, the one into sympathy, the other into alliance with the Protestants, and Europe no longer presented even the approximate outline of a religious cleavage. The political aspect of the conflict had destroyed the spiritual."[56]

On August 13, 1630, Emperor Ferdinand was prevailed upon at the Regensburg Electoral meeting to dismiss Wallenstein from command of the Imperial army. The mercurial Wallenstein had accumulated powerful enemies who feared that he was plotting to make himself dictator of Germany or king of Bohemia,[57] and they pressured the Emperor to relieve his best general from command. This choice was to prove unwise, for the appointment of the aging General Count Johan Tserclaes von Tilly to head all the Imperial forces, assisted by his second in command, Count Goffried Heinrich Pappenheim, a militant soldier eager to push for vengeance on the battlefield, represented a serious loss in military leadership.

On May 30, 1631, a second miscalculation occurred. In the hope of replenishing his starving troops' supplies, General Tilly ruthlessly sacked the prosperous Lutheran city of Magdeburg, ignoring the offer of a treaty of surrender. Tilly's atrocities in a total war of annihilation were facilitated by the continuing hesitation of the Protestant princes to join the Swedes, as well as by the delay caused by Gustavus's successful April 13, 1631 conquest of the Brandenburg fortress of Frankfort an der Oder—a strategic decision undertaken to protect Gustavus's forces from an attack by the Poles and to intimidate the two neutral Electors, George William of Brandenburg and John George of Saxony. Although Gustavus was unable to prevent Tilly's Imperial army from vanquishing Magdeburg in "an orgy of rape, murder and robbery . . . which horrified even contemporaries,"[58] the city's destruction ultimately provided Gustavus with political benefits.

The news came upon Europe with a shock of horror. At Vienna the thanksgivings were hushed, and in Protestant countries no words could describe the outburst of disgust and indignation. The appalling incident which robbed the conquest of its military significance was trumpeted to the world as the deliberate act of its conquerors, and Tilly's name was to pass into history forever coupled with Magdeburg. Years later, imperialist soldiers crying for quarter would be met with the answer "Magdeburg quarter" as they were shot down.

"Our danger has no end, for the Protestant Estates will without doubt be only strengthened in their hatred by this," Tilly wrote to Maximilian. He was right. Throughout Europe Magdeburg was the signal for Protestant action; on May 31st the United Provinces entered into an agreement with the King of Sweden, by which they undertook to add their subsidies to those of the French, and directly after made ready to invade Flanders.[59]

Gustavus had written the *Norma Futuranum Actionum* in April 1631 and immediately set about implementing his plan to unite all of Germany in a new confederation under Protestant leadership to resist the Counter-Reformation. As news of Tilly's slaughter of all but 5,000 of Madgeburg's 30,000 inhabitants spread across Europe, the prospects for Gustavus to carry out his plan improved. With the assistance of German allies, he was now able to move the Swedish army forward into the Palatinate. After the Madgeburg massacre, John George, the Lutheran Elector of Saxony who had previously lent his support to the Holy Roman Emperor, promptly reversed his alignment and joined the Protestant cause. On September 11, 1631, Saxony signed a military alliance with Sweden as the formerly lukewarm Elector of Brandenburg had already done earlier that year, following the news of Madgeburg's destruction.

When combined with French assistance, these alliances with Sweden led to the expansion of the Thirty Years' War. The conflict that had started as a civil war over religion in the German states now became a truly international fight over the redistribution of territorial possessions. One early sign was the decision by France in 1632 to ratify a defense treaty with Russia, not for religion but to politically oppose Hapsburg expansionism. As Gustavus explained, "All the wars of Europe are now blended into one."[60]

The military confrontation thereafter dominated diplomacy—a transition that was to become a prelude to the practices that would share the Westphalian conception of strategic priorities in international affairs. Surging with the confidence of allied support, the Swedish king, now joined by John George's army of 18,000 reinforcements, confronted Tilly's Imperial army at Breitenseld, four miles to the north of Leipzig, on September 17, 1631. The outnumbered Imperial army was dealt a crushing defeat by the small but efficient Protestant army—the first major breakthrough for the Protestants in the war. Two-thirds of Tilly's army was destroyed and Tilly, the aging seventy-three-year-old Imperial commander-in-chief, was fatally wounded.

Countering the Counter-Reformation

Gustavus's smashing defeat of the Imperial army "marks the turn in the tide of the Counter-Reformation. The whole Empire now laid at the feet of the Swedish King."[61] Protestant hopes soared by this reversal of fortunes: "What the German princes could not do for themselves, the King of Sweden had done for them." At the Battle of Breitenfeld Gustavus "liberated Europe from the fear of Catholic-Hapsburg tyranny which had haunted her since the time of Philip II."[62]

Gustavus now began a daring and victorious march through northern Germany, devastating the Emperor's best troops in a winter campaign and giving new strength to the Protestant cause. Many towns surrendered; others were pillaged and plundered. Following the Saxon conquest of Prague on November 15 by Hans George von Arnim, southern Germany stood exposed, and Gustavus triumphantly advanced from the Rhineland west on the *Pfaffengrasse* (*Priests' Alley*) into the center of the Catholic bishoprics in Bavaria, in a drive directed toward Munich and Vienna. Ferdinand II's desperate "appeals to Rome brought only the cold answer that the pope did not consider the war to be one of religion,"[63] and requests to Madrid went unanswered. The exhausted Spanish were unable to provide relief as they fought the Dutch, who took advantage of the eroding strength of the Hapsburg armies to end Spain's rule over the Netherlands.

Fate Restores the Empire's Fortunes.   On April 13, 1632 the desperate Emperor recalled Wallenstein from retirement to lead the Imperial troops—but on very advantageous terms. It is said that Wallenstein demanded

> not only for absolute control in the army, but for absolute control of all peace negotiations and the right to conclude treaties when and where he would, for the exclusion of the Emperor's son from any part in the command, and of Spain from any influence upon it, while he, Wallenstein, was to receive as his reward a part of the Hapsburg lands and the title of Elector—Bohemia and the Electorate of Brandenburg or the Palatinate.[64]

Whatever the true provisions of the agreement, the experienced but controversial commander was the Emperor's only hope to repel the Swedish troops. Wallenstein's skill posed a temptation which the Emperor, in a "might makes right" climate of opinion, found irresistible. In May, the newly recommissioned Wallenstein regained control of Prague and, in so doing, blocked Gustavus's march on Vienna. By August, Wallenstein had built a barrier around the outnumbered Swedish forces, which were in dire need of supplies and reinforcements. A month later Gustavus offered to make peace with Wallenstein. Gustavus's terms—the unconditional revocation of the Edict of Restitution—were deemed unacceptable, so the two armies prepared to settle the matter on the field of battle.

On November 1, 1632, Wallenstein masterminded the first major defeat that Gustavus Adolphus experienced, which allowed the Empire to recover much of Bavaria, Silesia, and Saxony. Although demoralized, the Swedes remained a significant fighting force composed of nearly 150,000 soldiers. Two weeks later, on November 16, 1632, the Swedes took on and withstood Wallenstein's Imperial army in the fog-shrouded Battle of Lützen, but the cost was immeasurable because Gustavus Adolphus was killed in the battle. According to legend, enemy soldiers first found the dying Gustavus Adolphus lying on the battlefield and asked him to identify himself. "I am the King of Sweden," he replied, "who do seal the religion and liberty of the German nation with my blood."[65] Searching the battlefield for their King, the shocked Swedes discovered Gustavus's "naked body under a heap of dead, a bullet hole though his head, a dagger thrust in his side, another bullet, ominously, in his back."[66]

The intervention of Gustavus Adolphus into the Thirty Years' War had "spared Protestantism in Germany from the annihilation that it suffered in Bohemia, and he had frustrated the Hapsburg attempt to establish Imperial supremacy."[67] However, the loss of Gustavus Adolphus was a disaster beyond measure. His death was celebrated in Catholic masses in Vienna, where the blood-stained uniform of Gustavus was later put on public display as a symbol of deliverance from destruction.

Gustavus's death set back the Protestant cause as the relative power of the belligerents again shifted back toward equilibrium.

> It was because it put an end to the brief Protestant tide of success that Lützen, although a drawn battle, was so important. Another Swedish victory like Breitenfeld or Rain would have destroyed the Imperial cause beyond all hope of recovery. Now the two sides were again more or less equal, leading each combatant to seek desperately for more foreign support which might tip the scales—the hopes of Sweden pinned ever more firmly to France, those of the Emperor fixed increasingly on Spain.[68]

The death of Gustavus Adolphus left the dispirited anti-Hapsburg coalition without a skilled, seasoned leader.[69] Command was transferred to General Lennart Torstensson and, later, Chancellor Axel Oxenstierna took direct responsibility for making Swedish strategic decisions, eventually reconstructing the Swedish alliances in the 1633 Treaty of Heilbronn with all the German Protestant princes except Brandenburg and Saxony. But without Gustavus, the momentum of Sweden's military forces expired.

Wallenstein further advanced the Imperial cause through his October 1633 victory against General Thuan's Swedish forces at Steinau in Silesia, but his accomplishment was counterbalanced when anti-Imperial forces under General Bernhard of Saxe-Weimar conquered Regensburg in November. Both sides became locked in a military stalemate. It was a fear of defeat, despair about victory, and the seemingly hopeless prospect of a quick end to the suffering that prompted many belligerents to begin talking about the need for a negotiated settlement.

The inscrutable Wallenstein then stepped into the breach and attempted to take advantage of the situation. In order to pacify the Empire under his own control and exact revenge against the Emperor for his dismissal in 1630, Wallenstein began his own secret peace negotiations with Sweden, France, Saxony, and Brandenburg. Emperor Ferdinand regarded these independent initiatives as treasonous, and his anger matched his resentment of the extraordinary payments Wallenstein demanded. The chief commander's previous inability to engineer a decisive victory had compounded the Emperor's frustration with his defiant general, whose loyalty was in doubt to everything except increasing his personal fortune.

Wallenstein's arrogant personality and excessive wealth had won him few friends.[70] When Wallenstein made peace overtures toward the Lutherans, Emperor Ferdinand decided to eradicate his untrustworthy commander and obtain "Wallenstein's army and Wallenstein's resources but without Wallenstein."[71] In retaliation for Wallenstein's alleged plans to take his army over to the Protestant side,[72] the Emperor declared Wallenstein guilty of high treason and secretly granted permission to have him assassinated if he resisted being returned to Vienna for questioning. On February 27, 1634, Wallenstein's entourage was murdered at a banquet by Imperial conspirators, who then killed the defenseless Wallenstein in his bedroom. After the loss of Wallenstein, the Emperor promoted his son Ferdinand, the King of Hungary, to the position of Supreme Commander, and named General Matthias Gallas as Imperial Generalissimo because, although "he was seldom sober and intent only on plunder, [Gallas] had not sufficient imagination to be dangerous."[73]

The Peace of Prague.   By the mid-1630s Germany was in economic ruin. Public opinion was strongly opposed to the continuing presence of foreign soldiers on their blood-soaked soil, and divisions within the Heilbronn League dimmed Protestant enthusiasm for renewing their quest for a military victory. A general desire for peace led to the 1635 Peace of Prague that reduced tensions between Protestant and Catholic princes. In making 1627 instead of 1552 the date for determining legal possession of ecclesiastical territories, this agreement drastically modified the Edict of Restitution and helped reconcile Catholics and Lutherans by allowing the latter to recover their land (while excluding the Calvinists once again). This act of conciliation ameliorated the fanatic religious animosity that had heretofore fueled the flames of war. As Geoffrey Parker notes: "No longer were Protestants ranged against Catholics in almost monolithic blocs; no longer did the ultra-Catholics monopolize Imperial policy."[74] A precedent was set for religious reconciliation that was to move Europe toward a separation of religion from politics and of church from state.

Peace seemed imminent, especially following the September 1634 Imperial victory of General Gallas's forces over those of General Bernhard of Saxe-Weimer at Nördlingen. In addition to retaking nearly all of Sweden's former conquests, the victory precipitated the collapse of the fragile League of Heibrunn, as war-weary German princes led by Saxony withdrew their soldiers from the Swedish army. Moreover, the Hapsburg victory at Nördlingen gave the Empire courage to pursue complete victory over the subdued Protestants rather than settle for a compromise settlement. "It looked like the end for the Protestant cause and the German Liberties; it was the end for Sweden."[75]

The Imperial cause gained a further boost when the Spanish Hapsburg King, Philip IV, counseled by his First Minister the Count-Duke de Olivares and emboldened by Russia's plan to withdraw from the conflict in the June 1634 Peace of Polyanov, chose to fully back his Austrian relatives and send the powerful Spanish army into the Rhineland. The looming prospect of complete subjugation reinvigorated the anti-Hapsburg coalition. France, guided since 1624 by its first Minister, Cardinal Richelieu, now entered the war as a full participant.

THE 1635–1648 FRANCO-SWEDISH PHASE

It was not difficult for Richelieu to convince King Louis XIII to fully engage French troops in the war because the French ruler believed that preemptive military action was required to prevent a Spanish invasion. On August 4, 1634, Louis XIII ordered his defense ministers to prepare for a "vigorous open war against Spain in order to secure a beneficial general peace."[76] The execution of the policy was assigned to Cardinal Richelieu.

Richelieu and the Ascendance of Raison d'Etat

As a Catholic clergyman, Cardinal Richelieu had no affection for Protestantism. As a seasoned practitioner of *realpolitik* (see Box 2.2), however, he put French national interests above his religion. Recognizing the harsh realities of amoral balance-of-power competition, Richelieu began to see advantages to subordinating the church to the state. The glorification of French power was valued as an end in itself, justified by the necessity of ensuring national self-preservation, even if the defense of state power required war. The Cardinal perceived grave danger for France in the shifting balance of power but also an opportunity to defeat the Spanish and Austrian Hapsburgs, the traditional enemies of France. The French decision to enter the war represented the culminating step in the transition of the Thirty Years' War from primarily a war of religion to a war of political position.

Alliances figured prominently in the new French strategy. Richelieu moved quickly to align France with other states whose national interests converged with those of the French throne. On February 8, 1635, Richelieu signed an offensive and defensive alliance with the United Provinces of the Netherlands when the Swedish Chancellor, Count Axel Oxenstierna, anxious to protect Sweden's interests in Germany, offered Richelieu support. Two months later, the allies cemented their coalition with the Treaty of Compiègne, aimed at preventing the Swedes from surrendering after being decimated in the battle of Nördlingen. This mutual defense treaty pledging support to the Protestant princes in Germany made French military involvement in Germany inevitable, although Richelieu's strategy originally had been aimed at a minimal participation so that the French could concentrate their intervention on the Spanish, whom Richelieu perceived to be a greater threat than the Emperor in Austria.

With the Franco-Swedish alliance in place, Richelieu forged an alliance with Savoy and Parma, negotiated a twenty-year truce between Sweden and Poland-Lithuania, and hired the experienced Lutheran General, Bernhard of Saxe-Weimar, to lead the French interventionary forces, who "hired Saxe-Weimar's entire army."[77]

On May 19, 1635 "the unscrupulous Richelieu, who had long been intriguing with both Bavaria and Sweden at the same time, scented the opportunity of making significant gains for France," and declared war on Spain.[78] The thirteen-year Franco-Spanish final phase of the Thirty Years' War was purely political. As one study observes, following French intervention, "The war lost nearly all connection with religious issues and became a dynastic struggle between Bourbon France on one side and Hapsburg Austria and Spain on the other."[79] The transformation of underlying motives for waging war represented a cultural shift that was to have lasting effects. War was for power, not principle, as the Swedish crown, the French Bourbon King, the Hapsburg King of Spain, and the Hapsburg Emperor in Vienna engaged in a zero-sum contest to establish geostrategic position, with other states aligning with or against one of these centers of power. As controversies over religious issues subsided, balance-of-power politics became a permanent obsession among rival monarchs. Indeed, the widespread practice during the war of forging *ad hoc* coalitions to block the ambitions of the powerful crystallized after the war as a norm which promoted flexible, nonideological, and amoral alliances of convenience solely for self-advantage.

Richelieu's strategy to weaken the power of the Hapsburgs in general and Spain and its Hapsburg ruler Philip IV in particular was symbolic of the new philosophy of expedience that was to dominate international politics for the next two centuries. Consistent with the rise of *realpolitik*, France wanted to ensure that the Holy Roman Empire would crumble "because a weak Empire divided into scores of independent principalities enhanced France's international stature."[80] The French war was to be fought on two fronts—in German states and in Spain. Richelieu felt that he could rely on German Protestant princes to wage the war in the Empire against Ferdinand II while the French fought against Philip IV in Spain. Richelieu was confident that strategic necessity compelled the Protestants to hold the same outlook which he himself had accepted.

France was motivated in the Thirty Years' War almost exclusively by geostrategic calculations emanating from a fear of encirclement by Hapsburg Spain and its Italian possessions to the south, by the Spanish territories of Franche-Comté and the Netherlands to the north, and the Austrian Hapsburgs to the east. For Cardinal Richelieu national survival meant pursuing three goals. First, he was determined to weaken the two branches of the House of Hapsburg and reduce their threat to French security. Second, he sought to expand French borders to include territories controlled by the Holy Roman Empire's Imperial armies. Third, he deliberately planned to delay the entrance of French troops into the war, subsidizing Hapsburg enemies such as Sweden in the hope that exhaustion would lead to an easy and profitable win once France intervened militarily.[81] When France formally entered the conflict in 1635 by declaring war against Spain, the decision was motivated by a rational estimate of projected costs and benefits. "French involvement in the war had been carefully calculated,"[82] and the timing of the decision for war occurred not coincidentally when the balance of power had most required it—"at the lowest point in the fortunes of the Protestant cause in Germany."[83]

The Final Phase of the War

The French decision to intervene in the Thirty Years' War expanded the conflict, with fighting in the Low Countries where the United Provinces of the Netherlands and France opposed Spain; in Italy, where France and Spain struggled for preponderant influence; in France, when Spanish and Imperial forces invaded; in Germany where the war began; in the Iberian peninsula in 1640, when Portugal saw an opportunity for independence and militarily revolted against Spain; and in northern Europe where Denmark and Sweden opposed each other. In short, the Thirty Years' War became a general, systemwide war: "Practically all the petty wars and disputes of continental Europe were thus united into one grand holocaust."[84]

The final phase of the Thirty Years' War was a long-drawn-out, highly destructive series of inconclusive battles. The era displayed all the properties characteristic of classic balance-of-power politics: distrustful allies, competition by great-power rivals for additional support from neutrals, and the pervasive threat of an opportunistic "separate peace" that would leave the remaining belligerents without a voice at a comprehensive peace conference.

The French assembled an army of 130,000 that grew to 200,000 by the end of 1635. The first French campaign, launched against Spanish territory in the Netherlands, Italy, and the Valtellina, resulted in complete failure. The second campaign in Alsace and Franche-Comté was equally unsuccessful. Meanwhile, in 1636 Spanish Imperial forces invaded France. The Spanish drove deep into France: "Champagne and Burgundy were ravaged and Paris itself was seized with panic. The Spanish also raided the south. The French had a taste of the plunder, murder, burnings, and stealing of cattle by which Germany had been afflicted."[85] Spanish gains were short-lived, however. The alarmed French rallied to defeat the Spanish troops, whereupon France turned its attention to Germany, where the Thirty Years' War had started and which had borne the brunt of the war's devastation.

In adjacent theatres, the Franco-Swedish coalition met with greater initial success. In Italy French Marshal Charles de Créqui and French ally Duke Victor Armadeus of Savoy won a major victory over the Spanish at Tornavento on June 22, 1636. In Germany during October, 22,000 Swedish and Scottish mercenaries under General Torstensson and General Johan Banér severely defeated 30,000 soldiers at Wittstock and restored Swedish domination in north and central Germany. The following year, the Dutch, under the command of Frederick Henry, recaptured Breda after a year-long siege. Spain then responded with an abortive second invasion of southern France from Catalonia which was turned back at Leucate, and the Imperial army held ground the next year to resist a French counterattack in an intervention that was blocked at Fuenterrabvia.

In March 1638 the anti-Hapsburg alliance resumed the offensive with Bernhard, engineering a victory in Alsace over Italian mercenary Count Savelli and Bavarian General Johann von Werth at Rheinfelden. "With French support, Bernhard then besieged Breisach, the key to the Rhine, which held out from June to December 1638 and until every cat, dog, and rat in the city and some of the deceased among the human population had been consumed."[86] The war continued throughout 1639 with a series of indecisive battles in Germany, Italy, the Netherlands, and Roussillon. Still, the belligerents persisted. Reputation and the desire to negotiate a peace settlement from a position of strength were uppermost in their minds. French victories had tipped the balance of the conflict in favor of the anti-Hapsburgs, but had not forced the Imperial armies to surrender nor clotted the bloodletting of the Germans.

In general, the closing phases of the war proved disastrous for the Holy Roman Empire. The Austro-Spanish Imperial army's last victory occurred at Thionville on June 7, 1639. The two most capable French commanders, Henri de la Tour d'Auvergne, the Viscount of Turenne, and the youthful but ingenious Louis II de Bourbon, the Prince of Condé, proved to be more than a match for the Emperor's Imperial troops (including the venerated Spanish infantry). Bernhard of Saxe-Weimar conducted a series of masterful campaigns, as noted, that culminated in the 1638 capture of Breisach, and the Swedish General Johan Banér also won important battles in Germany, including a major victory over Imperial General Melchior von Hatzfeld at Wittstock. As the prospects for the Protestant coalition's subjugation of the Hapsburgs appeared in sight, the feeble Emperor Ferdinand II died on February 15, 1637, and was succeeded by his son Ferdinand III. But only after the devout Bernhard of Saxe-Weimer died from fever at the age of thirty-five in 1639 and Johan Banér died in 1640 did earnest peace negotiations finally begin.

The Rocky Road to Peace

The seemingly endless rounds of combat steadily eroded whatever enthusiasm for war remained. Yet the belligerents continued fighting to achieve peace on advantageous terms, and remained dedicated to the growing popularity of the Machiavellian belief that war was an acceptable instrument of foreign policy to promote parochial national interests. Ever more blood was spilled to guarantee that no power would find itself in a poor position at the bargaining table. The maxim "always negotiate from a position of strength" compelled both sides to keep their war-weary forces on the battlefield.

On the other hand, the war's brutality continued to energize the cry for peace.[87] Pope Urban VIII, who anxiously prayed for the triumph of Catholicism but in an age of mistrust distrusted the Catholic Hapsburgs, is credited with taking "the first steps toward the organization of peace talks to bring the war to an end [when] a papal legate arrived at Cologne in October 1636 and invited all interested powers to send representatives to a general peace congress. But his efforts at mediation failed: neither France nor Spain trusted the pope to be impartial and the Protestants rejected papal mediation altogether."[88]

A window of opportunity in this horrible war of attrition finally opened following the onset in 1640 of revolutions in both Catalonia and Portugal that forced the Spanish to concentrate their military efforts on the Iberian Peninsula. When the Arras stronghold surrendered to the French during August, the Spanish position in the Netherlands was exposed, thus increasing Madrid's interest in a negotiated settlement. With the Valtellina artery severed, "the Spanish Netherlands were left a rudderless ship drifting before the gale."[89]

Prospects for a peace settlement were also affected by the deaths of Cardinal Richelieu in December 1642 and King Louis XIII of France five months later. The papal nuncio to the French throne, Cardinal Jules Mazarin, succeeded Richelieu as Chief Minister of the French Crown, and continued to pursue the French wartime policy of alignment with the Protestant coalition. Trained by Richelieu, Mazarin also placed French national interests ahead of his Catholic faith—a choice that led Pope Urban III, who resented Mazarin's opposition to his appointment as pope, to outrage. The papacy wished to end the war before the depopulation of Europe left Christendom with few souls to save, and the pope condemned French and Hapsburg intransigence and power politics as responsible for creating obstacles to peacemaking.

Although new proposals for peace negotiations continued to be voiced, progress proceeded haltingly through *ad hoc*, trial-by-error diplomacy while the fighting continued. A breakthrough did not come until the Imperial coalition began to crumble in northeast Germany. Key Electoral members of the Empire forged separate peace agreements that enabled them to withdraw as neutrals from the war. Brandenburg, for example, pursued its immediate self-interest by striking a separate peace with Sweden in July 1641, because it had become the victim of relentless warfare and the Elector, Frederick William, recognized that the Holy Roman Emperor could no longer protect his province. Similarly, the Duke of Brunswick in January 1642 negotiated the Peace of Goslar, which enabled Brunswick to become a neutral and to conduct Lutheran worship.

Losing ground, the new Emperor, Ferdinand III, had to abandon all hope of driving the Protestant anti-Hapsburgs out of the Empire and subjugating the French. Recognizing his vulnerability, Ferdinand sought to bargain for favorable terms, and he prepared the way for a general peace by convening a meeting of the Imperial Diet at Regensburg. Debate at the meeting concluded with the negotiated acceptance of the Emperor's authority, but the issue of secularized church lands was resolved in the Protestants' favor.

> Again the Emperor gave way. In spite of papal protests . . . the Emperor abandoned the Edit of Restitution: ecclesiastical property that had been in secular hands on 1 January 1627 was to remain. Although the papacy contrived to condemn all future settlements, including the final [1648 treaties of Westphalia] peace that included this abrogation of the Edict of Restitution, in effect the issue was resolved forever at Regensburg.[90]

Resolution of the religious controversy made possible the eventual resolution of the geostrategic issues that now preoccupied the belligerents.

Fighting continued as diplomatic discussions inched the combatants closer to peace. Portions of the Holy Roman Empire were reduced by the Swedish armies led by the Swedish Commander-in-Chief Lennart Torstensson and the French forces led by General de Condé and Marshal Turenne. Torstensson defeated the Hapsburgs at Breitenfeld in 1642 and, after a campaign in the north to subdue Danish resistance, the French Joint Commander Count Matthias Gallas engineered a climactic victory over Imperial General Franz von Hatzfeldt at Jankau in Bohemia on March 6, 1645. Meanwhile, French General Duc d'Engien (titled "the Great Condé) repulsed a Spanish counteroffensive at Rocroi on May 19, 1643, in a decisive victory that destroyed the core of the remaining Spanish infantry. The defeat "was the end of the Spanish army . . . almost, one might say, the gravestone of Spanish greatness."[91] Following several French setbacks, General de Condé and Marshal Turenne were again victorious near Nördlingen. The military balance tilted once again further toward the anti-Hapsburg coalition.

The Eleventh Hour of the Thirty Years' War

Within weeks of the Imperial army's defeat at Rocroi, Emperor Ferdinand III authorized peace negotiations with France and Sweden. The Austrian Hapsburgs had been stripped of all their previous conquests, Austria's strongest ally, Bavaria, was overrun, and enemy forces were approaching Vienna. With prostrate Spain no longer capable of fielding a significant military force, Ferdinand III was forced to bargain for the best peace terms possible.

It now appeared that the cherished goal of Cardinals Richelieu and

Mazarin—adherents to the increasingly popular realist strategies to target your closest rival for attack and to "divide and rule"—would be realized as the Austrian and Spanish branches of the House of Hapsburg were in the process of being severed. However, in a calculated strategy conceding to deteriorating geostrategic realities, Spain offered the Netherlands independence in exchange for a Dutch truce so France would lose an important military ally. The truce brought the Hapsburgs time, but Germany remained exposed to more suffering. The Swedes under Karl Gustav Wrangel and the French under their commander, the Viscount of Turenne

> . . . together laid waste to Bavaria. By now the German countryside was so looted, stripped bare, and defiled by the contending armies that it could not support long major concentrations of troops in the field. As a result armies grew smaller and lulls between operations grew longer, although the incessant raids and rapine by small independent bands of men, more brigands than soldiers, never seemed to diminish. Total exhaustion was beginning to wear down both sides.
>
> But a few last weary rounds remained to be fought. . . . In the last year of the war Turenne and Wrangel again collaborated in the further punishment of Bavaria. The Imperialist army of 30,000 under Marshal Peter Melander, accompanied by a horde of 100,000 refugees, fled before the invaders, but the Protestants and French caught the rearguard at Zusmarshausen on May 17, 1648, and routed it. Melander was killed in the action.
>
> The Swedes thrust again into Bohemia and took control of Prague. Spain tried one last invasion of France, coming through Artois, but Condé, back from Catalonia, met the invaders with 14,000 Frenchmen at Lens on August 10 and smashed them. It was almost a replay of Rocroi. The Archduke Leopold's army lost 4,000 slain and 6,000 taken captive.[92]

The devastation of Germany finally came to an end when the Austrian Hapsburgs were forced to negotiate a cease-fire, after which fighting narrowed to the unresolved contest of wills between France and Spain. Though exhausted by the rigors of three decades of warfare, neither side trusted the other. The belligerent rulers had become hardened by a culture of death, equating expedience with wisdom and ruthlessness with virtue. Horrific actions bred militant attitudes. Now, at war's end, the warrior's philosophy had become the statesman's creed. Due to a rigid, punitive mind-set, the end to the Thirty Years' War came slowly:

> In Prague, where the war had begun, they were still fighting [on 24 October 1648]. Monks, students, and townsmen were manning the Charles Bridge against an expected Swedish assault [when] with nine days' delay, news of the peace arrived. The clanging of church bells drowned the last thunders of the cannon.[93]

War truly had become a way of life.[94] But not everyone responded to its challenges in the same way. Lacking political dexterity, the Holy Roman Emperor saw the world through the lens of religious absolutes. Cardinal Richelieu, on the other hand, saw no difficulty in aligning with Protestants to advance French interests. He was unwilling to commit to any cause but those in accord with a dispassionate assessment of *raison d'état*, and he preferred to put his faith in French power and cunning rather than in moral law or the good will of others. Whereas Emperors Ferdinand II and Ferdinand III harkened back to the medieval past, Richelieu was a precursor to the modern age that lay ahead. In the period following the end of the Thirty Years' War, a normative system inspired by Richelieu's secular philosophy of statecraft took root in Europe. At Westphalia, the practice of amoral power politics, honed during a long, bitter war, took on the obligatory tone of a new rule for international behavior. The old idea of a unified European society would slumber for centuries, not to awaken until the twentieth-century Cold War ended and visionary leaders began to seriously contemplate the need to exorcise the ghost of Westphalia and reorganize international relations on an alternative foundation—one that balances principle with pragmatism, idealism with realism, and supranationalism with state sovereignty.

In the end, exhaustion combined with the sheer brutality of the protracted armed struggle to finally bring the reticent, weary belligerents to parlay in Münster and Osnabrück. The moods of the diplomats assembled in these two Westphalian towns cannot be understood without accounting for the burden imposed by war. In the next chapter, we examine the costs of the Thirty Years' War.

CHAPTER 3

The Costs
of the Thirty Years' War

Know, my son, with how little wisdom the world is governed.
—Count Axel Oxenstierna, Chancellor of Sweden

The destructiveness of the Thirty Years' War shaped the mood of the belligerents when they convened in 1648 to craft a peace settlement. Warfare had already become increasingly violent due to technological advances in the previous century, but now soldiers displayed a "callous disregard for restraints."[1] One cost of abandoning moral restraints in combat was immediately conspicuous: the German population was reduced by a third, perhaps more.[2]

The Thirty Years' War was in a descent into barbarism: "The facts are that hundreds of villages were left without a single inhabitant; that many towns were reduced to less than half their population; that dead men were found with grass in their mouths; that cannibalism broke out in several parts of Germany; and that . . . a prisoner might have reason to fear . . . a death more terrible than any which law could inflict."[3] Michael Howard aptly described the unrestrained conduct of the war when he wrote,

> A soldier . . . was well described as a man who had to die so as to have something to live on. His condition was no better than that of the peasants he tormented. Armies were in a continual state of deliquescence, melting away from death, wounds, sickness, straggling, and desertion, their movements governed not by strategic calculation but by the search for unplundered territory. It was a period in which warfare seemed to escape from rational control; to cease indeed to be "war" in the sense of politically-motivated use of force by generally recognized authorities, and to degenerate instead into universal, anarchic, and self-perpetuating violence.[4]

Through a scorched-earth strategy of annihilation, each side sought the complete subjugation of the other so the terms of the peace treaty could be dictated to the defeated. Wallenstein's call for his army to "live off the land"

and Gustavus's "swath of destruction" tactics were typical of the period. They stemmed from philosophies that denied limits in a just cause; a moral end justified brutal means, including what today would be classified as crimes against humanity. The destruction born of this mentality surpassed even the savagery of the Crusades, and "exceeded levels of direct and collateral damage of most wars either before or since."[5]

What made such ruthless behavior common was the gradual acceptance of total warfare as the fighting widened in scope. Habits grew into customs, and customs created complacency about war and its use as an instrument of state policy. Aggression for the glorification of state power had become so institutionalized after three decades of ceaseless fighting that it was difficult for many Europeans to visualize any alternative to a Hobbesian "war of all against all." Not surprisingly, expectations about reducing war's frequency and severity plummeted. Brutality had become legitimized on behalf of state aggrandizement. All assessments of the wages of the Thirty Years' War must be seen in the context of the changes in the climate of the opinion about international ethics that transpired as the war was fought. The Thirty Years' War left in its wake a culture permissive of warfare, indifferent to the justice of its cause or the means by which it was fought. Take, for example, Grotius's description of the kinds of customary practices which international law began to defend as legal:

> . . . according to Grotius' account the law of nations permitted belligerents to kill and injure all who are in enemy territory, including women and children; to destroy and pillage enemy property, even that which is held sacred; to kill captives and hostages; and to make slaves of prisoners of war (although it strictly forbade the use of poison). Grotius however, makes clear his dissent from the existing state of the law by saying that it prescribes merely what is permissive in the sense that it is done with impunity, even though it might "deviate from the rule of right." He then adds a series of pleas for modernization in the exercise of what the law permits.[6]

In this chapter we will describe the costs of this new normative climate of opinion. Our purpose is not just to revisit the cruelty that dashed the older medieval order, but, more importantly, to show how the war shaped the system of international relations codified by the Peace of Westphalia. To understand the war's system-transforming impact, it is useful first to look backward and briefly review how the conduct of the war brought on a bitter harvest for those toiling for peace in the killing fields of central Europe.

A WORLD DESTROYED

By any measure, the Thirty Years' War was a human tragedy of epic proportions. The devastation it caused had more to do with the desperate circumstances the disputants faced than with the intolerance each side felt for the other's religious convictions and practices.[7] As each stage of the war unfolded, the participants' motives shifted in reaction to the changing conditions. What had begun as primarily a religious conflict over confessional rights and liberties became in time a war fought over political, military, and mercenary considerations without regard for the ethical teachings of Christian doctrine. As the war became secular, the belligerents appealed to expedience and abandoned serious attempts to adhere to higher moral principles. Military necessity became the rationale for doing whatever would deliver an advantage on the battlefield.[8]

> The Thirty Years' War was the most brutal and destructive conflict in European history up to that time, . . . a crisis in the relations between states. The military ran amok, agreements were broken with impunity, and sheer chaos reigned for thirty savage years. With religious partisanship to excuse the worst perfidy, it seemed that all the traditional rules and courtesies of war had been abandoned to burgeoning armies.[9]

The cost of abandoning moral limits on behavior and thereby operating within a culture of mistrust can be seen in the alignments that the belligerents formed in pursuit of material gain and self-aggrandizement. For example, although many Protestants initially refused to attack other Protestants, over time this principle was relaxed, as can be seen in Sweden's war with Denmark over control of the Baltic. Protestants also put power over principle by siding with Catholics for mutual gain, as Saxony did when it aligned with the Catholic Emperor as the war spread to Germany. Similarly, some Catholics put politics ahead of religion by supporting alliances of convenience with Protestants, of which Catholic France's alliance with Lutheran Sweden and Pope Urban VIII's support of Protestant opposition to the Holy Roman Emperor are conspicuous examples.[10]

Arguably, the price of abandoning morality in the conduct of the war was an acceptance of military tactics that relied on terror. Massacre and pillage became widespread. Soldiers, often unpaid, were required to feed themselves and forage for supplies by plundering innocent civilian bystanders. To recruit and retain soldiers in the absence of financial compensation, "armed bands had roamed Germany like packs of wolves, slaughtering the populace sheep."[11] War-profiteers like Wallenstein reflected the opportunistic self-interest of the times by permitting his quasi-independent mercenary army to ravage "friendly and hostile regions alike."[12]

The people residing in Germany were the real victims (see Box 3.1). When the fighting finally ceased,

> Germany lay desolate. The population had fallen from 21 million to perhaps 13 million. Between a third and a half of the people were dead. Whole cities, like Magdeburg, stood in ruins. Whole districts lay stripped of their inhabitants, their livestock, their supplies. Trade had virtually ceased. A whole generation of pillage, famine, disease, and social disruption had wreaked such havoc that in the end

the princes were forced to reinstate serfdom, to curtail municipal liberties, and to nullify the progress of a century. The many exploits of Spanish, Swedish, Italian, Croat, Flemish, and French soldiers had changed the racial composition of the people. German culture was so traumatized that art and literature passed entirely under the spell of foreign, especially French, fashions.[13]

BOX 3.1
The Wages of War: Two Telling Cases

To illustrate the conditions that prevailed especially in the war's later stages, consider the following two infamous episodes. The first occurred in 1631 when the Imperial Army attacked Rothenburg-ob-der-Tauber along Bavaria's "Romantic Road." According to that feudal town's celebrated legend, General Tilly followed the accepted practice toward those who did not surrender unconditionally by ordering his soldiers to sack the town. The citizens begged for mercy, and Tilly agreed to spare the town providing a citizen would accept his dare to consume an unspeakably enormous tankard of wine. The *Bürgermeister,* Heinrich Toppler, accepted the challenge and saved the entire town by chugging the entire flagon of wine; but he passed out from intoxication and died. The mayor's brave feat is commemorated in a play, *Der Meistertrunk,* which by tradition is performed every Whit Monday in the Kaisersaal of the town's Rathaus.

The second episode speaks to the ordeal faced by many other German villages during a war in which "hundreds of villages were left without a single inhabitant."[14] In January 1634 a platoon of about twenty Swedish soldiers rode into Linden, in Franconia, demanding food and wine. They forced their entry into the cottage of Georg Rosch, raped his wife, and stole what they found available. The villagers ambushed the soldiers on their departure from the town and confiscated their clothing, loot, and horses. The next day, the Swedes returned with a constable who arrested four men for their assault and issued a report to General Horn that identified one of the soldiers as the rapist of Frau Rosch. This was followed by the soldiers' effort to escape criminal punishment: "shortly after the village was registered as uninhabited. Its inhabitants did not return to their prewar number until 1690."[15]

All historians accept the view that the Thirty Years' War was extremely destructive, although estimates of the war's damage vary with the criteria used. Some put the loss of life at about one-fourth of Germany's population; others estimate that Germany's population declined by as much as two-thirds. One account calculates that "some 12,000 towns and villages were destroyed," but that figure may be low given another estimate that of some 35,000 Bohemian villages "hardly more than 6,000 were left standing."[16] Whatever the actual loss of life, it is clear that at least half-a-million troops perished and that civilian casualties far exceeded that of the military.[17] The depopulation of central Europe also resulted from starvation and disease, from refugees fleeing the bloodshed, extraordinary taxes, and the threat of religious persecution. "The solace of cynicism seemed to transcend faith and unfaith alike."[18]

WHY DID THE WAR LAST?

Historical events like wars and peace settlements "are not random events; they are the products of decisions."[19] Although these decisions may have been driven by faulty assumptions, erroneous intelligence estimates, and other forms of miscalculation, nonetheless they stemmed from purposeful acts aimed at achieving desired goals. Looking back on the Thirty Years' War from this perspective we face a puzzling question: Why did the war continue for so long when the costs far exceeded the gains? The failure to cut huge losses by negotiating a compromised peace settlement defies logic (see Table 3.1). Could the belligerents not see the catastrophic failure their strategies were producing? Why did the warring parties persist against all odds? Why, indeed, did a climate of opinion develop that tolerated warfare, when so obviously only a handful of war-profiteers directly benefited while rich and poor alike suffered?

One explanation might be that the belligerents became callous in the pursuit of state power. They were obsessed with status and prestige, rendering acceptance of defeat impossible and evoking the conclusion that compromise would be an embarrassing acknowledgment of military mistakes. Pride seemed to have fathered denial. Experiencing cognitive dissonance, they disregarded information that presented them with the uncomfortable possibility that their choices might have been wrong.

A second factor was greed. Opportunistic pursuers of personal wealth, like Count Albrecht von Wallenstein, Bethlen Gabor, Ernst von Mansfield, and Christian of Brunswick, saw in the role of military entrepreneur a means of achieving social stature and financial gain. Such men had few incentives for a negotiated truce that would end their acquisition of territory and titles as spoils of war. Once set in motion, the mercenary machine could not retreat, in part because of the system of subsidizing military campaigns by paying commanders with the promise of territorial possessions. Conquest, of course, was costly: "The battles of the Thirty Years' War averaged 30 percent casualties for the defeated and 15 percent casualties for the victorious army."[20] Yet however sacrificial the battles were, conquest was required to recover expenses. Unpaid soldiers lived off the land and threatened mutiny if not assured future indemnities paid by the vanquished. The policy of leading generals to pay their subordinates with the promise of confiscated goods helped keep the fires of war burning long after many people recognized they were trapped in a military stalemate.

A third ingredient in the continuation of the war was the pervasive influence of tightly-knit autocratic groups whose closed collective decision making

TABLE 3.1 The Carnage of Combat: Casualty Estimates of the Major Battles of the Thirty Years' War

Battle	Date	Army	Size	Number Killed and Wounded
White Mountain	November 8, 1620	Imperialists	25,000	650
		Bohemian Protestants	15,000	5,000
Wimpfen	May 6, 1622	Imperialists	20,000	n.a.
		Protestants	14,000	2,000
Höchst	June 20, 1622	Imperialists	20,000	n.a.
		Protestants	16,000	6,000
Stadtlohn	August 6, 1623	Imperialists	15,000	n.a.
		Protestants	16,000	10,000
Breda	August 28,1624–	Spanish	60,000	n.a.
	June 5, 1625	Dutch	9,000	5,000
Bridge of Dessau	April 25, 1625	Imperialists	20,000	n.a.
		Protestants	12,000	4,000
Lütter	August 24–26, 1626	Imperialists	20,000	n.a.
		Danes	15,000	4,000
Werben	July 22, 24, 1631	Imperialists	23,000	6,000
		Swedes	16,000	n.a.
Breitenfeld	September 17, 1631	Imperialists	34,000	7,600
		Swedes/Saxons	26,000/16,000	700/1,500
Lech River	April 15–16,1632	Imperialists	20,000	2,000
		Swedes	26,000	n.a.
Alte Veste Castle (Nuremberg)	September 3–4, 1632	Imperialists	60,000	600
		Swedes	45,000	2,400
Lützen	November 16, 1632	Imperialists	27,000	6,000
		Swedes	18,000	6,000
Nördlingen	September 6, 1634	Imperialists	33,000	n.a.
		Protestants	25,000	12,000

(continued)

TABLE 3.1 continued

Battle	Date	Army	Size	Number Killed and Wounded
Wittstock	October 4, 1636	Imperialists	30,000	11,000
		Swedes	22,000	5,000
Casale	April 29, 1640	Spanish	20,000	3,800
		French	10,000	n.a.
Second Breitenfeld	November 2, 1642	Imperialists	20,000	5,000
		Swedes	15,000	n.a.
Rocroi	May 19, 1643	Spanish	26,000	8,000
		French	22,000	4,000
Freiburg	August 3–10, 1644	Bavarians	17,000	6,000
		French	17,000	8,000
Allerheim	August 3, 1645	Bavarians	12,000	5,000
		French	12,000	5,500
Lens	August 10, 1648	Spanish	15,000	4,000
		French	14,000	n.a.
MAJOR SEA BATTLES				
The Downs	October 21, 1639	Spanish	77 warships	14 captured
				51 destroyed
		Dutch	24,000 seamen/soldiers	7,000 killed
			105 galleons, 2 fireships	1 ship sunk
				500 sailors killed
Kolberg	October 13, 1644	Danes	17 warships	14 ships destroyed
		Dutch/Swedes	37 warships,	no ships lost

Source: Data from Clodfelter, 1992, pp. 8–9.

precluded the active participation of advisers earnestly seeking peace. Warfare rationalized the rise of absolute monarchs for desperate people who began
to value order over freedom and saw in autocratic rule "the only escape from
uncertainty, confusion, civil conflict, and hard times."[21] "The development of
absolution in Europe was a process . . . linked to the changing nature of European warfare which forced governments to alter substantially their administrative systems, including tightening control of their subject peoples."[22]
Paradoxically, the expansion of centralized governance crippled the capacity
to terminate the fighting. War had concentrated military might in the throne,
making state power unassailable for those religious and humanitarian groups
that otherwise could make a moral argument for peacemaking. Thus when
the modest organized opposition to the continuation of the war within the
belligerent societies vanished, the ruling monarchies possessed a free hand.
Consider the head-strong persistence of the autocratic Austrian House of Hapsburg, which ordered its troops to fight in no less than 86 separate battles
between 1618 and 1648 without real opposition to the continuation of war
from within either branch of the royal court.[23]

A fourth factor perpetuating the Thirty Years' War was the prejudicial
spirit of the age. It was "an age of intolerance," observes René Albrecht-Carrié,
"in many ways akin to our own, though we now choose to call our differences
ideological and political instead of theological in content."[24] The early seventeenth century's religious intolerance, fueled by military brutality in the conduct
of the war, served as a barrier to the resolution of conflict. Mutual disdain
encouraged suspicion about the enemy's motives, and these negative mirror
images heightened fears in a self-reinforcing cycle of mistrust that made it
exceedingly difficult for the belligerents to negotiate, let alone achieve peaceful reconciliation.

Put together, the values and interests animating European political culture
in the first half of the seventeenth century were not conducive to making coura-
geous choices for peace once decisions for war were reached. As one historian
concludes,

> Both the Catholic and Protestant coalitions were in a sense syndicates, the claims
> of whose members exceeded the possible profits available. The wars lasted so long
> largely because of the disproportion between princely and aristocratic ambition on
> the one hand and the resources of Germany on the other.[25]

What today is known as prospect theory in the study of political psychology
helps to explain why belligerents were hesitant to cut their losses when losing.[26] They were willing to take risks in the hope of avoiding losses, even though
the result may have been a greater loss. The kings and princes pursuing the
war clung to failed policies long after the prospects for recovering their losses
disappeared.

THE WAR'S CONSEQUENCES

After the Thirty Years' War, many Europeans began to think of warfare as a naturally occurring and appropriate institution. Battles became fashionable, especially among aristocrats who observed the fighting from the sidelines unexposed to danger. But for those with a lower station in life, armed conflict instilled a mood of cynicism and despair. The Thirty Years' War stripped people of hope for sanctuary from perpetual warfare because it seemed to be an entrenched, inevitable a way of life that afforded no hope for escape.

Sadly, the normative climate of European opinion acclimated itself to the barbaric violence that had become conventional military practice. Machiavellian attitudes that "might makes right" and that brute force was a moral means to military victory gained many adherents in royal courts who learned to prize their self-preservation above any other value. The resultant decay of concerns about the moral content of diplomacy may, in the last analysis, have been the highest cost of the armed struggle:

> The real significance of the Thirty Years' War lies not in its wastage, which was ultimately repaired, but in its indication of a stage in the evolution of this attitude of mind. The direction of history is ultimately determined by these attitudes of mind, revealed in apparently trivial matters, and in this sense everyone is still paying for the Thirty Years' War.[27]

Respect for moral conceptions of right and wrong in diplomacy became a casualty of war. The real cost of the Thirty Years' War was the moral legitimation of the drive for state power and acceptance of virtually any military or political means as a method of increasing power.

The Collapse of Civil Culture

Perhaps the most obvious consequence of the Thirty Years' War was the collapse of civil culture in Germany.

> Life was reduced to savagery in order to persist, over much of the land, sections of which went uncultivated, reverting to primitive brush; manners and morals, too, went primitive. Letters, the arts, and education, all those amenities that make civilization and culture, in great part disappeared under pressure of the elementary struggle for mere survival. The losses, material and moral, of the episode set the Germanic world back an appreciable period of time.[28]

Outside of Germany, the Thirty Years' War created strong states by placing ultimate political authority into the hands of absolute rulers and removing them from the supranational jurisdiction of the Church or the disorganized pluralistic interests of merchants and the mass populace. As a consequence of the

Thirty Years' War, rulers ceased to speak of themselves as the king *in* their territory and began to call themselves the king *of* their territory.

The rise of the absolutist state, with kings and princes claiming to be accountable to no human because they ruled by divine right as God's agent on earth, can be classified as a cost of the war because it retarded the emergence of democratic governance, perhaps for centuries.[29] The pursuit of war for self-preservation justified the growth of centralized administration to mobilize societies for total warfare; the concentration of political authority went hand-in-hand with the growth of powerful armies and the wars they fought. As Joseph Schumpeter put it, centralized states were "created by the wars that required it [and] the machine now created the wars it required."[30] The chaos led intellectuals such as Thomas Hobbes to justify absolutist governance as the best way to preserve order. Recall that in his influential treatise *Leviathan*, published in 1651, he concluded that there was no way to terminate warfare without the creation of a single sovereign empowered to deploy unlimited military power to enforce internal unity and control international competition (see Chapter 4). The Thirty Years' War may be said to have compelled "political leaders to centralize power in order to mobilize the resources necessary for its waging. This effect was critical to state formation in early modern Europe. War gave rulers both the incentive and the opportunity to concentrate power—and that power was the force that ultimately overcame the fragmentation of feudal society."[31]

The price of consolidating political power was extraordinary for the subsequent pattern of relationships between states. War reinforced authoritarian rule, and the growth of autocracies contributed to further warfare. Unlike democracies, whose shared procedural norms emphasize compromise and negotiated settlements, autocracies are more prone to use force for conflict resolution. Research has shown that wars are rare among democracies,[32] but the prospects for a democratic peace at this juncture were foreclosed as the demands of war inhibited the growth of democracy in those few quasi-republics that had previously experimented with government through the consent of the governed.

The Collapse of Prosperity

The wages of war proved extraordinary during the Thirty Years' War. Strained by obsessive competition for hegemony, the fortunes of the belligerents plummeted in a recession accompanied by inflation, falling tax revenues, and the decline of production. There were no financial winners: "Within some thirty years from 1610, every important state staggered from strength to weakness."[33] The war was responsible for the contraction of the European powers' economies that went far behind their immediate material costs, with severe social consequences that fomented a wave of civil unrest and peasant rebellions threatening to undermine the monarchs ensconced in royal courts. Worse still, economic collapse "disturbed the course of trade and industry, apparently to the profit of few and the loss of many [destroying in the process any] foundation for a lasting peace."[34] Wars for trade and overseas empires by great powers desperate to exploit others to subsidize recovery at home followed in the aftermath of the Thirty Years' War.

The Collapse of Christian Unity

The division of Christendom into competing confessional divisions during the Reformation in the sixteenth century was party responsible for the outbreak of the Thirty Years' War. However, rather than resolving theological disputes and reconciling the festering sectarian differences between Catholics, Lutherans, Calvinists, and the other splintered Moravian, Anabaptist, and Reformed movements, the Thirty Years' War had the effect of rendering the divisions permanent. The varieties of liturgical practices and Biblical perspectives undermined any chance to reunify the Church within a common institutional home.

During the war, and especially after the 1635 Peace of Prague, confessional division was chosen as a solution to religious strife in the spirit of mutual coexistence, with different religions assigned by their ruler to dominate their individual spheres of influence. Yet the cost of perpetual disunity was high. True, "Catholic and Protestant finally realized that neither was strong enough to destroy the other and that they must learn to live together [and] out of the forced compromise a spirit of toleration slowly grew."[35] Nevertheless, Scriptures' plea to adhere to a single, universal (catholic) and consistent liturgical interpretation was violated. The "story of the preservation of Catholic tradition within an evangelical Church"[36] became, after the Thirty Years' War, a truncated story, with the exceptions such as the Swedish Lutheran-Catholic liturgy far outnumbered by disintegrative tendencies in most countries. The Thirty Years' War was the death knell of Christian unity. Jennifer Jackson Preece writes that with the end of the Thirty Years' War, medieval Christendom was replaced by a society of sovereign territorial states. In effect, "the fundamental spatial organization of modern international relations had been established."[37] The war signaled the "dawn of the principle of nationalism," as the importance and autonomy of the nation-state came to take precedence over that of universal Christian morality restraining states' freedom to wage war.[38]

The Collapse of Legal Constraints on Warfare

A symptom of the moral decay produced by the brutal experience of the Thirty Years' War was the concomitant decay of the rule of law. Since classical times support had grown for the belief that international order could be constructed from rules that adhered to the immutable higher principles of natural law discovered through reason. "During the sixteenth century, and especially in the first half of the seventeenth century, when international conflict reached a level of barbarity perhaps never equaled, some legal writers began to devise a code of conduct for states which might restore to the community of nation-states some semblance of order."[39] However, the powers engaged in the fighting during the Thirty Years' War resisted these proposals; instead, they argued for the right to use war to increase their power and advance national security interests.

Following the Thirty Years' War, it "became easier than ever for sovereign states to justify themselves by the declaration that those wars which they fought were 'just' and those of others, 'unjust.'"[40] The legal liberation of states from moral restraints was a costly development, however. After 1648, "no widely accepted definitions of 'aggression' . . . [were] generally accepted among international lawyers or among states. And at no time have even the agreed provisions of the law been widely respected by states themselves."[41] The legality of state conduct was now reserved for the state itself to judge. Any war was permissible under the doctrine of *raison d'état* (reason of state), and any method of waging it was defined as acceptable under the corollary of military necessity.[42] The unrestrained acts of war between 1618 and 1648 cost the belligerents dearly, but it cost future generations even more by impeding the development of a code of conduct with moral restraints on warfare.

HOW THE WAR ENDED

Despite huge obstacles, the Thirty Years' War finally came to an end, largely because the warring parties faced exhaustion in the widening theatre of combat that spread throughout the continent after 1635 (see Figure 3.1). Treasuries were depleted and many mercenaries were no longer willing to accept plunder as compensation. The belligerents now began to explore ways to end the war on the best terms they could negotiate. Nevertheless, they would limp through four years of "preliminary" or "preparatory" discussions as each side sought to improve its bargaining position by winning just one more decisive battle. During this interregnum both Cathloics and Protestants searched for a pretext to avoid hard decisions; neither was willing to concede defeat as long as the other's strategic situation appeared better than its own.

It was not until Christmas 1641 that a preliminary treaty was signed in Hamburg by ambassadorial representatives from France, Sweden, and the Holy Roman Empire. This preparatory agreement to pursue a permanent peace settlement provided for two concurrent peace conferences to be convened at Münster and Osnabrück in Westphalia. It was not until January 1643 in Frankfurt that the warring parties actually began negotiating about the procedures that would be followed. A Catholic hard-liner confessed at the Frankfurt meetings, "In winter we negotiate, in summer we fight."[43]

The belligerents eventually concluded their debate about procedure. In November 1645, the representatives from France and the Empire began negotiating at Münster, and later, in June 1647, parallel negotiations between the Swedish and Imperial representatives began 50 kilometers away at Osnabrück.[44]

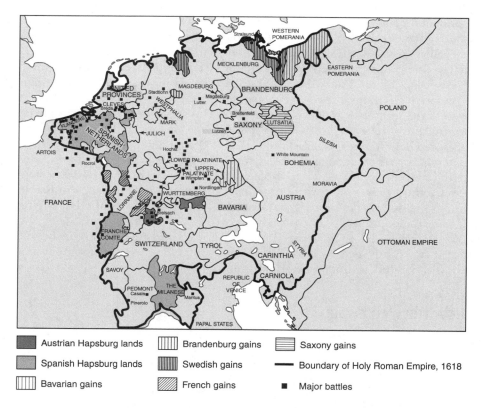

Austrian Hapsburg lands   Brandenburg gains   Saxony gains

Spanish Hapsburg lands   Swedish gains   —— Boundary of Holy Roman Empire, 1618

Bavarian gains   French gains   ■ Major battles

FIGURE 3.1   The Major Battles of the Thirty Years' War Fought between 1635 and 1648, and the Territorial Transfers of the Peace of Westphalia
In the period prior to the conclusion of the Thirty Years' War, the belligerents waged numerous campaigns over a wide area that brought death and destruction to many towns and cities in Europe. The inability of either side to engineer a decisive defeat of the other was an obstacle to negotiating an agreement to reach a peace settlement. This map shows the major theatre of combat as well as the new territorial borders that were drawn at the peace conference.
Source: Adapted from Chandler, 1998, p. 29.

When the brilliant French campaign of 1648 finally convinced the Holy Roman Emperor that further warfare was useless, dedicated efforts to reach a settlement finally commenced. The belligerents suspended their quibbling about etiquette and embarked upon the serious business of crafting an agreement. Out of this now-earnest attempt at peacemaking emerged "a revolutionary change in the way the states of Europe were to order their mutual relations in the future."[45] While most of the diplomats in Westphalia believed that the fighting had become so burdensome that warfare ceased to remain a viable option, several of them had a broader vision of the peace negotiations. Rather than merely ending the war, they hoped to build a new international order.

In Part II of this book we shall investigate how the Peace of Westphalia revised the rules for the conduct of international relations in profound ways, and, in so doing, legally supported the system to which rulers had grown accustomed. We shall illuminate how "the deplorable customs of the territorial princes thus received juridical sanction."[46] To anticipate the argument that will be advanced in the next two chapters, we ask our readers to consider how the practices of statecraft that were institutionalized during the Thirty Years' War were legitimated by the Westphalian Peace. Did Westphalia's confirmation of the secular sovereign state and its virtually unrestrained right to use military force actually serve to perpetuate warfare? Let us pursue the reasoning and evidence underlying this possibility by evaluating the process that produced the Westphalian conception of international politics.

PART II

The Peace of Westphalia's Blueprint for International Relations

As [a] survey of some of the salient features of the Peace Settlement of 1648 discloses, the actual terms of the settlement, interesting and novel as they may be, would hardly suffice to account for the outstanding place attributed to it in the evolution of international relations. In order to find a more adequate explanation it would seem appropriate to search not so much in the text of the treaties themselves as in their implications in the broad conceptions on which they rest and the developments to which they provided impetus.

—Leo Gross

Former U.S. Secretary of State John Foster Dulles is reported to have observed that "you have to take chances for peace, just as you must take chances in war." To break the cycle of carnage, the warring parties in 1648 made a series of fateful choices involving high risks for high stakes. They arrived at a settlement that set in motion diplomatic practices that continue today.

The Thirty Years' War is important because out of it emerged rules and institutions for international relations that have had a lasting influence. Among the list of contributions normally attributed to the Westphalian settlement that ended the war is, first, that it "gave birth to the first modern peace congresses,"[1] setting a precedent for future attempts to negotiate comprehensive settlements after general wars. Simply put, Westphalia changed diplomatic practice because its treaties "laboriously built up from a series of diplomatic conferences, and such a congress of ambassadors thereafter became the accepted method of treaty-making."[2]

Second, the Peace of Westphalia set another precedent by aspiring to write rules for international relations that were intended to be universal, applicable to all international agents. According to one student of international law, "it was the first of several attempts to establish something resembling world unity, on the basis of states exercising untrammeled sovereignty over certain territories and subordinated to no earthly authority."[3]

Third, Westphalia represents "the first faint beginning of an international constitutional law," as Randall Lesaffer has pointed out. "The Westphalia treaties formed the first positive act by the sovereign states of Europe that implied the recognition of a *société des nations* between them, and which helped rule that community. The Westphalia treaties were the inaugurating constitutions of the international community that came to succeed the medieval, hierarchical *respublica christiana.*"[4]

Fourth, the Westphalian settlement secularized law and politics. As Leo Gross observes, "The Peace of Westphalia marked an epoch in the evolution of international law. It undoubtedly promoted the laicization of international law by divorcing it from any particular religious background, and the extension of its scope so as to include, on a footing of equality, republican and monarchical states. Indeed these two byproducts of the Peace of 1648 would seem significant enough for students of international law and relations to regard it as an event of outstanding and lasting value."[5]

Fifth, the Westphalian Peace treaties broke with the past by providing world politics with a new, decentralized *structure*: "Westphalia is an icon for international relations scholars," notes Stephen Krasner. "The Peace of Westphalia of 1648 is routinely understood to have ushered in or codified a new international order, one based on independent sovereign states rather than on some earlier medieval concept of Christendom, or feudalism, or empires."[6]

If all of these contributions were not enough, Westphalia deserves a special place in the history of thinking about world affairs, inspiring such influential writers as Hugo Grotius and Thomas Hobbes. "Grotius together with Hobbes [are] key figures in international relations theory; [the former's] is the only work that has exercised a persistent influence on the theory of international relations."[7]

It is not by coincidence, therefore, that the Peace of Westphalia continues to receive the attention it does. It literally changed the world. Whether we agree with Leo Gross's claim that Westphalia is "the majestic portal which leads from the old world into the new world," or Hans J. Morgenthau's depiction of it as "metonymy for the modern international system,"[8] there is little risk of hyperbole in acknowledging, with Richard Falk, that Westphalia provides "the basic formal ordering conception in international society since the seventeenth century [for] the coordination of sovereign state units."[9]

The chapters in Part II move from the origins of the Westphalian plan for world order to a consideration of the meaning and consequences of the Westphalian legacy for international affairs. Before taking on the challenge of stipulating what, precisely, the Westphalian Peace meant philosophically, legally, and instrumentally, we first inspect the processes by which the peace treaties were drafted. Chapter 4, "Negotiating the Peace Settlement," looks inside the conference chambers at the diplomats representing war-torn societies who sought to orchestrate an end to the fighting, resolve their differences, and to rebuild a stable set of international relationships. Negotiations took years while intense fighting continued. Exhausted adversaries, drained of resources, eventually turned their mercenary armies loose on innocent noncombatants in brutal campaigns of pillaging and foraging. The land was stripped bare, leaving Germany desolate. These shocking tactics on the battlefield hardened the positions at the bargaining table. The poisonous atmosphere in the two Westphalian cities where the talks convened, Münster and Osnabrück, contributed to delays and growing distrust. The lack of a clear victor further complicated progress, inviting the conclusion that

> Where a war terminates in a draw, indecisively, the treaty ends the war but does not remove its causes, so that hostilities may be expected under a conjuncture of conditions which appear favorable to either party to the conflict; peace thus becomes a temporarily suspended war, a protracted truce. Treaties of peace are in reality treaties of war, and to the extent that international law is largely built upon such treaties, it is permeated with the spirit of war, of successful conquest. The law of nature and of nations within society is the law of social evolution; the law of nations as obtaining between states is largely the law of force. [10]

The troubled, halting steps to end the war help to explain the spiral of fear and mistrust that permeated the peace settlement. The harsh attitudes that developed on both the battlefield and at the bargaining table go a long way toward accounting for the international norms that the Westphalia Peace promoted.

Chapter 5, "The Consequences of the Peace Settlement," shows how the rules *of* warfare became rules *for* statecraft. Westphalia made a covenant with power. What was practiced between 1618 and 1648 was preached during the peace negotiations, and eventually enshrined as a new set of permissive norms. The chapter identifies the reasons why Westphalia empowered states to make war for purposes beyond self-defense. The dark vision of Hobbes was not softened by the largely humanitarian hope of Grotius; what emerged was a "new secularized political theory . . . justifying the naked power of the national sovereign state."[11]

The transformation of international society from one responsible to the dictates of morality to one that worshiped expediency was *not* reached by people who perceived themselves as innovators.[12] More accurately, they regarded themselves as preservers. They did not seek to act as visionaries, imaginatively creating new rules for a new world through reason guided by an overarching conception of justice. Rather the negotiators in Westphalia perceived their role as one that required them to define the competitive drive for power that had become socially sanctioned as an acceptable foreign policy goal. War, and the right to wage it for self-preservation or self-promotion, had become a way of life. There is substantial evidence that the mission the peacemakers defined for themselves was primarily to confirm earlier proclamations and pronouncements.[13] Westphalia demonstrates that when a practice (such as war making) becomes widespread, these customs tend to become obligatory. How states had begun to routinely behave determined conceptions about how they concluded they should act; behavior that was frequent became legal, and what the most powerful did established norms for what others should do. In this sense, Westphalia ratified and licensed the expedient self-help practices in statecraft that had become customary in the first half of the seventeenth century.[14]

True, the Westphalian principles put foreign affairs on an organized legal basis, designating sovereign territorial states as the preeminent actors on the international stage, delineating their rights and duties, and empowering states to exercise complete control over domestic conditions and foreign relations. "Only states were subjects of international law whereas individuals were objects, whose rights were derivative from the state and dependent on their government for their protection."[15] In addition to setting back development of the concept of human rights for centuries, Westphalia turned states loose from most moral moorings, for with respect to their interactions the only rule was that there were no moral rules. The state was supreme, accountable to neither a higher authority (such as the church, emperor, or a supranational organization) nor to the humanitarian norms of classical ethical and religious traditions. *Raison d'état* was elevated to the status of a virtue, an operating principle to which all other definitions separating right from wrong were made subservient. Indeed, after Westphalia "international law in the three centuries which followed . . . rejected the distinction between just and unjust wars. War became the supreme right of sovereign states and the very hallmark of their sovereignty."[16]

By exalting the autonomous state at the expense of a united universal empire built on a moral consensus, Westphalia paved the way for acceptance of the balance of power as the sole mechanism for maintaining international stability and deterring a would-be hegemon from subjugating the other states. Autonomy meant that states were "free to do what they wish," permitted a "complete freedom of action."[17] The rationale was to lubricate a system of flexible alliances to maintain peace. The negotiators in Westphalia were haunted by their dread of an imbalance of power—another potential unequal distribution in which one state, empire, or coalition might obtain sufficient resources to authoritatively dominate the rest. As a consequence, whether tacitly or purposely, they accepted the balance of power as a process on which states could count to prevent hegemonial domination. At its core was the belief that peace would result when states were free to combine forces against potential aggressors. If one state, or a combination of states, gained enough power to threaten others, compelling incentives would presumably exist for those threatened to disregard their superficial differences and unite in a defensive alliance, as Sweden and France had done to repel the Hapsburg bid for hegemony. The power resulting from such collaboration would, according to this theory, deter any would-be attacker from pursuing expansionism. Thus, from the unrestrained competition of rivals would emerge a balance of contending factions, an equilibrium, capable of maintaining the status quo.

The logic underlying balance-of-power theory was founded on the premise that weakness invites attack and that countervailing power must be used to deter potential aggressors. Because the Westphalian statesmen assumed that the drive for power guides every state's actions, it followed that all countries were potential adversaries, and each must strengthen its military capability to protect itself or recruit allies—regardless of a potential ally's ideology, religious preference, or type of government—for collective defense when necessary. Invariably, this reasoning rationalized the quest for military superiority because others were expected to pursue it as well.

The policymakers mesmerized by *realpolitik* reasoning in Europe, who resurrected and reconstructed classical balance-of-power theory after the Peace of Westphalia, were not irrational.[18] They reasoned that an anarchical system founded on suspicion and competition, in which all states were independent and could make choices freely to advance their perceived national interests, would curtail the temptation of any actor like the Holy Roman Empire to again seek to dominate others, because that relentless pursuit of hegemony and resistance to it had been experienced and observed in the years prior to and during the Thirty Years' War, and those perceptions fed the socially constructed reality that was conceived at Westphalia. A state system to facilitate a dynamic balance was thus created, which institutionalized the balance-of-power process into the European system and, eventually, the world system.

In interpreting the impact of Westphalia's embrace of balance-of-power logic, a word of caution is in order. The "balance of power" is a rather slippery, elastic concept fraught with ambiguities. As Inis Claude and others warn, it has been used before, during, and after Westphalia inconsistently to refer to a condition describing a particular power distribution, a process, a policy prescription, and a propaganda slogan.[19] The diplomats who use the term in the aftermath of Westphalia have injected these semantic problems into their vocabulary, exacerbating analysis of the meaning and effects of the balance of power. Just as in the chapters in Part I, here in Part II we shall refer to the balance of power in the primary way that those at Westphalia conceived of it; as a *process* flowing from a set of diplomatic rules, not as a description of a distribution of power in which military capabilities and political influence among the most powerful transnational actors are approximately equal. Therefore in reading these chapters keep in mind that we shall emphasize in our discussion the balance of power as a set of rules stipulating the behaviors to be followed to prevent nascent hegemonial actors from achieving preponderance, in conformity with Morton Kaplan, who summarized the six essential rules for state behavior in an effective balance of power regime by noting that in such a process each great power was obligated to

(1) increase capabilities but negotiate rather than fight; (2) fight rather than fail to increase capabilities; (3) stop fighting rather than eliminate an essential actor; (4) oppose any coalition or single actor which tends to assume a position of predominance within the system; (5) constrain actors who subscribe to supranational organizational principles; and (6) permit defeated or constrained essential national actors to reenter the system as acceptable role partners.[20]

Looking at the subsequent record of European and world history after 1648, the evidence suggests that this reasoning and constructed consensus was fatally flawed. Westphalia created a war called "peace." The balance-of-power process is one of the Westphalian ghosts that needs to be exorcised if a stable new world order is to develop. As the chapter documents, the claim that a balance of power would bring peace has since been largely false: although "there were periods when an equal distribution of power between contenders actually existed, these . . . were the exception rather than the rule. . . . Closer examinations reveals that they were periods of war, not peace."[21]

Perhaps the foremost expert on the balance of power, Inis L. Claude, comes to this sobering conclusion:

> Balance-of-power theory is concerned mainly with the rivalries and clashes of great power—above all—what we have come to describe as world wars, the massive military conflicts that engulf and threaten to destroy the entire multistate system. It is difficult to consider world wars as anything other than catastrophic failures, total collapses, of the balance-of-power system. They are hardly to be classed as stabilizing manoeuvers or equilibrating processes, and one cannot take seriously any claim of maintaining international stability that does not entail the prevention of such disasters as the Napoleonic wars or World War I. Mention of those and similar disasters, however, frequently evokes the reminder that the would-be universal emperor—be it Louis XIV or Napoleon or Hitler—was defeated; in accordance with balance-of-power principles, a coalition arose to put down the challenger and maintain or restore the independence of the various states. In short, the system worked. Or did it? Is the criterion of the effectiveness of the balance of power that Germany lose its bid for conquest, or that it be deterred from precipitating World War I? It is not easy to justify the contention that a system for the management of international relations that failed to prevent the events of 1914–1918 deserves high marks as a guardian of stability or order, or peace. If the balance-of-power system does not aim at the prevention of world war, then it aims too low; if it offers no hope of maintaining the general peace, then the quest for a better system is fully warranted.[22]

The question history asks is whether the balance of power is really a reliable mechanism to prevent war, as the architects of the Westphalian blueprint for international affairs implicitly assumed. As Inis Claude concludes, the balance of power hardly appears successful. More accurately, Westphalia's primary product would seem to be the continuation of warfare, not its long-term prevention. The balance of power checked the Hapsburg bid for domination, but it also enlarged the number of belligerents in the Thirty Years' War, added to the destructiveness, and arguably lengthened the war's duration. By legitimizing balance-of-power politics, Westphalia atomized international politics. Hence, we conclude, with Susan Strange, that Westphalia is more aptly termed "West-failure."[23] The balance of power "did not lead to greater stability nor to the supremacy of right above might. Quite the contrary. It led to the introduction of political interest as a leading principle in international relations."[24] Although Westphalia can be credited with terminating what had become the most widespread, large-scale general war in Europe up to that point in history, it did not create an effective process for preserving world order. "So the significance of the Treaty of Westphalia is not that it found a way for the maintenance of peace, for this it did not do, but rather that it accepted the conditions which made the ding-dong [cycle] of war and peace an acknowledged feature of the international life of Europe. In reflecting the balance of religious and political forces at the time, the Treaty established a diplomatic balance which only had to be disturbed to make further wars inevitable."[25]

   This sobering assessment of the Westphalian Peace settlement does not mean that the international community is today, more than 350 years later, free of the paralyzing grip of the Westphalian ghost. The national security strategies of most states continue to be predicated on Westphalian logic, and not even the United Nations Charter gave a funeral dirge for the Westphalian skeletal conception of international order. [26] The ghost of Westphalia still stalks. At times it is manifest in the gloomy vision of Thomas Hobbes who "compares princes to gladiators . . . in a posture of Warre."[27] Yet at other times it reflects the reform-minded vision of Hugo Grotius who longed for an international society of states under law while at the same time incorporating the state customary practices of his epoch into his definition of the legal boundaries of permissible state choice. There are many pressing problems on the global agenda for which the general Westphalian rules for the conduct of international relations need to be exorcised if they are to be effectively managed.[28] In the concluding chapters in Part III, we look to the future and assess which of these remnants of the Westphalian legacy[29] will prevail, and how an alternative conception of international order that combines the best features of Hobbes and Grotius might provide a stable foundation for world order in the twenty-first century.

CHAPTER 4

Negotiating the Peace Settlement

Wave goodbye to the medieval world view, the Counter Reformation, wars of reli-gion, the Holy Roman Empire, Germany's prospects for the next two hundred years, and Spain's prospects, period. Brace yourself for the triumph of secular thinking, the ascendancy of France (in the person of Louis XIV), and a new age of plural-ism, in which nobody will ever pretend Europe has any overriding unity, spiritual, political, or other, and in which states will behave like the discrete, self-interested entities they are.

—Judy Jones and William Wilson

Peacemaking can be likened to the game of chess. The players make a series of interconnected moves, each of which alters the costs and benefits of the next round of moves. Neither side can be certain of the opponent's sequence of moves over the course of the game, and each move opens the possibility of sub-sequent countermoves—thereby preventing anyone from knowing the long-term consequences of their choices.

Just as there is no single formula to win at chess, there was no doctrine to guide the warring states on how to craft a just and lasting peace settlement. Solutions to the policy problems and moral dilemmas involved in constructing a durable world order cannot be reduced to a few simple maxims. The nego-tiations at Münster and Osnabrück made this evident, which is why building a new security regime is aptly described as "an untidy affair."[1] To quote E. H. Carr: "peacemaking is not an event, but a continuous process which must be pursued in many places, under varying conditions, by many different methods and over a prolonged period of time; and anyone who supposes that it will be complete within six years should be regarded with the utmost suspicion."[2]

Decisions about terminating lengthy, system-wide wars force peacemakers to confront rival ideas about how choices should be made regarding issues for which there seldom exist obvious solutions or universally applicable ethical principles. Those gathered around the bargaining table face a tragic dilemma in which "there is decisive support for two more incompatible courses of action."[3] In 1648, the political leaders of the belligerent states were caught in an ineradicable tension between competing aspirations, one for justice and the other for self-advantage. They were forced to weigh difficult trade-offs between competing values as they inched their way toward a political settlement.

Although the belligerents had suffered heavy losses on the battlefield, neither side seemed willing to yield. As one historian has written, "Both sides had in fact been equally winners and losers."[4] Ultimately war weariness and depleted royal treasuries encouraged them to negotiate an end to the fighting. The initial talks in Cologne and Lübeck proceeded haltingly. Finally, by the end of 1641, a preliminary agreement to negotiate a comprehensive peace settlement was reached. Under the terms of the Treaty of Hamburg, entitled *The Preliminary Articles for the Universal Peace Conference,* two conferences were scheduled to be convened simultaneously in neighboring Westphalian cities, with the Catholic envoys assembled in Münster and the Protestant envoys meeting in Osnabrück.[5] Münster and Osnabrück are located on a fertile plain, "almost the only part of Germany which had suffered little from the ravages of war."[6] The two conferences were considered parts of one congress aimed at establishing a "Universal peace, and a perpetual, true, and sincere Amity"[7] among the belligerents. Since hostilities continued throughout the negotiations, the envoys were promised safe conduct and the two cities were declared neutral territory. Soon thereafter, houses in the two cities were rented by the chief negotiators, and nearby inns were filled with their assistants.

ENDING THE THIRTY YEARS' WAR

As in all eras when political leaders attempt to design new world orders, the delegates at the Westphalian peace conferences were heavily influenced by the culture in which they lived. During peaceful times, a political culture changes slowly through social learning and the diffusion of new values. Wars, however, accelerate the pace of cultural transformation. The Thirty Years' War had a profound impact on European political culture. Harsh lessons the belligerents learned in combat were carried with them to Münster and Osnabrück. The war bred a pessimistic mood: evil was seen as ubiquitous and *realpolitik* seemed to offer the only viable tactics for advancing one's interests in a callous world.

Enormous barriers impeded the quest for peace. In general, the longer fighting in a war continues, the wider the array of belligerents, and the greater the number of contested issues, the more difficult it becomes to arrive at a durable peace settlement.[8] Given the character of the Thirty Years' War, it is not surprising that negotiations over the rules to establish international security moved at a glacial pace. Quite simply, the methods of modern international diplomacy had not yet been formalized. The delegates at Münster and Osnabrück had to improvise rules for procedure and protocol; they literally had to make decisions on how they would later decide points of order at each step in the negotiations.[9] The task was formidable because the congresses involved no less than 194 separate territorial entities represented by 179 plenipotentiaries, with each principality supported by its own team of lawyers.[10] Further complicating matters, the negotiators were asked to arrive at a peace settlement satisfactory to all interests while they adhered to the instructions of those governments and religious institutions they represented.[11]

Forging a new architecture for world order requires vision and leadership. Although many of the delegates were concerned with simply ending hostilities by any means possible, several rose to the challenge and played decisive roles in producing the historic settlement. Maximilian Graf Trauttmansdorff (Lord Steward) made a pivotal contribution as the Chief Ambassador for the Imperial Court. Traveling between Osnabrück and Münster freely with instructions from the Holy Roman Empire "to make far-reaching concessions if necessary" to reach a peace settlement,[12] he is credited with primary authorship of the final draft of the Peace of Westphalia. Both he and Isaac Volmar, his chief secretary, were converts to Catholicism who appreciated the convictions motivating the Protestants. They understood the need for compromise and the importance of reconciling extremists who saw the treaty as a zero-sum contest between good and evil.

Various other representatives also deserve credit for their moderating influence during the negotiations. Included among these people were Johan Rudolf Weltstein of Basil, who spoke not only on behalf of the Swiss Protestant cantons but other cantons as well; Jacob Lampadius of Brunswick, who provided expert legal advice on many disputed issues; and David Gloxin, the Lübeck envoy who championed the interests of the powerful and independent mercantile enthusiasts. In addition, the Papal Nuncio Fabio Chigi (who later rose to become Pope Alexander VII) and the Venetian diplomat Aloisi Contarini did much as unofficial participants to mediate factional differences among the representatives.[13] These men of vision preserved a sense of mutual European comity for the higher purpose of reaching a peace settlement.

Ironically, their work was both complicated and facilitated by personal antagonisms within the French and Swedish ranks. The French delegation was divided by rivalry and suspicion, but blessed by skill and intelligence. All had to bend to the power of Cardinal Jules Mazarin. He distrusted Claude de Mesmes, Comte d'Avaux, who was one of France's primary negotiators along with Henry d'Orleans (the duc de Longueville) and Anne Genevieve de Bourban-Condé, his duchess, who questioned Cardinal Mazarin's motives and feared the other key member of the French delegation, Abel Servien, in whom Mazarin placed confidence. The other negotiators had to play these crafty representatives of the French throne off against one another in order to reach an agreement—a challenge that was heightened because, despite their personal differences and competitiveness, the French delegation was united in its desire to secure the best terms possible for their country.

The Swedish diplomatic mission meeting separately with the Protestants in Osnabrück was likewise divided internally. The Chancellor's son, Johan Oxenstierna, advocated a retributive settlement to secure Swedish gains and compensate for its injuries. Conversely, the experienced Swedish diplomat John Adler Salvius advocated the preference of Queen Christina for a restorative settlement that would cement a peace, even at the cost of Swedish sacrifices.

In summary, like all subsequent efforts to construct new rules for international peace and security, the Westphalian settlement was a complex affair involving many issues. Reaching a consensus on the shape of a comprehensive peace plan is seldom easy, and between 1641 and 1648 the conditions were not favorable, which explains why the belligerents "negotiated as hard as they fought."[14] Throughout the negotiations, they wrestled with fateful choices about the redistribution of power. The settlement they reached is remembered for its innovative solutions to what many onlookers feared were insoluble disagreements. Out of the struggle over competing political interests and moral values emerged an agreement that marked "an important turning point in the story of Europe, the emergence of the state system under which Europe has operated until our own time."[15]

This far-reaching impact notwithstanding, it is not at all clear that the recipe for international order that emerged from so complex and conflictual a negotiating process was sufficient. It *was* visionary, but it had its deficiencies. Westphalia, truly a turning point in the history of international relations, took statecraft into turbulent waters for which the world was unprepared. In the last analysis, "the entire settlement had something forced and makeshift about it. Ambiguities both accidental and intentional confused the situation."[16] Out of so messy and uncoordinated competitive maneuvering, it is hardly surprising that the final lengthy and inconsistent texts of the treaties are regarded widely as providing pretexts for war.[17] To better appreciate the solution that the Westphalian conception of international order embraced, we need to take a close look at its major provisions.

THE TERMS OF THE PEACE SETTLEMENT

The delegates at Münster and Osnabrück faced two basic types of decisions, the first pragmatic and the second philosophical. The former dealt with questions of reallocating territory, resources, and titles in a way that could settle the material issues underlying the brutalizing armed conflict. The latter dealt with the rules of statecraft that would govern postwar European diplomacy. These philosophical decisions were more difficult, but their results were longer lasting.

Decisions on Material Issues

The Peace of Westphalia contained two interlocking treaties, written in Latin, that ended the fighting in central Europe, one drawn up by envoys of the Catholic princes and states at Münster, and the other by the imperial ambassadors who negotiated with envoys of the Protestant princes and states at Osnabrück. Both treaties converged on principles for international order that were celebrated throughout Europe as the springboard to a peaceful future. Signed on October 24, 1648, and ratified during the following February, the details of their execution were worked out at a conference held in Nürnberg between April 1649 and June 1651. According to the military provisions of these treaties, a cease-fire would be declared, prisoners released, and troops returned home. Furthermore, an amnesty was granted "of all that has been committed since the beginning of these Troubles" (Article 2). Because the political terms of the treaties were complex, let us review them as they affected the members of the new international order.

France.   The Peace of Westphalia enabled France to become the dominant power on the continent, occupying the leadership position that Spain had previously held. The power of the Hapsburgs had been weakened, and France was now bordered by weak, fragmented states that posed no real threat to its security (see Figure 4.1; also review Figure 3.1 on p. 98). By acquiring German possessions, the French also gained a voice in German affairs when the new French territories became Electors of the Holy Roman Emperor.

From the disintegrating western frontier of the Holy Roman Empire, the French obtained sovereignty over three Lorraine bishoprics: Metz, Toul, and Verdun. Furthermore, Pinerolo, Breisach, and the Sundgau in southern Alsace came under French control. France also received so-called Landvostei or "Advocacy" rights of jurisdiction over ten additional Alsatian cities,[18] and was allowed to fortify a garrison at Philipsburg. In short, France acquired almost all of Alsace and was confirmed in the possession of its earlier gains in Lorraine.[19]

Austria received from France the county of Hawenstein, the Black Forest region, Upper and Lower Brisgaw, and the towns of Rheinselden, Seckingen, Laussenberg, and Waltshutum (Articles 87–88). Fortifications on the right bank of the Rhine River were to be dismantled (Articles 73–74) and navigation would be free (Article 79). Restitution was promised (Articles 6–7), and all contracts, exchanges, debts, and obligations extorted by threats would be annulled (Article 37–39).

Sweden.   France was not the only victor to benefit from territorial transfers. Sweden received control of the north German Baltic coast, annexed the western part of Pomerania including Stettin, obtained the port of Wismar, the territories of Rügen, Pöl, and Wollin, the bishopric of Bremen and the adjacent territory of Verden, and gained control over the mouths of the Oder and

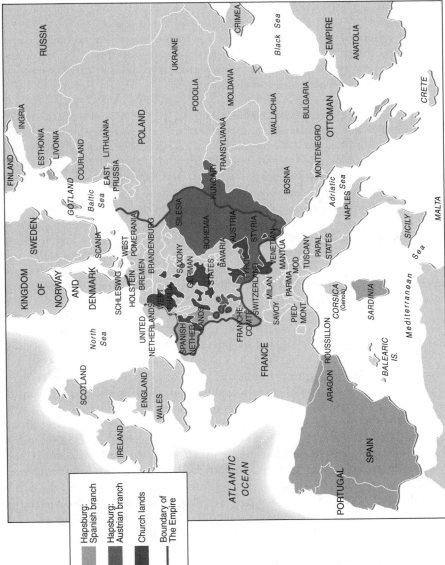

**FIGURE 4.1
Europe Following
the Peace
of Westphalia**

The Peace of Westphalia redrew the map of Europe, redistributing lands to newly created states in an innovative effort to sharply define borders; it was hoped that clear boundaries around states' territories would separate them and their jurisdictions and thereby allow frontiers to act as a barrier against intervention.
Source: Adapted from Blum, Cameron, and Barnes, 1970, p. 236.

Legend:
- Hapsburg: Spanish branch
- Hapsburg: Austrian branch
- Church lands
- Boundary of The Empire

Weser Rivers. Sweden also received monetary reparations from the Holy Roman Empire and the right to send representatives to the Imperial Diet. While the peace settlement did not resolve all of the conflicts in the Baltic, it did confirm Sweden as the dominant power in the region.[20]

The United Provinces of the Netherlands.   The general settlement that ended the Thirty Years' War also touched on territorial issues in the Low Countries. The United Provinces of the Netherlands became an independent state when the Dutch concluded the so-called Eighty Years' War with Spain. Although the Netherlands had enjoyed partial *de facto* independent status since the 1609 Treaty of Antwerp, it now had *de jure* recognition as a sovereign state. According to the peace treaty of January 30, 1648, Spain would destroy several forts in the Low Countries and both sides agreed to refrain from constructing replacements. In addition, the Dutch were allowed to close traffic in the Scheldt Estuary and on certain canals. Although the treaty guaranteed merchant rights and promoted free trade between the parties in Europe, restrictions were placed on commerce in the East and West Indies. The two countries agreed to cooperate in efforts to control piracy, keep waterways navigable, and make restitution to those who had lost property during the war. By terminating hostilities with Spain, the United Provinces could turn its energies to economic competition with its now-greatest mercantile rival, the colonial empire of Portugal.

Spain.   The government in Madrid had made peace with the Dutch early in 1648 to deprive France of an ally in the Franco-Spanish war which continued until 1659.[21] Because of these hostilities, Spain was excluded from the terms of the October 24 Treaty of Münster. Under Article 3 of the treaty, which stipulated that "one shall never assist the present or future Enemies of the other under any Title or Pretense whatsoever," Austrian Emperor Ferdinand III was prohibited from assisting Hapsburg Spain in its conflict with France. Generally humiliated at the Westphalian peace conferences, Spain still held the Spanish Netherlands (Belgium) and a large part of Italy, but it slipped into bankruptcy and was slowly isolated. By the time it signed the 1659 Treaty of the Pyrenees ending the war with France, Spain was finished as an aspirant to Europe hegemony.[22]

The Holy Roman Empire.   In the main, the settlement of Westphalia centered on the Empire, which was reduced to "purely nominal existence."[23] To create a balance of power, the Peace of Westphalia left the Holy Roman Empire greatly weakened, and limited its sphere of influence to Austria and parts of Germany. With the demise of the Madrid-Vienna axis, the power of the Holy Roman Emperor so declined that no Emperor after 1648 ever again tried to establish a central authority over all German territories. The "Empire" was no longer a continental dominion; it became a patchwork of diverse Christian religions, with Lutherans prevailing in the north, Catholics in the south, and Calvinists along the Rhine and in the Netherlands. Although the Holy Roman Empire continued to exist until Napoleon's conquests in 1806, "its authority was little more than parchment."[24] To issue laws, levy taxes, or recruit soldiers in the name of the Empire, the Emperor had to obtain the consent of the Imperial Diet, formed of representatives of the 350 princedoms, bishoprics, and free cities in Germany. Since the jealousies and ambitions "of the many German rulers made agreement on such matters impossible, these provisions ended any possibility of Imperial control over Germany and doomed German unification."[25]

By allowing the separate states to be involved in the negotiations, the Emperor lost what little power he had retained over the German princes. "The disintegration of the Holy Roman Empire, which had been advanced by the drawing of internal religious frontiers in the days of Luther, was now confirmed in politics, and international law."[26]

The Papacy. The Thirty Years' War cost the Roman Catholic Church politically. Formerly, the pope had exercised enormous influence over the secular relations of European nations, but in the wake of Westphalia this authority and jurisdiction decreased.

The Westphalian settlement was understandably resented by many church officials, who saw the treaty as "a public act of disregard of the international authority of the Papacy."[27] The 1555 Peace of Augsburg was retained permanently, with Calvinism added to Lutheranism and Catholicism as an acceptable religion throughout most of Europe. In the German states, the north remained Protestant and the south Catholic, and the wars of religion that had plagued the continent for over a hundred years finally appeared to have vanished as a precipitating factor in warfare. After the Peace of Westphalia, "people who could no longer bear to talk of 'Christendom' began to talk instead of 'Europe.'"[28]

The famous November 1650 *Zelus domus Dei* Bull reiterated the Vatican's universalist claims. Pope Urban VIII complained the treaties were "null, void, invalid, iniquitous, unjust, damnable, reprobate, inane, and devoid of meaning and effect for all time." Thus, while the pope refused to acknowledge the terms of the treaties, the clauses on sovereignty effectively ended his (or any other religious body's) dominion over Europe. The delegates at both Catholic Münster and Protestant Osnabrück put political considerations ahead of religious allegiances. The peacemakers systematically isolated confessional and denominational issues from geopolitical choices. This stance enraged Pope Urban VIII, who was more vocal in his opposition to the political leanings of Catholic Spain and the Catholic Holy Roman Emperor in Austria than he was to many of the similarly independent-minded Lutherans and Calvinists in Sweden, the Netherlands, and Germany. When during the Westphalia peace conferences Pope Innocent X protested against any contemplated compromise by the Catholic Hapsburgs to appease the Protestants, the Catholic delegates responded evasively. Later they joined with the other representatives to sign an "anti-protest" clause that labeled Innocent's complaints "invalid." The Peace of Westphalia ended ecclesiastical tutelage over secular affairs as well as the prospects for a common European polity united politically and religiously. Instead of the pope orchestrating political affairs on the continent, states became the highest recognized level of governance as well as objects of patriotic worship in their own right.

Germany.   Although the peace treaties enabled the Protestant princes in the north to conduct their own foreign and domestic policies without external interference, it should be remembered that Westphalia was an imposed peace. Territorial gains and losses were determined by the French, Swedish, and Austrian crowns, who regarded their weaker German allies as pawns to be shifted as required to keep the postwar balance of power in equilibrium. As one observer has put it, "if there were any true winners in this war, Germany . . . was certainly not among them."[29] The peace settlement "recognized 343 sovereign states in Germany, of which 158 were secular states, 123 were ecclesiastical principalities, and 62 were Imperial cities."[30]

The absence of a strong German voice at Münster and Osnabrück was made transparent by Westphalia's provisos: The Upper Palatinate was retained by Bavaria but the Rhenish Palatinate, with a new electoral vote, was assigned to Charles Louis (the son of Frederick the Winter King). The elector of Brandenburg received compensation for Pomerania, and the Duke of Mecklenburg for part of Wismar and Pöl. Saxony obtained what it had acquired through the 1635 Peace of Prague, Lusatia and Magdeburg. As compensation for other losses, Brandenburg was granted the greater part of eastern Pomerania up to the Polish frontier, the former Bishoprics of Halberstadt, Minden, and Kammin, and the city of Magdeburg. To assuage hard feelings, the Dukes of Mecklenburg-Schwerin, Brunswick-Lüneberg, and Hesse-Cassel each were given control over new territories in exchange for their losses, such as Mecklenburg's loss of Wismar.

Germany, the main battlefield of the Thirty Years' War, lay in ruins and its strategic position was greatly weakened. The French now held the middle Rhine. The mouths of Germany's three great rivers—the Rhine, Elbe, and Oder—were held respectively by the Dutch, the Danes, and the Swedes. The common interest of the Empire was subject to the separate interests of the larger German states: Austria, Bavaria, Saxony, and Brandenburg-Prussia. Destitution accompanied humiliation. Austria, which had begun the period as the wonder of the age, was reduced to being just one German state among many.[31] "Broken, divided, economically weak, and lacking any sense of national unity, Germany became virtually a French protectorate."[32]

Other Relevant States.   States on the periphery of the war had little influence over the peace negotiations. Denmark, for instance, lost its status as a European power of stature after the 1629 Peace of Lübeck ratified its withdrawal from the conflict. Having not been a formal belligerent because of internal strife, England made no meaningful contribution to the outcome. These nonparticipants were excluded from the deliberations, without influence over the decisions that established the principles underpinning the Westphalian world order.

Polish and Russian influence at the peace conferences were also limited. Russia's refusal to become directly involved in Germany, when it fought the War of Simolensk (1632–1634) with Poland, compromised its bargaining power. Following the Peace of Polyanov, which ended the war with Russia, Poland's resumption of hostilities with Sweden that contributed to the disastrous Swedish defeat at Nördingen essentially deprived Poland of a voice in the Westphalian peace negotiations.

Decisions on the Rules of Statecraft

The negotiators drafting the Westphalian Peace did something far more than reach decisions about the reallocation of territory and resources. They made *philosophical* choices over competing values about how states in the future should seek to survive in the anarchical world that emerged from the Thirty Years' War. The motive behind many of the territorial transfers was to redraw the map of Europe so that a new balance of power could keep the peace among sovereign states. The articles of the treaties comprising the Peace of Westphalia were to "serve as a perpetual law" (Article 120), defended by all signatory parties (Article 123).

The Thirty Years' War generated a verbal conflict over which ideas should guide the management of international relations after the guns had fallen silent. Working like engineers, the envoys to the peace conferences could draw from two contending sets of ideas, one subsequently represented by the philosophy of Thomas Hobbes and the other by Hugo Grotius (see Box 4.1). The former insisted that peace could be best preserved by concentrating power in the hands of a strong central authority; the latter averred that it could be fostered by building a society of states around a shared moral consensus. In making philosophical choices about which plans should guide the construction of a new world order, the envoys gravitated toward the decentralized vision of Grotius rather than toward a more centralized architecture.

BOX 4.1
A Clash of Visions: Hobbes and Grotius on the Prerequisites for International Order

---

The Thirty Years' War stimulated theoretical thinking about the rules for war and the preconditions for peace, thinking that continues to influence the way scholars, policy makers, and international lawyers view world order issues today. Thomas Hobbes and Hugo de Groot (later known simply as "Grotius") were arguably the two foremost international relations theorists of the early seventeenth century. Both men were deeply influenced by the political turmoil of their era, both recognized a need for a fresh interpretation of the sources of international violence, and both articulated proposals that had a lasting impact on theories of war and peace. Yet each of these seminal thinkers advanced a different set of recommendations for containing armed conflict and alleviating its devastating effects.

Hobbes recoiled in hostility to the papacy—"its lust for power, its immorality, and its covetousness"[33]—but concluded that degeneration was a product of flawed human nature and, because of the human tendency for aggrandizement, the idea of an ecclesiastical peace managed by the Church was absurd. Rather, peace would have to come from a strong secular authority. In effect, Hobbes extended the earlier Machiavellian thesis that international politics was an amoral struggle for power in which ethical considerations were largely irrelevant. To him, warfare was a product of human nature and not a condition produced through human choice.

The Hobbesian world view emanated from his belief in a raw and untamed state of nature. If we accept Hobbes's conception of the "state of nature," we find ourselves in a situation where might makes right, where only the strongest have their grievances satisfied.[34] As Mark Kauppi and Paul Viotti explain, Hobbes argues

> "During the time when men live without a common power to keep them all in awe, they are in that condition which is called war; and such a war, as is of every man, against every man." Hobbes is not suggesting that in such a state of nature there is constant fighting; rather, war represents a constant "disposition" or "inclination," just as threatening weather may promise the possibility of rain.
>
> This condition has devastating consequences, because in a state of nature such uncertainty over one's security means no industry, no culture, no trading, no cumulative knowledge, no arts, no letters, no society, and worst of all, "continual fear, and danger of violent death; and the life of man, solitary, poor, nasty, brutish, and short." In such a situation there is no such thing as right or wrong because "where there is no common power, there is no law; where no law, no injustice. Force and fraud, are in war the two cardinal virtues." In other words, it is only where a civil society has been created with a supreme authority to regulate disputes and enforce contracts that we can speak of such things as justice.
>
> Hobbes' description of the state of nature has been viewed as analogous to the international system. Just as in the state of nature where man stands alone, so, too, in the international system, do states strive to maintain their independence. Just as individuals in the state of nature have a predisposition toward war, so, too, is the international system marked by constant tension and the possibility of conflict. The single most important passage in which the comparison is made is:

> > But though there had never been any time, wherein particular men were in a condition of war one against another; yet in all times, kings, and persons of sovereign authority, because of their independency, are in continual jealousies, and in the state and posture of gladiators; having their weapons pointing, and their eyes fixed on one another; that is, their forts, garrisons, and guns upon the frontiers of their kingdoms; and continual spies upon their neighbors; which is a posture of war.

Both the state of nature and the international system therefore reflect a condition in which there is "no common power" to enforce order. In other words, it is a condition of anarchy, which means, as . . . [with] Thucydides, a system whose structure encourages suspicion and distrust. It should be noted, however, that for Hobbes such suspicion and distrust are due not just to the fact that no common power exists; rather, such attitudes and behavior reflect human nature unconstrained by any common power.[35]

In *Leviathan* (1651), Hobbes presented a theory for bringing order to a turbulent political world. His solution was to use power to combat power. "Hobbes's horror at civil violence led him to lose faith in ordinary human reason and thus in political deliberation. It is because he lost faith in the latter that scientific reason emerged as a powerful alternative. But if human beings are so unreasonable that we can no longer take seriously what they say, how can we expect them to be reasonable enough to accept Hobbes's prescriptions? The Hobbesian solution is that an absolute government must enforce the plan."[36] Distrusting democracy and the passions of the masses, Hobbes conferred great status on the concept of sovereignty, emphasizing "the conviction that the state is the ultimate arbiter of its own fate in relation to the outside world," and stressing the need for "unrestricted government authority within territorial boundaries."[37] Hobbes was willing to sacrifice liberty for order. His "Leviathan" or supreme sovereign was a plea for establishing of a centralized authority: "Before the names of just and unjust can have place, there must be some coercive power to compel men equally to the performance of their covenant by the terror of some punishment."[38] To this end, the concentration of power in the hands of a single, all-powerful hegemon was a political necessity for preventing the kind of ceaseless conflict exhibited in the Thirty Years' War. Hobbes stands as a founding figure in what became a growing body of modern realist thinking.

Thomas Hobbes

Hugo Grotius reacted to the destruction he witnessed in his lifetime by advancing a rival solution to the problem of war. Powerfully affected by his religious beliefs and the insecurity experienced by the new Dutch republic of which he was a citizen, Grotius sought to design a system of international law that would bring justice and order to a fractious world. Sentenced to life imprisonment in 1621 for his efforts to advance religious toleration, Grotius made a celebrated escape from the castle of Loevestein in a chest of books and spent most of the rest of his life in exile. In 1625 Grotius authored his most famous treatise, *On the Law of War and Peace,* which made a great impression throughout Europe. The Swedish leader Gustavus Adolphus is said to have carried a copy with him

Hugo Grotius

during his military campaigns in the Thirty Years' War. For this work, Grotius, shown in the photo below, is widely acclaimed as the "father of international law."

In his treatise, Grotius called on the great powers to resolve their conflicts by judicial procedures, rather than on the battlefield, and specified the legal principles he felt would encourage cooperation, peace, and a more humane treatment of people. But beyond this, "his work is significant" because it "provided a guide to the operations of this new system of sovereign states . . . one that accepts the sovereignty of states, and even their right in certain circumstances to wage war, but at the same time stresses the existence of shared values and the necessity of international rules."[39] Departing from the realist approach to peace advanced by Hobbes, Grotius did not believe humankind was doomed to perpetual strife in the absence of an all-powerful hegemon. Rather, he fashioned an approach to international relations that drew eclectically on natural and positive law to establish the ethical and legal underpinnings for a *society* of states. Believing that enlightened rulers would use their God-given reason and see that their self-interests would be served by a shared moral consensus,[40] Grotius labored to overcome the limitations of a world order rooted in territorial sovereignty.[41] Hersh Lauterpacht summarizes the main propositions underlying his approach to international relations by noting the following salient principles of the Grotian tradition:

- Grotius conceived "of the totality of the relations between states as governed by law . . .";
- In laying down "the distinction between just and unjust war Grotius rejected the claim to any such right. Neither did he concede to states the absolute faculty of action in self-preservation . . .";
- Grotius's "conception of . . . a law of nature [is] based on and deduced from the nature of man as being moved by desire for social life, endowed with an ample measure of goodness, altruism, and morality, and capable of acting on general principles and learning from experience. . . . For Machiavelli and Hobbes man is essentially selfish, anti-social, and unable to learn from experience; . . . human nature does not change . . . On this line of reasoning there is no salvation for humanity but irrevocable subjection to an order of effective force . . .";
- Grotius drew "the close analogy of legal and moral rules governing the conduct of states and individuals alike. . . . The analogy . . . is not asserted for the reason that states are like individuals; it is due to the fact that states *are composed* of individual human beings. . . . The individual is the ultimate unit of all law . . .";

- Grotius denied the "'*reason of state*' as a basic and decisive factor in international relations. . . . This means . . . that shameful acts ought not to be committed even for the sake of one's country. It means also that the hall-mark of wisdom for a ruler is to take account not only of the good of the nation committed to his care, but the whole human race. [In rejecting] *"raison d'état"* [Grotius rejected] the cruder forms of treacherous violence, of brazen perfidy, and of outright deceit [he sought to curb] the spirit of [Machiavelli's] *The Prince* . . .";

- Grotius denies the absolute right of war and differentiates between just and unjust wars. "For a war to be just, there must exist a legal cause for it—a reason which would be recognized by a court of law as a cause of action. As he points out, war begins where judicial settlement ends. . . . The causes of just wars are limited to defense against an injury either actual or immediately threatening. . . . He definitely excludes wars undertaken to weaken a neighbor who is a potential threat to the security of the state, [arguing] 'Advantage does not confer the same right as necessity.'" . . . In this sense Grotius articulates "a condemnation of a system of international law, fully in operation at that time, in which resort to war was an unlimited right of sovereign states . . .";

- Grotius stresses the "sacredness of good faith [and] the obligation to abide by pacts. . . . To him the binding force of treaties is the basis of international law. They must be kept even in relation to pirates and tyrants, in peace or in war . . .";

- Grotius "considers just resort to war to prevent the maltreatment by a state of its own subjects [and] permits a foreign state to intervene, through war, on behalf of the oppressed. . . . This [may be] the first authoritative statement of the principle of humanitarian intervention—the principle at the exclusiveness of domestic jurisdiction where outrage upon humanity begins. . . ."[42]

The remarkable feature of Grotius's *On The Law of War and Peace* is his effort to humanize the rules of war that were so transparently inhumane and militant at the time he was writing: "In general, there breathes from the pages of *De Jure Belli ac Pacis* a disapproval, amounting to hatred, of war."[43]

Grotius was fighting many of the customs of his time, while advocating the perpetuation of various other customary practices. By seeking to establish a universal moral order, Grotius put forth a code of ethics to be applied to states, seeking in the process to go beyond defining what existing laws were at the time and advocating the kind of norms that ought to prevail for future generations. It is no wonder that this vision still inspires peacemakers seeking to escape the "war of all against all" that Hobbes perceived. Grotius's ideas clashed with those of Hobbes in the mid-seventeenth century, and they continue to vie for acceptance now, at the start of the twenty-first century.

As much as he was a reformer, it would be a misrepresentation to see Grotius as an opponent of all the mores of his time. Unlike Hobbes, who advocated the concentration of power to tame war, Grotius assumed that international stability could exist on a decentralized footing. Simply put, he anticipated what Westphalia would later ratify:

The Westphalian international system is also best characterized as a laissez-faire system, inasmuch as it too proceeds on the assumption that unrestrained and coequal actors (here nation-states rather than individual persons) should be allowed to help themselves, to a great extent, to the values of their choice and thereby assist the achievement of the general welfare of all members of the society. The man known as the father of modern international law, Hugo Grotius, stands in relation to the world order system of Westphalia much as [John] Locke does to limited constitutional government and [Adam] Smith to free enterprise in economics. Each writer emphasized the good that would come to the whole of the respective domain he studied from an absence of strong centralized control and thus a relatively great amount of freedom for the individual actors within the system. Each was an advocate of *laissez-faire*.[44]

The philosophies which gained expression in the Peace of Westphalia reflect this perpetual tension between the vision of Hobbes, tinted by the dark shades of realism, and the vision of Grotius, painted in the bright colors of hope. This contest between competing approaches to international order grew out of the growing dissatisfaction across Europe with conditions that prevailed during the Thirty Years' War. In the "decades preceding the Peace of Westphalia, it is probably correct to say that the Peace merely finally sealed an existing state of affairs. Lord Bryce said the Peace of Westphalia 'did no more than legalize a condition of things already in existence, but which, by being legalized, acquired new importance.' It is probably also true, in a broad sense, that with the Congress of Westphalia the various states entered into the legal concept of a *societas gentium* which had long before been established by the science of natural law. It is equally correct that the so-called Grotian Law of Nature school continued to expound the concept of a society of states. . . ."[45] The world is still wrestling to create a truly global community in which states behave as Grotius wished. We can be assured that future leaders will continue to debate which picture of international reality, the Hobbesian or the Grotian, is the more accurate and the more useful in providing a foundation for world order.

The perpetual law enshrined by the Peace of Westphalia was the principle of sovereignty. Simply put, sovereignty means that no authority is legally above the state. That is to say, states have the exclusive right to make, implement, enforce, and adjudicate laws within their own territories, but they must refrain from prescribing laws outside of their jurisdiction. States are immune from the judicial processes of other states. No duty could be imposed upon them without their consent. States were only bound by international obligations that they *voluntarily* entered into; but once accepted, they were responsible for any breach of those obligations as well as for wrongful acts that violated the rights of other states. Consequently, international law as it evolved after the Peace of Westphalia was a law of coordination *between* states, not a law of subordination *above* states.[46]

Two corollaries followed from the principle of sovereignty. First, sub-state units (such as bishoprics, duchies, fiefdoms, or other principalities) were denied international legal personality. They could not declare war, make treaties, claim neutrality, or exercise any of the other legal rights possessed by states. Second, and more important, international intervention was prohibited. Uninvited involvement in one state's internal affairs by any other state or international body was defined as illegal. The norms of the new Westphalian order prohibited interference with the domestic policies and practices of others.

Whatever its advantages and disadvantages, the principle of sovereignty emerged from the Peace of Westphalia to color every dimension of international politics for centuries thereafter. Of course, the exercise of sovereignty was never absolute. But in the years following the Westphalian settlement, states were seen as enjoying certain "fundamental rights," namely, those of equality, independence, self-defense, respect, legation, and intercourse. These rights were thought to derive from a primordial entitlement to continued existence, which allegedly would be guaranteed by a rough equilibrium in the distribution of international power. As Leo Gross concludes, "the balance of power doctrine forms an important part of that body of political thought which came to fruition in the Peace of Westphalia."[47]

In summary, the practical decisions about material issues made by the architects of the Westphalian settlement were underpinned by deeper philosophical choices regarding the rules of statecraft political leaders should follow in the aftermath of the Thirty Years' War. Those choices reflected a shift in the international landscape from a heterogeneous feudal order to an anarchic world populated by sovereign states. To be sure, the disintegration of medieval Europe was well underway by the onset of the seventeenth century. The Thirty Years' War accelerated the process and the Peace of Westphalia legitimized nascent ideas about how political life should be structured in a new era. For sovereign states wishing to survive in a world without a higher earthly authority, the idea of a balance-of-power system seemed to offer much promise as a viable substitute for the chaos and bloodletting that had accompanied the waning days of the old medieval order. Acting like engineers, the envoys to Münster and Osnabrück designed a rough balance among the greater and lesser powers, surrounded it with a code of conduct, and hoped that it would preserve their creation.

CONTENDING INTERPRETATIONS OF THE PEACE SETTLEMENT

It might appear that the Westphalian settlement of the Thirty Years' War was visionary and constructive. This was the enthusiastic endorsement that the French philosopher, Jean Jacques Rousseau, was to pen in 1761 when he wrote:

> What really upholds the European state system is the constant interplay of negotiations, which nearly always maintains an overall balance. But this system rests on an even more solid foundation, namely the German Empire, which from its

position at the heart of Europe keeps all powers in check and thereby maintains the security of others even more, perhaps, than its own. The Empire wins universal respect for its size and for the number and virtues of its peoples; its constitution, which takes from conquerors the means and the will to conquer, is of benefit to all and makes it a perilous reef to the invader. Despite its imperfections, this Imperial constitution will certainly, while it lasts, maintain the balance in Europe; no prince need fear lest another dethrone him. The peace of Westphalia may well remain the foundation of our political system for ever.[48]

Other observers take a different position: the mixture of incompatible tenets within the Westphalian settlement made it seem to them as little more than a packet of "futile" and "meaningless" platitudes.[49] To these critics, the Peace of Westphalia was ineffectual in resolving the deep-seated problems of Europe.[50] The view of one historian captures this negative interpretation well:

> The peace, which had settled the disputes of Germany with comparative success because passions had cooled, was totally ineffectual in settling the problems of Europe. The inconclusive and highly unpopular cession of Alsace led direct to war; the seizure of half Pomerania by the Swedish Crown was only less disastrous because the Swedish Crown was palpably too weak to hold it. The insidious growth of Bourbon influence on the Rhine, and Mazarin's deliberate policy of seizing good strategic points on the frontier, vitiated the settlement. The Peace of Westphalia was like most peace treaties, a rearrangement of the European map ready for the next war.
>
> The peace has been described as marking an epoch in European history, and it is commonly taken to do so. It is supposed to divide the period of religious wars from that of national wars, the ideological wars from the wars of mere aggression. But the demarcation is artificial as such arbitrary divisions commonly are. Aggression, dynastic ambition and fanaticism are all alike present in the hazy background behind the actual reality of the war, and the last of the wars of religion merged insensibly into the pseudo-national wars of the future.[51]

Controversy persists to this day over the consequences of the Peace of Westphalia, which continues to cast its shadow over all thinking about how a group of dissimilar and unequal states should be organized to promote peace and justice. Was it a visionary plan to usher in a new international order? Or was it a flawed scheme that did little more than serve the immediate interests of the victors? Spirited arguments have been made on behalf of both positions. On the one hand, the period "is significant for the political analyst because, for all its apparent futility and lack of perfect or final settlement, it represented a new ordering of relationships."[52] Whereas the fortunes of France, Sweden, and the United Provinces of the Netherlands were on the rise, Germany lay in ruin, Spain declined to the status of a secondary power, and Austria would now have to fend off encroachments by the Ottoman Empire. Yet, on the other hand, the war and its settlement seems to have decided nothing: France and Spain continued fighting; Bourbons and Hapsburgs remained on their respective thrones; Austria, Bavaria, and what is today Belgium remained Catholic; and Brandeburg, the Netherlands, and Saxony maintained their Calvinist and Lutheran faiths.

Amidst these rival images of the Westphalian settlement, there is strong agreement that it "replaced most of the legal vestiges of hierarchy, at the pinnacle of which were the Pope and the Holy Roman Emperor."[53] The Peace of Westphalia dramatically changed the face of Europe through a multilateral process unprecedented in procedures and objectives. By introducing these far-reaching changes, Westphalia transformed the *normative order* of world politics. Although the newly emerging sovereign states were not accountable to the judicial authority of others, this does not mean that Westphalia bred anomie. Contrary to the assertion that "the independence of states implies that in international relations there are no rules,"[54] voluntarily acknowledged normative standards were respected after the Thirty Years' War, even in the absence of centralized mechanisms to articulate a code of conduct and enforce compliance.

Norms are ubiquitous. Studies of hunting and gathering bands, the most primitive political systems for which we have data, indicate that groups with minimal role differentiation routinely develop codes of conduct to govern their members.[55] Furthermore, the record of ancient multistate systems and segmented lineage societies show that these codes also develop in anarchies.[56] According to Evan Luard, "All groups of nations in regular contact have in practice adopted certain rules defining the conduct which could usually be expected among their members."[57] Adam Watson concurs: "No system has existed without rules and conventions of some kind, and it is difficult to see how one could."[58] "Every social system creates rules and laws for governing behavior," adds Robert Gilpin.[59] This was as true for the anarchical state system that emerged after the Thirty Years' War as it was for the hierarchical system of the late middle ages.

It should also be added that almost every social system emerges from controversies and debates over the rules and laws which will govern subsequent behavior. The system that came into being in 1648 was a product of an intense controversy about future rules. Moreover, it was a controversy that would reappear at all of the great peace congresses that followed Westphalia, including those convened at Utrecht (1713), Vienna (1815), Versailles (1919), in the aftermath of other catastrophic wars.

Ever since the Thirty Years' War, historians, publicists, and social scientists have debated the costs and benefits of the international norms engendered by the Peace of Westphalia. Emerging from a complex, multilateral war fought over three decades, the settlement was a product of mixed motives and clashing ambitions. Having described the negotiations that occurred at Münster and Osnabrück, we turn in the next chapter to consider the legacy of the Westphalia normative order as a structure for building world order in the twenty-first century.

CHAPTER 5

The Consequences
of the Peace Settlement

Farewell you generals
You have served me so many years,
With unremitting bravery,
In conquering cities, land and folk.
Adieu, adieu, you cavaliers
High and low officers,
Adieu you honorable soldiers,
What advice can I give you now
After serving me my years
In many a perilous adventure?
You receive great praise and honor,
But O what now remains of
My great power and glory
The great fear of land and folk?

—Speech by "War" on a copper plate engraving
inscribed by Matthias Rembold in 1648,
from the collection of the
Stadtbibliothek, Ulm

On January 30, 1648, the Treaty of Münster ended the Eighty Years' War between Spain and the United Provinces of the Netherlands. Nine months later, the Treaties of Münster and Osnabrück concluded the war between the coalition of France, Sweden, and the Protestant German princes against the Holy Roman Emperor and the Catholic German princes. To reach these accords, the negotiators used a multilateral process unprecedented in procedures and objectives.

Despite the diplomatic novelty of the peace conferences, an argument can be made that nothing really changed: "France and Spain continued fighting intensively for eleven years following the Peace of Westphalia and intermittently for a century-and-a-half thereafter. Bourbon and Hapsburg remained on their respective thrones. Bavaria, Austria, and the Spanish Netherlands remained Catholic. Brandeburg, Saxony, a segment of the Palatinate, and the Netherlands preserved a rugged harmony between the Lutheran and Calvinist faiths. Relatively little property, real or improved, changed hands permanently. Prosperity returned to Amsterdam and continued to languish in Antwerp."[1] In addition, many issues remained unresolved: "Many problems were left up in the air by the Peace of Westphalia, either because the negotiators did not perceive them or because they were not equal to dealing with them."[2]

While such an argument may appear plausible at first glance, it overlooks deeper, more fundamental changes that restructured Europe. "The disintegration of the Holy Roman Empire, which had been advanced by the drawing of internal religious frontiers in the days of Luther, was now confirmed in politics, and international law."[3] The small German states obtained the authority to establish whatever form of government they chose, as well as the freedom to conduct their own foreign policies. State leaders no longer acknowledged the papacy as the supreme ruler of Europe, therein paving the way for a new world order based on sovereign territorial states. Contrary to the argument that Westphalia did not change anything, the peace congresses are significant for students of international relations because, for all the apparent futility of the Thirty Years' War and lack of perfect settlement, Westphalia "represented a new ordering of relationships."[4]

EVALUATING THE NEW ORDER

To accept the Peace of Westphalia as a watershed in diplomatic history is not to suggest that it was necessarily a constructive system of world order, formulated by statesmen of such vision and acumen that it augurs well even in our time. When evaluating the peace settlement, we must ask which criteria can most meaningfully inform a discussion of its impact. One approach is to judge its principles against the behavior that resulted after their promulgation. What were the consequences of the Westphalian Peace? To what degree were the aims of the peacemakers realized by the strategy they implemented? Were the means that they selected moral?

By asking these kinds of questions, we can draw upon two traditions of ethical thought: consequentialism and deontology. The former evaluates moral choices on "only the basis of results or consequences of actions, including unintended effects," and the latter "insists that doing right requires morally good motives as well as acceptable means."[5] Thus while the consequentialist would evaluate Westphalia in terms of results, the deontologist would ask whether the settlement achieved those results by means that were also moral.

TEN TENETS FOR PEACE

The Westphalian settlement reflected a consensus about rival normative principles that would underpin a lasting peace. What makes the settlement so memorable is how the plenipotentiaries creatively fused diverse ideas to put international order on a new footing. The terms of the settlement contained ten philosophical tenets that still influence world politics today. In the previous chapter, we examined how the peace settlement was negotiated. Now we will turn our attention to evaluating the consequences, means, and motives of each of these underlying tenets.

Retributive Justice

As noted previously, the negotiators at Münster and Osnabrück were embittered by the brutality of the war[6] and had powerful reasons to justify punitive peace treaties. The incentives for revenge were strong, and that made formulating a lasting settlement appear highly unlikely. "Under the conventions of the day, states had the right to demand *satisfactio* and *assecurato*. Victors could require the enemy to pay for the costs of the war."[7]

Spain and Austria faced defeat, and therefore braced themselves for French and Swedish revenge. Indeed, both the French and the Swedes approached the bargaining tables with the aim of strengthening their international positions. For example, the Swedes demanded "compensation for *'Blut und Opfer'* in the form of outright cash reparations, access to Baltic tolls, certain territorial concessions, and the prospect of taxation rights in Upper Germany."[8]

Wanton vindictiveness had the potential to degenerate into an endless blood feud, for retaliation often involves more than "an eye for an eye, a tooth for a tooth;"[9] it overpays rather than evens the score, thereby adding new injuries that reinforce old hatreds.[10] Aware of the problems that could arise from spiteful, measureless retaliation, the peacemakers differentiated between *revenge* and *retribution*. The former is an attempt "to impose suffering upon those who have made one suffer, because they have made one suffer."[11] It is a personal act—a self-righteous returning of wrong for wrong in which the avenger seeks pleasure from the suffering inflicted on the culprit. In comparison, retribution lacks the resentful, vindictive spirit of revenge; it avenges a moral transgression dispassionately, without personal rancor.[12] Retributive justice attempts to halt unrestrained vengeance by distinguishing between crimes and their punishment, and placing limits on the penalties wrongdoers are asked to pay.

For the victors, a peace treaty that substituted retributive justice for outright revenge offered several important benefits. First, it defused the possibility that all members of the defeated adversary would be collectively condemned. Second, avoiding collective condemnation facilitated the normalization of relations between the belligerents after the war. Finally, by eschewing revenge, reconciliation and the pursuit of restorative justice became possible. The scars of war could begin to heal, the victors reasoned, by giving the defeated a stake in the postwar order.

Assimilating Losers into the Postwar System

In an effort to avoid a new wave of armed struggle, the victors at Westphalia attempted to assimilate the losers in the postwar processes of collective governance. Showing disrespect to an adversary by preventing it from participating in a discussion over the peace terms was deemed risky because such insulting treatment was likely to evoke future efforts to vindicate a wounded sense of honor. As a result, the Catholic parties were allowed to convene separately in the nearby town of Münster and participate on an equal footing in the negotiations through procedures that encouraged voluntary consent. The peace treaties looked forward rather than backward. Shared interests were not immediately obvious, but the negotiators found common ground so that the winners could satisfy some of their opponents' interests without compromising their own. The victors believed that the success of a multilateral peace conference depended on everyone's capacity to transcend the desire for short-term relative gains and support the new rules regulating the postwar system.

Of course, attaining peace is more difficult than desiring it; and sustaining peace once it has been attained is even more demanding, for a lasting accord must somehow be able to quash challenges to the new international order while developing procedures that allow complaints to be aired and peaceful change to occur. What the Westphalian settlement shows is an acute sensitivity to harmonizing competing concerns that are often fragile and require constant care. Nowhere was this position more visible than in the treatment of the Austrian Hapsburgs, who retained their dignity in defeat. "Largely purged of dissidents and cut off from Spain, the compact private territories of the Austrian Hapsburgs were still large enough to guarantee them a place among the foremost rulers of Europe, and to perpetuate their hold on the Imperial title until the Empire was abolished in 1806."[13]

Removing Religion from International Politics

As we have seen in Chapter 1, one of the searing problems in Europe at the onset of the Thirty Years' War was the struggle between secular and sacral authority. The Reformation had challenged the political authority of the papacy, thereby giving Protestant princes leverage for freeing themselves from domination by the Holy Roman Empire. When the schism widened, the 1555 Peace of Augsburg attempted to resolve the conflict by adopting the principle *cuius regio, eius religio* ("Whose the region, his the religion"), so as to permit each prince to regulate religious practices within his territory. Rulers could choose their religion and that of their subjects. The Peace of Westphalia reaffirmed the

Augsburg solution with amendments aimed at rectifying much of the religious intolerance that had formerly plagued Europe. To protect religious minorities, Westphalia made Protestant and Catholic states equal and for the first time ensured the rights of subjects within the northern Protestants' states to worship as they preferred. The Treaty of Osnabrück stipulated that subjects who in 1627 had been debarred from the free exercise of a religion different from than that of their ruler were now able to conduct private worship and educate their children in conformity with their own faith. Furthermore, the treaty prohibited worshipers in northern Germany from being denied a religious burial; they also were allowed to sell their estates or leave them for others to administer.

In addition, the Treaty of Osnabrück established that (1) Protestants princes would now possess full voting rights in the Diet; (2) religious questions would be settled by an amicable "composition" or majority vote between its two parts or *corpora* (the Corpus Evangelicorum of Protestant states administrated by a directorate in Saxony and the Corpus Catholicorum administered in Mainz); and (3) when possible there should be equality of voting power between the Protestants and Catholics on all Diet commissions. Moreover, the settlement sought to terminate religious strife in Germany by granting the same rights to the Calvinists as to the Catholics and Lutherans. To enhance the prospects for maintaining peace and equal treatment between Catholics, Lutherans, and Calvinists, Westphalia created a supreme court for the Empire staffed by twenty-six Catholics and twenty-four Protestants, and Protestants were seated on the Aulic Council in Vienna.

In an effort to alleviate bitterness over their political losses elsewhere, the settlement gave rulers in the Austrian wing of the Hapsburg empire more influence to direct religious practices than rulers received in Protestant principalities. Both sides agreed upon 1624 as the "standard year" for determining which territories would be defined as Catholic or Protestant possessions. Although Catholic Hapsburgs' lost control over religious practices in the north, religious freedom was restricted within their dominion. As K. J. Holsti notes,

> This was not an entirely satisfactory basis for universal religious toleration, as it left the matter of regulating religious practice to the state and excluded tolerance in the Hapsburg family territories. However, the relevant articles did confirm the right of private worship, and any subsequent change of religion by a ruler was not to affect that right. . . . With these latter provisions, the settlement went beyond the principles of 1555. Indeed the congress also recognized Calvinism as a legitimate branch of the Christian faith, and established a Lutheran Church with bishops, titles, and honors modeled on the Churches of Sweden and England, though its head was not to be a crown.[14]

Religious questions could no longer be decided by a majority of the imperial estates; confessional and bishopric administrative issues hereafter were to be resolved though compromises between confessions. The treaty strengthened the sovereignty of the German princes by allowing them to make treaties without the pope's approval, and "following the Peace of Westphalia, states only rarely forcibly interfered in the religious affairs of other states."[15]

State Sovereignty

If Westphalia is known for its innovative approach to reconcile religious differences, it is also known for its rules stipulating the rights and responsibilities of sovereign political units. "Before Westphalia there was no sovereignty; no legitimate authority was supreme within its territory."[16] After Westphalia, no concept was more central to international law than state sovereignty. Jean Bodin's 1576 influential treatise *Six Books of a Commonwealth* had set the tone for the deliberations at Münster and Osnabrück over state power versus the claims of feudal and ecclesiastical authorities. Bodin argued cogently for the supremacy of the territorial state and against religious dominion over Europe. In international affairs, sovereignty means that no authority stands above the state, except that which the state voluntarily confers on any organizations it may join. Nearly every legal doctrine in the aftermath of Westphalia supported the principle that states were the primary subjects of international law, holding "a complete freedom of action" to preserve their independence.[17] Accordingly, most international legal norms address the rights and duties of states, not people.[18]

In line with the principle of state sovereignty, all 355 German states were recognized as independent members of the Imperial Diet.[19] Those princes who fought the Emperor were returned their lands from 1624, and the Edict of Restitution was formally withdrawn. By bestowing sovereign authority on every German prince, the Westphalian settlement is said to mark the birth of the modern nation-state. For the first time, territorial states were legally permitted to interact with each other without interference by a higher authority. They could now freely manage their domestic affairs and their diplomatic relationships. Thus, Article 65 gave all states an opportunity to

> . . . enjoy without contradiction, the right of suffrage in all deliberations touching the affairs of the Empire; but above all, when the business at hand shall be the making or interpreting of laws, the declaring of wars, levying or quartering of soldiers, erecting new fortifications in the territories of the states, or reinforcing the old garrisons; as also when a peace or alliance is to be concluded, and treated about, or the like, none of these, or the like things shall be acted for the future, without the suffrage and consent of the free assembly of all the states of the Empire; above all, it shall be free perpetually to each state of the Empire to make alliances with strangers for their preservation and safety; provided, nevertheless, such alliances be not against the Emperor, and the Empire.

Henceforth all imperial legislation became contingent on the Diet's approval rather than the pope's.

The Westphalian system made citizens subservient to their governments and challenged Christianity's fundamental teachings that bonds of human solidarity backed by universal standards of justice recognized no national boundaries. Christianity posited that moral responsibilities should be honored by all states at all times, in both war and peace, and that *raison d'état* (reason of state) did not warrant the neglect of moral duties. Westphalia rejected the view that states should be held accountable to moral commands in the same way that ordinary people are in their personal conduct. By granting states independence from any higher authority, Westphalia engendered a weak system of international law. States, under this legal system, were permitted "a complete freedom of action."[20]

The Equality of States

By challenging any supranational authority's claim of *totius orbis dominus*, the Westphalian Peace accepted a conception of international society that embraced states on a footing of equality, irrespective of religion and form of government.[21] All states possessed the same rights and responsibilities as equal members in a family of nations, though they were obligated to adhere to only those laws to which they gave their consent.

The Westphalian Peace closed one era and opened another when it overturned the preexisting vertical order of centralized authority and replaced it with a horizontal order of independent units. Hereafter, all states were (1) equal under the law, (2) equally able to make the laws that would govern international society, and (3) equally independent from any higher supranational authority to manage their relations. Whether, indeed, this set of rules served justice was debatable, however. Like all compromises, the sovereign equality of states was a regime of, by, and for heads of states; it sought justice for them, not their subjects. The regime fell short of protecting the equal rights of individuals or assuring for people equal protection under international law, as Westphalia assigned monarchs the right to control domestic affairs within their territories. Westphalia protected rulers against people, not people against the human rights abuses of rulers. When taken to the extreme, the state became a kind of secular deity. As one speech in 1661 put it,

> Just as the sun in the heavens above is made and fashioned by God, and is a truly wondrous work of the Almighty, so are kings, princes and lords placed and ordered by God in the secular estate. For that reason they may themselves be called gods.[22]

The Balance of Power

The Westphalian peace settlement redistributed power to compensate winners for wartime losses without rewarding them with gains that would heighten fears of their future expansionism. Facing the threat of civil war, France demanded *satisfactio* in the form of the Hapsburg province of Alsace as compensation for its losses, as well as to provide a buffer against external aggression. Similarly, the Swedes "requested *assecuratio*—that is, the formation of a German league to defend Swedish territorial security and the Protestant religion in northern Germany."[23] All these territorial redistributions were geared to the goal of enabling states to counter any future hegemonial threat. All states were encouraged to unite against any aggressor state, and France was empowered with the capability to perform the role of "balancer"—to intervene unilaterally or with allies to prevent the domination of Europe by any single power.

Collective Security and Multilateral Diplomacy

The major security threat faced by the victors of the Thirty Years' War was the emergence of another expansionist power bent on hegemonical conquest. The Hapsburg empire was still viewed as a danger, so the victors in the Thirty Years' War encircled it with a ring of alliances and tried to institutionalize their containment strategy by building a rudimentary concert of great powers. This plan followed the thinking of Cardinal Richelieu, who advocated "a continental system of collective security."[24] It also anticipated the thinking of Charles de Montesquieu and other Enlightenment philosophers who later advocated a checks-and-balance system policed by an equal balance of power, under the belief that "the balance of power distilled unity out of diversity."[25]

For unity to emerge from the fragmented landscape of national power, the architects of the Westphalian settlement envisioned the eventual creation of a European society, with a shared understanding of the need for collective security and the pacific methods of dispute settlement. "The Peace of Westphalia was notable for inculcating the idea of a society of states, a type of body politic with communitarian characteristics, including reciprocal delegations based on equality, that falls midway between a structure of hierarchical authority and a system of pure anarchy."[26] This vision of a society of states drew inspiration from the writings of Hugo Grotius (see Chapter 4), who called for the resolution of interstate conflicts by judicial procedures and specified a body of legal principles to encourage cooperation, peace, and more humane treatment of people. However, the Westphalian settlement rejected the argument that for a peace system to function effectively, *organized* collective security was required. Instead, Westphalia supported the use of *ad hoc* collective defense alliances to maintain peace.

Selective Nonintervention

From sovereignty came the principle that states could manage affairs within their territorial boundaries without external interference. Sovereignty could mean nothing if independence was not guaranteed. Rulers were therefore given freedom to regulate the practices of the people subject to their authority. True, their control was not unlimited; but the Westphalian settlement "sought to restore order by establishing rules that defined the control that rulers could legitimately exercise over religion."[27]

The delegates at Osnabrück and Münster had to face the problem of enforcing the rules of the settlement, including the cardinal norm of the now-sacred principle of state sovereignty. Sanctions were required to back the treaties' provisions, but no formal collective security institutions were created to punish violations of those rules. As a substitute, intervention was condoned to defend the political goals expressed by the treaties' provisions. For example, "the chief political idea underlying the Franco-German settlement of 1648 was . . . that the best guarantee of French security lies in a divided and impotent Germany, and that this division and impotence must be secured by appropriate provisions such as those that gave France a right to intervene when necessary in order to vindicate the principle of the sanctity of treaties."[28]

Yet nonintervention was a corollary of the sovereignty principle. It defended states against the threat of interference in their internal affairs. Nevertheless, the Westphalian treaties took an ambivalent posture toward nonintervention, prohibiting it for the purpose of modifying religious practices within other states but permitting states to intervene for military purposes to promote their national security, protect their independence, and preserve established international law. "The signers of the Münster treaty had clearly struck a balance," observes Charles Doran, in adopting the nonintervention norm to prohibit intervention with a purpose of religious persecution, while at the same time legalizing intervention for geostrategic purposes. Consequently Westphalia "circumscribed" rather than eliminated rights of intervention.[29] The use of force was not prohibited, and the pursuit of national power through foreign activism was seen as a natural and necessary priority, a prerequisite for the functioning of the balance of power.

Legitimizing *Realpolitik*

Westphalia made a covenant with armed force, in part because it was written by diplomats schooled in the ways of *realpolitik* during the Thirty Years' War. Power was seen as a product of military capability, and preparing for war was understood as the best way of keeping peace. The mood at the peace conferences seemed to accept Cardinal Richelieu's warning that "many princes have lost their countries, and ruined their subjects by failing to maintain sufficient military force for their protection, fearing to tax them too heavily."[30] Not only did the peacemakers reject proposals to construct a formal collective security organization to restrain the competition of states, but they refused to impose many legal restrictions on the use of military force. In short, protection provided for weak states was provisional and precarious, requiring the aid of stronger allies willing to offer military assistance.

Many historians see Westphalia as a settlement that created rules fostering hegemonic struggles. As Harvey Starr has observed, in stressing state auton-omy and independence the Westphalian settlement viewed "the balance of power as the key mechanism for the maintenance of world order."[31]

> Very clear *trade-offs* were made between autonomy and self-control on the one hand and the lack of order inherent in the anarchic international system on the other: princes who were striving for independence of action from the control of religious or Imperial authority (the Pope and the Holy Roman Empire) were will-ing to create a system of states that had no found source of authority or higher order.[32]

The Demise of Moral Constraints

The diplomats meeting in Münster and Osnabrück had to make moral choices. Building peace requires weighing competing values and contending visions, all of which inextricably involve defining the place of morality in international statecraft. They found their answer in realist thought. Looking askance at the applicability of noble ideals to international affairs, the diplomats and the army of lawyers advising them abandoned any notion of grounding the search for peace in a philosophy guided by religious or moral precepts. As Henry Kissinger observes, the negotiators replaced morality with the principle of *raison d'état* (reason of state), which "asserted that the well-being of the state justified what-ever means were employed to further it." In the world of power politics coun-tenanced by *raison d'état*, states do not receive credit "for doing what is right, they are only rewarded for being strong enough to do what is necessary."[33]

In making the principle of *raison d'état* paramount, the Westphalian Peace endorsed a norm that was already gaining popularity during the course of the Thirty Years' War, one that protected royal authority, territorial borders, and gave rulers the unrestrained right to pursue expansionist policies for their state's aggrandizement. It was a principle predicated upon the assumption that all political action should be "constantly directed towards one major, compre-hensive end: state building."[34]

Having made glorification of the state acceptable, Westphalia paved the way for the beliefs that "the end justifies the means" and "might makes right" that were to later rationalize the use of war as a tool of foreign policy. What mat-tered was the expedient pursuit of egocentric interest, not lofty ideals, absolute moral values, or unbending religious principles. Realism substituted *raison d'é-tat* for morality, secularized international affairs, and pushed it outside the realm of religion. *Raison d'état* and the doctrine of the balance of power were "deeply offensive to the universalist tradition founded on the primacy of moral law" since they cut foreign policy loose from all ethical moorings.[35] As one critic complained shortly after the signing of the Treaties of Münster and Osnabrück, "Reason of state is a wonderful beast, for it chases away all other reason."[36]

THE NORMATIVE LEGACY OF THE PEACE SETTLEMENT

In retrospect, the postwar record of the Westphalian settlement presents a mixed picture of achievement and failure. On the *positive* side of the ledger, Westphalia can be credited with:

- *Providing more concrete religious guarantees for Protestant and Catholic princes.* The Diet could no longer decide on religious policies with a simple majority. In addition, guarantees were provided for the people regarding religious rights: Where the ruler changed his religion, subjects were allowed to retain theirs, tolerance being allowed by the individual prince.
- *Terminating wars bred by religious conflict.* The Thirty Years' War would be the last great religious contest in which all powers of western Europe were more or less involved. "No war occurring after 1648—wars against the Ottomans excepted—derived primarily from religious issues. The Westphalia religious formula . . . was so successful that it served as a model for numerous other treaties, such as the Peace of Oliva (1660) ending the Swedish-Polish War."[37]
- *Repressing the threat of the hegemonic domination in Europe.* Westphalia formalized the collapse of the Hapsburg bid for supreme control of European affairs. Although efforts by expansionist powers to establish imperial rule would occur in later decades, Westphalia succeeded in legitimizing the balance of power as a means of preventing the conquest of the continent by a single power. The centerpiece of this effort was Westphalia's "effective elimination of Spain from the circle of Great Power diplomacy [though] the final deconsolidation of political, financial, and administration ties with the Hapsburg family complex."[38]
- *Defining legally the concept of sovereign power, which prohibited interference from any authority above the state.*
- *Creating a system for mediating international disputes and for making peace treaties after wars under the rule of law.* "The influence [of Westphalia] can be seen in the constant attempt to fashion peace settlements for bilateral and multilateral wars in western Europe on the basis of the Westphalian peace."[39]
- *Creating the basis for the modern state system and planting the seeds for the eventual birth of democratic governance.* The Peace of Westphalia could also be thought of as the ". . . consolidation of the first bourgeois republican state in the north of the Netherlands," which prepared the war for the contest between ". . . the outdated 'imperial-universal' path of development and the 'nation-state' approach, as embodied by France in particular."[40]

On the *negative* side of the ledger, however, Westphalia may be said to have failed in a number of important respects to provide an adequate blueprint for international relations. It is blamed for:

- *Failing to secure complete religious freedom.* Westphalia made no attempt to force the Emperor to grant religious toleration in Hapsburg lands, and any German ruler was entitled to expel religious dissidents who had not been free to practice their faith in 1624. The Westphalian peace treaties left a tangled web of religions throughout Europe, though it marked the start of religious stability on the continent. The belligerents had agreed to disagree in terms of religion, but toleration was incomplete.
- *Fomenting nationalist sentiments that were later to arouse public pressure to redress perceived injustices within the settlement.* For example, many Germans felt victimized and betrayed by Westphalia, which seemed to punish the victim by reducing Germany to disunited inferiority. The devastation and dislocation caused by the treaties "were used by various nationalist political groups who wished to represent the Peace of Westphalia, and indeed the entire war, as a monstrous iniquity perpetrated on Germany by foreign powers, especially France."[41] From nationalistic resentment were later to come cries for wars of revenge.
- *Guaranteeing hegemonic rivalry.* By legitimating the race for predominant power, Westphalia is said to have assured competition. Consider the fate of the "losers" and their subsequent reactions. Austria suffered the most of all European powers from actual destruction, and gained nothing except the right to withhold religious toleration in the lands the Hapsburgs controlled during the Thirty Years' War. The provisions of the settlement were not harsh enough to repress eventual Austrian recovery. Though denied direct access to Baltic, Austria expanded eastward through the declining Ottoman Empire, absorbed Hungary, and began a new rise to power.
- *Placing the maintenance of international peace on the precarious footing of a great power balance.* Freedom and flexibility were praised, but critics note that the Westphalian reliance on the balance of power was responsible for continued bloodshed: "It was precisely this flexibility, frequently regarded and praised as [the balance of power's] chief virtue which ultimately brought about its ruin . . . when it was most desperately needed. The policy of freehands reaped a large harvest in World War I."[42]

Westphalia's Grim Military Legacy

Like all peace settlements, in the final analysis Westphalia must be judged by its ability to preserve peace. And in that regard, the Westphalian design for the conduct of relations between sovereign states must be judged as the settlement's greatest deficiency. True, the Peace of Westphalia suspended fighting in the central German-speaking theatre, but not elsewhere. The French war with Spain dragged on for another eleven years, and the Spanish refused to remove their forces from the Frankenthal stronghold in the Palatinate until 1653. Furthermore, the Swedish forces did not withdraw from that troubled hot spot until

1654. Beyond that limitation was a more severe inadequacy: "Europe did not enter upon an era of peace in the latter part of the seventeenth century, for both Sweden and France—the unquestioned victors of the Thirty Years' War—continued to fight their neighbors for another sixty years."[43] Hence, the Peace of Westphalia did not bring true peace. Because "the post-Westphalian order was punctuated by frequent war: our conclusion must be that the order included some elements of stability, but it did little to reduce the incidence of war."[44]

In many respects, the Westphalian Peace was written in the language of Thomas Hobbes with the spirit of Hugo Grotius. Hobbes, of course, saw war as natural, and he perceived few incentives to place legal limits on what sovereign states could do to defend themselves or to expand their influence. Grotius tried to temper warfare by creating a law of nations that derived its obligatory character from natural law as well as "from the will of all nations or many nations."[45] However, his effort to identify rules of and for warfare that were "universal and immutable" did not reject waging war for "just causes," a view that later became a integral part of the Westphalian outlook on the rules for statecraft that states were expected to follow. The upshot was that Hobbes justified the sovereign's right to use military force, Grotius accepted it within limits, and Westphalia endorsed a concept of war that prepared the way for it to become prevalent in the future:

> Grotius's theory was that judgment by states not party to the controversy would tend to support the just cause and deter unjust wars. However, in many circumstances it is very difficult to determine which cause is just. Moreover Machiavellian considerations may enter into the calculations of states not originally participating in the war. Thus the formula offered by Grotius tended to spread war to the states that took sides regarding the justice of the controversy rather than to deter violence. As a result, it was ineffective to control the outbreak of war, and, once it had broken out, the principle tended to increase the extent and consequences of the war.[46]

Over time, states acted in ways that further undermined the Grotian plea to abide by a code of diplomatic conduct that would mitigate the horrors he witnessed. As Kaplan and Katzenbach elaborate:

> since no state could sit in judgment on the acts of other sovereigns, there was no way of determining whether the war was just or not. This action did not preclude states from continuing to invoke the older doctrine and plead the justice of their cause. States continued to do so, in part to build up domestic support for military intervention, in part, perhaps, to reassure other states as to their limited intentions. But it was clearly understood . . . by governments and scholars alike that there was no necessary or legal relation between statements of the grounds for war and the peace that might lawfully be enacted. [47]

Evidence for the criticism that the Westphalian conception of international behavior bred more war than it deterred is suggested by events that unfolded in the three-and-a-half centuries after 1648. Of course, it is difficult to make a clear causal connection between the Westphalian Peace settlement and the pattern of international behavior that followed. Conceptually, Westphalia "secured all the essentials and most of the trappings of sovereignty; thereafter every prince was emperor in his lands. All the powers they had acquired as a result of the Reformation and of the Thirty Years' War were confirmed in the Treaty of Peace, in particular their authority in matters of religion and their right to form alliances."[48] But what was the impact of this innovation? How do we estimate the extent to which the fluctuating level of international instability can be ascribed to the principles which Westphalia enshrined?

Cause and effect are difficult to establish. Chronology provides some telling clues, even though prior circumstances do not necessarily determine subsequent conditions. But the more elongated the period of observation, the more confidence can be placed in assessments of the ramifications of Westphalia for world order. Taking a profile of the long-term sweep of history following the Peace of Westphalia, we observe that warfare remained a chronic problem. Figure 5.1 traces the outbreak of 2,566 individual wars between 1400 and 2000. As the trends in this chronological profile show, the number of wars plummeted immediately after the exhausting Thirty Years' War—but has risen

FIGURE 5.1   The Number of Wars by Decade, Prior To and After Westphalia between 1400 and 2000

Westphalia appears to have produced a system of war. Its values worshipped sovereign freedom without restraints, and it is hard not to conclude that a major consequence of this value system was international insecurity in a ceaseless stream of warfare.
Source: Adapted from Brecke, 1999, p. 10.

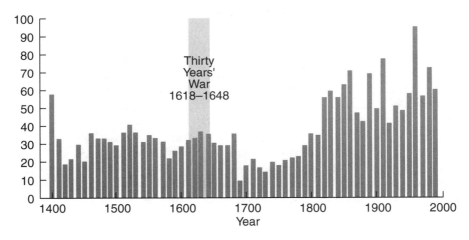

steadily thereafter. The legacy of Westphalia, this suggests, is one of continual warfare, a Hobbesian "war of all against all."

Much of the fighting in the immediate aftermath of the Westphalian settlement involved struggles over the consolidation of political power within the 355 newly established sovereign states that emerged in German lands. The central problem in the Westphalian system was converting sovereignty from a proposal to a reality. The challenge of the period was state building. Figure 5.2 shows that as the seventeenth century progressed, dynastic confrontations based on frontier adjustments with nationalistic, economic, and colonial overtones replaced religious clashes, although in southern Europe intermittent Ottoman-Hapsburg conflict retained religious significance.[49] While rulers attempted to exercise sovereign control over the territories Westphalia defined as their borders, the newly legitimated states were, in fact, still fragile, and the challenge of forging internal unity and nationalistic loyalty was formidable. Indeed, the period "was dominated by almost ceaseless wars between combinations of the major European states, many of which also faced grave internal struggles linked with religious or constitutional issues."[50] The continuous stream of internal and international warfare in the late seventeenth century escalated in frequency and destructiveness on through the twentieth century. It is noteworthy that many of the problems experienced during the mid-to-late seventeenth century, such as civil strife and waves of refugees, foreshadowed difficulties that continue to produce massive human suffering at the dawn of the twenty-first century.[51]

To put the period following Westphalia into sharper focus, we need to look more closely at the international situation that unfolded, in order to illuminate how, why, and the extent to which the Westphalian rules of statecraft legitimated power politics.

Westphalia's Turbulent Political Legacy

When the Thirty Years' War ended, Amsterdam stood at the center of world commerce and finance. Possessing a fleet larger and less expensive to operate than any other navy, the Dutch used their maritime strength to dominate seaborne trade. With the Hapsburgs defeated, France and Spain still fighting, and England distracted by civil war, the United Provinces of the Netherlands held an economic hegemony.[52] Dependent upon trade and vulnerable to privateering, the Dutch promoted international maritime law and fought less often than other great powers during the late seventeenth century.[53] Indeed, they "looked down with pitying contempt" on the wars of dynastic ambition waged elsewhere on the continent, seeing themselves "as the advocates of a rational, enlightened world order based on peace and justice."[54]

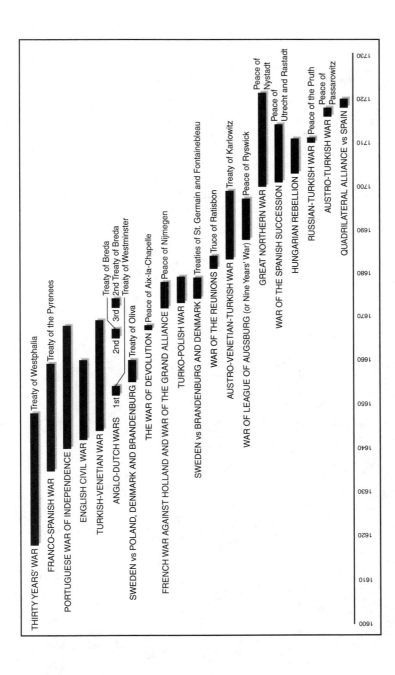

FIGURE 5.2 The Aftermath of Westphalia: Major Interstate Wars and Peace Treaties, 1618–1721

The Westphalian settlement did not create an era of stability. On the contrary, following the end of the Thirty Years' War armed conflicts between the most powerful states became a persistent feature of the international landscape.

Source: Adapted from Chandler, 1998, p. 18.

The United Provinces were a decentralized, patrician republic. Under the leadership of William of Orange (better known as William the Silent because of his ability to keep the purposes of his political maneuvers hidden), the Dutch had thrown off Spanish Hapsburg rule in 1609, though military campaigns continued between 1621 and 1648 (see Figure 5.3). After independence, no chief executive governed the United Provinces as a whole. Each province elected its own "stadholder" to function as an executive, though normally they all chose a prince from the House of Orange. Political power oscillated between the Orangists and the wealthy burghers who comprised a merchant patriciate. The former gained influence whenever foreign threats arose; the latter, when danger subsided and international business flourished. Following the conclusion of the Peace of Westphalia in 1648 and the death of Prince William II of the House of Orange two years later, the power of the burghers increased. Twenty-two years would pass before a new stadholder would be elected.

FIGURE 5.3   The Signing of the Westphalian Peace Treaty
The Treaty of Münster was signed in 1648, signaling the beginning of peace in war-swept Europe. To commemorate the signing of this peace treaty, Gerhard ter Borch painted a view of the historic event, which was greeted by celebration throughout most of Europe.

Over the course of these two decades, the United Provinces faced growing competition from England and France. In 1651, the British passed a Navigation Act calling for all imports to be carried on English ships or on ships from the country exporting the commodities. Since Dutch prosperity rested on shipping, financial services, and a complex system of "warehouse" trade that routed goods from one region of the world to another through Amsterdam, the Navigation Act represented a serious threat.

The Anglo-Dutch Naval Wars. The two maritime powers faced off in a series of wars between 1652 and 1674. In the first war (1652–1654), the English won convincing naval victories at Beachy Head, Gabbard Bank, and Scheveningen. The second encounter (1665–1667) was less conclusive. While the English were victorious at Lowestoft and North Foreland, the Dutch fleet prevailed elsewhere, and was able to blockade the Thames during the early summer of 1666. Dutch forces were also successful during the third war (1672–1674), earning victories at Sole Bay and Schoonveld Channel. Although the Republic of the United Netherlands won its share of naval battles during the three rounds of naval warfare against the upstart English, the protracted struggle eventually sapped Dutch military strength.[55]

The Wars of Louis XIV. At the same time that the Dutch sailed against the British, the French began pressuring them on land. Under King Louis XIV, France possessed the largest army in Europe, reaching some 400,000 troops at its zenith. In contrast to the undisciplined armies of the Thirty Years' War which relied on pillaging for supplies and compensation,[56] the French army was professionally trained, amply provisioned, and efficiently administered. Its generals were links in a vast chain of command that extended from the foot soldier to the Crown. Rather than being a hodgepodge of semiautonomous companies loyal only to the officers who recruited them, the French army in the second half of the seventeenth century was a highly centralized instrument of national policy, headed by a civilian war minister who worked for the king.

Louis XIV inherited the throne in 1643, though owing to his youth he did not rule until the death of Cardinal Mazarin eighteen years later. An ostentatious leader who traced his ancestry to Charlemagne, Louis sought grandeur and adoration. He selected the sun as his personal emblem, ordered the construction of a magnificent palace at Versailles, and surrounded himself with the pomp and splendor of court life. "The love of glory assuredly takes precedence over all other [passions] in my soul," he once proclaimed.[57] True to his thirst for glory, the "Sun King" used France's formidable army to push the boundaries of his domain toward the "natural borders" of the Alps, the Pyrenees, and the Rhine. His thirst was whetted by the status, prestige, and wealth that France could win by defeating other great powers on the field of battle.

The first expression of the Louis's territorial ambitions came in 1667 with an attack on the Spanish Netherlands (modern Belgium), a region seen by the Dutch as a buffer against French aggression. Alarmed by the Sun King's designs on the lower Rhine, the Dutch forged the Triple Alliance with England and Sweden, which prompted Louis to negotiate a diplomatic settlement. Yet even as the Treaty of Aix-la-Chapelle brought this so-called War of Devolution to an end,[58] Louis began planning for his next war.

To prevent another coalition from blocking French expansion northward, Louis concluded treaties with England (1670) and Sweden (1672) that deprived the Dutch of potential allies. After recruiting additional soldiers and building a navy, Louis attacked the Netherlands in 1672. French forces quickly overwhelmed the Dutch and marched toward Amsterdam. The city was saved only by opening the dikes to flood the surrounding countryside. With the threat to Amsterdam neutralized, the Dutch initiated a diplomatic counteroffensive. Under the leadership of William III, prince of the House of Orange, they pieced together a new anti-French coalition, consisting of Brandenburg, Denmark, and the Austrian and Spanish Hapsburgs. Faced once again with concerted opposition, the King Louis XIV reverted to negotiation. Under the terms of the Treaty of Nimwegen, he obtained territory to the east, but his political objectives in the north were not realized.

His ambitions in Holland frustrated, the Sun King changed tactics. From the Peace of Westphalia through the Treaty of Nimwegen, France had acquired many adjacent territories and, in the process, enlarged the French sphere of influence. Proposing that France might also hold the title to any lands previously owned by these territories, Louis established *chambres de réunion* to evaluate the case for French suzerainty over each parcel of land. Invariably, the judges in these courts ruled in his favor, and troops were quickly dispatched to cement the reunion of one parcel after another. Suspecting that the French monarch sought to swallow Europe incrementally, the Dutch Republic tried to counterbalance this new threat by joining with Austria, Bavaria, Holland, the Palatinate, Savoy, Saxony, Spain, Sweden, and ultimately England in the League of Augsburg. The long, inconclusive War of the League of Augsburg erupted in 1688 over the issue of succession to the electorship of the Palatinate and the archbishopric of Cologne. By the time the war ended with the Treaty of Ryswick nine years later, France had retained its acquisitions from Nimwegen but lost most of the lands procured through reunion.

The last of the armed conflicts comprising the Wars of Louis XIV was fought over the inheritance of King Carlos II of Spain. In an age where most monarchs ruled as unrestrained sovereigns, succession was a potentially disruptive issue in international affairs; indeed Westphalia had made it so in its quest to create unitary territorial state actors under the jurisdiction of strong rulers. Since the physically feeble Spanish monarch lacked an heir, whoever was bequeathed the crown and its territorial possessions would acquire enormous resources. Both King Louis XIV of France and Emperor Leopold I of Hapsburg

Austria claimed the right of inheritance for having married a sister of Carlos. Since neither the English nor the Dutch relished the prospect of having Spain's holdings given to either the House of Bourbon or the House of Hapsburg, the great powers of Europe agreed upon a treaty for dividing the possessions among several states. Angered by the plan to partition his empire, Carlos bequeathed his entire inheritance to Philip of Anjou, the grandson of Louis XIV. Even though Louis was a party to the Treaty of Partition, upon the death of Carlos on November 1, 1700, he reneged on his promises and accepted the crown on behalf of his grandson.

Shocked by the danger of a Franco-Spanish union, England, the Dutch Republic, and Hapsburg Austria joined together in a Grand Alliance, which later included Brandenburg, Savoy, and Portugal. The War of Spanish Succession began in 1701 when Leopold sent an army under the command of Prince Eugene of Savoy into Italy, where he routed the French in the Battle of Chiari. In addition to the outstanding leadership provided by Prince Eugene, the Allies could count on the brilliant military strategist John Churchill, Duke of Marlborough. Together, the two commanders orchestrated smashing victories at Blenheim (1704), Oudenarde (1708), and Malplaquet (1709). After eight years of fighting, France was exhausted and prepared to make sweeping concessions for peace. Yet the Allies responded by increasing their original demands, which so enraged the Sun King that four more years of bloodshed resulted. When the French earned a pivotal victory at Denain in 1712, the two sides returned to the negotiation table. Ironically, the final settlement accepted Philip of Anjou as king of Spain, though he had to renounce any claim to the French throne. Furthermore, Spain's territorial possessions were divided among several European powers. At one level of interpretation, the Treaty of Utrecht (1713) ended Louis XIV's bid to dominate Europe; at another, it reaffirmed the basic tenets of the Peace of Westphalia, which had sought to prevent any country from dominating Europe, by legitimizing the competitive drive to increase national capabilities while at the same time relying on the balance-of-power mechanism to keep any one state from emerging from the competition supreme.

Wars on Europe's Periphery.   As if to confirm the logical consequences of a *realpolitik* approach to international relations that endorses truculent, balance-of-power politics, while the Dutch, English, and French were vying for control of western Europe, a tangled web of conflicts in the Baltic region led Sweden to take up arms against Denmark, Poland, and Russia in the First Northern War (1654-1660). Victory over Denmark allowed the Swedes to add the provinces of Skåne, Blekinge, Halland, and Bohus to the lands in northern Germany that they had gained in the Peace of Westphalia. By the early eighteenth century, however, Sweden's position began to erode. Defeat in the Battle of Poltava (1709) by Peter the Great of Russia resulted in territorial losses in the eastern Baltic, and, by 1720, the northern German territories were ceded to Prussia and Hanover.

In southeastern Europe, war flared up between the Hapsburg and Ottoman Empires. Since the reign of Suleiman the Magnificent (1520–1566), the two powers had been skirmishing intermittently on the Hungarian plain. Serious fighting broke out in 1657 and intensified six years later when the Turkish military began to march up the valley of the Danube River. Its progress was stopped, however, by a multinational Christian army that had come to aid the Hapsburgs in their struggle against the Islamic onslaught. With neither side able to subdue the other, a twenty-year truce was arranged.

However, the precarious nature of balance-of-power politics, the bedrock of the Westphalian vision, was soon displayed. Encouraged by Louis XIV to resume their attack on France's traditional rival, the Turks marched into Austria as the truce expired and promptly besieged Vienna. When the siege was lifted in 1683 by a multinational relief force under the command of King John Sobieski of Poland, other European states capitalized on the unexpected turn of events and started whittling away at Turkish possessions. The Ottoman Empire lost Dalmatia and much of southern Greece to the Venetians (1685–1688), and it was decisively beaten by the Austrians at Szalánkemen (1691), by Peter the Great of Russia at Azov (1696), and by Prince Eugene of Savoy at Zenta (1697). Staggered by these losses, the Turks surrendered large portions of Hungary, Transylvania, and Croatia to the Hapsburgs, who then turned their attention westward toward France.

WESTPHALIA AS A WAR SYSTEM

As events from the Peace of Westphalia to the Treaty of Utrecht reveal, a multipolar balance-of-power system took root in Europe after 1648. With the economic hegemony of the Republic of the United Netherlands slowly deteriorating, challengers arose from the Atlantic and on the European continent. England supplanted the Dutch Republic as the world's foremost maritime power and began laying the foundation for her own economic hegemony.[59] France deposed Spain as the dominant land power and began a quest for military supremacy that resulted in a series of increasingly severe wars.[60] Whereas the War of Devolution killed some 4,000 combatants, battle deaths climbed to 342,000 in the Dutch War, 680,000 in the War of the League of Augsburg, and reached 1,251,000 in the War of Spanish Succession.[61] Meanwhile, other great powers squared off in both the Baltic and Balkan regions of Europe.

The permissive normative order established by the Peace of Westphalia underpinned this turbulent system. Its tenets were inherently unstable and are blamed by some scholars for magnifying instabilities that rocked the European political landscape over the next three centuries. One can readily reach this conclusion by inspecting the lethal history that unfolded after the ink on the Treaties of Münster and Osnabrück had barely dried. Amoral alliances, territorial compensation, policies of "divide and rule," the opportunistic disavowal of promises, and secret agreements like the 1670 Treaty of Dover between France and England were justified by appeals to sovereignty and *raison d'état* (reason of state). In memoirs he wrote for his son, King Louis XIV explained how he lulled potential targets into believing they were safe from attack: "For even though it was impossible to prevent someone from guessing the truth, I gave so many indications to the contrary that even those who had been the first to suspect it sometimes had their doubts, and those who had been told of it could not believe it."[62] Assuming that international politics was driven by the pursuit of power, and leaders had no obligations beyond their selfish interests, the *realpolitik* norms emerging from Westphalia supported such guileful practices as a means of generating world order without an orderer. If everyone followed their own interests, national vigilance and unfettered international competition would allegedly produce a self-regulating equilibrium. With an "invisible hand" maintaining a delicate system of national counterweights, no one country was expected to dominate the others. As expressed in the Treaty of Utrecht, a balance-of-power system "is the best and most solid foundation of . . . lasting general concord."

In summary, the Peace of Westphalia, like all settlements reached by an *ad hoc* process, produced mixed results.[63] It involved difficult trade-offs among rival values, the results of which could only accommodate some needs at the expense of others. On balance, the critics seem to have a better case than the celebrants. As Lynn Miller has written:

> We should draw two conclusions from this experience to guide our thinking about the Westphalian order's likely future. First, any legal order that claims rights for some cannot resist indefinitely the logical conclusion that they must be granted to all like actors if it is to maintain a claim to any semblance of being a system of justice. As the history of Westphalia shows, those served by the system can deny the logic of such an idea for a very long time simply by defining unequal participants as not truly like themselves and therefore not entitled to participate on an equal footing. Nonetheless, the very idea of equality—whether of sovereigns or of individual citizens within a domestic order—has proved to be an extremely dangerous idea to let loose upon a hierarchical society, for as larger numbers of actors meet whatever requirements are demanded are to be treated like equals, the tendency is irresistible to qualify still other members of the society as well.
>
> The second conclusion, which reinforces the first where global ordering arrangements are concerned, is that the concept of sovereign equality, with its comparatively simple and concrete tests to qualify as such an actor, remains the only alternative the modern world has been able to devise in opposition to hierarchical governmental principles. The result has not been an unmixed blessing from the standpoint of effective control over social disorder, but it undoubtedly has guaranteed greater freedom for more groups of people than any other kind of legal order known in history.[64]

Paradoxically, it could be said that the victors won the war and lost the peace. France, Sweden, and the Netherlands successfully curtailed the power of the Hapsburgs, but after Westphalia the Austrian side of the House of Hapsburg rose to a position of formidable power in Europe. Although the Holy Roman Empire was greatly weakened, it still retained influence over much of north central Europe, where German princes won greater independence from the Emperor and received the right to determine the state religion, but were not compensated for losses suffered during the war.

In another sense, with the containment of the Hapsburg bid for European hegemony, it might appear that the victors were rewarded in a way that permitted their rise as great powers. Yet the plight of Sweden suggests that the wages of war were high. Sweden reached its apex in 1648, having gained territory and the right to vote in Diet, but slipped into gradual decline due to the inability to take advantage of these gains and the devotion of too many resources to securing its German territories. The military might established by Gustavus Adolphus could not be sustained by an army whose mobility and size demanded that it pillage and plunder to maintain itself. "The victory of the anti-Hapsburg forces was, then, a marginal and relative one. They had managed, but only just, to maintain the balance between their material base and their military power better than their Hapsburg opponents."[65] Thus, the Peace of Westphalia ended a war fought for mixed causes, by belligerents pursuing mixed military objectives, and whose mixed motives at the peace congresses led to a mixed record of results. It is hardly surprising that ever since 1648, philosophers, historians, and statesmen have debated the settlement's costs and benefits and reached divergent conclusions about the value of the Westphalian vision. Given this controversy, let us turn our attention in the next chapter to evaluating the relevance of the Westphalian vision as a guide for maintaining world peace and justice in the twenty-first century.

PART III

The Westphalian Ghost and the Future of World Order

It is widely recognized that the notion of international order that European modernity continually proposed and reproposed, at least since the Peace of Westphalia, is now in crisis.

—Michael Hardt and Antonio Negri

Delegates to the peace conferences in Münster and Osnabrück witnessed the end of one era and the onset of another, a transformation from a time when "political authority was incompatible with sovereign statehood" to a time when the "landscape came gradually to be filled with sovereign states over the next three and a half centuries."[1] We are currently living through a transformation that promises to be just as significant. Revolutionary innovations in information and communications technology are eroding the boundaries of the sovereign territorial state, and the spread of democracy throughout the world is creating the possibility that a global civil society may arise from the growing transnational contacts among the world's nongovernmental organizations.

Following Winston Churchill's advice that "the farther backward you look, the farther forward you are likely to see," we have looked backward to 1648 when the Peace of Westphalia gave birth to the modern system of international politics. Our efforts are inspired by the conviction that, to understand the prospects for world order in the future, we need to learn from those periods in the past that experienced the challenge of building new blueprints for international security in the wake of wrenching political change. While we must guard against being seduced by superficial analogies between then and now, cautious historical inquiry can suggest what peacemakers today should and should not do to craft a durable world order.

In the remaining chapters of *Exorcising the Ghost of Westphalia*, we examine the policy problems of the present in the light of the lessons on world order-building suggested by the seventeenth century. As described in Part I, arrogance, mutual suspicion, and a general disregard for the human dignity of others characterized the conduct of the Thirty Years' War. To quote Hugo Grotius, the influential Dutch legal scholar, who wrote *De Jure Belli Ac Pacis* (*The Law of War and Peace*) in the midst of the savagery and slaughter:

> I have seen a lawlessness in warfare that even barbarian races would think shameful. On trifling pretexts, or none at all, men rush to arms, and when once arms are taken up, all respect for law, whether human or divine, is lost, as though by some edict a fury had been let loose to commit every crime.[2]

Sadly, genocide and a tendency to dismiss the human rights of others continues today, as seen in the explosion of civil wars and separatist revolts since the end of the Cold War. We still can find evidence of "the banalization of war and the celebration of it as an ethical instrument."[3] Indeed, the horrors that Grotius observed in his age anticipate what journalist Robert D. Kaplan now reports about entire regions of the planet.[4] As the chapters in Part II elaborated, there are many compelling reasons to investigate the prospects for future world order by comparing today's circumstances with those that prevailed during the seventeenth century. We agree with Richard Falk when he notes that "the basic postulates of the Westphalian conception continue to hold . . . [despite] its increasing inability to satisfy the needs of individuals." "At each stage of international history," he points out, "there has existed a peculiar tension between the logic of sovereign equality central to Westphalian thinking and the actualities of inequality in national wealth, power and disposition."[5] In Part III, we extend his critical interpretation of the state-centric foundation for international relations of the past three and a half centuries by arguing that the historic tension between Westphalian logic and international realities is now at a breaking point. In addition, we explain why we feel the Westphalian approach to international security offers more peril than promise for the twenty-first century, and why it is necessary to extirpate those features of the Westphalian order that are counterproductive for a new age of globalization.

"The best qualification of a prophet," George Savile (Lord Halifax) once quipped, "is to have a good memory." How we conceptualize the past has direct relevance for how well we can extrapolate from current trends and forecast probable futures. The challenges which we face in inspecting the past to foresee the future as a basis for conducting this kind of diagnostic and prescriptive analysis are many. To begin with,

> . . . there is always some element in history which can only be called chance. There is also the factor of human will. . . . There is never merely one broad dialectical process which can be defined in simple, clear-cut terms, but rather many interwoven and intersecting dialectical processes. The relevance of historical study for

the political scientist is that he must analyze the strongest of these processes, examine their points of intersection and significant overlap, and gauge from his conclusions the probable total direction in which events are moving.[6]

Simply put, it is extremely difficult, with so many imponderables, to attempt anything more ambitious than to lay down a general framework for a durable system of world order.[7] Like the negotiators at Westphalia, facing many uncertainties as they wrestled with the challenge of designing a skeletal blueprint for the future conduct of international relations, so we, too, are necessarily unable to proceed confidently with a proposal for a twenty-first century blueprint, let alone a complete architectural design that can provide order in the uncharted sea of the global future. Hence our most modest goal is to delineate the minimum requirements for a viable post-Westphalian world order rather than to specify a set of maximum preconditions.

As a first step toward this goal, Chapter 6, "Challenges to World Order at the Dawn of the Twenty-first Century," traces unfolding trends in contemporary world politics that are transforming the Westphalian system and, in the process, reducing its efficacy. Paradoxically, both integrative and disintegrative trends are occurring simultaneously, with each undercutting the capacity of the Westphalian security regime to foster international stability and order. On the one hand, globalization, democratization, and humanitarianism are bringing people together in ways that make the Westphalian image of independent territorial states anachronistic. On the other hand, the implosion of failed states, a surge in separatist movements driven by the enduring force of nationalism,[8] and the rise of outside intervention into civil wars,[9] has shattered the Westphalian illusion of sovereign states holding complete control of their internal affairs.

The dilemmas produced by the erosion of the Westphalian order are discussed in Chapter 7, "Westphalia's Problematic Contribution To Contemporary World Order." Here, we compare the environmental setting of the seventeenth century with the conditions prevailing today, and question whether the international norms embodied in the Westphalian code of conduct can remain applicable in the early twenty-first century. "Westphalia marked the end of a world of universal values and the rise of national interests in its place," enshrining the concept of *raison d'état* that "ushered in the modern state system that governs our world."[10] But now that world is changing[11] because state sovereignty is being undermined by a congeries of challenges. For various reasons sovereign autonomy and countries' internal cohesion are declining, and these trends increasingly call into question the capability of states to promote mutual security and well-being.[12] At the same time that interdependence is ushering in a nascent sense of universalism, a spirit of independence is defiantly resisting the specter of cultural homogenization. In short, we face a choice between incompatible norms for preserving international security, a choice that entails a tragic separation between opposed values—between unilateralism and multilateralism, between autonomy and collectivity. Inis Claude aptly poses the challenge which the post-Westphalian normative culture must confront, and the mixed reactions which such a choice provokes among scholarly experts:

> Sovereignty arouses ambivalence in the community of academic specialists in international relations. For many of us, the term seems unfortunate because it suggests separateness and independence in an era increasingly marked by togetherness and interdependence; it stands for freedom of action by states when the need is for central coordination and control; and it evokes the fear of unpredictable and irresponsible state behavior instead of progress toward the international rule of law. On the other hand, we value sovereignty as a protective mantle and deplore such disrespect for it as is entailed by acts of aggression against states and arbitrary interventions into their affairs. Moreover, we tend to react favorably to invocations of the principle of national self-determination by peoples previously swallowed up by colonial or other empires—usually without reflecting on the fact that we are actually endorsing sovereignty, for the typical objective and result of the drive for self-determination is the acquisition of sovereign status.
>
> Sovereignty, however, is not merely something to be embraced or deplored, supported or opposed, in accordance with the disposition either to associate it with such values as national freedom and immunity from improper interference or to emphasize the danger of its being abused to impede useful international cooperation and to justify domestic tyranny or violations of international order. Rather, the claim to and acknowledgment of sovereignty are significant facts of life in the multistate system, elements of reality that students of the system need to understand and take into account. . . . [However] the definition of sovereignty—if that is taken to include the delineation of the implications of being a sovereign state—is a perpetually tentative undertaking; one can only cite the latest edition and anticipate . . . recent and probable future developments in the meanings associated with the venerable concept of sovereignty.[13]

According to many scholars, the sovereign territorial state "is today weaker than it has . . . ever been since its first firm establishment in the Treaty of Westphalia in 1648, and no new kinds of political structures have arisen or are arising to take its place."[14] As market forces draw the world together, "the parochial and particularizing pull of new and renewed forms of spiritual solidarity"[15] is returning questions of identity to world politics. With the very meaning of sovereignty changing as the forces of globalization rush forward, traditional national loyalties will be increasingly supplemented by new, crosscutting affiliations linking people to actors beyond the nation-state.

The future, we conclude in Chapter 8, "The Importance of Trust in Global Governance for World Order," will be determined by the kinds of norms that are embraced and the principles around which state *and* nonstate actors build a new consensus. The capacity to build trust among mixed actors, as opposed to continuing international life under a *laissez-faire* culture predicated on giving states maximal freedom to pursue egoistic interests, will be decisive. But building trust among a welter of state and nonstate actors with multiple loyalties will be difficult. We contend that it must begin on a basis of reciprocity, and subsequently include a sense of common identity.[16]

Which will be the primary organizing principle of world politics in the future, a *network* of global governance composed of state and nonstate actors that gives voice to people who would otherwise be unrepresented, or an *anarchy* of sovereign territorial states? We ask you to join us in contemplating what is preferable, and urge you to evaluate our arguments in favor of rejecting many elements of the Westphalian system. Much of the world has become disenchanted with the culture of mistrust engendered by the Westphalian order and has begun to recover faith in cosmopolitan values. Human civilization has clearly evolved, and the hope expressed by Immanuel Kant in his late eighteenth century essay, *Idea for a Universal History with a Cosmopolitan Purpose,* is now emerging.[17] As Robert Wright observes, "In the long run, over millennia, the worldwide trend has been toward consolidation, toward higher and higher levels of political organization."[18] In the larger scheme of things, trend may indeed be destiny. Given this cultural trajectory, it seems to us that the time has come to cease thinking about the waging of war in Westphalian concepts and to begin thinking about the waging of peace with a cosmopolitan perspective. We invite our readers to consider with us the question on which this book centers, namely, if it is now time to exorcise the ghost of Westphalia and pursue an alternative formula for building an enduring world order. We contend that there "is need for a new synthesis that can make possible an informed public discourse about those matters in terms that are both realistic and responsible."[19]

CHAPTER 6

Challenges to World Order at the Dawn of the Twenty-First Century

> *A novel redistribution of power among states, markets and civil society is under-*
> *way ending the steady accumulation of power in the hands of states that began*
> *with the Peace of Westphalia in 1648.*
>
> —Jessica T. Mathews

The Peace of Westphalia codified political developments that had been evolving for many years. In place of the medieval ideal of a hierarchically ordered universal society, the settlement negotiated at Münster and Osnabrück inaugurated a decentralized *laissez-faire* system of autonomous states. As we have seen in the previous chapter, many of the elements of this system—sovereignty, *raison d'état* (reason of state), and balance of power—predated the peace settlement of 1648. But because they were welded together in a new structure of world order, the settlement has been called "a statutory landmark" in the growth of public international law.[1]

According to the logic underpinning the Peace of Westphalia, the governments of sovereign states possessed exclusive jurisdiction over their respective territories. Although they might negotiate voluntary agreements with one another on matters of common concern, uncertainty over the promises voiced by others often led them to forgo mutually beneficial collaboration. Equals in the eyes of international law, they did not always match up evenly on the battlefield. Together, uncertainty and material inequality reinforced self-help behavior. Rather than pursuing long-term benefits that would accrue from consistent cooperation, ruggedly independent states jockeyed for immediate gains to enhance their relative power and status. The atmosphere was polluted with mistrust.

In an anarchic world, where self-interested governments continually vie for advantage, problems that defy unilateral solutions will fester. So long as foreign policy difficulties arise infrequently, remain uncoupled, and involve few stake holders, "going it alone" may appear attractive, especially for those who are confident in their skills and strength. But as challenges multiply, become intertwined, and cross many national frontiers, the logic of unilateralism weakens. Noting how profoundly international affairs have changed since the end of the Thirty Years' War, many scholars question Westphalia's capacity to make a constructive contribution to world order in the twenty-first century. Richard Falk, for example, has complained that the Westphalian system of world order seems unable to address humanity's vital needs: "It no longer provides sufficient security against attack, nor permits reasonable progress in attaining social and economic justice; it cannot protect the environment from deterioration, or satisfactorily allocate and conserve the scarce minerals and resources that will be taken from the oceans."[2]

Every historical period is marked to some extent by change. However, the pace of change seems more rapid today and its consequences more destabilizing than ever.[3] The shock of these disruptive changes has raised anew the ageless problem of how to build the modicum of order on which peace and justice depend. New conditions call for new responses. However, as has been argued in Parts I and II of this book, most peace plans today draw their inspiration from the Westphalian blueprint for international order. The vocabulary in contemporary discourse about the global future is laden with concepts that arose in the wake of the Thirty Years' War. Indeed, the chief legacy of the Peace of Westphalia is that it still structures most thinking about the code of diplomatic conduct that should govern world politics. The irony is that the Westphalian principles were deficient for preserving peace even during the century in which they were formulated, because they legitimized the drive for power and position rather than providing a substitute for military self-help. The major clauses of the Westphalian treaties implicitly accepted a free-floating political struggle for predominance among competitive sovereign states and only vaguely "hint[ed] at the intention to establish a more permanent international order or system."[4] Westphalia made the idea of a balance of power "the ruling concept in international politics."[5] In retrospect, the Westphalian blueprint has failed as a formula for international peace because peace was never the primary objective of the balance of power. Survival of the members of the state system was the goal, and to survive it was assumed that wars would have to be fought, especially to block states with hegemonic ambitions. Westphalia "did not lead to greater stability nor to the supremacy of right above might. On the contrary, it led to the introduction of political interest as a leading principal of international relations."[6]

We contend that the ghost of Westphalia needs to be exorcised. In its place, a new set of rules for international relations and a new security architecture should be constructed. The cogency of this conclusion will depend, of course, on the defining properties of the global future: "The question is whether the Grotian scheme will still do the trick in whatever becomes of the new world order of the twenty-first century."[7] In order to evaluate the feasibility of a neo-Grotian model of twenty-first century world order, we need to first identify the major trends that are shaping the global future which any post-Westphalian security regime must manage. Toward that end, in this chapter we shall examine two sets of trends that are shaping our global future. The first set is integrative: globalization, democratization, and humanitarianism are deterritorializing much of the political landscape. The once impermeable, hard-shell boundaries separating states have become porous. Channels of contact among distant peoples have grown exponentially, owing to an unprecedented revolution in information technology. The world of the past, writes Thomas Friedman, "was chopped up, and both threats and opportunities tended to grow out of whom you were divided from." Today, threats and opportunities grow out of "whom you are connected with." In short, "we have gone from a system built around walls to a system increasingly built around networks."[8]

INTEGRATIVE TRENDS THAT ARE TRANSFORMING WORLD POLITICS

Unlike the governments of sovereign states, networks are not wedded to an established chain of command or a fixed geographic space. They contain multiple nodes of interaction, where different combinations of people coalesce for different purposes. "After three and a half centuries," suggests Jessica Mathews, "it takes a big mental leap to think of world politics in any terms other than that of occasionally cooperating but usually competing states." Yet "states may simply no longer be the natural problem-solving unit."[9] Globalism, democratization, and humanitarianism are reducing the relevance of the Westphalian territorial state in world politics during the new millennium.

Globalization and the Erosion of State Sovereignty

Until the fifteenth century, most civilizations remained relatively isolated from one another. Circumscribed by slow, costly, and often dangerous transportation routes, international intercourse tended to occur within self-contained regions of the world.[10] Except for intermittent trade, occasional waves of migrants, and periodic clashes with invaders, contact with distant peoples was rare.

What distinguishes contemporary world politics from earlier eras is its global scope. As suggested by the various definitions provided in Box 6.1, globalization can be understood as a set of processes that are widening, deepening, and accelerating worldwide interconnectedness. It is a multifaceted phenomenon that produces complex networks of exchange which are not solely organized according to any territorial principle.[11] Rather than being the endpoint of a uniform linear evolution, globalization involves several distinct types of activity, each with its own temporal and geographical dynamics. Sometimes events in one area of activity affect another, sometimes not; consequently the process of globalization is uneven both in intensity and geographic breadth.[12]

Robert T. Kudrle distinguishes among three domains of globalization: the first pertains to the staggering growth in worldwide telecommunication; the second, to the increased mobility of goods and services, capital, and labor; and the third, to the burgeoning number of environmental problems like acid rain, deforestation, and global warming that cross national borders.[13] Let us examine each of these phenomena in turn.

BOX 6.1
Defining Globalization

"Globalization" is a trendy word whose meaning is not self-evident. As with any term that refers to more than one type of process, it can connote different things to different people. Listed below are some representative examples of how globalization has been defined.

Globalization refers to processes whereby social relations acquire relatively distanceless and borderless qualities, so that human lives are increasingly played out in the world as a single place.
—Jan Aart Schote

[Globalization is] a gradual and ongoing expansion of interaction processes, forms of organization, and forms of cooperation outside the traditional spaces defined by sovereignty.
—Victor D. Cha

By globalization we simply mean the process of increasing interconnectedness between societies such that events in one part of the world more and more have effects on peoples and societies far away.
—Steve Smith and John Baylis

[Globalization involves] the compression of the world and the intensification of consciousness of the world as a whole.
—Roland Robertson

Globalization means the increasing scale and importance of exchanges of people, products, services, capital and ideas across international borders.
—Byron G. Auguste

Communication Globalization. Recent advances in information technology underpin perhaps the most striking form of globalization. Satellite broadcasting and the Internet have obviated the spatial distance separating the peoples of our planet, linking ever more humans in an electronic virtual community. Sounds and images from distant lands can now be experienced as events unfold. In addition, cellular phones, fax machines, and e-mail give a worldwide audience the opportunity to communicate with participants in those events. Not long ago, the quickest way to inform others of important happenings was to send a handwritten letter by ship or mounted courier. Today millions of people are connected by fiber-optic networks, giving them instantaneous access to myriad computer bulletin boards, chat rooms, and databases. Tomorrow they are likely to be connected by wireless systems based on low earth orbit satellites and High Altitude Long Endurance (HALE) platforms.[14] For some futurologists, this telecommunications revolution is turning the planet into a vast "global village," where everyone will share a common supranational identity. For others, however, it is creating a "global metropolis" that lacks the social intimacy of a well-integrated community.[15]

Regardless of whether humanity eventually lives in a global village or a global metropolis, the telecommunications revolution is radically changing existing power structures. "Borders," writes the former president of Citibank, "are no longer barriers to information."[16] As the torrent of online information ruptures one national frontier after the next, the significance of territorial sovereignty will erode. "The same information superhighway that moves the currencies of the global economy around the planet at the speed of light," insists former U.S. Deputy Secretary of State Strobe Talbott, "also transports the ideas and images of freedom across the boundaries of politics and ideology."[17] By providing immediate access to the outside world, modern communications technology has weakened the control that states previously held over the dissemination of information while facilitating transnational contacts among people.

The domestic implications of communication globalization are not lost on governments. Fax machines provided a steady stream of outside information to the opponents of the attempted 1991 coup against Mikhail Gorbachev in the former Soviet Union. Cellular phones helped Thailand's pro-democracy movement remain organized in 1992 when the military regime repressed its members. As these examples illustrate, "globalization has ended the nation-state's monopoly over internal sovereignty, which was formerly guaranteed by territory."[18] Although reestablishing state control over the flow of information across national borders will not be easy, several governments have tried. During the 1980s, for example, leaders from various less developed countries called for a New World Information and Communication Order (NWICO) to stem what they saw as a deluge of images from the industrialized world promoting crass commercial values that were perceived as alien to their local, indigenous traditions. Roughly a decade later, Saudi Arabia banned satellite dishes and the People's Republic of China sought to restrict access to the Internet.

The telecommunications revolution is still in its infancy, and its impact during the twenty-first century remains difficult to predict. Nevertheless, certain patterns are already clear. First, communication globalization is decreasing the relevance of geographic location for service providers. The Information Age has produced what may be termed without fear of exaggeration, "the death of distance." This sea change is rapidly making every place more like every place else, making news anyplace instantaneously news every place. Nor is there an end in sight to the universalization of information: "Computing power has doubled every eighteen months for the past thirty years. . . . Similarly growth of the Internet and the World Wide Web has been exponential. Internet traffic doubles every 100 days."[19] As the infrastructure for rapidly transmitting heavy streams of multimedia traffic improves, international outsourcing will expand to include a wide array of financial, managerial, and technical activities. If global telecommunications continue developing along these lines, clients could bypass service providers within their own countries and contract with a matrix of professionals from around the world.

A second emerging pattern is the rising importance of what Joseph Nye calls "soft power."[20] As it is traditionally understood, power refers to the capacity to control the behavior of others: a powerful state can make a target continue some course of action, change what it is doing, or refrain from acting. National leaders have long assumed that the capacity to control others is a function of the resources they possessed, especially those military assets that enhanced their war-fighting capability. While military prowess remains a key source of national strength, "soft" co-optive power is becoming more important because the costs of using coercion are higher today than they were during earlier, less economically interdependent periods. Soft power, the ability to shape the preferences of others through the attraction of one's culture and ideas, is easier to exercise in the Information Age where knowledge becomes, truly, power. Those who control information, as well as those who control access to information and who enjoy stature as producers of information and ideas, have clear-cut advantages in international bargaining over those whose major source of influence is confined to the threat to use armed force. Hence, more and more states are investing in nonmilitary methods of obtaining soft power, under the assumption that "if a state can make its power legitimate in the eyes of others and establish international institutions that encourage others to define their interests in compatible ways, it may not need to expend as many costly traditional economic and military resources."[21]

Finally, a third pattern born of the telecommunications revolution involves an increased difficulty for governments to maintain a consistent agenda of priorities.[22] Many national leaders have grumbled about a "CNN-effect," the alleged capacity of round-the-clock news services to highlight certain issues by immediately televising heart-wrenching scenes of famine, atrocities, and other human tragedies to millions of viewers throughout the world. When combined with the use of electronic mail by grassroots activists to mobilize people in other countries quickly on a particular issue, governments may find their formerly low-priority problems (such as global warming or preservation of rain forests) rising in importance, and the time for deliberation reduced.

Economic Globalization.   In the years immediately following the Peace of Westphalia, many states sought to increase their power by acquiring additional territory. Aside from territory that held precious metals or offered access to navigable waterways, the most valuable land in an age without refrigeration contained cereal grains, a source of food with sufficient nutrition to sustain peasants as well as people not engaged in agriculture. Rulers who wished to exercise independent power needed high-yield crops that could be easily transported and stored. Exotic spices and oils might command higher prices than wheat, barley, oats, or rye, but these cereal grains were staples that could be grown in Europe and did not depend upon distant suppliers and dangerous trade routes.

With the onset of the Industrial Revolution, capital increased in value as a factor of production, although the demand for coal, iron ore, and later oil continued to underscore the importance of land. Only after World War II did some states shift their emphasis from territorial expansion through military conquest to international commerce. These "trading states" recognized that manufactured goods were more mobile than capital or labor, and that expanding exports would fuel economic growth.[23] Soon they also realized that exporting was only one path to prosperity; products could be designed at home but produced abroad for both foreign and domestic markets. Not only would labor costs decline, but shifting manufacturing overseas reduced the likelihood of foreign tariffs.

Offshore manufacturing can be carried out in several ways. First, a corporation can forge an alliance with a foreign firm to make its products through temporary co-production agreements. Second, it can merge with the foreign firm to realize more advantageous economies of scale. Third, it can eschew partnerships or mergers and establish an overseas subsidiary. Finally, it may set up a production facility and contract with foreign companies to manufacture according to their specifications. According to Richard Rosecrance, this kind of interdependence of production creates far stronger bonds than an interdependence of trade. In his opinion, we are entering a world where individual states "cannot guarantee favorable economic outcomes for their peoples . . . [without cooperating] with foreign factors of production economically and with other states politically."[24] It is a world where traditional territorial considerations will be less important than an educated populace, where holding stocks of goods will be less important than having access to their flows, and where parochial national interests "become less important than the international economy as a whole."[25]

For Rosecrance, the most influential states in the twenty-first century will be "virtual states," those with the financial and managerial skills to create products, provide services, and control assets elsewhere. Signs of virtualization in the world economic system abound. At present, we find an unusual mixture of technology from the late twentieth century, arguments for free trade that are reminiscent of the nineteenth, and a rebirth of the kind of centers typical of world trade during the Middle Ages.[26] Consider the following example. Computer programmers in Beijing who are employed by an American firm revise the software on a computer system in Seattle. Once they have gone home for the evening, programmers in India add several refinements, which are further modified by a Latvian task force after the Indians have ended their work day. By the time the Chinese return to the project the next morning, the software has also been edited by programmers in Canada. In short, technology is changing our conceptions of time and space. Interlaced electronic networks, market segmentation, flexible production systems, and matrix organizations raise the question of whether it is meaningful to continue thinking of geography as a basis for organizing economic activities. "Economic governance in the modern state system," notes Stephen Kobrin, "assumes that all transactions take place somewhere; that all income streams, production, sales loans and currency exchanges can be located precisely in geographic space." With the emergence of a digitalized global economy, however, the boundary between domestic and international transactions is "becoming ambiguous and blurred."[27]

Economic globalization, insists Susan Strange, is no myth.[28] Rather than goods and services being produced by and for people living within a particular territorial state, they are now increasingly produced by people in several states for world trade. Similarly, where the creation and use of credit once occurred within the societies of those states, it now emanates in global markets electronically linked into a single system. Nearly two trillion dollars are traded every day in a global foreign exchange market that is always open. As one business executive has put it: "Out-moded, nationalistic chauvinism and geocentric thinking have no place in the one-world economy."[29] As Strange elaborates, the world has left behind the Westphalian state-centric system because it is unable "to govern and control the institutions and markets that create and trade the credit instruments" essential to the twenty-first century economy.[30]

The transformation of the automobile industry illustrates the changes that undermine Westphalia's lasting usefulness. At the end of the Second World War, three American companies—General Motors, Ford, and Chrysler—dominated the world market. By the 1990s, however, American and foreign companies became intertwined by equity ownership, jointly manufacturing cars and assembling them with components from multiple countries. For example, General Motors owns half of Saab, Ford's Explorer is virtually identical to Mazda's Navajo, and DaimlerChrysler assembles its LH series in Canada with parts from several countries. In the years ahead, it will be even more difficult to determine what is a national product or a national firm. It is already very difficult for countries to levy taxes on the revenues of these truly multinational conglomerates, and calculating measures of states' balance-of-payments and balance-of-trade ratios is rapidly becoming a lost art. Countries don't trade; companies trade. And today about half of so-called "international trade" is actually the movement of goods *within* a single multinational corporation across the borders where it conducts operations.

In summary, markets no longer correspond with national boundaries. Conducting business in cyberspace compounds the problem of determining the jurisdiction in which a transaction takes place because transactions are disconnected from geography. The NASDAQ market, for example, is not a physical location like the New York, London, or Tokyo exchanges.[31] Electronic commerce is a symptom "of an increasing asymmetry between economics and politics, between an electronically integrated world economy and territorial nation-states and between cyberspace and geographic space."[32] These developments create conditions for which the Westphalian model is unsuitable as an instrument for managing global affairs.

Ecological Globalization.   Many scholars use the Peace of Westphalia to mark the transition from feudalism to modern nation-states. According to Dennis Pirages, the three centuries following the end of the Thirty Years' War also "produced a new international order predicated upon rapid growth and the expansion of Western European economic and political dominance."[33] During this period, world population increased eightfold, fossil fuel consumption rose from nearly nothing to more then seven billion metric tons of coal equivalent annually, and the use of nonfuel minerals skyrocketed. Demographic pressures combined with resource-intensive industrialization to place enormous stress on the global environment. By the end of the twentieth century, sustainable yield thresholds for many natural resources were in danger of being crossed, which would result in a depletion of the resource base itself. Simultaneously, the absorptive capacities of the world's atmosphere and oceans were becoming overwhelmed by pollution, which caused biodiversity loss. As the Worldwatch Institute summarized the situation: "Forests are shrinking, water tables are falling, soils are eroding, wetlands are deteriorating, rivers are running dry, temperatures are rising, coral reefs are dying, and plant and animal species are disappearing."[34] Environmental degradation foreshadows scarcity, and, as Richard Barnet warns: "A world of scarcity is a world of inevitable struggle."[35]

Some of these environmental problems are localized and can be addressed through unilateral action. Yet many others span the boundaries between existing states and require either bilateral or multilateral action. For example, sulfur oxide emissions from industries in one country may fall as acid rain on a neighboring land. Greenhouse gas emissions (carbon dioxide, chlorofluorocarbons, methane, and nitrous oxide) from numerous countries may contribute to global climate warming, which could disrupt weather patterns across the planet and expose coastal lowlands everywhere to the threat of rising seas. The political world may be a checkerboard of sovereign states, but the natural world is a seamless web. "All things are connected," Chief Seattle of the Suquamish tribe once told the U.S. government. "Man did not weave the web of life; he is merely a strand in it. Whatever he does to the web, he does to himself."[36] For those who acknowledge this interconnectedness, the "emergence of major environmental problems and efforts to address them call into question in a very radical way the modern Westphalian sovereignty system."[37] Damage to airsheds and other components of the ecosystem often transcend national jurisdictions; hence concerted international efforts are needed to cope with these long-term problems.

Because damage caused by environmental degradation accumulates slowly, is unequally distributed, and remedies remain expensive, many states— still wedded to the Westphalian conception of sovereign autonomy— hesitate to join environmental-preservation efforts unless they are sure that others will act as well. The atmosphere and oceans are common-pool resources: controlling access by potential users is difficult, negligent users decrease the value of the resource for everyone, and protecting the resource yields benefits that are available to all regardless of whether or not they help pay the costs of preservation. As a result, countries are tempted to be free riders, negotiating treaties that "reflect the lowest common denominator of perceived interests" that "maximize the responsibilities of other nations while minimizing their own obligations."[38]

Ever since the Peace of Westphalia, states have been understood to possess sovereign rights over their natural resources. Questions regarding environmental degradation were a national matter. Indeed, many rulers viewed land, airspace, and territorial waters as elements of their own private estates, with which they could do as they pleased. Over the past few decades, however, these territorial rights have been tempered by two international norms: the first directs states to not use their territory in ways that adversely affect others; the second enjoins them to warn others if some activity under their jurisdiction has caused an environmental danger.

The norm that "no State has the right to use or permit the use of territory in such a manner as to cause injury . . . to the territory of another"[39] draws upon the ancient Roman maxim *sic utere tuo ut alienum non laedas* (one must use his own so as not to injure others). As expressed by Principle 21 of the Stockholm Declaration from the 1972 United Nations Conference on the Human Environment: "States have in accordance with the Charter of the United Nations and the principles of international law, the sovereign right to exploit their own resources pursuant to their own environmental policies, and the responsibility to insure that activities within their jurisdiction or control do not cause damage to the environment of other states or of areas beyond the limits of national jurisdiction."[40] Frequently, pursuing the former clashes with the latter. Given the tension between state sovereignty and ecosystem integrity, globalization poses a major problem for the progressive development of international environmental law.

The norm that states have a right to be warned of known dangers can be traced to the *Corfu Channel* adjudication (United Kingdom *v.* Albania, 1949) and the *Lac Lanoux* arbitration (France *v.* Spain, 1957). Applying the norm to the world's oceans, Article 19 of the 1982 Law of the Sea Convention provides that "where a state becomes aware of cases in which the marine environment is in imminent danger of being damaged or has been damaged by pollution, it shall immediately notify other states likely to be affected by such damage." Nonstate actors are now playing greater roles in making the environmental actions of states more transparent. By some estimates, the total number of environmental nongovernmental organizations (NGOs) runs into six figures.[41] They have served as "information-brokers," disseminating research on potential environmental hazards, and as "whistle-blowers" who monitor the implementation of environmental treaties. Still, national governments vary enormously in their commitment to international institutions aimed at promoting environmental protection. Nor do these institutions seem adequately equipped. "Getting action in the United Nations," a diplomat once complained, "is like the mating of elephants. It takes place at a very high level, with an enormous amount of huffing and puffing, raises a tremendous amount of dust, and nothing happens for at least 23 months."[42] As one observer has pessimistically concluded, "It is difficult to conceive of circumstances in which states would be willing to relinquish or pool their sovereignty to substantially strengthen global institutions charged with mounting a more effective response to the deepening environmental crisis confronting humanity."[43] Here again, the Westphalian formula acts as a barrier to the successful management of collective problems.

Democratization and the Emergence of Global Civil Society

A second integrative trend in contemporary world politics is the spread of democratic governments across the planet. The surge in democracy has come in three waves.[44] Led by the founding of the United States, the first wave culminated with the establishment of democratic regimes in countries carved out of the Austro-Hungarian, German, and Russian empires after World War I. The second wave began with the defeat of the Axis powers in World War II and continued until the early 1960s. Finally, the third wave of democratization started with the collapse of authoritarian rule on the Iberian Peninsula and spread through Latin America, Africa, and parts of the former Soviet bloc.

Of course, democracy can be reversed. Authoritarianism briefly returned to Italy and Germany following the first wave; it took hold for a short time in Argentina, Brazil, and Peru after the second wave; and, most recently, it has reemerged in many of the former Soviet republics. However, several democratic states and liberal nonstate actors have attempted to arrest future reversals. Most conspicuously, of course, have been the European Union, NATO, OSCE, and Group-of-Eight (G-8), which made liberal democracy and civil rights requirements for membership. In addition, the World Bank and the International Monetary Fund have designated democratic reform as a condition for loans and developmental assistance, and in its 1991 *Santiago Commitment to Democracy and the Renewal of the Inter-American System*, the Organization of American States supported the policy of exporting democracy. Finally, in its 1993 Bottom-Up Review and its 1994 National Security Strategy of Engagement and Enlargement, the Clinton Administration called for using American military power to guarantee the results of free elections.[45]

The significance of this trend lies in the possibility of building a global civil society. Recent research has found that while democratic states have been involved in foreign conflict as frequently as nondemocratic states and are only slightly less likely than nondemocratic states to initiate wars, democracies almost never wage war against one another.[46] The flood of scholarly literature on the virtual absence of war among constitutionally secure democracies indicates that conflict-resolution practices used at home are also employed when dealing with international disputes. Leaders socialized within democratic political cultures share a common outlook that stresses tolerance, compromise, and a non-zero-sum view of politics. Viewing international politics as an extension of domestic politics, they externalize their norms of regulated competition. Disputes with kindred governments rarely escalate to war because each side accepts the other's legitimacy and expects it to rely on peaceful means of conflict resolution. These expectations are reinforced by the transparent nature of democracies.[47] The inner workings of open polities can be scrutinized by anyone harboring doubts about the way disputes are resolved within their borders; hence it is difficult to demonize them as outgroup enemies.[48] In contrast, autocratic regimes do not offer potential critics an unobstructed view of their domestic conduct, and actively shield from view the processes by which decisions are reached regarding foreign and domestic policies.

As the proportion of democracies in the world passes a certain threshold, norms of nonviolent conflict resolution may cascade through the international system, superseding the Westphalian justifications for the right of states to use force to resolve disputes. A critical mass of democratic states, argue Zeev Maoz and Bruce Russett, might make it possible to construct a new world order, radically different from the Hobbesian state of perpetual war that has existed for the past three-and-a-half centuries. If every country became a stable democracy, the standards of behavior that developed in the seventeenth century when the state system was populated by autocracies could undergo dramatic change.[49] Major democratic states would function as norm entrepreneurs, using their resources, expertise, and moral stature to persuade others that the old order should be overhauled. Once a sufficient number of states agree, more might follow suit, which would result in a greater percentage of the system's membership embracing nonviolent norms of conflict resolution, therein triggering yet another round of adoptions, and so on.

This transformation, if it takes root, could alter the previous pattern of interstate diplomacy since the Peace of Westphalia. Competition and military confrontation, endemic for the past 350 years, could be replaced by a system in which cooperation and compromise between democratic states become routinized, anchored by the security resulting from democracies' ability to resolve their disputes at the bargaining table instead of on the battlefield. Moreover, just as public policies in democratic states are molded by interest groups and voluntary associations that are not agencies of the state, global public policies may be increasingly shaped by transnational federations of nongovernmental organizations, such as Amnesty International, EarthAction, and Médicins sans Frontières. Preliminary signs of the emergence of a global civil society can be seen in several of the world conferences organized by the United Nations over the past decade. For example, at the 1992 UN Conference on Ecology and Development, representatives from over 1,400 nongovernmental organizations showed up in Rio de Janeiro to lobby the assembled heads of state. A year later in Vienna, some 3,000 representatives took part in the UN Conference on Human Rights. The figure climbed to almost 4,000 NGO representatives attending the 1994 International Conference on Population and Development in Cairo.[50] What is more, nongovernmental organizations have begun to convene global fora that run parallel to official United Nations conferences, where they frame the discussion of the policy problem in question and articulate recommended solutions.

At the beginning of the twenty-first century, more than 27,000 NGOs were active, worldwide, "influencing decisions and helping to set agendas that were once determined solely by governments."[51] Since most nongovernmental organizations are embedded within national societies, the development of a global civil society may depend on having a growing number of constitutionally secure democracies that are congenial to transnational political participation by voluntary associations. One trend is very clear, therefore: NGOs are sapping the traditional authority monopolized since Westphalia by sovereign states. Any objective reading of contemporary global circumstances must take account of the rising influence of NGOs; to view the world as only consisting of territorial states each exercising supreme authority within its borders is no longer accurate.[52]

Humanitarianism and the Decay of the Nonintervention Principle

The third integrative trend shaping world politics can be found in the rising emphasis on humanitarian intervention. In the aftermath of the Peace of Westphalia, most national leaders claimed that reason of state, not moral considerations, should guide foreign policy. Statesmen were said to be driven by forces beyond their control, forces that compelled them to advance national security interests even when their actions contravened the ethical standards most people follow in their daily lives. As the seventeenth-century scholar Daniel de Priezac put it: if while conducting foreign policy something happens contrary to ethical principle, "it is not a crime of will but of necessity whose laws are most harsh and commands most cruel."[53]

Since the end of the Cold War, a different conception of necessity has entered into debates about world affairs. Rather than defending the resort to arms on the grounds of strategic necessities entailed by *raison d'état* (reason of state), it is repeatedly justified nowadays in terms of a categorical moral imperative to stop brutal governments from violating the human rights of their citizens. As one champion of this point of view (echoing Hugo Grotius's justification for humanitarian intervention) has insisted, the military defeat of rulers who initiate massacres "is a moral necessity."[54] It is an absolute duty, one that holds at all times and in all places, regardless of whether it advances the strategic interests of the intervening state.

Allowing the use of coercion by one state to modify the authority structure in another state would significantly transform the normative climate of world politics. Ever since the Thirty Years' War, the twin principles of sovereignty and nonintervention have underpinned international relations. The only widely accepted exception to the prohibition against interfering in the domestic affairs of other nation-states was military intervention to liberate one's own nationals when they were being held hostage. What is noteworthy about recent appeals to moral necessity is they do not focus on whether the suffering are the intervening state's own citizens. As expressed in Article 7 of the Universal Declaration of Human Responsibilities, proposed by the InterAction Council of twenty-four former heads of state from five different continents: "Every person is infinitely precious and must be protected unconditionally." When massive human rights violations occur, "intervention from the outside is not only legally justified but morally required."[55]

The argument supporting the claim that it is permissible to intervene with armed force in order to stop egregious violations of human rights rests on three propositions. The first proposition asserts that human rights are an international entitlement. Article 55 (c) of the United Nations Charter requires member states to promote "universal respect for, and observance of, human rights." Over the past fifty years, the UN has developed a detailed list of inherent, inalienable rights of all human beings. The most important legal formulation of these rights is expressed in the so-called International Bill of Human Rights, the informal name given to the Universal Declaration of Human Rights (which was passed by a vote of the UN General Assembly in 1948), the International Covenant on Civil and Political Rights, and the International Covenant on Economic, Social, and Cultural Rights (which were both opened for signature in 1966 and entered into force a decade later). The legal rules governing these rights are regarded as *jus cogens* —peremptory norms from which no derogation is permitted.

The second proposition maintains that governments committing grave violations of human rights lose their legitimacy. Although Article 2 (7) of the UN Charter prevents member states from interfering in the "domestic matters" of one another, the Charter's legal protection does not extend to genocide, torture, or other horrific acts shocking to the conscience of the international community. As one legal theorist has expressed it, any government involved in egregious human rights abuses "betrays the very purpose for which it exists and so forfeits not only its domestic legitimacy, but its international legitimacy as well."[56] By forfeiting its political legitimacy, adds another scholar, it becomes an international outlaw—a rogue state that "forfeits the protection of international law."[57]

The third proposition declares that the international community has a legal responsibility to stop human rights violations. According to the International Court of Justice in the *Barcelona Traction Case*, there are some obligations that a state has "towards the international community as a whole," and all members of that community "have a legal interest in their protection." Advocates of humanitarian intervention maintain that the entitlement for protection against genocide, slavery, and the like gives rise to these legal obligations *erga omnes*. Since under this doctrine any member of the international community has legal standing to call for a state to observe these obligations and to impose sanctions if wrongful acts continue, it introduces "a vertical legislative element and a decentralized enforcement regime" to world politics.[58] As such, it represents a significant step away from the Westphalian normative order.

DISINTEGRATIVE TRENDS THAT ARE TRANSFORMING WORLD POLITICS

According to one eminent British diplomat, the era of the strong state began in 1648 and is now being replaced by a post-modern system of overlapping roles and responsibilities with governments, international institutions, and various nonstate actors all involved. Whereas a zone of safety exists among the participants in this open, transnational system, elsewhere people face danger and chaos.[59] As Max Singer and Aaron Wildavsky describe it, beyond the peaceful world of mass, high-wealth democracies lies "an immense, slowly boiling cauldron, agitated by powerful internal forces."[60]

Two trends that have led various observers to characterize much of the world as a zone of turmoil are the implosion of what have been called "failed states" and the rise of parochialism. Disagreement abounds over the causes of these disintegrative trends, as well as over their long-range implications.

The Implosion of Failed States

The Peace of Westphalia marked the "coming of age" of the state system,[61] a time when general rules of behavior were set forth to solidify a new international order. Far from eradicating warfare, however, these rules merely articulated when it was appropriate to wage war and how to fight. By one count, sixty-three wars involving great powers occurred between the Westphalian settlement and the end of World War II, with almost one-third pitting great powers against each other.[62] Although great powers continued to engage in armed conflict with lesser powers after the Second World War, they did not go to war against one another. The years since 1945 entail the longest period of great-power peace since the birth of the modern state system.[63]

While the great powers avoided testing each other's strength in head-to-head combat, proxy wars between their clients, foreign interventions, and hostilities among minor powers continued to plague the peripheral regions of the international system.[64] More deadly have been civil wars. The carnage from *intra*state wars has eclipsed that of *inter*state wars, causing torrents of refugees to stream across national frontiers in search of sanctuary. The UN High Commissioner for Refugees estimates that between 1960 and 1999 more than 350 million refugees had crossed state borders and another 56 million "displaced people" were uprooted from their homes and forced to live as persecuted members of their own countries.[65] By the end of the twentieth century (like the chaotic state-formation process in the violent seventeenth century), civil war had become the most frequent, lethal, and protracted form of organized violence in world politics.

Age-old hatreds are often blamed for this tragedy,[66] but the sources of civil war are far more complex. Whereas a *nation* is a collection of people who, on the basis of ethnic, linguistic, or cultural affinity, perceive themselves to be members of the same group, according to international law a *state* is a legal entity that possesses a permanent population, a defined territory, a functioning government, and the capacity to engage in formal relations with other states. Although the term "nation-state" combines the concepts of "nation" and "state," as Figure 6.1 illustrates, most states contain many nations, and some nations overlap the borders between different states. Indeed, one study found that only nine percent of the world's nation-states are ethnically homogeneous.[67]

FIGURE 6.1   Configurations of Nations and States
Few nation-states are ethnically homogeneous. In the year 2000, ethnographers estimated that there were 3,000 to 5,000 indigenous peoples sharing a common ancestral heritage and language living within 207 sovereign nation-states.
Sources: Center for World Indigenous Peoples, 2000; Davis, 1999; Enriquez, 1999.

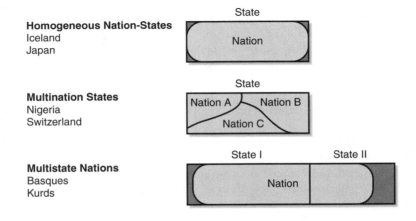

The choice of an official language, the location of educational institutions, and even decisions on where to construct new roads or bridges may be seen as conferring unfair advantages on one group or another in multinational states. Perceived inequalities in the government's allocation of benefits can activate previously unmobilized groups, igniting fierce competition and separatist demands. Distributional conflicts are common in nation-states characterized by cultural pluralism, especially when they contain two or more homelands for different ethnopolitical groups. People living within an ancestral homeland tend to exhibit greater animosity toward other citizens of the same multinational state.[68] When urbanization and industrialization bring them into close proximity, demagogues may attempt to exploit lingering resentment and orchestrate savage confrontations. The likelihood of violence is greatest if a people who strongly identify with their ethnic brethren live within a poor, autocratic multinational state and have experienced chronic discrimination and intermittent repression.[69]

Ethnic, religious, and regional schisms within multinational states are just a few potential sources of civil war. As the fratricidal conflict in Cambodia demonstrates, civil wars can occur in states without deep ethnic fissures. Economic deprivation brought on by corruption or mismanagement, as well as scarcities in fuel, water, and land, may also provoke internal rebellion.[70] By simply attributing collective violence on the periphery of the international system to atavistic antagonisms within divided states, cleavages created by economic, demographic, and environmental hardships can be overlooked.

In summary, civil wars stem from a wide range of conditions and they frequently resist negotiated settlement. As the fighting persists, countries are torn into smaller units anchored in gang, clan, or other primordial affiliations. As illustrated by recent events in Somalia and Liberia, under these conditions government atrophies to the point that it is incapable of caring for its citizens and fulfilling its obligation to maintain law and order. In these failed states, much of the territory shown on standard maps escapes central control. Beyond the core districts of major cities lie rings of shanty towns and a countryside divided among an unruly rabble of warlords, each with his own private militia. To Robert Kaplan, the civil strife in these regions resembles the premodern formlessness of the European battlefield prior to the Peace of Westphalia.[71] If this trend toward state disintegration continues, separatism and secession could, as U.S. President Bill Clinton warned in Ottawa a few years ago, result in as many as 800, and possibly even 8,000, states.[72]

The Reassertion of Parochialism

From the Enlightenment onward, the Western world has professed faith in a credo of progress. Among its tenets is a belief in the directionality of change. History moves forward. Advances in knowledge and technology would usher in a brighter future. Some writers described this great ascent as a rising spiral; others, as an upwardly oscillating process alternating between innovations and temporary regressions; and still others, as a dialectical struggle moving through certain developmental stages. Despite their variations, a progressive linear trend underpins each description.[73]

Unlike most theorists who propose linear interpretations of human destiny, Francis Fukuyama proclaims that we are now at "the end of history."[74] With the collapse of communism, ideological conflicts are receding into the past. In his opinion, Western democratic polities and market economies are now the only viable alternatives for modern societies. As U.S. President Bill Clinton assured the leaders of the world's industrial powers at a conference in Denver on June 19, 1997, "globalism is irreversible."

From some vantage points, globalism appears neither inevitable nor benevolent; it looks like a hegemony. Whether it is French intellectuals complaining that the Disney theme park on the outskirts of Paris constitutes a "cultural Chernobyl" or irate farmers protesting against opening Kentucky Fried Chicken restaurants in India, many people detest the vision of "one McWorld tied together by communications, information, entertainment, and commerce."[75] For them, a vile uniformity threatens to displace cultural distinctions and destroy traditional local values.

In contrast to the claim that an amalgamated global culture is emerging in the wake of the Cold War, Samuel Huntington submits that modernization and Westernization do not travel in tandem.[76] While technological innovations from the Silicon Valley rapidly diffuse throughout the world, the individualist values of Western democratic thought face stern opposition. "History is not at an end," adds Raymond Aron. We live in an age of contradictions: "the means of production perfected by science and technology, although they possess universalist potentials and do in fact tend to spread over the continents, divide humanity as much as they unite it." They "have brought the scattered parts of the human race closer together physically," but they have not sown the seeds of community.[77]

According to Huntington, the fundamental source of conflict in the future will be a clash of civilizations. As he sees it, world politics will be shaped by the interaction of seven or eight major civilizations: the Western, Confucian, Japanese, Islamic, Hindu, Slavic-Orthodox, Latin American, and possibly the African civilization. Acknowledging that the lines separating civilizations are seldom sharp, he predicts that wrenching conflicts will occur either in "cleft countries" (states with large populations belonging to different civilizations) or along the "fault lines" that separate civilizations.

Of course, such clashes were not unknown in the seventeenth century, as evidenced by the protracted hostilities between the Hapsburg and Ottoman Empires. Certainly, cultural differences between people can generate friction and frustrate efforts to resolve disputes. But there is scant evidence that they cause war by themselves. Nor is there evidence that collective loyalties are shifting from the nation to whole civilizations. Instead, they appear to be turning toward smaller ethnic units, which, as the civil war in Rwanda demonstrates, can descend into genocide even though the parties belong to the same civilization. Rather than fostering solidarity within civilizations spanning the periphery of the international system, the cultural strains brought on by the spread of secular Western values are fomenting a resurgence of parochialism.

People engulfed by modernization are often perplexed by the changes they witness. With traditional values under siege, they cannot always make sense out of their daily lives. Uncomfortable with social turbulence and offended by what they see as moral decline, many of them gravitate toward fundamentalism. Although the term "fundamentalism" originally pertained to a conservative Protestant movement in the United States during the nineteenth century, it now is applied to conservative movements in virtually all of the world's major religions. Of course, fundamentalism is not monolithic; there are pietist and militant strains within most movements. Yet whatever their faith, fundamentalists from the Ayatollah Ruhollah Khomeini of Iran to Hassan Turabi of the Sudan generally possess the following traits: "authoritarianism, messianic spirit, subordination of secular politics to their religious beliefs, belief in the infallibility of holy scripture, belief in the supernatural, charismatic leadership, and enforced morality."[78]

Religious fundamentalism, whether in the form of the Islamic Salvation Front in Algeria or the Bharatiya Janata Party in India, is one manifestation of a localizing reaction to global interdependence. As complex globalizing forces become more pervasive in everyday affairs, the loss of autonomy felt by many people encourages a retreat to a favorably remembered or imagined past, where orthodoxy is expected to hold the vices of modernity at bay. In many ways, the quest for timeless, spiritual values to combat the secular, homogenized commercialism of globalization reflect a desire for the kind of pre-Westphalian religious order that prevailed throughout the Middle Ages in Europe, when the distinctions between good and evil, justice and injustice, and virtue and vice seemed more clear.

BEYOND THE WESTPHALIAN MODEL OF WORLD POLITICS

Every year, the ski resort of Davos in eastern Switzerland hosts the World Economic Forum, a conference attended by selected corporate and government leaders. Between visits to the town's chic cafés and elegant boutiques, the world's rich and famous spend their time listening to speeches about international interdependence and discussing financial opportunities in a global marketplace. During the 2000 conference, several hundred protestors attempted to disrupt the meetings. Like the demonstrators who derailed the 1999 Seattle ministerial meeting of the World Trade Organization, they complained that a borderless world threatened local control over the fate of ordinary people. Globalization, they insisted, entrenches the power of the world's "haves" while marginalizing the "have-nots." Although the Davos protesters failed to shut down any meetings, their criticisms reminded conference participants of the backlash against globalization (see Box 6.2).

Protests from Seattle to Davos underscore the paradox of our age: disintegrative trends are splintering the political landscape at the very time that integrative trends are shrinking the planet. Subnational fragmentation and transnational integration are occurring simultaneously. Whereas some states are imploding and their populations are becoming more parochial, globalization, democratization, and humanitarianism are pulling people together as never before. "A new pattern of international politics is emerging," Zbigniew Brzezinski predicted a few decades ago. "The world is ceasing to be an arena in which relatively self-contained, 'sovereign,' and homogeneous nations interact." International politics "is increasingly shaped by forces whose influence or scope transcend national lines."[79]

BOX 6.2
Globalization and Inequality

Although globalization tends to be portrayed as a force that will close the gap between the world's rich and poor, many people fear that it will have the opposite effect. Below are excerpts from speeches expressing this concern that were delivered by several world leaders at the United Nations "Millennium Summit," held in New York City during September 6–8, 2000.

> *A new world order is indeed dawning. The capacity of globalization to transform our economies and societies is enormous. But, unless shaped by a value system, globalization will mean an even more lopsided world.*
>
> —Bertie Ahern
> Prime Minister, Ireland

> *Globalization and a borderless world are not a panacea for all social and economic ills. While they can reinforce the rich and powerful, they can also impoverish the weak and the vulnerable.*
>
> —Hasina Wazed
> Prime Minister, Bangladesh

> *Our world is becoming more globalised, yet at the same time more fragmented. Technological advances have brought the world closer. But they have also opened up divides between those who are able to cope with the resultant challenges, and those who lack the capacity to do so. . . . Our world risks being sharply divided between countries which are able to take advantage of globalisation and others which cannot.*
>
> —Goh Chok Tong
> Prime Minister, Singapore

We are living in the same house, whether you are developed or not developed. . . . We are saying, "Look, in the interest of all of us, let us living in the superluxurious rooms pay a bit of attention to those who are living where the pipes are leaking, or we'll all be badly affected."

—Olusegun Obasanjo
President, Nigeria

Source: http://www.un.org/millennium/webcast/statements/

To acknowlege that contradictory forces are buffeting the nation-state is not to proclaim that it is about to disappear. The actors on the world stage today are many and varied. At the time of this publication, there are 207 nation-states, over 38,000 transnational corporations (with approximately 250,000 foreign affiliates), some 250 intergovernmental organizations (IGOs), and more than 27,000 nongovernmental organizations with significant international activities.[80] Clearly, we are moving away from a world dominated by a single type of actor and toward what Oran Young has called "a mixed actor system" containing many qualitatively different types of actors.[81]

Nonstate actors are important not only because they pursue their own interests, "but also because they act as transmission belts, making government policies in various countries more sensitive to one another."[82] When they take actions that transcend geographic frontiers, the lines between foreign and domestic politics become blurred. World politics is swayed by the relative strength of domestic interests within the countries, which can influence the global agenda by framing an issue in a particular way and rallying citizens' groups to pressure national governments. In 1995, for instance, Greenpeace was able to prevent Royal Dutch/Shell from disposing of the Brent Spar oil platform at sea by mobilizing public opinion in several European countries.

Although the vast number of nonstate actors influencing the global agenda today challenges the Westphalian state-centric vision of world politics, nation-states still lay claim as the principal source of security and identity in most peoples' lives. Nonetheless, it is worth remembering that "the state has not always been the *primary* actor in global politics and it has never been the *sole* actor."[83] As the lead performer sharing the stage with a panoply of other actors, the nation-state is in a position unlike any time since its emergence after the Thirty Years' War. An age of eroding state sovereignty is underway. Consequently, a new post-Westphalian way of conceptualizing world politics is needed if we are to understand the character of international affairs in the twenty-first century, despite the fact that the Westphalian territorial state continues to cast a long shadow over the political horizon.

If the Westphalian world view could be symbolized by a two-dimensional map depicting territorial units on a horizontal grid, then a post-Westphalian world view might be represented by a holographic projection that showed a lattice-like structure of networks surrounding territorial states. World politics, suggests James Rosenau, has become bifurcated into an anarchic system among nation-states and a multicentric system of nonstate actors.[84] But the salience of these two systems is not uniform from one issue to the next, or from one region of the world to another. To borrow a metaphor from the study of federalism within the United States, the structure of contemporary world politics looks more like a marble cake than a layer cake.[85] That is to say, world politics is increasingly shaped by networks of coordination, where state and nonstate officials who hold similar values and concerns address international problems without a formally legislated charter, fixed membership, or large bureaucracy. The Paris Club, an ad hoc forum of creditors that reschedules the debt of developing countries, exemplifies this form of transgovernance, in which states are part of complex networks that include corporations, banks, international organizations, and a rich array of nongovernmental organizations.[86]

Figure 6.2 shows how state and nonstate actors intermingle in an intricate web of relationships. Table 6.1 summarizes the main differences between the Westphalian model of world politics and a post-Westphalian model that conceives of nation-states as enmeshed within such webs of transgovernance.

FIGURE 6.2   The Web of World Politics
Rather than focusing exclusively on relations among sovereign, territorial states, a post-Westphalian model of world politics depicts how various types of state and nonstate actors form a complex web of interactions.

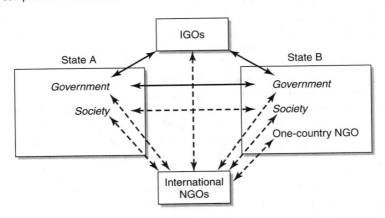

Types of Interactions in World Politics
——— Interstate relations
– – – – Transnational relations

TABLE 6.1   Two Models of World Politics

	Westphalian Model	Post-Westphalian Model
Primary units	Nation-states	Nation-states and various nonstate actors, including multinational corporations and civil society organizations
Unit boundaries	Firm	Permeable
Membership identity	Single unit	Multiple types of units
Principal objective	Increase military power	Promote policy coordination
Global structure	Anarchy	Anarchy among states and transnational networks linking nonstate actors
Role of regional and world organizations	Limited	Prominent
Vision of the future	Continuity	Change

In brief, the Westphalian model is predicated upon continuity: the twenty-first century will resemble the mid-seventeenth. Sovereign, territorial states will remain the only actors of consequence in world politics. They will undergo unequal growth and seek security through self-help and power balancing as they incessantly compete with one another for relative gains in an anarchic environment.

By way of contrast, our post-Westphalian model is predicated upon change. Global governance will involve a complex, interlocking mix of supranational, national, and private subnational actors. Instead of being exercised within an autonomous monistic legal order, sovereignty will be diffused across a polycentric order. With international regimes playing an ever greater role in world politics, traditional military capabilities alone will not guarantee satisfactory outcomes for states pursuing individual gain.

Having sketched how the Westphalian state system is being transformed by integrative and disintegrative trends, and having suggested how a post-Westphalian world might differ from its predecessor, we turn in the next chapter to explore the ways that these insights might organize our thinking about a new set of ideas, ideals, and institutions to build a more peaceful and just future. If the trends identified in this chapter persist, and if they promote the kinds of transformations that we postulate will likely result, then what will this mean for global governance at the dawn of the new millennium?

We submit that effective global governance in the twenty-first century will require weaving together diverse networks of sovereign and sovereignty-free actors. To make this claim is to extend the Grotian tradition beyond its statist roots. As discussed in Chapter 4, both Grotius and Hobbes saw sovereign states as the principal actors in world politics; however, Grotius rejected the Hobbesian depiction of their interaction as a brutal zero-sum contest ruled by expediency, believing instead that states which shared common values and were bound together by voluntarily acknowledged normative standards were members of an international society. Given the growing importance of intergovernmental and nongovernmental organizations in world politics, we propose extending the concept of an international society to include salient nonstate actors that also feel bound by prevailing values and norms.[87] This neo-Grotian conception of international society does not suggest that a universalist community of all humankind will soon transcend the political units to which people currently devote their loyalty. Rather it implies that as long as we continue to think of international society exclusively in terms of sovereign territorial states, the ghost of Westphalia will continue to haunt the world, undermining the prospects for a peaceful and just twenty-first century world order. In the next chapter, we shall further pursue the reasoning behind our thesis that this ghost needs to be exorcised.

CHAPTER 7

Westphalia's Problematic Contribution to Contemporary World Order

Today, many things indicate that we are going through a transitional period,
when it seems that something is on the way out and something else is painfully
being born. It is as if something were crumbling, decaying, and exhausting itself,
while something else, still indistinct, were arising from the rubble.

–Václav Havel

Contemporary world politics is being shaped by centripetal and centrifugal forces. At the same time that globalization, democratization, and humanitarianism are pulling many of the planet's inhabitants together, fragmenting processes are pushing people apart. The world is simultaneously becoming more cosmopolitan and more parochial. Nonterritorial, sovereignty-free organizations now vie with territorial, sovereignty-based states. Intricate webs of transnational exchange compete with the emotional ties of national identity.

Due to the interplay of these contending forces, many scholars believe that international life in the twenty-first century will differ significantly from that of the past three-and-a-half centuries, when the Peace of Westphalia created new rules for interstate relations and world order. "We no longer live in the world of the Westphalian treaties," asserts Stanley Hoffmann.[1] Humanity, adds Harvey Starr, is "moving from the Westphalian system into something not yet clearly defined or understood."[2]

The Peace of Westphalia settled a grisly seventeenth-century war. Over the next three hundred and fifty years, the norms embodied in the Treaties of Münster and Osnabrück gradually spread from Europe to the rest of the world.

The entire globe became, in a word, "possessed" by the Westphalian conception of international relations which it inherited, and its spirit has literally provided the ground rules for international interaction for countless state and nonstate transnational actors who had no voice in their creation. The rules of the Westphalian ghost continue to cast their shadow over the global landscape.

The Westphalian problematique centers on the issue of the consequences of the Westphalian spirit's lasting grip on diplomacy. How relevant are these norms today? Can a code of conduct derived centuries ago from a Eurocentric, state system be grafted on a pluralistic, global society where shifting, *ad hoc* networks of state and nonstate actors abound? We have serious doubts. As we have shown in Chapter 5, the Westphalian rules for statecraft were woefully inadequate for securing peace in the aftermath of the Thirty Years' War. Although the diplomats of 1648 succeeded in stopping most of the fighting associated with that ghastly war, their patch-work settlement did not put into a sealed coffin the smoldering rivalries that soon ignited into future wars, even after the rules articulated by the settlement were refined sixty-five years later in the Treaty of Utrecht.

The Westphalian code of conduct did not bury the state machinery for waging war; rather, it sought to enshrine the sovereign state as an autonomous actor, and it interpreted war as a legitimate tool that states could use to preserve their existence by thwarting the ambitions of aspiring hegemons who dreamed of replacing the system of sovereign, independent states with a structure based on supranational organizational principles. Over time, the Westphalian ghost changed its colors when war also came to be seen as a permissible means of enhancing national security by allowing states to imperialistically acquire territory that contained valuable resources or a strategically important position. Paradoxically, a balance of power among these rival states was supposed to maintain peace, yet war was one of the instruments accepted by the Westphalian code for maintaining the balance.

If the international norms that emerged from the Peace of Westphalia were unable to secure peace in the early modern era, they are even more problematic as an anchor for world order in the twenty-first century. The trends described in Chapter 6 are eroding the underlying postulates of the Westphalian conception of international relations. A state-centric system premised on sovereign control is increasingly at odds with a world characterized by ever-increasing transnational ties among banks, corporations, investors, and other agents that lie beyond the purview of state authorities. It is axiomatic that Westphalia and state interdependence under globalization are incompatible.

To locate firm ground on which a future world order might be based, it is instructive to compare the conditions of the early twenty-first century with those that the Westphalian code of diplomatic conduct attempted to address. By making such a comparison, we will be able to highlight changes over time in salient discrepancies between the code's professed principles and its applied rules, the degree to which international actors internalized those rules, and whether those rules are congruent with one another. Gaps in the normative consistency, consensus, and congruence of the Westphalian code can alert us to the kinds of alternative security architecture that will be needed in the years ahead.

COMPARING TWO POSTWAR ERAS

The Peace of Westphalia was a regional settlement whose norms for interstate relations slowly diffused throughout the entire world. Table 7.1 compares some of the major characteristics of the period following the conclusion of the Thirty Years' War with those existing at the dawn of the twenty-first century. In 1648, as well as today, political leaders recognized the need to prevent future wars and arrest the threat of internal revolts, or at least limit their destructiveness should efforts at preventive diplomacy fail. The gruesome human toll exacted by the Thirty Years' War led Thomas Hobbes, Hugo Grotius, and other seventeenth-century theorists to prescribe contending approaches for preventing such horrors from ever occurring again. Equally shocked by the carnage, monarchs in the latter half of the seventeenth century began to prune field commanders of their latitude to initiate massive offensives and target and plunder innocent noncombatants. Strategies of maneuver and evasion replaced frontal assaults, when much of the fighting was confined to ritualized siege operations conducted so an honorable surrender was expected once the zigzagging trenches of the besieger snaked close enough to make a breach in the defender's fortifications inevitable. Other restrictions on military strategies and tactics altered the methods by which wars were fought, while the Westphalian legal right to wage war continued without interruption into the twentieth century.

Just as the Thirty Years' War displaced countless people in central Europe, in the last decades of the twentieth century, violence in Afghanistan, Bosnia, Cambodia, East Timor, Kosovo, Rwanda, Somalia and elsewhere have forced nearly 47 million noncombatants to flee their homes.[3] Compounding the problem, famine, rampaging private militias, and a countryside seeded with land mines now continue to threaten civilians long after military units have disengaged. To reduce the destructiveness of warfare and to relieve the suffering of people trapped in war zones, some weapons stockpiles have been reduced, periodic great-power summit conferences convened, and a host of dispute-settlement and truce-monitoring mechanisms installed in volatile regions. But these measures have not produced peace or stability; humanitarian disasters and small wars abound, and the peacekeeping mechanisms operative today are no more capable of containing genocides and gross abuses by militarized state governments of their subjects than were the nonexistent collective peace-maintaining processes in the wake of Westphalia. That is why the strident cry is heard to exorcise the Westphalian concept of inviolable state sovereignty that stands in the way of humanitarian intervention.

Reaction to the chronic violence sweeping the contemporary world, for example, prompted UN Secretary General Kofi Annan, at the *Millennium Summit* in September 2000, to enunciate a plea for global acceptance of a doctrine that would authorize "the United Nations to intervene to stop massive human rights violations wherever in the world they happen, irrespective of sovereign state borders or local government objections."[4] As a sign of the changing spirit of the times, the UN Security Council in September 2000 took a historic step to solidify the emerging consensus that a major change was necessary, even if it undercut the Westphalian prohibition of external interference in the internal affairs of sovereign states. Its unanimously supported resolution endorsed an overhaul of UN peacekeeping operations to create a more potent, better financed rapid-deployment force that could quickly respond to threats to peace and to human rights violations.

To better picture the magnitude of this potential departure from the legacy of Westphalia, it is useful to survey comparatively the major properties of the post-Westphalian and post-Cold War global settings. Table 7.1 highlights the key similarities and differences between the two periods, and illuminates why the instabilities prevailing both then and now exert the same kind of pressure to place international security at the top of the global agenda. The primary reason why the Westphalian conception continues to hold a paralyzing grip on thinking about international politics is because the problem of war remains, as it was in 1648, *the* most pressing concern, given the prevalence of aggression, especially within states in contrast to wars between states.

Neither the late seventeenth nor the early twenty-first centuries enjoyed a respite from military hostilities. As a result, curbing the potential excesses of armed combat topped the diplomatic agendas of both periods. Security had to be conceived as the most vital concern in the aftermath of the Thirty Years' and Cold Wars because then, and now, without it no other values could be addressed successfully. What differs were the codes of diplomatic conduct that were adopted to legitimate the evolving practices in each period, because the pressures percolating then and now are in many respects making for radically different environments and for problems beyond national security defined in military terms with which the international community has been forced to cope.

Other salient similarities also can be identified in the policy challenges arising after the conclusions of the Thirty Years' and Cold Wars. For example, both were periods when the status of the sovereign state was uncertain, when military self-help was highly regarded by the major powers, and when the question of international ethics was hotly debated. These commonalities help to account for the stubborn persistence of Westphalian logic, which was born by a piecemeal attempt to cope with international conditions as confusing and chaotic as today, amidst substantial uncertainty about viable solutions to the management of orderly world affairs. At Westphalia, the devil was in the details,

TABLE 7.1 Two Postwar Eras in Comparative Perspective

	Aftermath of the Thirty Years' War	Aftermath of the Cold War
Background Conditions	Great-power war	Long great-power peace
	Growth of autocratic governments	Growth of democratic governments
	Declining role of religion in international relations	Increasing role of religion in international relations
	Mercantilist efforts to expand state economies through trade protectionism	Promotion of free trade and liberalization of the global marketplace
	Declining concern about theology, rising concern about political ideology	Declining concern about political ideology, rising concern about theology
	Multipolar balance-of-power state system emerging from demise of bipolarity	Unipolar state system, evolving toward multipolarity and global governance
	Rising nationalism	Rising supranationalism alongside rekindled nationalism
	Minimal transnational contact, mostly restricted to political and economic elites	Significant transnational contacts among members of the mass public facilitated by the digital revolution
	Low rate of weapons innovation concomitant with a revolution in military tactics	Rapid rate of weapons innovation, including weapons of mass destruction
		Rising tide of cynicism
		Postmodern age of doubt and intellectual chaos
Power Contenders	Austrian and Spanish Hapsburgs, England, France, the Netherlands, the Ottoman Empire until 1699, Sweden	China, the European Union, Japan, Russia, the United States

(continued)

TABLE 7.1 continued

	Aftermath of the Thirty Years' War	Aftermath of the Cold War
Major Military Resources	Shipbuilding and sea transport following revolution in military technology and battle tactics	Aeronautics, nuclear weapons, ballistic missiles, precision-guided munitions and nonlethal weaponry amidst revolution in military affairs (RMA)
Valued Commodities	Gold, textiles, spices	Information, petroleum, electronics
Policy Challenges	Consolidating emerging state sovereignty through centralized state governance	Coping with the erosion of state sovereignty, failed states, and separatist revolts
	Managing the security dilemma in the geopolitical realm of high politics	Managing the low politics of environmental preservation and the geoeconomics of trade-bloc rivalry and market interdependence and integration
	Refugees and displaced people	Refugees and the global migration crisis
	Achieving economic recovery	Maintaining economic growth
	Transition from the medieval period's cosmopolitan ideal to state rivalries	Transition from interstate competition to interstate interdependence and global governance
	Reconciling state autonomy with international anarchy	Reconciling local fears of cultural homogenization with globalization

183

and it is safe to conclude that the overwhelmed negotiators largely abandoned the challenge of innovatively creating institutions to police international affairs and instead licensed the sovereign state to act unilaterally, without meaningful legal or moral restraint, in a turbulent sea of anarchy. They were unprepared to imagine any basis for international relations other than the perpetuation of the *laissez-faire* state behavior that had become customary during the Thirty Years' War. It is not surprising that today, in the face of similar uncertainties, many leaders of sovereign states are unwilling to entertain any alternative to the Westphalian conception and why, because they see it as the least of two evils, they are highly resistant to accepting the kinds of major changes that the UN Security Council has defined as necessary.

Inasmuch as the mid-seventeenth and early twenty-first centuries are strikingly similar, it might appear on the surface that architectural continuity rather than change is probable. However, the trajectories of history favor change— and the ultimate rejection of the Westphalian blueprint. Changing times call for changing approaches, and it is in the disparities between the conditions that prevailed in the seventeenth century and the conditions which prevail today that the prospects for moving beyond Westphalia are improving. On the whole, differences between these periods abound.[5] The contemporary era, for example, was not born in the shadow of a general systemic war; it followed the longest span of great-power peace since the Peace of Westphalia.[6] Another important difference involves the role of religion in world politics, which declined after the Thirty Years' War, but has recently resurfaced, especially among Islamic countries and their relations with countries that are home to other universalistic religions. The rate of weapons innovation, the relative importance of various military resources, and the value placed on many commodities also differed. The world population stood at roughly 600 million in the middle of the seventeenth century, compared to more than 6 billion inhabitants living at the beginning of the new millennium. Whereas three centuries ago most people were governed by autocratic monarchies wedded to economic protectionism, today liberal democracy and support for free trade in a capitalistic global marketplace without borders are commonplace. Relentless military competition occurred among the strongest states during each period, but the power contenders of yesterday have long since been superseded in the international pecking order, as uneven economic growth and major wars propelled some states to the top of the global hierarchy while others experienced significant decline. Today the great powers are undergoing another power transition potentially as profound in proportion.

Of high potency in the equation that predicts whether continuity or change will be prominent in international relations is the extent to which power is concentrated or diffused internationally. Indeed, global norms historically have adjusted themselves to changes in the global distribution of power.[7] Transformations in the international balance of power are influential agents in shaping of the international system's political culture.[8] For that reason, it is critically important to pay particular attention to this factor in any assessment of the global future and Westphalia's likely place in it. The argument we advance proceeds from several basic assumptions: (1) dramatic changes in relative capabilities sometimes cause power to be concentrated in the hands of one preponderant state; (2) at other times, they result in rough parity among two or more states as movement up and down the global hierarchy creates different configurations of power; and (3) international norms that mesh with unipolar configurations may not provide a suitable code of conduct in bipolar or multipolar configurations, nor will norms that guide behavior when power is dispersed always function adequately in environments where it is concentrated. These assumptions point to a fundamental thesis that speaks to the coming obsolescence of the Westphalian rules for statecraft. We shall argue that the Westphalian settlement was situated in a multipolar balance-of-power system. Although the idea of balancing power dates back to antiquity, "it was not until the Treaty of Westphalia had been signed that it took its full and modern form."[9] According to Michael Glennon, the delegates at Münster and Osnabrück "sought to balance one equal, independent state or group of states against another, in the belief that the resulting *principe d'équilibre* would secure a stable, lasting peace."[10] Since the establishment of a set of international norms that lubricated the balance of power system is one of the "paramount and lasting contributions" of Westphalia,[11] we must position our appraisal of the current relevance of this landmark peace settlement on the premise that it greatly hinges on whether such norms mesh with the power structure of the contemporary international system.

WESTPHALIA AND THE CHANGING WORLD SYSTEM

In contrast to the multipolar balance-of-power system of the seventeenth century, the hierarchical structure of the current international system can be described as nonhegemonic unipolarity.[12] With the collapse of the Soviet Union, the United States emerged from the Cold War as the world's sole remaining superpower. To be sure, Russia still possesses a formidable nuclear arsenal, Japan and the European Union continue to maintain high levels of capital accumulation, and China has enormous military and economic potential. Yet the scope of American power today is unique. As described by Zbigniew Brzezinski, militarily, the United States "has an unmatched global reach; economically, it remains the main locomotive of global growth . . . ; technologically, it retains the overall lead in the cutting-edge areas of innovation; and culturally, . . . it enjoys an appeal that is unrivaled."[13] The United States eclipses all other states in the global traffic of information and ideas. "American music, American movies, American television, and American software are so dominant, so sought after, and so visible that they are now available literally everywhere on earth."[14] Because it ranks so extraordinarily high across the entire range of power resources, the United States is "able to sustain reverses in any one area while maintaining its overall influence stemming from other sources."[15]

Complementing America's power resources is an immunity to external threats. The United States enjoys a privileged geostrategic position. Geographically, the United States is insulated from any rival's expansion into its sphere of influence, and, except for a heavy reliance upon Middle Eastern oil, it is almost invulnerable to economic coercion. Strategically, the United States is impermeable to conventional attack, and, at least for the discernible future, it is impervious to the actions others might take to slash the margin of American military superiority. As Eric Nordlinger has put it, "America was markedly immune to many diverse threats when facing an enormously powerful, globe-straddling Soviet Union." Today, "without a threat on the horizon that at all approximates the Soviet one in scope and power, the United States is consequently far more immune than in the recent past."[16]

While Washington, infatuated with the Hobbesian assumption that global stability is contingent upon hegemony, may regard its current privileged position of global preeminence as benign, others disagree. As the world's paramount power, the United States inspires awe as well as anxiety, respect as well as rebuke. "Unipolar moments," cautions Christopher Layne, "cause geopolitical backlashes."[17] Well after the end of the Cold War, "hundreds of thousands of American troops, supplied with the world's most advanced weaponry . . . , are stationed on over sixty-one base complexes in nineteen countries worldwide."[18] However, military might does not necessarily translate into proportional political influence. Although it claims to be an "indispensable nation" standing taller and seeing farther into the future than anyone else, the United States "can no longer do whatever it wants even if it is the only superpower."[19] And the United States cannot pacify the globe as a hegemonic policeman if it is unwilling to perform a leadership role or deploy its military muscle to empower the United Nations, NATO, and other security organizations to perform a peacekeeping and preventive diplomacy mission.

Today the United States holds "a more diversified portfolio of power resources than any other country," observes Joseph Nye. But the world order of the immediate future "will not be an era of American hegemony."[20] Indeed, even those who describe the early twenty-first century in unipolar terms acknowledge that power will not remain concentrated in American hands indefinitely. The hierarchy of international power is dynamic, with states changing positions as their economies grow at different rates. "No doubt, multipolarity will come in time," concedes Charles Krauthammer. "In perhaps another generation or so there will be great powers coequal with the United States."[21] China, Japan, the European Union, Russia, and conceivably India might achieve such status. Nevertheless, such power shifts are unlikely to beget a multipolar future that fits with Westphalian norms any more closely than the current unipolar world. As described in the previous chapter, potent centripetal and centrifugal forces are changing the way we must think about the future structure of the international system.

Following the Westphalian way of constructing a picture of international reality, nearly all traditional conceptions of system structure have tended to focus exclusively on the discrete, autonomous great powers that vigorously compete with one another, guard against intrusions into their internal affairs, and dominate less muscular neighbors. This socially constructed reality—and images of stability within it—have customarily assumed that what matters most was the distribution of military capabilities among great power rivals and potential changes in their positionality; everything else at the lower tiers of international society was deemed relatively uninfluential as a determinant of war or world order. Polarity—the distribution of capabilities among these great powers—ever since Westphalia has been depicted in its *realpolitik* framework as the crucial variable that affects the stability of the international system.[22] That vision reflected the actual realities in the seventeenth century, when different opportunities and constraints arose for large and small alike, depending upon whether the global system contained one preponderant state, two major power centers, or several roughly equal great powers. As states came into being as legally the only players of note on the world stage, it was then useful to concentrate on the number of great powers and the propensity of weaker countries to cluster around them in alliances.

However, many dimensions of that Westphalian global structure have been fading in significance. Training a statist lens on world affairs in Westphalian terms will be increasingly less revealing if the twenty-first century international system continues to move in the direction of coming to resemble what Manuel Castells calls a "network society."[23] Rather than being composed of the singular, hard-shelled units of Westphalian sovereign states, a global network society will contain a web of interdependent, heterogeneous units, including states, quasi-states, multinational corporations, virtual communities, interest groups, professional bodies, and a welter of other nongovernmental organizations.[24] If, as many scholars and policymakers expect, the current unipolar system evolves toward a more diffused configuration of power, the rapidly growing network of transnational relations among interdependent state, quasi-states, and nonstate actors will greatly differentiate such a multipolar future from the system that developed in Europe during the second half of the seventeenth century.

History does not follow a consistent path, in a continuous linear direction; it branches off here and there forming identifiable periods, each with its own characteristics. Although the Westphalian period continues to color the way scholars and policymakers think about world politics, the signs of the times point unmistakably toward the conclusion that the world now stands on the threshold of a new era. A historic watershed has been reached, inasmuch as we are clearly in a transition away from the Westphalian system and toward a post-

Westphalian global system with fundamentally different properties. As one student of digital-electronic telecommunications has concluded, whereas "determinations of world order in the Westphalian system were largely contested by states, today they are being hammered out by a constellation of nonstate actors, who see territorial boundaries as mere inconveniences to their larger aims." States are not about to disappear, but they have been "interpenetrated by social forces and technologies now partially beyond their control."[25] The consequence of a transformation of such magnitude is certain to be profound, for it will render obsolete the Westphalian conception of international relations. To evaluate the extent of such a system-shattering discontinuity, it is necessary to identify the *norms* inherent in the Westphalian worldview and to enumerate the important ways in which those norms fail to speak to the conditions and challenges of the globalized twenty-first century.

INTERNATIONAL NORMS AND THE PEACE OF WESTPHALIA

Having described the principal differences between the late seventeenth and early twenty-first century international systems, we can now take up the question of how the normative consistency, consensus, and congruence of the Westphalian code of conduct has changed over time. International norms are social phenomena with deontological content. They advance a collective, socially sanctioned set of perspectives of what ought to be done, a collective expectation as to what will be done, and pronouncements backed by consensus about the costs regarding compliant versus noncompliant behavior with respect to potential norm violations. Communicated through a rich lexicon of legal symbols and reinforced by diplomatic ritual, international norms are more than modal regularities; they are intersubjectively shared understandings which, when formed, communicate a consensus about the obligations of international actors to behave in a specified way. Conformity with a norm's instructions elicits approval from nearly all other relevant international actors; deviance, disapproval. Moreover, these voices of praise and protest encourage conformity by influencing every actor's affective image of itself and its reputation among others.[26]

International norms do not exist in isolation. They fit together in a complex mosaic to form a normative order. The Peace of Westphalia marked the consolidation of a normative order whose sundry rules of behavior had been gradually accumulating since the onset of the Protestant Reformation.[27] When the peace settlement of 1648 crystallized in a collective spirit of enthusiasm about the norms by which states were thereafter expected to abide in their relations with one another, that spirit took possession of international society and bequeathed to the modern world a new conception of world politics based on sovereign, territorial nation-states. The communications between diplomats at Westphalia were "laced with references to state autonomy, the equality of states, and an equilibrium of states, and even an early version of collective security–all notions that were unintelligible apart from a sovereign states' system."[28] Before we examine the gaps in the consistency, consensus, and congruence of the Westphalian normative order, that, from the start, diminished its effacy and now is dysfunctional to international order, let us briefly summarize its key components.

The Westphalian Normative Order

At the base of every normative order is a set of foundational norms that define its axiology, or value orientation. As described in Chapter 4, the Westphalian axiology hinges on the concept of sovereignty. The idea that there is a final and absolute political authority within the state (internal sovereignty) was first enunciated by the Romans.[29] The complementary idea that no supreme authority exists over the community of states (external sovereignty) emerged between the late sixteenth century and mid-seventeenth centuries, where it supplied the normative foundation for the Treaties of Münster and Osnabrück. By enshrining this external facet of sovereignty, the Peace of Westphalia encouraged a horizontal vision of international relations. States were no longer seen as parts of a vertical system headed by Church authority over both secular and religious affairs; henceforth sovereign states' interactions would be governed by laws of coordination rather than subordination. In short, sovereignty provided the cornerstone for modern international law, which rested on the supremacy of state independence and autonomy as its *ground norm*. Indeed, it has been said that international law in its early stages of development was "the reasoned extrapolation of the consequences of sovereignty for the mutual adjustment of states."[30]

The philosopher and mathematician Gottfried Wilhelm Leibniz was one of the first people to explore the legal consequences of sovereignty. While working for the Duke of Hanover, he addressed an issue that puzzled many leaders of the small German states occupying central Europe after the Thirty Years' War. The Peace of Westphalia had conferred sovereign independence on the duchies and principalities within the Holy Roman Empire, but it did not abolish the political machinery of the Empire itself. How had the peace settlement affected the political status of these dukes and princes? Did they lead sovereign states, or were they still under the jurisdiction of a higher authority? Leibniz responded by establishing rudimentary criteria for statehood: true sovereigns possessed the "actual and present power to constrain" subjects on their own territories.[31] A sovereign state, in other words, had a defined territory, a population, and effective governmental organs to control the territory and its population. The pope or the emperor might have majesty, the moral authority to demand fidelity from the Germans, but neither possessed sovereignty over the German states.

The Rights of Sovereign States.   Under the Westphalian normative order, political entities that met the criteria of sovereign statehood held certain rights. In the words of one legal theorist, they formed "the statutory basis of the law of nations, and the common constitution of our political civilization."[32] Over the course of the next two centuries, several "fundamental rights" were recognized by publicists as inherent in sovereignty. First, states possessed the right to continued national existence, which really meant the prerogative to use force in self-defense for the acclaimed higher good of self-preservation. Whereas the subjects living within a sovereign state were expected to submit their differences to adjudication, no earthy judge was thought to be in a position to make a binding judgment on disputes between states, unless they had given their prior consent. As a result, war served as the court of last appeal among sovereigns. During the period after the Thirty Years' War, most people "regarded war in much the same way they regarded a hard winter—uncomfortable, certainly, but part of the settled order of things, . . . even the wounded soldier did not regard war as wrong, any more than the skier with a broken leg regards skiing as wrong."[33]

A second widely understood right within the Westphalian normative order was independence. States could manage their domestic affairs without external interference, and they could act as free agents in foreign affairs, negotiating commercial treaties, forming military alliances, and entering into other types of agreements without the supervision of another state. Independence did not mean that they were exempt from a generally accepted code of conduct, however. Among the most important components of any normative order are rules enumerating what constitutes "civilized" behavior and how such behavior differs from the "uncivilized" action of outsiders.[34] These norms of inclusion/exclusion reinforce a state's identity as part of a wider international society. They not only describe what practices society members follow, but they imply that this is the way anyone who is civilized ought to behave.[35] Restrictions on a state's freedom of maneuver, arising from a common cannon of civilized behavior, were not considered to be a violation of independence.

Finally, the Westphalian order promoted the right of equality. Though unequal in size and strength, states were said to be equal before the law in the sense that they all (1) possessed the same privileges and responsibilities, (2) could appeal to the same rules of conduct when defending themselves and seeking to exercise influence over others, and (3) could expect to have these rules applied impartially whenever they consented to having an arbitrator settle their quarrels. By defining equality in this manner, no state could claim jurisdiction over another, nor could it sit in judgment over the validity of the public acts other states initiated under their own laws. Moreover, heads of state and their diplomatic representatives were immune from prosecution in foreign courts.

The Duties of Sovereign States.

Beside recognizing the rights of existence, independence, and equality, the norms embraced in Westphalia acknowledged certain corresponding duties. A sovereign state had the right to maintain its corporate personality as a state (and control religion within its borders), but it also possessed a corollary duty not to meddle in the internal matters of other states. Indeed, the Westphalian code of conduct made rulers supreme by strictly prohibiting any interferences or intervention by another state or supranational collectivity in the internal affairs of the state, including the unrestricted right of rulers to treat their own citizens any way the monarch chose (including the gross violation of their subjects' basic human rights). Fearing a relapse into the fractious environment that spawned the Thirty Years' War, the victors at Münster and Osnabrück supported the territorial integrity of states by prohibiting intervention by one state into the internal affairs of another state, except in cases of self-defense. The negotiators agreed to the norm that any action aimed at modifying the government, the leadership, or the foreign or domestic policies of another sovereign state was to be regarded as an illicit interference. Such interference threatened dire repercussions from the larger international community, and France and the Holy Roman Empire were authorized to use military force to assure compliance with this rule. National autonomy was considered a prerequisite for the smooth functioning of a balance-of-power system; intruding into political life elsewhere was thought to hinder the ebb and flow of alignments needed to maintain a stable equilibrium among contending great powers.

Another Westphalian-decreed duty of states adhered to the Grotian belief about the importance of carrying out promissory obligations in good faith. A sovereign state had the right to act as a free agent when dealing with others, but it also had a duty to honor agreements that were not signed under duress. As expressed in the norm *pacta sunt servanda* (treaties are binding), promises made voluntarily by parties to international treaties must be upheld: They are irrevocable pledges. This lofty aspiration notwithstanding, the Westphalian norms also reflected the growing acceptance of the view that states should be entitled to release from their promissory obligations prior to an agreed-upon expiration date if their national interests seemed to justify the expedient termination of their treaty agreements. According to the *clausula rebus sic stantibus*, an escape clause believed by many at the time to be tacitly incorporated within every treaty in conformity with the diplomatic customs of the seventeenth century, promissory obligations were situational. A radical change in the circumstances that existed when a commitment was made could be invoked as a ground for unilaterally terminating an agreement, if those circumstances which constituted the original basis for granting consent were perceived to have changed; then, the change significantly altered the obligations to be performed under the agreement.[36] The Grotian duty of good faith was therefore legally undermined by norms which stressed state autonomy and voluntary compliance with agreements, as the diplomatic culture condoned the *realpolitik* principle that the first duty of states was to advance their national self-interest. (Note once again how the Westphalia norms regarding treaty compliance captured the essence of, and codified, the growing tendency during the fluid Thirty Years' War for parties to agreements to renounce their pledges when circumstances in the war had changed.)

In summary, what we have termed the "Westphalian normative order" was born between 1517 and 1648, and grew by accretion over the next three centuries. Venerating sovereignty, it contained a set of foundation norms that identified states as the subjects of international law, stipulated that they were bound only by voluntary consent, and delineated a set of interrelated rights and duties that stressed national self-preservation, political independence, juridical equality, nonintervention, and showing good faith in adhering to international agreements only when territorial circumstances were stable and when national interests were clearly advanced by treaty compliance. Over time, many other norms were linked to this foundation: some reinforced its original injunctions, others modified their thrust, and still others extended their application to new issue areas.[37] Westphalia has been called "the majestic portal" that leads from the medieval to the modern world order.[38] Standing on the edge of a post-modern era, however, the Westphalian conception now seems deficient as a continued source of normative guidance.

Deficiencies in the Westphalian Normative Order

The interlocking norms that comprise a normative order vary along several dimensions. Westphalia, like earlier normative orders, varied over time in terms of (1) the amount of discrepancy between its professed principles and applied rules, (2) the degree to which the members of the international system internalized those rules, and (3) whether the rules complemented or contradicted one another. Variations along these three dimensions affect the strength of a normative order. Those orders with high levels of normative consistency, consensus, and congruence have a greater probability of influencing international outcomes than those ranking lower on these dimensions, and, to a considerable degree, the levels of consistency, consensus and congruence extant in 1648 have declined as the international system has evolved at an accelerating pace over the past three hundred and fifty years. Thus, in the incipient stage of the new millennium, the Westphalian skeleton is less capable of carrying its weight to support global order than at any time since the Westphalian normative structure was constructed.

Normative Consistency.   What levels of consistency, consensus, and congruence exist within the Westphalian order? Have they fallen over the past three-and-a-half centuries to levels that make them incapable for the demanding task of guiding international society toward a fairer, safer future? Looking first at the normative consistency within the Westphalian order, we can see its strength and spirit sapped by the growing gap between its statist principles and the influence of nongovernmental organizations in developing rules that apply to economic, environmental, and humanitarian problems. Although states remain the dominate actors in world politics, a twenty-first century normative order cannot be tied solely to the interaction of sovereign, territorial states. Many observers have joined Richard Falk in asserting that the state has lost much of its problem-solving credibility. Challenged from above by global market forces, the Westphalian order built on a state-system structure seems to have abdicated custody over the global public good to corporations, banks, and other international financial institutions. Challenged from below by an emerging transnational civil society, it also seems to have ceded guardianship over environmental and humanitarian concerns to grassroots activists. In short, we face what Falk calls a "profound moral vacuum" at the very time that states "can no longer be counted upon as the principal agency for achieving normative adjustments."[39]

Normative Consensus.   International norms are a medium of communication through which prevailing opinions about acceptable patterns of behavior are transmitted to members of the state system. Of course, not everyone will internalize these norms, even though their existence may be acknowledged. The consensus expressed by norms is imperfect; national leaders often agree on certain values at the same time as they fail to recognize the implications of these values for their own behavior. Nowhere is this more clear than in norms pertaining to nonintervention. Although intervention was prohibited by the Westphalian order, at various times great powers have attempted to establish conditions under which it could be justified. Consider the case of debt recovery. During the nineteenth century, the great powers disregarded the nonintervention norm to collect debts owed their nationals. For example, France landed forces at Vera Cruz in 1838, due to the financial liability of the Mexican government; the British and Spanish joined the French in sending troops in 1862; and between 1902 and 1903, Germany and Great Britain blockaded the Orinoco River, bombarded forts at Puerto Cabello, and sank several Venezuelan gunboats. By the early twentieth century, however, intervention for the collection of debts from delinquent states was no longer accepted as permissible. Based on Argentine Foreign Minister Luis Maria Drago's insistence in a 1902 memorandum that insolvency should not be considered a form of misconduct, the parties to the Second Hague Peace Conference agreed not to rely upon military force to recover what was owed to foreign bondholders, unless the debtor state refused to arbitrate the financial dispute.

Other norms within the Westphalian blueprint have also experienced alternating periods of observance and disregard. At times, noncompliance has been due to brash opportunism, but often it has occurred because of ambiguity in a norm's prescriptions or proscriptions, as they pertain to emerging situations. As nonstate actors continue to challenge the sovereign state from both above and below, the normative consensus underlying Westphalia is likely to erode for a more serious reason: nonterritorial, sovereignty-free actors will simply conclude that the foundation norms of state independence, equality, and the like are illegitimate. Rather than cheating or prescriptive ambiguity causing noncompliance, increasing numbers of nonstate actors may openly disregard certain international norms because they believe them to be morally wrong, and they may voice support for alternative norms that better serve global interests and international morality in the new realities of the new millennium.

Norms stressing state autonomy and independence received support in the seventeenth century when those values were in short supply; now post-Westphalian norms, stressing collective action for common values, are receiving support and are increasingly receiving it from broad spectrums of public opinion worldwide, in a consensus that challenges the continuing hold of the Westphalian conception. Measure by measure and treaty-resolution by treaty-resolution, emerging practices and global conventions are exorcizing the Westphalian ghost.

Rival norms may be building a consensus for a post-Westphalian conception (just as rival norms in the late sixteenth and early seventeenth century built a consensus for the Westphalian norms). Consider U.S. President Bill Clinton's statement at the September 2000 UN Millennium Summit: "If I have learned anything in these last eight years, it is, whether we like it or not, we are growing more interdependent. That will require us to develop greater sensitivity to our diverse political, cultural, and religious claims. But it will require us to develop even greater respect for our common humanity." Such a normative perspective was arguably premature and out of step with the spirit of the times when Hugo Grotius promoted humanitarian norms for international society in the seventeenth century.[40] Now, however, the vision Grotius, then unsuccessfully advocated for his times, has gained, three hundred and fifty years later, a large following around which a new, post-Westphalian consensus is forming, and the logic of the Westphalian order is crumbling.

Joseph Nye has argued that "the real problems of a post-Cold War world will not be new challenges for hegemony, but the new challenges of transnational independence."[41] If his reading of the trajectories of world history is correct, as many today believe, then it is likely that the growing support for a new normative consensus will continue to gather momentum. At the Millennium Summit in September 2000, leaders from throughout the world convened to reach agreement on new norms for the new realities of the twenty-first century, and they gave enthusiastic voice in support of a new normative order to underpin world order, in an innovative conference as potentially system transforming as were the norms that were supported at Westphalia in 1648 (see Box 7.1).

BOX 7.1
The Imperative of a Post-Westphalian Global Future:
New Consensus Emerges?

"An invasion of armies can be resisted," Victor Hugo wrote in a passage that became a popular epigram, "but not an idea whose time has come." Has the time now come for a new normative consensus, built on the proposition that it is time to shed the Westphalian principles for international relations and replace them with a new normative ethos—one based on a moralistic concern for ideals and a dedication to collective problem solving through global governance? At the so-called UN Millennium Summit in September 2000, widespread support was voiced about the need to moderate and mitigate the ultimately unrewarding struggle for power by states, legitimated by Westphalian norms, and to create a new code for statecraft to promote justice, security, and morality in the twenty-first century. As in the seventeenth century, so again today "behind all the issues of security we find questions about values."[42] The Summit entailed "three days of braining by the leaders of all the world's nations [in] a brave attempt to agree on a set of goals for the next millennium, and common values by which to govern."[43] Consider some expressions that reflect the emerging normative consensus to move beyond Westphalia at the dawn of the new century:

> *Now let's set a new course for the world, no less. We face global challenges that oblige us to work together. If that is true in the economic and social sphere, it applies even more to the challenge of massacre and war. The instinct of human solidarity that impels some states to come to the aid of each other's citizens or to indict each other's former dictators is laudable. But when such actions are taken by one or a few states on their own authority, they bring with them a danger of world anarchy.*
>
> *[At the Millennium Summit] the leaders will adopt a declaration reaffirming our shared values and setting goals for the next fifteen or twenty years. A declaration by itself is of little value, I know. But a declaration containing firm pledges and precise targets, solemnly accepted by the leaders of all nations, can be of great value to the world's peoples as a yardstick by which to judge their rulers' performance. I hope it will be seen not as a mere statement of principles but as a plan of action.*
>
> —Kofi Annan
> U.N. Secretary-General

> *If the new millennium, like the last, remains an age of hegemonic empires and conquerors doing the same old things in new technological ways, remains the age of the master race, the master*

> *economy and the master state, then I am afraid we in developing countries will have to stand up as a matter of principle and say, "Not again."*
>
> —Robert Mugabe
> President of Zimbabwe
>
> *This has been the mother of all summits. It also confirmed that the UN provides the only viable setting to develop a village council for a global village.*
>
> —Kishore Mahbubani
> Singapore's Ambassador to the United Nations
>
> *Multilateralism is too often overlooked or unfairly disparaged in . . . political debates on foreign policy. Yet there is a marked consensus across the political spectrum in favor of it—and therefore a tremendous opportunity . . . to achieve significant progress in strengthening multilateral arrangements.*
>
> —Princeton N. Lyman and Michael H.C. McDowell
> Overseas Development Council

Because global interdependence alongside continuing international anarchy is real and its consequences potent, the world community has little choice but to respond collectively to the high probability that "welfare, not warfare, will shape the rules [and] global threats like ozone holes and pollution will dictate the agenda."[44] These threats require leaders to contemplate substituting an ethic of "shared sovereignty" and mutual assistance for the orthodox *realpolitik* Westphalian ethics of self-help and national competition. Cooperation has become imperative, for most of the new global dangers are *shared* problems that cannot be addressed unilaterally by independent actions; a Westphalian "us-versus-them" zero-sum competition will assuredly undermine the long-term security of the competitors. The emergent problems necessitate acceptance of new norms replacing Westphalian self-help with ones that stress the advantages of state and nonstate actors "working collectively to achieve common objectives."[45] The Westphalian distinction between individual versus collective welfare, always exaggerated, is less clear than ever. There is no contradiction between nationalism and concern for the world. For if everyone's welfare increasingly depends on the welfare of others, and we can only help ourselves by helping others also, an ethic that emphasizes the advantages of contributing to others' welfare must be seen as enlightened self-interest.[46] The new global setting is thus provoking a direct challenge to the Westphalian conception of international norms condoning national competition and downplaying national responsibilities. A normative consensus is emerging that the future international landscape need not necessarily be painted in the single color of the Westphalian order, showing only the dark side of the *animus dominandi*, the lust for power. The cluster of diverse threats to contemporary global order calls for a new ethic, predicated on the hope for—even the expectation of—international cooperation that undermines the anarchical circumstances which discouraged collaboration within the Westphalian structure. The international community must, as Secretary of State James A. Baker asserted in 1990, "use the end of the Cold War to get beyond the whole pattern of settling conflicts by force," because only concerted international cooperation can avert slipping "back into ever more savage regional conflicts in which might alone makes right."[47]

Normative Congruence. A central theme in the Westphalian order was the priority given to the rights of the state over those of the individual. In an effort to free the rulers of states from the moral confines of religious doctrine, the Westphalian norms made rulers supreme, and thereby went against Biblical scripture which warned "Put not your trust in rulers" (*Psalm* 146). Originally, those unrestricted rights of rulers over secularized sovereign states included the resort to military force as an instrument of self-help. Except for rescuing nationals caught in civil disturbances abroad, force rarely served humanitarian ends. Nonintervention, the correlative duty to the right of independence, excluded others from involving themselves in disputes over how a state treated its own citizens. Although early publicists like Hugo Grotius endorsed the use of arms to help foreign citizens facing "manifest oppression,"[48] international law through the nineteenth century gave up "the attempt to regulate recourse to war, the most extreme form of the use of force, and made no distinction between a just and unjust war."[49]

The Westphalian norms were the product of a brutal age, when the fighting warlord states in the Thirty Years' War set aside the medieval just-war principles for the humane conduct of war and liberated rulers by giving them "a complete freedom of action"[50] to wage wars, by any means, to preserve their sovereign independence. In the Westphalian norms, there was no regard for human rights and, instead, enthusiastic endorsement of the concept of the "divine right of kings" to rule over their subjects' authoritatively: "Laws were made to protect the state from the individual and not the individual from the state."[51] Needless to say, the Westphalian conception drafted by princes, to serve the parochial interests of princes, was silent about any such activity of what would today be called "state sponsored terrorism" by rulers practicing genocide against people within their territories, and such medieval concepts as noncombatant immunity in Christian just-war doctrine, which attempted to protect innocent civilians by restricting military targets to soldiers and supplies, were outright repudiated in the savage era of the seventeenth century.

The progressive development of international law in the twentieth century has modified the Westphalian system in two important ways by which the states of global society have distanced themselves from the norms of the Westphalian past. First, the right of states to resort to force was limited by Article 2 (4) of the United Nations Charter, which allows for the use of force only in cases of self-defense (Article 51), actions authorized by the Security Council (Chapter VII), and actions taken by regional organizations that are consistent with the principles of the United Nations (Article 52). Second, respect for fundamental human rights was encouraged by Articles 1 and 55 of the Charter, as well as by the Universal Declaration of Human Rights (1948), the International Covenant on Civil and Political Rights (1966), and the International Covenant on Economic, Social and Cultural Rights (1966).[52] While the formation of these rules may have created a new legal regime,[53] it was situated within an older normative order and "left essentially unchanged the *framework* of the state system and of international law resulting from the Peace of Westphalia."[54]

The new UN Charter regime led to serious incongruities by being nested within an ordering framework premised upon the sovereign right of independence and a parallel duty of nonintervention. On the one hand, human rights are perceived as a legal entitlement worthy of being supported by the force of arms if necessary. On the other hand, the traditional prohibition against military intervention has been reiterated by the 1933 Montevideo Convention on Rights and Duties of States (Article 8); the International Court of Justice in the *Corfu Channel* (1949) and *Nicaragua* (1986) cases; the UN General Assembly in resolutions 2131 (December 21, 1965) and 2625 (October 24, 1970); and in the charters of the United Nations (Article 2 [7]), Organization of American States (Article 18), Organization of African Unity (Article 3), and the League of Arab States (Article 8).

Given the difficulty of reconciling respect for human rights, limitations on the use of force, and nonintervention within the Westphalian framework, a growing chorus of leaders in the global community have called for a new, post-Westphalian normative order. They see Westphalia as an obstacle to peace and human rights, which ought to be exorcized. "We have returned," observes Inis Claude, to the pre-Westphalian "medieval view that it is permissible . . . to fight to promote justice, broadly conceived. Evil ought to be overturned, and good ought to be achieved, by force if necessary."[55] Note how far a world disgusted by war crimes, acts of barbarity, and atrocities committed by leaders has begun to distance itself from the Westphalian license given to heads of states to use armed force against their own populations. The doctrine of "sovereign immunity" flowing from Westphalia that liberated leaders from supervision has been replaced by a new set of norms that now accepts humanitarian military intervention to prevent rulers from committing war crimes, and holds them accountable as criminals who now can be persecuted before the International Criminal Court (ICC) for genocide and other crimes against humanity. In removing the Westphalian protection rulers had previously received, by making it legally possible for a head of state to be charged with war crimes, the global community has turned its back on the spirit of the Westphalian past. The future is painted in the optimistic colors and reform language of Hugo Grotius, and the dark "might makes right" nihilist perspective of Thomas Hobbes (and Niccolò Machiavelli a century before him) is ceasing to guide an interdependent global community—a community increasingly dissatisfied by the *realpolitik* philosophy of Westphalia, which held that "the conduct of nations is, and should be, guided and judged exclusively by the amoral requirements of the national interests."[56]

In summary, the Westphalian normative system suffers from a number of critical deficiencies that, despite some similarities between the conditions of 1648 and those today which rationalize those norms' persistence, greatly diminish Westphalia's capacity to remain a diplomatic code of conduct for the maintenance of a just world order. First, by only allocating legal competence to sovereign actors whose role in addressing global problems is decreasing, the Westphalian order lacks normative consistency. Second, because many of its foundation norms are seen as illegitimate by sovereignty-free actors, a normative consensus that honors the Westphalian spirit has dissipated. Finally, since it is unable to reconcile conflicting values within its very structure, the orthodox Westphalian conception lacks normative congruence. Without consistency, consensus, and congruence, the Westphalian order will be unable to provide normative guidance in the decades ahead.

TOWARD A POST-WESTPHALIAN NORMATIVE ORDER

"Peace hath her victories no less renowned than war," wrote John Milton at the conclusion of the Thirty Years' War. But given that the world presently lacks a higher authority that is empowered to prevent the mighty from imposing their will over others, how can global governance over states triumph? The question has haunted women and men of good will throughout history.

Political leaders with blueprints in mind for a peaceful twenty-first century face the same task today that confronted the diplomats assembled at Münster and Osnabrück over three centuries ago. They must devise a framework for maintaining order that also fosters justice, and construct an architecture compatible with the customary practices of the time which defines the normative boundaries of permissible international conduct.

The vision of international relations which emanated from Westphalia is often metaphorically represented by a game of billiards, with hard-shelled states endlessly colliding on a single spatial plane. In the light of the contemporary challenges from home and abroad to the supreme authority of the "sovereign" state,[57] a more appropriate metaphor now would be that of a dynamic, multi-level network linking a vast constellation of heterogeneous actors. Such a reconceptualization of the world has been called as significant as that which occurred when the hierarchical vision of medieval times was replaced in the sixteenth century by the idea of a society of sovereign states;[58] it would be equally revolutionary in impact and would, ironically, represent a reversal of history full circle by signaling the coming return to the medieval conception of a single unified international society—a "neomedieval" system.[59]

Any normative framework for promoting order and justice in world affairs must begin by recognizing the limitations of the billiard ball metaphor. Rapid, unanticipated changes often create apprehension. As policymakers attempt to understand the unsettling events swirling around them, it is difficult to cast off old habits of mind; yet it is imperative that they do so. In a world inhabited by hard-shelled states, order tends to be given priority over international justice. Given the uncertainties they faced, the architects of the Westphalian settlement sought order through equilibrium, even though balance-of-power politics elevated expediency over justice. Today's leaders could easily respond the same way. In a global network society, however, upholding norms that promote international justice will become as important in the future as protecting territorial borders has been in the past, "requiring a degree of international cooperation and even integration that civilly constrains state sovereignty."[60]

What architecture for global governance can facilitate such levels of cooperation? Traditionally, discussions of this question are framed in terms of three general courses of action available to the most powerful states in the international system (the great powers, which continue to exert disproportionate influence over determining the rules for the entire international community). The great powers can act unilaterally; they can develop specialized bilateral relations; or they can engage in some form of collective collaboration. Of course, each option has many possible variations, and the foreign policies of most great powers contain a mix of acting single handedly, joining with a partner, and acting in concert. What matters for any architecture of global governance is the relative emphasis placed on "going it alone" versus "going it with others," and whether joint action is defined in inclusive or exclusive terms.

Unilateral policies (such as those at one extreme advocated by Thomas Hobbes for a great power to seek preponderance and, through achievement of global hegemony, maintain international order by force), are unlikely to be viable in the twenty-first century. No single great power can shoulder the financial burden of acting alone, and no great power can afford to withdraw isolationistically from active involvement in today's globalized economy, on which their prosperity through economic and military participation are heavily dependent. Most of the transnational problems faced by humanity require collective management, which renders unilateralism a hopeless substitute for multilateralism. Moreover, any attempt by a great power to unilaterally assert its authority is certain to provoke stiff resistance by the others, as the history of the Thirty Years' War (recall Chapter 2) and all other periods of attempted hegemony readily reveal.[61]

An alternative to acting unilaterally is joining with selected states in a series of special relationships, as envisioned at Westphalia as a *laissez-faire* process to maintain international stability through the balance of power. Recall the Westphalian logic, which assumes that

> . . . states will align in a manner that will prevent any one state from developing a preponderance of power. This is based on two assumptions: that states exist in an anarchic system with no higher government and that political leaders will act first

to reduce risks to the independence of their states. The policy of balancing power helps to explain why in modern times a large state cannot grow forever into a world empire. States seek to increase their powers through internal growth and external alliances. Balance of power predicts that if one state appears to grow too strong, others will ally against it so as to avoid threats to their own independence. This behavior, then, will preserve the structure of the system of states[62]

Unfortunately, the past three centuries have not validated this Westphalian recipe for international order; each previous balance of power has eventually collapsed in a catastrophic war, and the interregnum between 1648 and the start of the twenty-first century attests to the inadequacy of alliance formation to police international aggression (recall Chapter 5). In addition, the "networks of intrigue," as Woodrow Wilson referred to the diplomacy of alliance building, are flawed in principle. The alliances and counter-poised blocs resulting from these exclusive associations have significant drawbacks. In a world lacking the stark simplicities of bipolarity, differentiating friend from foe is exceedingly difficult, particularly when, as today, allies in the realm of military security are frequently trade competitors, in a cutthroat global marketplace. Instead of adding predictability to world affairs, a series of special bilateral relationships would foster a fear of encirclement among those who perceive themselves as the targets of these combinations.

Beyond forming special bilateral alliances, great powers have the option of establishing the kind of broad, multilateral associations which the Westphalian architects regarded as anathema—the very kind of medieval common international society for united collective action that those negotiators in Westphalia sought to overthrow and to replace with the modern system of independent states. Two common variants of multilateral options are concerts and collective security organizations. The former involve regularized consultation among those at the top of the global hierarchy; the latter, full participation by all states. A concert constructed to manage the international system jointly offers the benefit of helping control great-power rivalries that often spawn polarized blocs, though at the cost of ignoring the interests of those not belonging to the elite group. Alternatively, the all-inclusive nature of collective security allows every sovereign voice to be heard, but exacerbates the problems of providing a timely response to threatening situations. Since all decision-making bodies tend to become unwieldy as their size expands, what may be needed, to make multilateralism a viable option, is a hybrid that combines elements of a great-power concert with elements of collective security.

One way of combining the advantages of a concert with those of collective security is to create a two-tiered, modular structure that rests on a shared commitment to cooperation and common security. Under such a scheme, countries at the center of policy deliberations would shift as different kinds of problems arise. The system would be concert based, with some great powers taking a leadership role on certain issues and others on a different set of issues. At the same time, this great-power concert would be anchored in a larger collective security framework, where small and medium powers would have a voice in pending matters if their interests were affected or if they possessed expertise in dealing with the issue in question.

On the surface, such a hybrid system appears attractive. But in a world where sovereign territorial states will increasingly share the world stage with nonterritorial, sovereignty-free actors, this form of multilateralism is too limited. While inclusive from the perspective of states, it does not bring relevant nonstate actors to the table. Thus two additional features are needed to craft a truly post-Westphalian architecture of global governance. First, such a structure of world order must embrace a norm of transparency. From the end of the Thirty Years' War through the Cold War, states have cloaked themselves in secrecy. Calls for the voluntary disclosure of economic and military information were interpreted as an intolerable invasion of sovereignty. But making sensitive information accessible allows for accountability, which, in turn, signals cooperative intentions. At a time when many different types of international actors are linked in a community of shared fate, transparency should extend beyond the nation-state. Private corporations, intergovernmental organizations, and other nonstate actors should also adhere to the norm of transparency.

The second modification to a hybrid system of concert-based collective security would involve a formal role for nonstate actors. Just as small and medium powers would have a voice as their interests and expertise warrant, nonstate actors need to have an avenue to bring their unique skills to bear on pressing global problems. Indeed, these heretofore excluded actors frequently have more knowledge and experience dealing with global problems than the representatives of nation-states. The virtue of a modular structure is that it allows for a diverse mix of participants, which can rotate as the issues under consideration change.

A new world order "is fast upon us," writes Stuart Kauffman. "We will live through its birth, ready or not."[63] In a global network society, where states share the world stage with assorted nonstate actors, global governance will become a plural, multilevel enterprise, where effective working relationships hold more importance than the specific types of actors that are interacting. Some global issues may be best dealt with by several states working in concert, others by two or more nongovernmental organizations, and still others by some combination of state and nonstate actors. What will matter more than whether the actors have sovereign status or not is the specific combination of human and nonhuman resources they are able to marshal. The concept of state sovereignty "was more useful in those bygone days when the greatest part of economic life, as well as cultural issues, was confined to a single state and there was relatively little movement of people, goods, capital and even technology and ideas . . . and therefore less likelihood that the internal affairs of one state would impinge on another."[64] Unlike the single sovereign territorial state, networks of diverse actors have the advantage of being able to respond quickly to emerging problems while giving a voice to a broad spectrum of people with a stake in the outcome, many of whom would otherwise be excluded if the issue was only dealt with by the official representatives of sovereign states.

With working relationships among diverse actors gaining unprecedented emphasis, we will need to devote greater attention to the normative aspects of human interaction. In this context, two classical issues have resurfaced: whether morality is relevant to the affairs of states, and, if so, whether in a culturally pluralistic global community there exists a common normative principle that statesmen from diverse ethical traditions might embrace, to discipline diplomatic behavior. Let us consider the controversies that surround these timeless issues which were debated in the medieval period and are now likely to be debated in the postmodern twenty-first century.

As a preface to our concluding chapter, we shall contend that "Globalization increasingly demands that we trust people we never see or, perhaps, hear; pluralism forces us to trust people close by who are very different from us."[65] As we see it, in the last analysis a fatal drawback to the Westphalian system was the striking degree of mistrust that it bred. Collective problem solving suffers when the Westphalian logic of *realpolitik* counsels against firm commitments and encourages unilateral, opportunistic self-help behavior; the Machivellian "invitation to immorality" embedded in Westphalian logic, we maintain, counterproductively reduces "the conduct of good men to the standards of the worst."[66] To be sure, cooperation can occur without trust, and exploitation can thrive in an atmosphere of trust.[67] But as one prescient observer of world politics has concluded, without a "presumption of trust" by the various actors now playing diverse roles on the world stage, it will be difficult to maintain minimally tolerable conditions for social life globally.[68] Stability and prosperity, Francis Fukuyama has convincingly shown, are likely to depend, more than ever, on trust: on the Grotian social solidarity of a cohesive global community instead of on the Westphalian rugged individualism of unrestrained competition that ignores the moral basis of community.[69] Following this principle, let us turn our attention in the final chapter to the issue of how to build trust among diverse international actors,[70] which will be critical for operating the kind of post-Westphalian system of global governance necessary for international security and world order.

CHAPTER 8

The Importance of Trust in Global Governance for World Order

Every kind of peaceful cooperation among men is primarily based on mutual trust.
—Albert Einstein

In the previous two chapters, we have described how various integrative and disintegrative trends are changing international affairs. Because of these trends, the world of the early twenty-first century differs markedly from that of the mid-seventeenth century. The sovereign territorial state will not disappear in the foreseeable future, but its preeminent position is gradually eroding as nonterritorial, sovereignty-free actors play increasingly important roles on the global stage. The metaphor of a network captures the essence of contemporary world politics better than the traditional image of colliding billiard balls. Viewing world politics as a complex web of state and nonstate actors highlights the need for a modular, multilayered system of global governance. Whereas the Westphalian normative order privileged myopic, self-directed great powers, we contend that a post-Westphalian order should be more inclusive, bringing different types of actors into global policy deliberations as required by the nature of the problem at hand. Exorcising the ghost of Westphalia is crucial for resolving policy problems that transcend national jurisdictions—because *who* makes decisions about world order issues is inseparable from *what* gets decided.[1]

Despite all of the changes that have occurred in world politics since the end of the Thirty Years' War, some entrenched continuities persist. Perhaps the most important continuity concerns the persisting mistrust that pervades today's self-help international system, whose diplomatic culture remains imbued in Westphalian logic. As Mikhail Gorbachev once observed, without trust "it is difficult to make headway in politics."[2] Certainly, limited cooperation can take place without trust, and treachery can occur among those who trust one another; however, building international trust is critical if we are to move beyond the atomistic, competitive system of politics that arose in the wake of Westphalia. Regardless of how a post-Westphalian system of global governance might be structured, its long-term stability will be enhanced if it is anchored on a bedrock of trust.

TRUST AND STATECRAFT

In some respects, today's endemic insecurity mirrors the distrust that characterized the torturous peace negotiations of the seventeenth century. The Thirty Years' War was punctuated by several unsuccessful efforts to stop the carnage. Although Protestant forces were defeated in the battle of White Mountain within eighteen months of the defenestration of Prague, the fighting dragged on for decades because the victors could not convert their military triumph into a viable political settlement. Neither side had faith in the other, and a culture of mistrust took root.

A lack of mutual trust continually hampered attempts to end the bloodshed. For example, the terms offered in 1635, by a compact known as the Peace of Prague, were rejected by many on the Protestant side because the proposed settlement did little to curb Hapsburg power. A year later, the pope invited the Catholic princes to send delegates to a peace conference in Cologne but France refused to send envoys. In 1640, the emperor convened a Diet at Ratisbon, but it too was unable to arrive at terms that the Protestants could accept. Despite mounting battlefield losses and mediation offers from Brandenburg, Denmark, and Luxemburg, the war continued. As horrible as it might be, armed combat seemed less onerous to the belligerents than a living under a noxious political settlement.

During the tumult of war, when the air is heavy with apprehension about the future, sincere peace proposals can easily be mistaken for ruses. All negotiations are influenced by the sense of trust that the belligerents bring to the bargaining table. Whether or not they believe in one another's willingness to abide by the promises they make has an enormous impact on structure of the agenda, the sequence of offers and concessions, and the ability to narrow differences toward a mutually acceptable agreement. In the case of the Thirty Years' War, the pervasive fears caused by years of brutal combat shaped expectations about real motives underlying each side's peace proposals. This belief in the inherent bad faith of the enemy helps to explain why the Westphalian settlement stressed (without success) the importance of "the restoration of friendship between the treaty parties."[3]

Trust is a social adhesive. The performance of all groups is affected by shared expectations held about the behavior of their members in contingent circumstances. Without trust, we harbor uncertainties about the intentions of others, and we avoid placing ourselves at their mercy unless we can identify common interests, verify that commitments are being fulfilled, and retaliate in a manner that makes betrayal unprofitable. Cardinal Richelieu, the architect of French foreign policy from 1624 until his death in 1642, counseled King Louis XIII about the dangers posed by a climate of international mistrust. "It is necessary to sleep like the lion, without closing one's eyes," he warned, "so that one may instantly ward off the slightest misfortune which may arise."[4]

In the grim political cauldron of the mid-seventeenth century, it is easy to understand the pessimism that pervaded European society, and why the belligerents made the assumption that because they could not trust each other the natural order of international life was a state of war.[5] To understand the importance of trust as a foundation for a post-Westphalian world order, it is helpful to first delineate the meaning that we ascribe to the concept. Let us therefore explain our conception of trust, and then discuss different forms that it may take in world politics.

The Concept of Trust

As a property of collective units (dyads, groups, communities, and societies), trust is a social-psychological concept. Indeed, "individuals would have no occasion or need to trust apart from social relationships."[6] Because human interactions are influenced by the degree of trust that the parties have in one another, "whenever philosophers, poets, statesmen, or theologians have written about man's relationship to his fellow man, . . . the phenomena of trust and betrayal, faith and suspicion, responsibility and irresponsibility, have been discussed."[7] Yet despite all of this attention, until recently little has been done by social scientists to develop a theory of trust.[8] Since building trust among a welter of diverse state and nonstate actors is crucial for laying the foundation for a just world order, let us briefly explore the elements of this concept which are so central to both interpersonal and international relations.

The concept of trust blends risk with an expectation of forbearance. We accept the risk that someone could injure us at the very time we expect they will not take advantage of opportunities created by our acceptance of that risk. Trust, in other words, entails optimism about the good will and competence of other parties as they pertain to our interaction with them. When we trust someone, we expect them to care about our welfare and to fulfill any commitments they might make on our behalf. But trust is more than just a reliance upon the benevolence and capabilities of others. In relationships anchored on trust, the party being trusted (trustee) is directly and favorably moved by the thought that he or she is being counted on by the party doing the trusting (truster).[9] In short, the trustee feels *obliged* to fulfill the truster's expectations.

Trust, in other words, is a complex, multidimensional concept. Though frequently equated with credibility, its meaning extends beyond having one's statements accepted as factual. For example, someone would be considered credible if we believed his or her promise to forgo the exploitation of a specific situation. Within a relationship based on trust, even when the latter party could gain from opportunistic behavior in situations *not* covered by formal promises, he or she would refrain from doing so. Thus in addition to the dimension of credibility, trust includes beliefs about the good will, competence, and reliability of another party.[10] When trusting someone, we believe: (1) what they say is true; (2) they have concern for our welfare and are moved by the knowledge that we are counting on them; (3) they possess the capability to follow through on their pledges; and (4) there is consistency between their words and deeds. The stronger our beliefs along each of these dimensions, the greater our overall trust in the other party.[11]

To acknowledge that each of these four dimensions can vary in strength is to recognize that trust is not dichotomous—something that either exists or does not exist. The strength of our trust in another party can be conceptualized as a point on a distribution of expectations that represents the level of *subjective* probability with which we assess that the other party will perform a particular act. The probability score can range from complete trust (i.e., a value of 1.00) to complete distrust (a value of 0.00), and is a product of our evaluation of the other party's credibility, good will, competence, and reliability. Trusting is a matter of degree, and the magnitude of trust required for political leaders to accept different kinds of international agreements varies. The greater the potential injury arising from an act of betrayal, the higher someone's subjective probability score must be in order to reach a significant agreement with another party.

Types of Trust

Trust may be narrow or wide. It might be confined to straightforward transactions within a single issue-area, or extended to more diffuse exchanges spread across several issues on which there are deep divides.[12] When it stretches across many different issues, the degree of trust in another party can be uniform, or it may vary from one issue-area to the next. For example, states may develop a relatively high level of trust that their trade agreements will be honored at the same time that their confidence in the arms control treaties they have negotiated with each other remain relatively low.

Two approaches have been taken to explain the contours of trust between international actors who can behave freely within an anarchical setting. The first stems from research inspired by "rational choice" theory; the second, from "social contextualist" theory. Rather than representing alternatives, these two approaches are complementary: the former provides a cogent account of the most bounded forms of trust, while the latter offers a better account of deeper, more extended forms of trust. Let us briefly discuss each of these theoretical approaches and the types of trust they illuminate.

What we shall call "reciprocity-based trust" arises from recurring, out-of-the-ordinary interactions. States are only selectively attentive to the actors in their environment,[13] but those experiencing high levels of continuous interaction tend to exhibit a pattern of reciprocity in their exchanges. Reciprocity means responding in kind to the behavior of another party, returning good for good and ill for ill. Although these responses may resemble the behavior received (e.g., friendly acts from one party returned by friendly acts from the other party), the responses may not match precisely what the other side has done.[14]

As an explanation for behavior within a process of sequential action, the concept of reciprocity has long been popular among students of social and economic exchange.[15] In recent years, numerous studies have documented that reciprocal exchanges characterize the usual pattern of relations between frequently interacting states.[16] Drawing upon the findings reported in this literature, Martin Patchen has proposed that the reciprocation of cooperative actions becomes more likely as:

A. The actor has a higher expectation that his own cooperative action will result in continued mutual cooperation.
   Such expectations will increase as:
   1. The recent behavior of the other has been cooperative, especially compared to the actor's own behavior.
   2. The other's outcomes are (seen as) positively correlated with the actor's own outcomes (common interests).
   3. The other is *not* (seen as) stronger than the actor.
   4. Third parties are providing incentives for the other to continue cooperation.
B. The value of mutual cooperation to the actor is high.
   This value will increase as:
   1. The actor has a strong need for the rewards that the other can provide.
   2. The actor lacks alternatives for meeting his needs.
   3. The actor is not disadvantaged in its exchange with the other.
   4. The actor wishes to maintain, rather than to challenge, the status quo with respect to the distribution of privileges.
   5. The interaction between the actor and the other will continue for some time in the future.
C. The value of (possible) advantages to the other is not strongly negative.
   This value will depend on the magnitude of the loss (if any) to the actor that may result from a competitive or conflictive response by the other to his own cooperation and on the irreversibility of his own cooperative action or concession.

D. The intrinsic value of cooperation is high.
   This value will increase for the actor as:
   1. The direct cost of his cooperation decreases.
   2. Domestic political support for cooperation increases.
   3. The support of third nations for cooperative action increases.
   4. The norms requiring reciprocation of cooperation are stronger and more accepted by the actor.[17]

High levels of cooperative reciprocity between adversaries reinforce the international norm that states should not injure those who have helped them.[18] According to rational choice theory, during an iterated chain of contacts, as self-interested actors choose alternatives with the highest expected utility, the norm of reciprocity induces restraint and creates trust in others.

In contrast to the rational choice approach to conceptualizing trust, a social contextualist approach depicts individuals as social decision makers whose level of sociability varies across different contexts.[19] Trust, from this perspective, is embedded within a larger cultural milieu where ritual, symbolic behavior, and affective attitudes are important.[20] We shall call this phenomenon "identification-based trust." It is predicated on the assumption that certain kinds of behavior emanate from one's perception of self in relation to others, and this identity sets the domain of choice for an individual.

Identity formation is a binding of self with society. According to Kenneth Hoover, although individual identities may differ in content, they all consist of some combination of claims that refer to (1) competence in certain vocations or avocations, (2) location in the social firmament (as believers in a particular religion, natives of a particular region, partisans of a certain ideology, and so on), and (3) personal interconnections or attachments.[21] People sharing the bonds of identity generally possess an empathetic understanding of one another's desires and interests. Moreover, they tend to hold an in-group bias that portrays those who are similar in positive, trustworthy terms.[22] As a result, social categorization based on identity provides a robust form of trust that can sustain cooperation across multiple issue-areas, even in the absence of reciprocity.[23]

One of the benefits of viewing trust through the prism of social identity is that it emphasizes the affective aspects of trust—the ways in which someone is prone to act on his or her feelings of love or hate toward another party. Although most of the scholarly literature on trust stresses the role of cognitive processes in predicting how others will behave, Lawrence Becker reminds us that noncognitive trust frequently colors our everyday experiences.

> In ordinary life there is massive anecdotal evidence that most of us have personal relationships in which we remain trustful despite the known untrustworthiness of others. Whether this is with an unfaithful spouse, an alcoholic lover, a backbiting friend, . . . it is not uncommon for people to be both vividly aware of the problem in reflective moments and helplessly credulous, reliant, or secure in action.[24]

Applying Becker's insight to world politics, it can be argued that decisions involving trust are not only about weighing material costs and benefits; they are also about image, which has emotionally powerful implications for how state and nonstate actors present themselves and how they perceive their standing within the world community.[25]

To summarize, trust is a multifaceted phenomenon with distinct cognitive *and* affective manifestations.[26] Whether generated by reciprocity or identity, trust is a unique resource whose supply increases with use. The higher the level of trust and the longer the time horizon that someone faces in a relationship, the less he or she "would be apprehensive about being harmed as well as tempted to take short-term gains."[27] Given that the most powerful form of trust exists within groups that share certain fundamental values,[28] the dilemma for the architects of world order is how to build a culture of trust between groups that are so antagonistic and lacking in shared values that they take up arms to resolve their disagreements. What, if anything, can be done to break this barrier of mutual suspicions?

GLOBAL CULTURES OF TRUST AND MISTRUST

Within a global culture of trust, mutually beneficial problem-solving ventures are common since information is readily shared, transaction costs are low, and scarce resources do not have to be expended to assure compliance with promises. With credibility taken as a given, agreements become largely self-enforcing. Trust permits habits of cooperation to develop and expand—a process of learning that builds still new levels of trust. Attention can be focused not just on one's own interests but also on the obligation of everyone to the common good.

These benefits notwithstanding, most wars end under a shroud of suspicion. As we have seen in the Thirty Years' War, multiple fears swirl around the peacemaking process: the fear that trusting an adversary will open oneself to exploitation; the fear that tying one's fate to others will create expectations that cannot be fulfilled; and the fear that commitments will create an entangling position from which it will be impossible to extricate oneself without prohibitively high costs and risks. These kinds of fears encourage states to pursue unilateral policies under the banner of national self-sufficiency. By elevating unrestrained sovereign autonomy above the respect for promissory obligations upon which fiduciary relationships depend, postwar apprehensions can easily spawn a culture of mistrust.

International interactions within a culture of mistrust are motivated by a felt need to engage in self-protective behavior to counter the threats of predatory challengers. Deceit is justified as a tactic of statecraft because competition is believed to be zero-sum, and unscrupulous practices allow one to take advantage of others and accrue more power. Unsure of the aims of rivals but convinced that power furnishes protection, each state takes measures to enhance its own security, only to find that these precautions are regarded elsewhere as evidence of hostile intent. The drive to establish absolute security for one state creates the perception of absolute insecurity for the others, with the result that everyone becomes locked into an upward spiral of hostile countermeasures that jeopardizes the security of all. Simply put, mistrust is contagious: it breeds the very behaviors that accelerate its diffusion.

Westphalia and the Culture of Mistrust

A "culture of trust" and a "culture of mistrust" describe two very different normative climates for the conduct of international relations. The history of the complicated negotiations that led to the Peace of Westphalia reminds us how difficult it is to extinguish the flames of war and to forge a new set of rules for world order that break the chains of mutual mistrust. As we have shown, the diplomats at Münster and Osnabrück attempted to build a more peaceful, orderly world through a system of *laissez-faire* competition. But rather than eradicating the suspicions that had enveloped Europe during the Thirty Years' War, such a system only served to perpetuate the culture of mistrust that the traumatic war bred.

The Westphalian settlement gave states freedom to act, unbounded and unburdened by strict normative restraints. Holding supreme power over their land and its populace, the rulers of these sovereign states no longer owed allegiance to the idea of a universal Christian commonwealth under papal authority. Yet with sovereignty came the security dilemma of international anarchy: in the absence of a central arbiter wielding the legitimacy and coercive capability to maintain peace and enforce international law, state leaders had no alternative but to remain vigilant, rely upon self-help to deter aggression, and punish encroachments on their territory whenever deterrence failed. Hence the art of statecraft in this increasingly secular world required pursuing vital interests within the limits imposed by available resources, regardless of whether such pursuits violated traditional moral standards. National self-interests stood above collective, community interests.

When the delegates at Münster and Osnabrück canceled the Hapsburg bid for hegemony in Christendom, they replaced the politics of vertical world order with those of a horizontal world order. Whereas a vertical order contains national units that are linked together in superior-subordinate relationships, a horizontal order contains autonomous, legally equal national units of differential power and prestige. Because a horizontal world order lacks a central arbiter to regulate competition among its members, even well-intentioned leaders acquire arms and allies to guard against rapacious neighbors. Unable to decipher the intentions of others, they often hedge their bets by maintaining high levels of military readiness. As the imperial general Count Raymondo Montecuccoli asserted, "statesmen cannot doubt that there can be no real peace between powerful competing states; one must suppress or be suppressed, one must either kill or perish."[29]

The propensity of political leaders in decentralized, horizontal orders to seek peace through military preparedness was seen as inevitable by the authors of the Westphalian settlement. Those jockeying for competitive advantage were expected to maintain constant watch over one another, which allegedly allowed threats to be recognized early enough to parry acts of aggression. If an aggressor like King Louis XIV of France proved too strong for a potential victim to contain, a coalition would form and block his expansion. In this way, mutual suspicions combined with a joint fear of aspiring hegemons to create a security architecture that rested on a foundation of unremitting scrutiny and countervailing alliances. Paradoxically, a culture of mistrust became part of the balance-of-power system designed to prevent another catastrophic war. With each state pressing for national advantage, a tenuous equilibrium was expected to emerge as ambition checked ambition and self-interest countered self-interest. The state system would be preserved, not due to a general desire for a thriving international community, but as a byproduct of each state ruthlessly striving to advance its own cause.[30]

Although the Westphalian security regime attempted to place mistrust in the service of peace, history has cast doubt on the wisdom of this world view. A large body of evidence on the causes of war suggests that *realpolitik* balance-of-power policies are far less successful than their advocates claim.[31] Rather than harnessing mistrust for beneficial ends, these policies have increased international tensions and made disputes more apt to escalate to war.

Weighing the Evidence on Cultures of Mistrust

When war, imperial overstretch, or uneven growth produces profound changes in the distribution of national capabilities, the interests of rising states generally diverge from the interests of those suffering from decline. In multipolar environments, where capabilities are dispersed in a pattern of rough parity among three or more great powers, these shifts cause enormous difficulties in assessing the relative strength of allies and adversaries. These difficulties are magnified when international norms support a flexible interpretation of alliance commitments. If prevailing norms allow states to disregard treaty obligations and realign as expediency dictates, predicting who will be in league with whom whenever conflicts occur becomes problematic and mistrust soars. Uncertain about one's own military might, the loyalty of friends, and the backing enjoyed by foes, foreign policy miscalculations are more likely. As revealed by research on permissive alliance norms, the international system experiences a rise in serious disputes when states are engulfed by cultures of mistrust.[32]

Upswings in the frequency of serious disputes are dangerous because they increase the probability of war. One way this has been demonstrated is through the tendency of leaders in successive crises to employ more coercive bargaining tactics in each subsequent encounter.[33] The problem with relying on coercive diplomacy to communicate resolve is that bullying tactics and physical threats to vital interests have been found to be associated with the escalation of crises to wars.[34]

Another way the build-up of serious disputes can raise the probability of war is through the tendency of those involved in confrontations to seek allies and acquire additional arms. During a series of disputes, numerous distinct political stakes easily become linked into a single overarching issue.[35] In effect, the disputes no longer remain independent of one another.[36] As a result, the conflict becomes more intractable; the prospects for an amicable settlement decline, and the disputants acquire assistance by forming alliances. This strategy ultimately can be destabilizing because alliance aggregation has been found to be related to subsequent increases in arms expenditures,[37] perhaps as insurance against the ever-present fear of defection among one's allies when they are most needed.

The difficulties posed by arms acquisition are twofold. In the first place, serious disputes that take place during arms races tend to escalate into wars, especially when they occur within enduring rivalries.[38] In the second place, if war occurs, the effect of alliances will be to spread the hostilities and create a larger, more complex conflict.[39] Should these alliances polarize into rigid, adversarial blocs, the magnitude and severity of any war that erupts will be greater than if they had remained flexible, disaggregated coalitions.[40]

To sum up, serious disputes accumulate within cultures of mistrust. Ever suspicious about the intentions of others, political leaders overestimate the hostility they face and exaggerate the susceptibility of their opponents to ultimata. Mistaken about relative strength and the reliability of allies, they can easily underestimate the risks of issuing threats and slip into a self-aggravating conflict spiral.[41] Moreover, the very environment that evokes this behavior thwarts efforts to deescalate. Without a modicum of trust, garbled information about the actions taken by an adversary can lead fearful states to assume the worst, cling to negative images of their rival's character, and discount initiatives aimed at reducing tension. In such a foreboding environment, the Leninist dictum is widely accepted: "Trust is good, but control is better."

APPROACHES TO BUILDING A GLOBAL CULTURE OF TRUST

The transition from peace to war is a multistage process, where chance, various contextual factors, and the sequence of choices made by the interacting parties affect the aggregate outcome. More than one combination of these ingredients may lead to war, and different combinations may lead to different types of wars. Understanding why wars occur may be likened to knowing how to open "a highly sophisticated combination lock" that has "several different number sequences that will release it." To disengage the lock, one must know "not only the individual numbers and the sequences in which they should be entered, but also the movement instructions."[42] Just as our hypothetical lock has more than one set of number sequences that can open it, there are multiple combinations of chance, context, and choice that can lead to war.

Up to this point in our discussion, we have sketched how certain ingredients spawned by a culture of mistrust may combine to produce wars of rivalry.[43] We focused on this particular combination because it is a consequence of forces set in motion by the Peace of Westphalia, forces that still haunt us as we begin the new millennium. Ironically, by placing international security on the precarious foundation of a balance of power, and by legitimating the use of *realpolitik* tactics as the means for maintaining international equilibrium, the Peace of Westphalia assured that warfare would persist. As John Vasquez has argued, the realist "practices of power politics not only lead rivals to take steps that lead to war, but to follow practices, which, under certain conditions, make the wars that do occur into world wars."[44]

To exorcise the ghost of Westphalia, it is necessary to build a global political culture of trust. Of course, trust cannot eradicate conflict.[45] It prevents some disputes, curbs others before they escalate, and facilitates mutual problem solving when disagreements turn violent. However, it is wrong to assume that diplomacy can always resolve international disputes if there is trust on both sides. The temptation to behave opportunistically can arise, even with full trust, when the anticipated time horizon of a relationship is short.[46] Trust, as Deborah Welch Larson points out, is "a necessary (though not sufficient) condition for states to cooperate."[47]

What factors can contribute to building trust in the twenty-first century international arena? Research on this question is still in its infancy; nonetheless, preliminary evidence suggests that the central problem for peacebuilders is to establish reciprocity-based trust and then gradually develop ways to expand it into identity-based trust.

Establishing Reciprocity-Based Trust

When trust has been broken, the betrayed party can experience a wide array of emotions. Feelings of humiliation, sadness, and indignation are common, though the exact combination and sequence of emotions appears to depend upon the form of betrayal.[48] Deceit by those we trust unleashes these powerful emotions because more is felt to be at stake than the immediate, tangible losses emanating from the act of ill will. Violating a relationship of trust disturbs what the aggrieved party thought was a larger reservoir of shared ethical values. Under certain circumstances, this can trigger a reexamination of the mental images heretofore used to order the social cosmos, as well as engender fears that still others will take advantage of one's vulnerabilities.

Building trust, especially after one has been betrayed, is a slow process.

Trust does not arise spontaneously in a cold, uncertain environment; it must be earned. Both state and nonstate actors can gradually establish reputations for being trustworthy—by making unconditionally supportive gestures, by eschewing opportunities that a perfidious actor would have seized, and by consistently reciprocating acts of cooperation.[49] According to what is called the "augmentation principle," the greater the costs entailed by such behavior, the less a recipient will view it as the product of ulterior motives.[50]

The most constructive approach to building reciprocity-based trust is a firm-but-conciliatory strategy that communicates amicable intentions, rewards cooperation, and punishes exploitative behavior. In brief, the strategy calls for a calculated program of unilateral conciliatory initiatives, followed by "tit for tat" responses to actions taken by the other side.[51] While there are many variants of reciprocating influence strategies, this approach contains four key attributes. First, it begins with an overt cooperative action coupled with an invitation for the adversary to respond in kind. Evidence from laboratory experiments[52] and comparative studies[53] indicates that such actions are effective except when an adversary seeks total domination.[54] As Roger Fisher and William Ury propose, one of the most productive ways to change negative perceptions held by a rival "is to send them a message different from what they expect."[55] Acting inconsistently with ingrained enemy images and acknowledging the interests held by one's counterparts help break cycles of mistrust and mutual competition.

The second attribute in a firm-but-conciliatory strategy is clarity. All unilateral actions aimed at eliciting cooperation from an adversary should be simple, unambiguous, and verifiable. They should be announced publicly prior to their execution, explained as components within a deliberate series of moves aimed at reducing tensions, and completed on schedule even if the adversary does not immediately respond.

The third attribute is provocability. Conciliators should demonstrate resolve in protecting their interests and vigorously resist attempts by the other party to take advantage of unilateral concessions. Policies that combine rapid responses to an adversary's collaborative behavior, with slow replies to provocations, encourage exploitative maneuvers.[56] The available evidence suggests that mutual cooperation is more easily resumed after punishing a provocation if the retaliation is slightly less than the infraction and is accompanied by a positive inducement.[57]

The fourth attribute of a firm-but-conciliatory strategy is forgiveness. Opportunistic noncooperation is penalized, but it is not allowed to harden into a permanent obstacle to reconciliation. Of course, genuine forgiveness is neither simple nor is it necessarily permanent. It is a demanding, protracted process characterized by several often-neglected features.[58] First, forgiveness is not a moral pardon; it incorporates a memory of past evils suffused with a judgment of injustice. Second, forgiveness entails forbearance; past wrongs are neither overlooked nor excused, but punishment is not reduced to revenge. Third, forgiveness involves empathy for the enemy; it recognizes the offender's humanity. Finally, forgiveness is restorative; it seeks to repair fractured human relationships and promote social healing.

By itself, forgiveness is not reconciliation. For social healing to occur, in many cultures wrongdoers must apologize for the injuries sustained by others. When accepted, apologies can be therapeutic, mending rifts between people, reviving faith in organizations, and resolving conflicts among states. They are a sign of character: evidence that a wrongdoer has the integrity to admit fault. Like forgiveness, a sincere apology entails several things. First, it involves feelings of sorrow and regret for the injurious act.[59] Second, it expresses shame over what was done and repudiates that kind of behavior.[60] Third, it contains an avowal henceforth to conduct oneself in the proper way.[61] Finally, it includes a gesture of penance to atone for the transgression. In some societies, apologies are part of a ritual of verbal remediation, where joint declarations of contrition defuse a confrontation by creating enough ambiguity regarding its origins to permit the offender to withdraw without losing face. In other societies, apologies inaugurate a process of lustration (or purification), where the offender is reintegrated into the fold through a public ceremony of reacceptance.[62]

In summary, reciprocity-based trust is slowly built through a series of graduated, cumulative actions. It is closely connected with our conceptions of equity and fairness in exchanges.[63] Reconciliation after the rupture of relationship is a dynamic process of conciliatory accommodation that requires actions by those who have had their trust betrayed, as well as by those who have committed the betrayal.[64] The greater the nature of the loss suffered by the party that had the courage to trust, the greater the asymmetry in the outcomes from previous encounters favoring the party making promises, and the greater the vested interests on either side in continuing the conflict, the less likely full reconciliation will be achieved. Sometimes the hurdles may be so great that what passes for reconciliation may be nothing more than a one-sided acquiescence to circumstances. At other times, however, enemies can become friends. Former adversaries may create bilateral and multilateral joint ventures that facilitate working together on shared goals.[65] A common sense of purpose can foster a common identity, and allow the parties to move beyond reciprocity-based trust to warmer relations, a more active partnership, and a broader basis for trust.

Developing Identity-Based Trust

Movement from reciprocity-based trust within a narrow domain of interaction to the more secure footing of identity-based trust will not eliminate conflicts of interest. Disputes can erupt, but psychological and institutional mechanisms can defuse most of them before they turn violent. When two or more parties enjoy identity-based trust, they cultivate an appreciation of the individual needs and wants of each. They know one another well enough to anticipate their respective responses to emerging problems, and this feeling of mutual understanding resists challenges from contradictory information. It is more difficult to attribute diabolical intentions to an abstraction called "the other side" than to someone with whom you share the bonds of a common identity.[66]

How Identity-Based Trust Has Been Built at the Regional Level.   Perhaps the best example of how identity-based trust can be developed lies in the European Coal and Steel Community (ECSC) formed by France, Germany, Italy, Belgium, Luxemburg, and the Netherlands in 1952. Europe emerged from the Second World War a devastated continent with a demoralized population. Over 35 million Europeans perished during the fighting. Much of the urban landscape was reduced to bomb craters and rubble. Countless buildings were uninhabitable, the transportation infrastructure lay in ruins, and food was scarce. Not since the Thirty Years' War had a conflict in Europe caused so much damage. Shocked by the destruction, some people believed that the Continent was infected with a virulent strain of nationalism that periodically caused epidemics of warfare. Indeed, three times in the span of seventy years, the French and the Germans had squared off on the battlefield, and twice in the first four decades of the twentieth century. Jean Monnet, the chief spokesman for a movement dedicated to pan-European economic integration, reacted to the horrors of the war by asking: "How could Europeans escape from the pattern of their history? How could nations suddenly learn to behave like civilized men?"[67]

Following Germany's unconditional surrender in Reims, France on May 7, 1945, the country was partitioned into American, British, French, and Russian occupation zones, with the military commanders-in-chief of each zone given complete administrative authority. According to General Charles de Gaulle, head of the provisional government that ruled France after its liberation in 1944, "the fate of Germany was the central problem of the universe."[68] From 1944 until 1948, France sought to deal with this problem by carving a French sphere of influence out of Germany that would extend to the "natural frontier" of the Rhine River. However, the French received little support from these wartime allies for dismembering Germany. When territory east of the Oder and Neisse Rivers was given to Poland after the war, de Gaulle complained: "Germany was amputated in the East but not in the West. The current of German vitality is thus turned westwards. One day German aggressiveness might well face westwards too."[69] Although France signed a Treaty of Mutual Assistance with the Soviet Union in 1944 that called upon the two countries to take "all the necessary measures in order to eliminate any new menace coming from Germany" (Article 3), de Gaulle and his successors in the Fourth Republic failed to detach the western regions of Germany. French territorial ambitions were not countenanced by the United States or the Soviet Union, since each superpower hoped to bring a unified Germany into its own political orbit.

In response to growing friction with the Soviet Union, the Federal Republic of Germany (FRG) was established in 1949 by merging the American, British, and French occupation zones. Controlled by an Allied High Commission that superseded the military governors of each zone, this truncated "West Germany" had little leeway to craft its own foreign or domestic policies; consequently the primary goal of Konrad Adenauer, the tall, austere Rhinelander who served as the Federal Republic's first chancellor, was to regain sovereignty over German land.

From Adenauer's perspective, the future of Germany hinged on rapprochement with France. Immediately following the war, a variety of informal ties between the two countries were forged by private citizens. Subsequently, local and regional officials launched their own outreach activities, which were supplemented by other initiatives undertaken through nongovernmental organizations. In addition to promoting cultural, scholarly, and people-to-people exchanges, these efforts to connect leery residents on both sides of the border supported sister city programs and a host of joint activities for French and German youth groups. Over time, they created a dense cross-national network, rich with frequent and multiple contacts.[70]

At the same time that this "human infrastructure" for "trustworthy relations"[71] was being established, the status of the German economy came under review. Under the terms of the 1949 Petersberg Protocol (named after a mountain outside Bonn, where the Allied High Commissioners had their headquarters), the occupying powers agreed to end the dismantling of German industry and remove the production ceilings that had been in place since 1946. In exchange, Adenauer accepted a proposal to establish an International Authority for the Ruhr basin, Germany's most important industrial region. Concerned that external restraints over German industry would one day be removed, French Foreign Minister Robert Schuman endorsed an idea suggested by Jean Monnet: all French and German coal and steel resources would be placed under a joint authority, and other European states would be allowed to take part in the new organization. For many people, this so-called "Schuman Plan" evoked the old saw that the Pas de Calais-Saar-Ruhr industrial enterprises were always prescribed by geography but prevented by history. For Germany, the replacement of the International Ruhr Authority by the ECSC would mean a partial restoration of German sovereignty since Bonn would participate in the organization as an equal.

The ECSC contained a supranational body called the High Authority, which made legally binding decisions by majority vote on the production and marketing of coal and steel. As part of the ECSC, Germany could revive its heavy industry after World War II without alarming its neighbors, who now possessed some degree of control over key German resources by virtue of their representation in the High Authority. As David Calleo summarized the logic behind the ESCS:

> It was impossible . . . to tie together France and Germany through classical diplomatic arrangements. The basic problem was that neither could afford to concede much to the other without feeling its own security and prosperity endangered,

and thus the old cycle of competition and fear had continued endlessly. The only solution was to fuse the two countries in such a way that each would lose its independent power to do mortal harm to the other.[72]

Fusing the two countries was not easy. The ECSC was "established in the face of significant distrust."[73] Not only were reservations expressed by major portions of the trade union movement, but Adenauer was attacked by Social Democratic Party leader Kurt Schumacher as "the Chancellor of the Allies."[74] A strident nationalist who had survived twelve years in a Nazi concentration camp, Schumacher saw the ECSC as a tool for bolstering capitalism and preventing German reunification. Rather than being tightly integrated within the Western alliance, he favored a neutral, socialist Germany that hopefully would be able to reach a political accommodation with the Soviet Union.

Further complicating matters was the political future of the Saar basin. A region rich in natural resources, the Saar had been occupied by France at the end of the war. Between 1948 and 1950, the French attempted to unite the Saar economically with France, and later proposed that it be admitted into the ECSC as an autonomous entity. Insisting that the Saar territories were an integral part of Germany, the Adenauer government eventually reached a compromise agreement with the French. In exchange for the restoration of German political sovereignty over the Saar, France would be given twenty-five years to phase out its mining operations in the region as well as other economic considerations. The resolution of the intensely contested Saar dispute was ultimately accomplished "because both countries recognized how crucial it was to nurture a Franco-German reconciliation."[75]

Recognizing that reconciliation was a long-term process that would require the creation of a new sense of identity, Adenauer weathered criticism of the Coal and Steel Community and pushed to integrate Bonn as an equal member within a tightly knit European community. As he later wrote:

> I was convinced that the *Montanunion* (as the Germans called the ECSC) in its results would change, not only the economic relations of our continent, but the whole manner of thinking and the political feeling of Europeans. I was convinced that they would lead the Europeans out of the confines of their national State existence into the broad reaches of the European area. . . . People whose feelings were still in our time determined by suspicion, the desire for advantage, and resentment would become neighbors and friends.[76]

His reflections on the birth of the ECSC paralleled the thoughts of many integration theorists. According to Ernst Haas, various scholars have hypothesized that the progressively rewarding experiences derived from institutions like the ECSC result in social learning, which, in turn, produces ever more complex patterns of intergroup loyalties and trust.[77]

Working in tandem with France and other Western European countries, Germany could do things it could not accomplish alone.[78] Similarly, France was able to harness German capabilities to buttress its international standing. Franco-German reconciliation terminated a fierce rivalry that had been described as an *Erbfeindschaft* (hereditary enmity). Looking back over the past half century, we can see that the gradual development of identity-based trust through the ECSC solidified the postwar peace and made possible the creation of other European institutions that evolved into the current European Union.[79]

Extrapolating from the Regional to the Global Level.   Moving from reciprocity to identity-based trust is a long, painstaking process. There is no guarantee of success. Given the profusion of state and nonstate actors that now fill the world stage, building a feeling of common identity will be far more difficult at the global level than it was at the European regional level within the context of the ECSC (see Box 8.1). Nor is there assurance that relations among diverse international actors sharing a common sense of identity will not suffer through periods of crisis and strain. However, a culture of trust encourages habits of cooperation to blossom and expand. It is a prerequisite for the growth of global civil society. As Robert Keohane has argued, *ad hoc* efforts to cooperate in the absence of trust yield inferior results compared to those within a culture based on the expectation of trust.[80]

BOX 8.1
The Difficulty of Building Trust in an Era of Economic Globalization

During the September 2000 meeting of World Bank and International Monetary Fund officials in the Czech Republic, demonstrators clashed with police not far from the site of the "Defenestration of Prague" which ignited the Thirty Years' War. Whereas the Bohemians of 1618 were resisting the power of the Hapsburg Holy Roman Empire, the demonstrators massed in the Czech capital 382 years later were denouncing what they saw as a different kind of hegemonic threat. In their opinion, a new form of international domination was lurking beneath the veneer of economic globalization. At a time when 20 percent of the world's population commands over 80 percent of its wealth, globalization would perpetuate existing inequalities by strengthening corporate interests in wealthy societies and expanding their worldwide reach.

The complaints raised by the demonstrators in Prague echoed concerns expressed in recent years by leaders of developing countries and countries undergoing a transition from command to market economies. Many of these leaders fear globalization will make their countries' economic fate dependent upon foreign production, marketing, and investment decisions, thereby increasing their vulnerability to external pressures and exploitation. Globalization, they insist, does not foster equity. It empowers economically advantaged states and constrains weak states, widening the gap between rich and poor in an already stratified global hierarchy.

Contrary to the wealthy investors and corporate managers who welcome the thought of a borderless planet, the leaders of some countries regard sovereignty as a source of legal protection in a world where the benefits of globalization are unevenly shared and its costs unequally distributed. From their perspective, international norms that support sovereignty should be strengthened. Wary of the motives of those who stand to gain disproportionately from economic globalization, they have little faith in assurances that new opportunities will trickle down to their countries. In the words of Theo-Ben Gurirab, the foreign minister of Namibia: globalization can be a "destructive force because it is being driven by the very people, the colonial powers, who launched a global campaign of imperial control of peoples and resources in what we call now the third world. *Can we trust them?*"[81]

As the violent protests in Prague and the suspicions voiced by Foreign Minister Gurirab reveal, building international trust in the early twenty-first century will involve more than reconciling old Cold War adversaries. Deep apprehensions exist among some people over the policies and procedures of global financial institutions, as well as over the economic aims of the world's richest nations and corporations.[82] Just as in the period between 1641 and 1648, when the delegates to the Westphalian peace conferences literally had to invent a set of rules and protocol to guide their negotiations, representatives of the diverse actors in today's world society must begin crafting rules of engagement to guide the complex interaction of states, intergovernmental organizations, global firms, advocacy groups, and the like. Without such a normative framework, globalization will continue to generate as much anxiety as ardor, and may prove difficult to sustain in the absence of an underlying presumption of trust.[83]

The unsettling changes currently transforming the world make imperative the construction of a new normative order to move beyond the vision endorsed at Westphalia. The giddy optimism that accompanied the end of the Cold War has been replaced by dire prophecies about not just renewed clashes between sovereign states, but also clashes of civilizations. Even if the prophets are wrong, it seems clear from the welter of interstate conflicts, stretching from Kosovo to Korea, that utopia will not be a child of the new millennium. Yet to assume that atomized competition within a culture of mistrust can yield a durable peace is to ignore the history of the past three-and-a-half centuries.

SUMMARY AND CONCLUSIONS

The Peace of Westphalia codified various political practices that originated in the Italian city-state system of the late fifteenth century and diffused throughout Europe during the Thirty Years' War. The earlier medieval order was a stratified, hierarchical society under the jurisdiction of universal canon law. At the apex of the pyramid stood the pope and the rmperor of the Holy Roman Empire, and under them were archbishops and kings, bishops and nobles, monsignors and merchants, priests and peasants—each social unit with its own place in the hierarchy. No monarch, however strong, could defy the pope or emperor "without incurring the material risks involved in excommunication, the release of his feudal vassals from allegiance, and of his subjects from paying taxation."[84]

The social units that the delegates to the peace conferences in Münster and Osnabrück dealt with were completely different from those of the Middle Ages; they were "territorial units, separated not only by local customs and traditions and jurisdictions, but by divergent loyalties to separate governments or to conflicting religious beliefs."[85] In essence, the 355 sovereign states that had been consolidated in the Peace of Westphalia (from more than 900 separate principalities) were more than units of social life; they had become units of political power.[86]

The Westphalian system of world order was designed to regulate the interactions of these sovereign, autonomous territorial units that we now know as nation-states. It was supported by six pillars:

1. The cost/benefit ratio of waging war made military force a legitimate instrument of foreign policy.
2. Activities within states had few negative side-effects on neighboring peoples, resulting in little collaboration to control transboundary environmental problems.
3. Low levels of economic interdependence did not require a concerted effort to manage international commercial and financial transactions.
4. Authoritarian governments limited the flow of information across national frontiers.
5. Slow, sporadic communication flows retarded cultural diffusion and reinforced a sense of national distinctiveness.
6. Social heterogeneity made policy coordination difficult.[87]

Each of these pillars is currently undergoing decay: the destructiveness of thermonuclear weaponry has made great-power war more perilous than ever before; serious environmental problems from global warming to ozone depletion have touched large portions of the planet; economic interdependence has reduced the ability of national leaders to manage their economies in isolation from the wider world; the spread of democracy beyond Western Europe and North America has facilitated the free flow of information among nations; a revolution in telecommunications has linked disparate peoples as never before; and, as more and more interconnected peoples face common problems, interest in global governance has increased.

Perhaps no recent event more clearly highlights the erosion of the Westphalian framework than the 1999 military intervention by the North Atlantic Treaty Organization (NATO) into Kosovo. "Although the international rules of the road set out in the Treaty of Westphalia have been modified over the years," explains U.S. Ambassador Edward Marks, "they remained more or less intact until June 10, 1999, when the UN Security Council approved Resolution 1244 . . . [which] redefined the sovereign character of the nation state."[88] NATO, pointing to egregious human rights violations by Serbian forces in Kosovo, drew upon Resolution 1244 to declare that the government in Belgrade had forfeited its authority to rule over one of its own provinces. For Ambassador Marks, the hitherto inviolable sovereignty of the nation-state had now become conditional, with the result that the "post-Cold War world has segued into what might be called the post-Westphalian world."[89]

To be sure, the Westphalian state "is as legally sovereign as ever," observe Yale Ferguson and Richard Mansbach, "but being so seems to guarantee less and less in terms of effective control over persons, resources, and issues."[90] Powerful centripetal and centrifugal forces are pushing and pulling at the nation-state as never before. We are entering a world where "the logic of governance does not necessarily follow hierarchical lines," notes James Rosenau. Events are cascading "through, over, and around the long-established boundaries of states" and, in so doing, authority is being relocated "upwards to transnational and supranational organizations, sidewards to social movements and NGOs, and downwards to subnational groups."[91] As another observer of the decaying pillars of Westphalia observes:

> Each time a new user acquires a TV dish or links up to the Internet, the nature of politics undergoes a subtle change. Each time a new international organization arises, more states find themselves caught in its coils. The splintering process has led to vast increases in the power of organizations other than states, such as multinational corporations, nongovernmental organizations, and the media. With each passing day these groups are a little more independent of government. With each passing day, the influence they exercise in world affairs grows.[92]

Whereas some people insist that the Westphalian principles "have endured and remain at the heart of contemporary international politics,"[93] others contend that we are in a "Grotian moment,"[94] a time in which sovereignty is at a crossroads pushing history from one type of world order to another.[95] Nation-states will not vanish in the near future, "but new channels of interaction will so proliferate that governments' preeminence will wane."[96] What will be needed as this transformation from one epoch to another unfolds is a way to bring together diverse international actors in an open, transparent system of global governance.

By conceptualizing the structure of such a system as a network of state and nonstate actors who pursue multilateral, multilevel solutions to common problems in the spirit of collective responsibility,[97] responses to ethical questions in world politics take on a more cosmopolitan overtone. Following the Peace of Westphalia, the cosmopolitanism in much of early and medieval Christian thought was superseded by two alternative interpretations of the role of morality in world politics: nihilism and national communitarianism. Let us briefly describe each of these schools of thought before comparing them with cosmopolitanism.

Nihilism involves "a critical negation, not an indifference to values."[98] Rather than claiming that guileful practices are a regrettable choice forced upon political leaders by the unsavory nature of international anarchy, nihilists deny the existence of any moral standards for evaluating foreign policy. Like beasts in a jungle, they believe that one must fight for survival, unencumbered by rules limiting the sovereign right to do whatever is expedient. For nihilists, ruthless behavior that advances one's interests is venerated; conversely, benevolent acts undertaken out of a sense of altruism are ridiculed.

Unlike the nihilists, national communitarians concede that normative standards exist, but they assign ultimate moral value to particularistic political collectivities rather than to humanity as a whole.[99] After the Thirty Years' War, communitarians depicted states as the primary collectivities in world politics "claiming exclusive authority and the monopoly of legitimate violence within their territorial limits."[100] Owing to this view, they were hesitant to override the norm of sovereignty on behalf of humanitarian claims made by individuals. For them, autonomous, independent sovereign states were the primary source of interests and values for their citizens. Indeed, some communitarians found it difficult to think of individuals in isolation from the communities that constituted them as citizens; they held that the concrete ethical customs of those communities trumped the abstract moral demands of personal conscience. In effect, states were not answerable to one another for the morality of their foreign policies; the only legitimate moral constraints on what they might do in world politics were those that arose from their own communities themselves.

In contrast to the national communitarian emphasis on the Westphalian territorial state, cosmopolitans submit that people have certain transcendent moral obligations to humanity as a whole. The roots of cosmopolitanism lie in Stoic philosophy. From Zeno (335–263 B.C.E.) and Chrysippus (250–207 B.C.E.) through Seneca (4 B.C.E.–65 C.E.) and Marcus Aurelius (121–180 C.E.), Greek and Roman Stoics believed in the equality and unity of humankind. Modern cosmopolitans subordinate state sovereignty to considerations of human welfare, and they insist that states lose their legitimacy and moral standing by violating humanitarian norms. Visualizing the twenty-first century in terms of a panoply of state and nonstate actors, each possessing unique resources, many with overlapping authority, and all connected by transnational networks, contemporary cosmopolitanism returns a moral perspective to world politics that was lost during the Thirty Years' War. In the centuries following the Peace of Westphalia, national communitarianism all too often degenerated into a justification for *realpolitik,* with the state frequently becoming a mystical entity unbridled in its pursuit of self-aggrandizement. To recognize the limitations of a purely statist approach to ethical questions in international affairs—and to acknowledge that we owe certain obligations to others simply by virtue of our shared humanity—is to begin laying the ideational foundations for a new structure of world order. This is not to deny that our membership in national communities has ethical relevance. Rather it is to assert that, in an era of increasing globalization, those identities are likely to become nested within wider affiliations and loyalties, which also have ethical relevance.

Of course, building a post-Westphalian system of world order on these foundations will not be easy. Currently, global politics and economics are disconnected. "Although we live in a global economy characterized by free trade and the free movement of capital," writes George Soros, "our policies are still based on the sovereignty of the state. International institutions exist, but their powers are limited by how much authority states are willing to confer on them. At the same time, the powers of the state are limited by the freedom of capital to escape taxation and regulation by moving elsewhere."[101]

Yet sovereignty, Stephen Krasner reminds us, has always been problematic. Most states since the Peace of Westphalia have actually been "semi-sovereign," insofar as they lacked full autonomy in both the political and economic arenas.[102] What the process of globalization has done in recent years is to further disaggregate sovereignty, creating multiple layers of authority which are interlaced in ways that blur jurisdictional distinctions between foreign and domestic, and public and private, entities. To be sure, some observers protest that the political impact of globalization has been superficial. The Westphalian framework, they argue, is "not a brittle stalk."[103] Democracy, economic interdependence, and the growth of international institutions have not transformed international politics.[104] But to other observers, the emerging global networks of governance are reminiscent of political and economic arrangements prior to the birth of the Westphalian territorial state.[105] They hint at the possibility of a neomedieval world, a "secular reincarnation" of a system of overlapping authority and multiple loyalty that existed in western Christendom during the Middle Ages.[106] People within such a system would look to different layers of authority to meet different needs. In effect, governance would be distributed across a range of subnational, transnational, and supranational organizations that operate alongside the territorial state.

Research on collaboration in nested multiorganizational systems indicates that policy coordination among different layers of authority can be effective in the absence of hierarchical command structures when reciprocity-based trust exists.[107] However, trust will be difficult to build in the years ahead since many of the new, sovereignty-free actors on the world stage have not been part of the general normative framework within which sovereign states have long interacted. Until a presumption of trust takes root among these heterogeneous actors, compliance with international agreements is likely to be "provisional, tentative, and unstable."[108]

The Westphalian blueprint for international affairs remains a powerful mindset in the world's political culture. Yet it has not met the challenge of providing security, despite its longevity. For the past 350 years, international trust has been fleeting, largely because the systemic conditions arising out of the Thirty Years' War led to a permissive normative order that has haunted the world ever since. We concur with Susan Strange's conclusion, that "from a globalist, humanitarian . . . perspective, the system known as Westphalian has been an abject failure. Those of us engaged in international studies therefore need to bend our future thinking and efforts to the consideration of ways it can be changed or superseded."[109] It is time to exorcize the ghost of Westphalia, and get on with the task of building world order on an alternative ideational foundation. As the *Millennium Report* of United National Secretary-General Kofi Annan points out, better governance does not mean replacing nation-states with a world government composed of "centralized bureaucratic behemoths." It means opening up the international public domain "to the participation of the many actors whose contributions are essential to managing the path of globalization," while at the same time adhering to the principles of multilateralism and accountability.[110] If this book has convinced its readers that new realities require a new normative framework for securing a just world order, and enabled them to appreciate the window of opportunity that has opened under today's changing global circumstances, it will have succeeded in its primary goals. We must recognize what Hugo Grotius called "the common tie of humanity" and reject myopic, egoistic policies devoid of a moral mooring, "lest by too much imitation of the beasts we forget how to be human."[111]

Endnotes

Preface

1. Zakaria, 1999, p. 99.
2. Holsti, 1991, p. 25. Porter, 1994, p. 71, similarly labels the Westphalian peace "the first grand settlement in European history, covering every important issue of the war and endorsed by all the major powers of the day." Ogg, 1948, p. 169, concurs, in describing Westphalia as "Europe's first great peace conference."
3. Lang and Lang, 1998, p. 209.
4. Kuhn, 2000, p. 2.
5. Kaplan, 2000.
6. Zakaria, 1999, p. 99.

Introduction

1. Albrecht-Carrié, 1953, p. 101, concludes that "the settlements of 1648 rank in importance with those that follow the Napoleonic wars or those that rose out of the First World War . . . because they mark an important turning point in the story of Europe."
2. Giraud, 1847, pp. 12–13.
3. Zeller, 1955, p. 16. Critics of the Westphalian treaty are numerous, and point to many deficiencies. Falk, 1998, is representative of those who, with Zakaria, 1999, p. 99, contend that "the twenty-first century may well bring a struggle [to find] another universal system."
4. As Blum, Cameron, and Barnes, 1970, p. 218, note, "The first six decades of the seventeenth century have no universally recognized label, such as the Renaissance or the Reformation. . . . It was an age of crisis, filled with uncertainty, confusion, civil conflict, and seemingly endless war."

5. Reinhold Niebuhr, as cited in Wight, 1968b, p. 108.
6. Steinbruner, 2000, p. 3.
7. Gilpin, 2000, p. 315.

Part I

1. Hoagland, 1999, p. 5.
2. James Michener, in Kegley and Raymond, 1990, p. 118.
3. Bull, 1977, pp. 173.
4. Ikenberry, 1987, pp. 1–2.
5. Falk, 1998, p. 4.
6. We are grateful to Robert A. Denemark, University of Delaware, for emphasizing this point to us and providing these illustrations.
7. We thank Robert A. Denemark for encouraging us to emphasize this aspect of our treatment.
8. Barzun, 2000, p. 178.
9. Philpott, 2000, p. 209.
10. Will Durant, in Kegley and Raymond, 1990, p. 118.
11. Valentin, 1946, p. 212.
12. Barzun, 2000, p. 179.
13. Hardt and Negri, 2000, p. 4.
14. Falk, 1985b, p. 122.
15. Lauterpacht, 1985, p. 31.

Chapter 1

1. Rosenthal, 1998, p. 363.
2. Philpott, 2000, p. 208.
3. Mowat, 1928, pp. 104–105.
4. Kissinger, 1994, p. 62.
5. Doran, 1971, p. 65.
6. Porter, 1994, p. 64.
7. See Neustadt and May, 1986, on the role of history for policy making.
8. Royal, 1999, p. 33.
9. Albrecht-Carrié, 1964, p. 67.
10. Blum, Cameron, and Barnes, 1970, p. 217.
11. Hackman, Kegley, and Nikander, 1957, p. 438.
12. Morgenthau, 1985, p. 294.
13. Fields, Barber and Riggs, 1998, p. 706.
14. Mattingly, 1971, p. 122.
15. Dehio, 1962, p. 23.
16. Dehio, 1962, p. 35.
17. Hackman, Kegley, and Nikander, 1957, p. 443.
18. In Kegley and Raymond, 1990, p. 153.
19. See Raymond, 1998–1999.
20. Quinton, 1994, p. 310
21. Dawson, 1996, p. 179.
22. Quinton, 1994, p. 308.

23. In Pangle and Ahrensdorf, 1999, p. 110.
24. In Dawson, 1996, p. 184.
25. In Dawson, 1996, p. 182.
26. In Kegley and Raymond, 1990, p. 41.
27. In Dawson, 1996, p. 181.
28. Hollingshead 1998, p. xv.
29. Hackman, Kegley, and Nikander, 1957, p. 447.
30. Hardt and Negri, 2000, p. 94.
31. Blum, Cameron, and Barnes, 1970, p. 195.
32. Parker, 1984, p. 214.
33. Albrecht-Carrié, 1964, p. 67.
34. Reddaway, 1948. p. 116.
35. See Beller, 1940; Gutman, 1988; Krasner, 1993; and Philpott, 2000.
36. Blum, Cameron, Barnes, 1970, p. 110.
37. For an analysis of the current clash between religion and the state in world politics, see Juergensmeyer, 1993.
38. Tuchman, 1984, p. 111. This eminent historian documents her thesis by citing Machiavelli, who "found proof of decadence in the fact that the nearer people are to the Church of Rome, which is the head of our religion, the less religious are they. Whoever examined the gap between the principles upon which the Christian religion was founded and their present application by the Church 'will judge that her ruin and chastisement are near at hand.' Machiavelli's anger was at the harm done to Italy. 'The evil example of the court of Rome has destroyed all piety and religion in Italy,' resulting in 'infinite mischief and disorders' which 'keep our country divided.' This is 'the cause of our ruin.' Whenever fearing loss of temporal power, the Church, never strong enough to be supreme, calls in some foreign aid, and "this barbarous domination stinks in the nostrils of everyone. The indictment was summarized in one sentence by Guicciardini: 'Reverence for the Papacy has been utterly lost in the hearts of men.'"
39. Blum, Cameron, and Barnes, 1970, p. 121.
40. Tuchman, 1984, p. 111–115.
41. Tuchman, 1984, p. 113.
42. Blum, Cameron, and Barnes, 1970, p. 127.
43. Blum, Cameron, and Barnes, p. 129.
44. Kennedy, 1987, p. 32.
45. Hatch, 1989, p. 179.
46. Hatch, p. 179.
47. Blum, Cameron, and Barnes, 1970, p. 128.
48. The Anabaptist movement survived under the leadership of Menno Simons, who preached strict pacifism, asceticism, and rejection of worldly practices, as well as the independence of religion from the state.
49. Hatch, 1989, p. 59.
50. Wedgwood, 1938, p. 19.
51. Blum, Cameron, Barnes, 1970, p. 129.
52. Gay and Webb, 1973, p. 145.
53. Wedgwood, 1938, p. 21.
54. Blum, Cameron, and Barnes, 1970, p. 141.
55. Ogg, 1948, p. 94, p. 92.

56. On the tension between the secular state and religious identity, see Huntington, 1996, and Melloan, 2000.
57. Wedgwood, 1938, p. 93.
58. Wedgwood, 1938, p. 90, observes "As befitted its founder, the society was military in organization; its head was called a General and it carried to extremes the military virtue of unquestioning obedience. As in no other religious order, the Jesuit had to surrender, not so much his time and property as his personality and intelligence; he had to submit to his superior *perinde ac cadaver*, and thus it was in its unity of organization and tenacity of purpose that the society was best fitted to deal with Calvinists."
59. Reddaway, 1948, p. 10.
60. Wedgwood, 1938, p. 95.
61. Blum, Cameron, and Barnes, 1970, p. 145. As Senn, 1997, p. 388, observes, it was only after the Council of Trent that "conformity to Roman use mandated by Rome (as opposed, say, by local rulers) [became] a new idea. It is in this sense that 'Roman' Catholicism emerged."
62. When the Imperial Diet met in 1555 at Augsburg, Protestants gained religious freedom as the Austrian Hapsburgs chose a tolerant policy. The states within the Austrian empire were no longer forced to be Catholics; rather, the assembly allowed Protestant princes to choose the religion of their states and were no longer required to accept Catholic law. Those Protestants living in states controlled by Catholic princes were allowed to move from such a state to one ruled by Protestants (Schiller, 1799, pp. 15, 16). One conflict arose during the assembly at Augsburg as Protestants requested that Catholic Bishops and Abbots be free to convert to Protestantism and adopt Protestantism as their religion. The Catholics refused, taking the position that any Catholic Bishop or Abbot who accepted another religion would be expelled and/or excommunicated (Gardiner, 1895, pp. 10, 11). Given this unresolved issue, some historians interpret Augsburg an "extraordinary compromise [that] saved the theory of religious unity for each state while destroying it for the Empire" (Wedgwood, 1938, p. 42).

    Though the assembly at Augsburg was very progressive in its tolerance and inclusion of Protestants in the Austrian Empire, most Protestants remained dissatisfied with their status. Protestants complained that they were doomed to perpetual repression by a Catholic Emperor. Both sides were dissatisfied with the policies generated from Augsburg, as Catholics felt the Protestants had received more than they had, and the Protestants felt that the Assembly did not make enough changes (Schiller, 1799, p. 23). Despite the dissatisfaction with the Assembly, the Peace of Augsburg prevented civil war between the divided religious groupings from erupting, Schiller, 1799, p.73.
63. Palmer and Colton, 1984, p. 79.
64. Albrecht-Carrié, 1964, p. 96.
65. Lee, 1986, p. 99.
66. Parker, 1984, p. 5.
67. Palmer and Colton, 1984, p. 138.
68. For example, see David Martin, 1998.
69. Johnson, 1998, p. 46.
70. Johnson, 1998, p. 46

71. Johnson, 1998, p. 48, citing Martin, 1998. For a penetrating discussion of this timeless problem, see Appleby, 2000.

72. The dilemmas caused by religious fervor and fanaticism are, of course, ageless. The dangers resurfaced in August, 2000, when more than 1,000 religious leaders from throughout the world convened in New York. This occasion provoked George Melloan, 2000, p. A27, to observe,

> Most of the violent conflicts in the world today have some religious element. Muslims and Christians are at odds in eastern Indonesia. Hindus and Christians or Hindus and Muslims clash in India. Northern Ireland seethes with Catholic and Protestant strife. Jews and Muslims, of course, continue their centuries-old quarrel over the Holy Land. If somehow religious leaders could advise all their communicants to just cool it. who knows what miracles could be worked?
>
> But, of course, one must not forget the role of temporal authorities. Many of them are highly suspicious of their spiritual brethren. The mixture of religion and politics is potentially explosive, as has been made evident by the clashes enumerated above. Both spheres are arenas of intense human emotions and they can never be entirely divorced, however persuasive the arguments for church and state separation might be. There are few places in the world where there is no interplay between religion and politics.

73. Kissinger, 1994, pp. 62, 59, 58.

74. Krasner, 1995, p. 235.

75. Cavendish, 1988, p. 50.

76. Parker, 1984, p. 220.

77. See Butterfield, 1968; Dehio, 1962, and Gulick, 1955.

78. Lee, 1986, p. 50.

79. Jan Huss lectured in theology at Prague, where he was influenced by the writings of John Wycliffe. In 1411 Huss was excommunicated by the pope, and after defiantly writing *DeEccelesia (On the Church)* Huss refused to disavow his plea for church reforms and, in 1415, Huss was burned at the stake. The wrath of Bohemian followers over this Catholic atrocity and the violation of freedom of speech and religious liberties led to the Hussite Wars which lasted until the middle of the fifteenth century.

80. Royal, 1999, p. 35.

81. Parker, 1998b.

82. Kamen, 1998.

83. Palmer and Colton, 1984, p. 124.

84. McKay et al., 1991, p. 474.

85. McKay et al., 1991, p. 474.

86. In later years, the seven northern provinces declared their independence from Spain, forming the Union of Utrecht, a mainly Protestant union; the southern provinces remained Catholic and under the control of the Spanish Hapsburgs.

87. Parker, 1998b. We are referring to the balance of power as a process designed to correct a perceived imbalance of power; see Part II, especially p. 105.

88. Blum, Cameron, and Barnes, 1970, p. 163, report that in the fifteen-year period between 1588 and 1603 more bullion flowed into Spanish coffers for overseas imperialism that in any period in Spanish history.

89. Blum, Cameron, and Barnes, p. 153.

90. McKay et al., 1991, p. 490.

91. See Dunan, 1964, p. 51.

92. Dunan, 1964, p. 51.

93. Viault, 1990, p. 72.

94. Cited in McKay et al., 1991, p. 472.

95. Dunan, 1964, p. 52.

96. Asch, 1997, p. 38.

97. Lee, 1986, p. 103.

98. Limm, 1984, p. 11.

99. Lee, 1986, p. 97.

100. Schiller, 1799, p. 70.

101. Gardiner, 1895, p. 21.

102. Rempel, 1998.

103. Pages, 1970, p. 250.

104. Parker, 1984, p. 22.

105. Davies, 1996, p. 563, citing Wedgwood, 1944.

106. Parker, 1984, p. 220.

Chapter 2

1. Chandler, 1998, p. 24.

2. Parker, 1984, p. 2.

3. Doran, 1971, p. 69. Chandler, 1998, p. 24, summarizes, "This dire and confused struggle in Central Europe, 1618–1648, was partly an internal struggle for the succession to power within the unwieldy Holy Roman Empire, partly on ideological and territorial conflict between Catholic and Protestant interests, and partly a dynastic struggle involving the royal houses of Hapsburg, Vasa and Bourbon."

4. Lee, 1986, p. 105.

5. Chandler, 1998, p. 24.

6. Lee, 1986, p. 100.

7. Hradcany Castle, or Hradschin Castle as the Bohemia Czechs called it then, has played a major role in the history of the modern Czech Republic. It is the country's traditional residence of Czech heads of state. In addition to the dramatic events that transpired in 1618 there in the Defenestration of Prague, it was adjacent to Hradcaony in the Obecni Dum municipal building where Czechoslovakia proclaimed its independence in 1918 following the collapse of the Austro-Hungarian Empire. The Hradcany castle was also the place where, in March 1939, Adolf Hitler of Nazi Germany proclaimed that "Czechoslovakia has ceased to exist."

8. Wedgwood, 1938, p. 84.

9. The Protestants were disunited, with many Lutherans more supportive of the Catholic Emperor Ferdinand than of the Calvinist Frederick, and looked to the leadership of Elector John George from Saxony, who preferred to maintain peaceful relations with the Emperor.

10. Ogg, 1948, p. 124.

11. Wedgwood, 1938, p. 33.

12. Blum, Cameron, and Barnes, 1970, p. 220.

13. Tilly's troops are described by Wedgwood, 1938, p. 121 as "mercenaries of many tongues. They marched to the encouragement of Jesuit preachers, the twelve largest cannon were each called after an apostle, and their general's especial

patroness was the Virgin Mary. As a young man, Tilly had wished to enter the Society of Jesus, but later, deciding to fight God's battles in another field, had maintained throughout his life in camps so strict a morality and so unfailing a devotion to his Patroness that he was popularly known as the 'monk in armor'."

14. It is interesting to speculate whether the outcome would have been different if Frederick had won the support of the peasants and merchants in Bohemia by engineering reforms, instead of backing the feudal nobility.

15. Chandler, 1998, p. 25.

16. Gay and Webb, 1973, p. 250.

17. Doran, 1971, p. 67.

18. Wedgwood, 1938, p. 141.

19. Blum, Cameron, and Barnes, 1970, p. 220.

20. Blum, Cameron, and Barnes, p. 220.

21. Schiller, 1799, p. 138.

22. Davies, 1996, p. 564.

23. It is probably unfair to blame the rest of the Thirty Years' War on Emperor Ferdinand's actions after capturing Prague, because it is almost surely the case that the Catholic-Protestant dispute would have erupted sometime in the future. The recapture of Prague and flight of Frederick did not end the ultimate question of religious competition in Austria. However, Frederick bears responsibility for the immediate continuance of a war that could have been concluded.

24. Ogg, 1948, p. 128.

25. Ogg, 1948, p. 134.

26. Ogg, 1948, p. 135.

27. The success of the French intervention was undermined by domestic opposition within France from the Parti Dévot Catholic zealots and from the Protestant Huguenots who both favored, for different reasons, support for the Spanish.

28. Parker, 1984, p. 66.

29. Parker, 1984, p. 70.

30. Palmer and Colton, 1984, p. 140.

31. Parker, 1984, p. 76, illustrates Wallenstein's primal values by noting that Wallenstein "made enormous profits from the sale of confiscated lands in Bohemia and raised his army by extorting contributions from his own troops." Wallenstein displayed, in the character assessment of Wedgwood, 1938, pp. 170–173 "a peculiar mixture of weakness and strength, vice and virtue, fulfilling the prophecy of the horoscope commissioned by Johan Kepler that, born September 14, 1583, Wallenstein would be a restless, exacting mind, impatient of old methods and forever striving for the new and the untried, secretive, melancholy, suspicious, contemptuous of his fellowmen and their conventions. He would be avaricious, deceitful, greedy for power, loving no one and by no one beloved, changeable in his humors, quarrelsome, friendless and cruel."

32. "Wallenstein regarded war simply as a business proposition," Ogg, 1948, p. 139, observes, adding that "it is evident of Ferdinand's destitution that he decided to accept the services of a man so little influenced by religious motives."

33. Chandler, 1998, p. 25.

34. Parker, 1984, p. 79.

35. Wedgwood, 1938, p. 213.

36. Parker, 1984, p. 81.

37. Ogg, 1948, p. 141.
38. Parker, 1984, pp. 101–102, 86.
39. Blum, Cameron, and Barnes, 1970, p. 222.
40. In Parker, 1984, p. 106.
41. Chandler, 1998, pp. 25–26.
42. Ogg, 1948, p. 150, Wedgwood, 1938, p. 271, describes Gustavus Adolphus as "the most successful administrator in Europe."
43. Lee, 1986, p. 104.
44. Wedgwood, 1938, p. 275.
45. Ogg, 1948, p. 150.
46. Ogg, 1948, p. 142, observes that "In his departure from the principles of warfare Wallenstein had made his greatest mistake." The retaliation by Sweden was to cost him dearly.
47. Reddaway, 1948, p. 135.
48. Blum, Cameron, and Barnes, 1970, p. 222.
49. Wedgwood, 1938, p. 190.
50. Kennedy, 1987, p. 65.
51. Chandler, 1998, p. 20.
52. Kauppi and Viotti, 1992, pp. 162–163.
53. In Kissinger, 1994, p. 63.
54. Roelofsen, 1997, p. 119.
55. Kissinger, 1994, pp. 58, 65.
56. Wedgwood, 1938, pp. 279–280.
57. Blum, Cameron, and Barnes, 1970, p. 223.
58. Ogg, 1948, pp. 154–155.
59. Wedgwood, 1938, p. 291.
60. In Holsti, 1991, p. 28, citing Roberts, 1967, p. 202.
61. Ogg, 1948, p. 156.
62. Wedgwood, 1938, p. 302.
63. Wedgwood, 1938, p. 307.
64. Wedgwood, 1938, pp. 315–316.
65. In Blum, Cameron, and Barnes, 1970, pp. 222–223.
66. Davies, 1996, p. 564.
67. Blum, Cameron, and Barnes, 1970, p. 222.
68. Parker, 1984, p. 132.
69. The death of Gustavus Adolphus alarmed the French and saddened Pope Urban VIII who, "as an opponent of the Hapsburgs was reported to have said a private mass for the soul of the deceased [ardently Lutheran] King," Ogg, 1948, p. 152, reports.
70. Wallenstein was estimated to have "owned one-quarter of all the land in Bohemia" which he accumulated by increasing the fortune left him by his wealthy wife. Described as "a lonely and sinister man, loving no one and loved by no one, driven by unfathomable ambition, believing in nothing except astrology and his own destiny" (Blum, Cameron, and Barnes, 1970, p. 221), it is understandable why Wallenstein was distrusted and resented throughout Europe despite his capabilities and intelligence.
71. Wedgwood, 1938, p. 544.
72. Gay and Webb, 1973, p. 253. Blum, Cameron, and Barnes, 1970, p. 223, report

that when the Emperor's counselors turned on Wallenstein, the commander "ordered his army to desert to the enemy. While in flight, he and four of his closest associates were murdered by officers loyal to the Emperor and anxious for reward."

73. Ogg, 1948, p. 159.
74. Parker, 1984, p. 143.
75. Wedgwood, 1938, p. 377.
76. Parker, 1984, p. 144.
77. Chandler, 1998, p. 26.
78. Chandler, 1998, p. 26.
79. Blum, Cameron, and Barnes, 1970, p. 223.
80. McKay et al., 1991, p. 478.
81. Although France and Spain continued to wage war until 1659, in fact each of Richelieu's three major goals were ultimately reached by the time the Treaty of Westphalia was signed in 1648.
82. Lee, 1986, p. 103.
83. Parker, 1984, p. 149.
84. Ogg, 1948, p. 163.
85. Palmer and Colton, 1984, p. 141.
86. Clodfelter, 1992, p. 6.
87. A party of English traveling through war-torn Germany reported mass starvation that had driven some peasants to cannibalism; they "came across one village," Geoffrey Parker, 1984, p. 164, reports, "that had been pillaged eighteen times in two years, even twice in one day."
88. Parker, 1984, p. 160.
89. Wedgwood, 1938, pp. 431, 435.
90. Parker, 1984, p. 167.
91. Wedgwood, 1938, pp. 458–459.
92. Clodfelter, 1992, p. 7.
93. Davies, 1996, p. 508.
94. The militant attitudes that prolonged the Thirty Years' War did not die after the withdrawal of the Austrian Hapsburgs from the conflict following the 1648 Peace of Westphalia. Despite the fact that the Holy Roman Empire was no longer a fixture of the European landscape, and the religious conflict between Christians was becoming a memory, the Franco-Spanish War continued for another eleven years, until the two rivals "resembled punch-drunk boxers, clinging to each other in a state of near exhaustion and unable to finish each other off" (Kennedy, 1987, p. 59).

Chapter 3

1. Holsti, 1991, p. 28.
2. Kissinger, 1994, p. 59. Estimates of civilian and military casualties vary widely.
3. Ogg, 1948, pp. 161–168.
4. Howard, 1986, p. 37.
5. Albrecht-Carrié, 1964, p. 101.
6. Bull, 1968a, p. 58.
7. Judgments differ about the extent to which religious fervor intensified the ruth-

lessness of the soldiers doing the fighting. Charles Doran (1971, p. 72) is skeptical: " religion may have hindered assimilation by enhancing the passions of the military—the catastrophe at Magdeburg being an example. Yet discipline within armies and the nature of the military payroll seem to explain the ruthlessness or beneficence of the soldiers as well. Swedish troops showed unequaled religious zeal on the battlefield, but looting was kept to a minimum by the iron rule which Gustavus Adolphus exercised over his men. By contrast, Bethlen Gabor was famed for the harshness of his campaigns and occupations, although neither he nor his men demonstrated much religious hatred."

8. See Raymond, 1998–1999, for an analysis of arguments from necessity in foreign policy.
9. Pages, 1970, p. 11.
10. See Lee, 1986, p. 108.
11. Clodfelter, 1992, p. 7.
12. Chandler, 1968, p. 25.
13. Davies, 1996, p. 568.
14. Ogg, 1948, p. 168.
15. Davies, 1996, p. 565.
16. Holsti, 1991, p. 29, citing Ward, 1966, p. 17. This carnage is described by Clodfelter, 1992, p. 7, who estimates that "Bohemia was the worst scarred region of the empire . . . at least 700,000 of the province's 2 million died. In one county of Bohemia, 75 percent of the people, 80 percent of the livestock, and 66 percent of houses were destroyed by the war. Other areas of the empire were nearly as badly hit."
17. This grim ratio of the death rate of soldiers in comparison to civilians was to become increasingly characteristic of war in the late twentieth century.
18. Blum, Cameron, and Barnes, 1970, p. 218. It is worth considering why the belligerents abandoned morality and religion with such alacrity. Surely it was not simply because expedience was so tempting and religion so superficial. Part of the justification undoubtedly stemmed from the fear that had grown during the 1500s that religion was a cause of conflict, not a cure for it. To some observers, the question to ask was, What happens when you unite religion and politics? The answer: Political goals become divinely sanctioned, with human agendas masquerading as God's agenda. The merger of religion and politics brings a spirit of absolutism into political life, destroying the art of compromise. For an analysis the relationship of the sacred to the sword, see Appleby, 1996 and 2000.
19. Welch, 1993, p. 9.
20. Clodfelter, 1992, p. xxx.
21. Blum, Cameron, and Barnes, 1970, p. 219.
22. Fields, Barber, and Riggs, 1998, p. 730.
23. Clodfelter, 1992, p. xxxii.
24. Albrecht-Carrié, 1964, p. 65.
25. Kaiser, 1990, p. 88.
26. For overviews of prospect theory, see Bostdorff, 1993; Levy, 1992; and Stein and Pauly, 1993.
27. Ogg, 1948, p. 169.
28. Albrecht-Carrié, 1964, p. 102. Reddaway, 1948, p. 205, notes that the devastation of the Thirty Years' War caused civilization in Germany to perish; to restore their

"ruined" depopulated country, "In some regions laymen were allowed two wives apiece, while only the elderly might become monks or nuns."

29. Any hopes for the advent of a new age of democracy were extinguished for another 150 years after the Thirty Years' War. Democratization was postponed and weak by 1795, at the time when Immanuel Kant wrote *Perpetual Peace* and averred that republican governance was a viable antidote for war. Fragile democratic governments then existed in only three countries: the United States, republican France and Switzerland.
30. Schumpeter, 1955, p. 25.
31. Porter, 1994, p. 12.
32. Gleditsch, 1992, pp. 369–370; see also Doyle, 1998; Hermann and Kegley, 1996 and 2001; Kegley and Hermann, 1997; Ray, 1995; Russett, 1993, 1995; Weede, 1984.
33. Reddaway, 1948, p. 97.
34. Reddaway, 1948, p. 117.
35. Blum, Cameron, and Barnes, 1970, p. 225.
36. Senn, 1997, p. 447.
37. Preece, 1997, p. 76.
38. Pages, 1970, p. 250.
39. Luard, 1968, p. 270.
40. Luard, 1968, p. 270.
41. Luard, 1968, p. 270.
42. See Raymond, 1998–1999.
43. Parker, 1984, p. 179.
44. The Swedes were insistent that France should not be given precedence and required that the Protestants negotiate with the Empire's Imperial diplomats separately.
45. Miller, 1985, p. 19.
46. Valentin, 1946, p. 212.

Part II

1. Ogg, 1948, p. 118.
2. Strong, 1945, p. 162.
3. Gross, 1969, p. 25.
4. Lesaffer, 1997, p. 73.
5. Gross, 1969, pp. 30-31.
6. Krasner, 1993, pp. 235–236.
7. Roelofsen, 1997, p. 120.
8. In Philpott, 2000, pp. 208–209.
9. Falk, 1985b, p. 120.
10. Henkin, 1934, p. 147.
11. Bowle, 1948, p. 203.
12. Osiander, 1994, p. 44.
13. Gay and Webb, 1973.
14. By arguing that the Westphalian treaties concretized evolving practices into a set of rules for the conduct of international relations, we adopt a perspective which assumes that norms have consequences for subsequent behavior. In contrast to some nihilists or hard-core proponents of *realpolitik* who believe that moral norms

are irrelevant because they are subservient to power politics, we concur with the philosophical view that norms provide a powerful regulatory mechanism for the conduct of relations between people and state. Consistent with the evidence in political sociology, norms influence patterns of behavior. International systems, just like genetic systems for humans, maintain behaviors within boundaries of variation. They operate just like "motor memory" does in helping individuals perform tasks such as typing, brushing our teeth, or running to catch a bus so effortlessly. Repeated behaviors are "learned" by the development of pathways through which environmental signals—such as seeing the sky above and the ground below—more rapidly reached the motor nerves which are coordinated in humans' spinal cords and not their brains. (Consider how animals can run around on instinct even when their brains have been removed through decapitation, as captured by the comment "He ran around like a chicken with its head cut off." With time individuals' pathways become fixed. This is one reason why it is so difficult for people to change their handwriting styles and even their thinking habits, even when they seek to, neurobiological science informs us. Likewise, just as with sufficient practice and repeated habits, people's routines become fixed, so in international relations by analogy when interstate customs are repeated they encourage certain norms to become accepted, which then perpetuate the established practice. In this sense, principles for behavior once established as norms exert power over interstate behavioral patterns.

15. Falk, 1985a, pp. 38–39.
16. Lauterpacht, 1985, p. 24.
17. Sørensen, 1968, p. 4.
18. Gulick, 1955.
19. Claude, 1962.
20. Kaplan, 1957, p. 23.
21. Organski, 1968, p. 293.
22. Claude, 1989, p. 78.
23. Strange, 1999.
24. Lesaffer, 1997, p. 73.
25. Strong, 1945, p. 102.
26. Falk, 1985b.
27. In Bowle, 1948, p. 202. Roelofs, 2000, p. 517 elaborates on the Hobbesian outlook and its relationship to the acceptance of the modern sovereign state by noting that "Hobbes tried with some desperation to tilt the balance of such calculations always in favor of the sovereign by making him armed, absolute, arbitrary, and, above all, awful—so that by the terror of his ways his subjects would all be held in awe."
28. The UN's Millennium Summit in September 2000 inventoried the many global issues that are in dire need of attention, in a survey which dramatized the extent to which Westphalia provides an inadequate solution. The chapters in Part III call attention to these inadequacies in the new environment of the twenty-first century.
29. As the careful reader of Chapter 5 will discover, the Westphalian legacy is not a neat package. The Westphalian Peace comprised a myriad set of general rules for international statecraft and, because of its multiple message it might be more accurate, as Robert A. Denemark of the University of Delaware usefully suggested in a

review of an earlier version of this book, to "imagine that it is 'ghosts' and not the singular 'ghost' that we are trying to exorcise." As we shall argue in Part III, the Westphalian rules collectively created a ghost that has a long shadow, but that some of those rules are less dysfunctional than others for the maintenance of international security in the twenty-first century, and for that reason we shall highlight the rules most in need of exorcism.

Chapter 4

1. Kennedy, 1987, p. 41.
2. E.H. Carr, as cited in Mowat, 1928, p. 104.
3. Nagel, 1979, p. 128.
4. Valentin, 1946, p. 209.
5. The authors of the Treaty of Hamburg originally hoped to convene the peace conferences on March 25, 1642; however, delays in ratifying the treaty pushed the starting date forward to July of the following year, then unresolved issues regarding the method of representing the estates and princes of the empire postponed it again to July 11, 1643 (see Mowat, 1928, p. 107). In truth, the Congress of Westphalia never had an official opening; after many preliminary planning conferences, the deliberations simply took on a more formal tone by the middle of 1645.
6. Mowat, 1928, p. 108.
7. Article I of the Treaty of Münster (October 24, 1648). Unless otherwise noted, all subsequent references to treaty articles in this chapter will refer to the Treaty of Münster. Copies of the Münster and Osnabrück treaties can be found in *Collection of Treaties of Peace and Commerce*, 1714; *The History of Treaties*, 1712. Also see Ogier, 1893.
8. See Randle, 1973, pp. 36–52, 478–480.
9. An example of the kinds of problems that arose in the absence of formal protocol can be seen in the following episode involving the Count d' Avaux of France: "When saying good-bye after receiving a visit from the Venetian mediator, Aloisi Contarini, [the Count] only accompanied his guest to the foot of the stairs; but Contarini demanded that he be escorted by his host to the carriage. D'Avaux could not settle this point without corresponding with Mazarin in Paris; eventually the Venetian delegate was accorded full diplomatic honors." Mowat, 1928, p. 108.
10. Limm, 1984, p. 45.
11. Mowat, 1928, p. 108, describes the setting by recording that "The two towns were neutralized and placed under the protection of their own magistrates and burgher militia. The intermediate routes were also regarded as neutral. Houses in the two towns were rented by the chief delegates, and the inns and lodgings were full of their retainers. Every state in Europe, except England, Poland, Russia, and Turkey, is said to have been represented."
12. Asch, 1997, p. 135.
13. Mowat, 1928, p. 109, applauds their performance as mediators able to overcome difficult obstacles: "These mediators received the written proposals of either side and handed them on to the other side. At Osnabrück, negotiations were carried on directly by exchange of notes. All communications were translated into Latin. It was at Osnabrück that the most difficult questions, those of religion, were

thrashed out; for this purpose the Catholic and Protestant delegates formed themselves into separate conferences, and communicated with each other by writing. Although most of the negotiating was done by exchange of notes, there were occasional oral conferences among the plenipotentiaries, at least at Osnabrück. Sometimes months elapsed between the delivery of a note and the reply, for the plenipotentiaries might have to send to Paris or Vienna for instructions."

14. Parker, 1984, p. 179.
15. Albrecht-Carrié, 1953, p. 101.
16. Valentin, 1946, p. 212.
17. This is the summary verdict of Ogg, 1960, among many others.
18. The cities included Hagenau, Colmar, Schlettstadt, Wissembourg, Landau, Oberenheim, Rosheim, Münster, Kaisersberg, and Türckheim.
19. Limm, 1984, p. 42.
20. Limm, 1984, p. 42.
21. Kennedy, 1987, p. 41.
22. Albrecht-Carrié, 1953, p. 104.
23. Albrecht-Carrié, 1953, p. 99.
24. Philpott, 1995, p. 356. Recall that Ferdinand II had attempted to augment his Imperial authority by terminating the Imperial Diet's legislative authority; the 1635 Peace of Prague had put all troops of the princes under the Emperor's supreme command and abolished the traditional right of princes to make alliances with each other or with foreign powers. The Westphalian settlement overturned the Emperor's controls and established a decentralized system of governance among the sovereign membership of the Empire. After 1648 the Emperor was required by the terms of Westphalia to abide by the decisions reached by the Imperial Diet in all matters of war and peace. The Emperor's loss of power in the Empire was further reflected in Westphalia's provisions that gave the bishopics administered by Protestants full voting rights in the Diet and restored their rights to make any alliances they perceived in their interests "except against the Emperor and *Reich*."
25. Blum, Cameron, and Barnes, 1970, p. 225.
26. Palmer and Colton, 1984, p. 144.
27. Gross, 1969, p. 33, citing Epstein, 1935, p. 192.
28. Davies, 1996, p. 568.
29. Clodfelter, 1992, p. 7.
30. Strong, 1945, p. 161.
31. Davies, 1996, p. 568.
32. Barraclough, 1946, p. 384.
33. Meyjes, 1984, p. 61.
34. Miller, 1990, p. 253.
35. Kauppi and Viotti, 1992, p. 165.
36. Johnson, 1993, p. 148.
37. Falk, 1993, pp. 852 and 853.
38. Hobbes, in Kauppi and Viotti, 1992, p. 166.
39. Roberts, 1993, pp. 368, 369.
40. See Johnson, 1983.
41. Falk, 1985b, p. 8.
42. Lauterpacht, 1985, pp. 12–28.

43. Lauterpacht, 1985, p. 28.
44. Miller, 1990, p. 30.
45. Gross, 1969, pp. 38–39.
46. Brierly, 1963, p. 46.
47. Gross, 1968, p. 53.
48. In Parker, 1984, p. 216.
49. This is the verdict of Wedgwood, (1938, p. 39), who argues that "the war solved no problem. . . . Morally subversive, economically destructive, socially degrading, confused in its causes, devious in its course, futile in its result, it is the outstanding example in European history of meaningless conflict."
50. Wedgwood, 1938, p. 39.
51. Wedgwood, 1944, p. 525.
52. Doran, 1971, p. 70.
53. Holsti, 1991, p. 25.
54. Fromkin, 1981, p. 81.
55. Maine, 1861; Numelin, 1950.
56. Barkun, 1968.
57. Luard, 1976, p. 61.
58. Watson, 1992, p. 312.
59. Gilpin, 1981, p. 35.

Chapter 5

1. Doran, 1971, p. 70.
2. Valentin, 1946, p. 213.
3. Palmer and Colton, 1984, p. 144.
4. Palmer and Colton, 1984, p. 144.
5. Harbour, 1999, p. 3. The term "deontology" comes from the Greek *deon*, meaning duty.
6. As noted in Chapter 2, military discipline on both sides deteriorated during the course of the war, especially in dealing with the people living in the regions where armies were quartered. According to one account, "Soldiers treated men and women as none but the vilest of mankind would now treat brute beasts. . . . Outrages of unspeakable atrocity were committed everywhere. Human beings were driven into the streets, their flesh pierced with needles, or cut to the bones with saws. Others were scalded with boiling water, or hunted with fierce dogs. The horrors of a town taken by storm were repeated every day in the open country." S. Rawson Gardiner as cited in Petrie, 1949, p. 146.
7. Holsti, 1991, p. 36.
8. Doran, 1971, p. 83.
9. *Exodus* 21: 24–25; *Leviticus* 24: 17–20. Compare *Matthew* 5: 38-42 and the comments on returning a wrong made by Socrates in Plato's *Crito*.
10. Wolgast, 1987.
11. Elster, 1990, p. 862.
12. Golding, 1975, p. 85, observes that two basic schools of thought exist on the nature of retributive justice. The *maximalist* school holds that there is a duty to punish anyone who is guilty and culpable for wrongdoing, and the punishment should be equal to the seriousness of the offense. *Minimalism,* the second school of thought,

also expresses moral indignation over the behavior of the culpably guilty. However, it asserts that punishment should be relative to the seriousness of the offense, and, unlike in a strict liability system that does not admit mitigating circumstances, the offender can be partially or completely absolved.

13. Parker, 1984, p. 217.
14. Holsti, 1991, p. 34.
15. Philpott, 1995, p. 359.
16. Philpott, 1995, p. 360.
17. Parry, 1968.
18. Indeed, "Laws are made to protect the state from the individual and not the individual from the state," observes Gidon Gottlieb, as cited in Kegley and Wittkopf, 1999, p. 505.
19. Limm, 1984, p. 38; Morgenthau, 1985, p. 360.
20. Sørensen, 1968, p. 3.
21. Gross, 1969, pp. 38–39.
22. In Parker, 1984, p. 223.
23. Doran, 1971, p. 83.
24. Doran, 1971, p. 82.
25. Kissinger, 1994, p. 67.
26. Holsti, 1991, p. 39.
27. Krasner, 1995, p. 235.
28. Gross, 1969, p. 26.
29. Doran, 1971, pp. 101–102.
30. In Porter, 1994, p. 64.
31. Starr, 1997, p. 108.
32. Starr, 1997, pp. 18-19.
33. Kissinger, 1994, p. 58, p. 61.
34. Church, 1972, p. 173.
35. Kissinger, 1994, p. 63.
36. In Parker, 1984, p. 219.
37. Holsti, 1991, p. 38.
38. Doran, 1971, p. 95.
39. Holsti, 1991, p. 44.
40. Langer, 1980, p. 11.
41. Parker, 1984, p. 215.
42. Gross, 1969, p. 25.
43. Parker, 1984, p. 218.
44. Holsti, 1991, p. 47, p. 46.
45. Grotius, 1949, writing in 1625.
46. Kaplan and Katzenbach, 1961, p. 203.
47. Kaplan and Katzenbach, 1961, pp. 206–207.
48. Barraclough, 1946, p. 382.
49. Chandler, 1998, p. 18.
50. Chandler, 1998, p. 18.
51. For surveys of global trends in the use of armed force and the toll they exact, see Mazarr, 1999; Reynolds, 2000. For information on the current refugee crisis, see Brown et al., 1999; Goldsborough, 2000.
52. The concept of "hegemony" derives from the ancient Greek term *hegemonia* (leadership), which differed from imperial rule (*arche*). Today the concept has

multiple meanings: some writers emphasize political preponderance, others stress economic superiority, and still others highlight the role of dominant ideas (compare Gilpin, 1981; Keohane, 1984; and Cox, 1987). Perhaps the most common usage is associated with world-system theory, which posits that hegemony exists when one state possesses a significant competitive advantage in commodity production, commerce, and finance. Based on this definition, the United Provinces of the Netherlands achieved hegemonic maturity between 1620 and 1650. See Wallerstein, 1984, pp. 38–39; Hopkins, Wallerstein, and Associates, 1982, p. 118.

53. Kaiser, 1990, pp. 168–170.
54. Dehio, 1962, p. 60.
55. For an analysis of the Anglo-Dutch rivalry, see Levy, 1999.
56. A testament to the horrors of pillaging can be seen in the following caption from a 1642 print in Nürnberg that describes the miseries of the peasantry:

> If there is anybody in the whole world
> Whom everyone wishes to flay and scalp
> It is we the little peasants! We are the poorest folk,
> For our cattle and horses are the soldiers' booty.
> Whatever the peasant possesses, is at once made a prize,
> Brother bailiff is the master of our lives.
> Houses are burned, churches are destroyed,
> Villages are turned upside down, provisions are consumed,
> As consolation for the countryside one sees great cities burn.
> The splendor of the land can no longer be recognized,
> By war, robbery, murder and arson, it is becoming a desert.

Reprinted in Beller, 1940, p. 45.

57. Cited in Craig and George, 1990, p. 6.
58. The war takes its name from an old legal principle giving daughters of a first marriage priority over sons from a second marriage. Louis had been promised a dowry of 500,000 crowns when he married Maria Theresa of Spain. Since the dowry was in default, Louis claimed the right to the Spanish Netherlands.
59. Based on data pertaining to capital ships, the Dutch controlled at least 40 percent of the system's naval-power capabilities from 1609 through 1644. No state held a comparable position until the end of the War of Spanish Succession, when Great Britain emerged as the world's premier naval power. According to other data sources, the British rise to economic hegemony occurred between 1798 and 1815, and reached maturity by 1850. See Modelski and Thompson, 1988, pp. 105, 110; Hopkins, Wallerstein, and Associates, 1982, p. 118.
60. Based on data pertaining to comparative army sizes, Spanish land power peaked during the early 1560s and then declined through 1800. Rising French power intercepted the Spanish downward trajectory at the end of the Thirty Years' War and peaked in the early 1690s. Thompson, 1992, pp. 139–140.
61. Levy, 1983. The nature of the latter wars of Louis XIV has prompted some scholars to describe the period between 1672 (Dutch War) and the Treaty of Utrecht as one of general systemic war. Others use 1688 (War of the League of Augsburg) as their historical watershed. Compare Toynbee, 1954; Thompson, 1983.
62. Louis XIV, 1992, p. 161.
63. Phillimore, 1917, p. 19, advances the following overall assessment of Westphalia's achievements and deficiencies:

[Westphalia] principally affected Germany, which it pacified. It did good inasmuch as it pacified, and inasmuch as it made an advance towards religious toleration; and it made the absolute dominion of the Emperor over the whole of Germany impossible, and in that way contributed to the balance of power.

But the mischief was that it established a number of Princes and States in an anomalous position of quasi-independence, most of them so weak that they could not resist the encroachments of France or Sweden, and yet unwilling, through mutual jealousies, to combine for the common interests of Germany.

And a still greater evil. It gave right to France and Sweden . . . in their capacity of guarantors of the treaty, to interfere with the internal affairs of Germany, taking to themselves allies out of Germany against the common interests of the bulk of the country.

It was framed largely in the personal interests of sovereigns and dynasties, and, except in the matter of religious toleration, paid scant regard to the interests of the people.

64. Miller, 1985, p. 49.
65. Kennedy, 1987, p. 72.

Part III

1. Philpott, 2000, pp. 209–210.
2. Grotius, 1949, pp. 10–11, writing in 1625
3. Hardt and Negri, 2000, p. 12.
4. Kaplan, 2000.
5. Falk, 1985b, pp. 122–123.
6. Thomson, Myer, and Briggs, 1945, p. 12.
7. Thomson, Myer, and Briggs, p. 13.
8. See Anthony Smith , 1999.
9. See Regan, 2000.
10. Zakaria, 1999, p. 99.
11. We do not mean to contradict ourselves by implying that so many discontinuities in international relations are evident that the remnants and legacies of the past have vanished. Indeed, as we document (especially in Chapter 7), many continuities with the past prevail alongside important, system transforming discontinuities; the historically minded observer may experience a sense of *déjà vu* when comparing periods—the illusion of having already experienced something actually being experienced for the first time. Because cycles do appear between seventeenth century and the early twenty-first century, commonalities abound which make the emerging international system appear to resemble that which occurred in the earlier period: everything old looks new again. However, the discontinuities overwhelm many of the continuities, and these global changes have created new issues which undermine the ability of the Westphalian rules to provide a sturdy foundation for managing the threats on the horizon. Hence, in advancing our theses that Westphalia is a faulty design for the new realities, we endeavor to identify those problems for which Westphalia provides imperfect solutions and are in need of exorcism from those rules which still have a contribution to make to international security, given the similarities between the mid-seventeenth century and the international system of today.
12. There is a huge literature on the erosion of state sovereignty and the probable decline of the territorial state as the global system's exclusive legal entity. Sassen,

1996, and Camilleri and Falk, 1993, are representative; for a critique of the thesis that states are increasingly powerless, see Weiss, 1998.

13. Inis Claude, in Fowler and Bunck, 1995, pp. ix–x.
14. Pangle and Ahrensdorf, 1999, p. 3.
15. Pangle and Ahrensdorf, 1999, p. 4.
16. "As a Kelsenia*ng grundnorm* or peremptory ethic centered in traditional thought about international affairs, the norm of *reciprocity*," Kegley, 1992a, p. 30, explains by citing S. S. Komorita, J. A. Hilty, and C. D. Parks, "'is universal and the basis of stable relationships. The reciprocity norm prescribes that people should help those who have helped them, and should not injure those who have helped them. Similarly, the reciprocity norm prescribes that people should retaliate against those who injure their interests—that bad deeds should be punished and exploitation of cooperation should not be tolerated.' By extension, the principle of reciprocity recommends that the impact of one state's policies on the other's be made the starting point of consideration, and that the Kantian injunction to treat others as ends but never as means replace the social Darwinist ethic rationalizing competitive struggle by taking advantage of others. Reciprocity draws attention to the extent to which states are partially responsible for the reactions of their allies and adversaries, and identifies the 'security dilemma'—that one nation's security can be a cause of others' *insecurity*—as a key precept for policy planning. It prompts us to think in terms of recursive causation by recognizing the interactive effects of each state's actions on the subsequent reactions of the others. An ethic predicated on reciprocity and mutuality would place the Golden Rule—that states treat others as they wish to be treated in return—at the center of their strategies for enhancing their security and welfare."
17. A major reason why we believe that it is now auspicious to give the Kantian vision on peace the fair test it has never received stems from the rapid expansion of the size of the liberal democratic community; today more than three-fourths of the state governments in the world are ruled through democratic institutions that protect the civil liberties of their citizens (see Freedom House, as summarized in Kegley and Wittkopt, 2001, p. 64 and pp. 423–427). Modern democracies have externalized their internal values and are joined together in actively promoting the further spread of democratic governance throughout the world through the many democratically governed international organizations they have created. Not only has this fueled acceptance of a cosmopolitan liberal ethos, it has also increased the prospects for peace because democracies have rarely, if ever, waged war against one another. Another reason to project that the Kantian proposal for perpetual peace might now be fulfilled in the twenty-first century, under a post-Westphalian cosmopolitan consensus, is because periods of peace have been conducive to the growth of democratic governance, in contrast to periods of warfare such as the Thirty Years' War that fostered the growth of absolute monarchies, which were legitimated by the Westphalian peace treaties.
18. Wright, 2000a, p. 58.
19. Dawson, 1996, p. 191.

Chapter 6

1. Fenwick, 1965, p. 15.

2. Falk, 1975, p. 68.
3. See Rosenau, 1990.
4. Lesaffer, 1997, p. 78.
5. Lesaffer, 1997, pp. 85, 73.
6. Lesaffer, 1997, p. 73.
7. Janis, 1993, p. 400.
8. Friedman, 1999, p. 111.
9. Mathews, 1998, p. 10.
10. Two important exceptions can be found in the second and thirteenth centuries. The former involved trade between the Roman Empire and Han China that passed through a welter of intermediaries as it moved by caravan and ship from one end of the Eurasian land mass to the other. The latter also comprised a complex system of exchange, stretching from the commercial centers of Flanders, the Champagne fairs of France, and the ports of Genoa and Venice to Malacca, Palembang, Hangchow and Ch'uan-chou in Asia. See Bozeman, 1960, pp. 168–169; Abu-Lughod, 1989, pp. 33–35.
11. Held, et al., 1999, pp. 14–27.
12. Holm and Sørensen, 1995, pp. 4–7.
13. Kudrle, 1999.
14. Most communications satellites today are in geosynchronous orbit, some 36,000 kilometers above the earth's surface. Placing satellites at an altitude of only 1,600 kilometers would allow signals to travel back and forth at a higher rate of speed, thus enhancing the capabilities of interactive networks and video teleconferencing. But because they circle closer to the earth, more satellites would be needed to obtain continuous global coverage. Given the cost of building and launching so many low orbit satellites, pilotless dirigibles and other types of HALE platforms are being considered as alternatives. Equipped with phased-array antennas and hovering at even lower altitudes, these drones could deliver information directly to the user, rather than through a commercial data hub. For an extended discussion of this technology, see Pelton, 1998.
15. Frederick, 1993. Compare Guéhenno, 1995; Hirst, 1997.
16. Wriston, 1992, p. 141.
17. Cited in Moore, 1998, p. 207.
18. Reinicke, 1997.
19. Keohane and Nye, 2001, p. 28.
20. Nye, 1990, pp. 31–33, 191–195.
21. Keohane and Nye, 2001, p. 31.
22. Nye, 1999, p. 13.
23. Rosecrance, 1986.
24. Rosecrance, 1999, p. 211.
25. Rosecrance, 1999, p. 3.
26. Hobsbawm, 1990, p. 174.
27. Kobrin, 1998, p. 368.
28. Strange, 1996.
29. Peterson, 1990, p. 529.
30. Strange, 1999, p. 346.
31. Rothkopf, 1998, p. 335.
32. Kobrin, 1997, p. 76.

33. Pirages, 1989, p. 16.
34. Brown et al., 1998, p. 4.
35. Barnet, 1980, p. 17.
36. Cited in Swift, 1993, p. 18.
37. Deudney, 1999, p. 301.
38. Soroos, 1999, p. 47.
39. *Trail Smelter* arbitration (United States *v.* Canada, 1938/41). An application of the tribunal's position can be found in the 1979 Geneva Convention on Long-Range Transboundary Air Pollution, which was supplemented by binding protocols in 1985 and 1988.
40. Principle 21 was reaffirmed with a significant change at the 1992 UN Conference on Environment and Development in Rio de Janeiro (also known as the Earth Summit). Concerned that it might be used to limit their sovereign right to encourage industrial growth, several less developed countries proposed new language that read: ". . . pursuant to their own environmental *and developmental* policies. . . ." See Principle 2 of the Rio Declaration on Environment and Development.
41. McCormick, 1999, p. 60.
42. Cited in Gardner, 1972, p. 70.
43. Soroos, 1999, p. 48.
44. Huntington, 1991.
45. For a further analysis of this trend, see Kegley, Raymond, and Hermann, 1998.
46. For a summary of the vast literature on the democratic peace, see Chan, 1997. Although several critiques have been made of this literature, one analysis concludes that none of them has refuted the consistent, robust finding that democracies almost never go to war with one another. On the contrary, "some of these critiques required new empirical analysis of the basic fact of democratic peace which actually strengthen the result." Maoz, 1998, p. 73.
47. Starr, 1997, pp. 156–158.
48. Hermann and Kegley, 1995, pp. 517–518.
49. Maoz and Russett, 1993, p. 637.
50. Axtmann and Grant, 2000, p. 41.
51. Curtis Runyon of Worldwide Institute, in Kegley and Wittkopf, 2001, p. 203.
52. Falk, 1993, p. 853.
53. Cited in Kissinger, 1994, p. 64.
54. Walzer, 1977, p. 105.
55. D'Amato, 1995, p. 90.
56. Tesón, 1988, p. 15.
57. Ellerman, 1993, p. 348.
58. Coffman. 1997, p. 297.
59. Cooper, 1997.
60. Singer and Wildavsky, 1993, p. 37.
61. Wight, 1977, p. 152.
62. Levy, 1983.
63. For an early interpretation of this achievement, see Gaddis, 1987; see also Kegley, 1991 and 1992b.
64. Singer, 1991; Brecher and Wilkenfeld, 1991.
65. See Brown, Renner, and Halweil, 1999, p. 106. For an assessment of the global migration crisis, see Goldsborough, 2000.

66. See especially Kaplan, 1993 and 2000.
67. Said and Simmons, 1976, p. 10; see also the Minorities at Risk Project, as summarized in Gurr, 2001.
68. Conner, 1987, p. 209.
69. Gurr and Harff, 1994, p. 92.
70. Homer-Dixon, 1994.
71. Kaplan, 1994 and 2000.
72. Brooke, 1999, p. 4.
73. For an analysis of these variations of progressive linear history, see Sorokin, 1963.
74. Fukuyama, 1992 and 1999.
75. Barber, 1995, p. 4.
76. Huntington, 1996.
77. Aron, 1968b, pp. 216–217, 229.
78. Husain, 1995, p. 44.
79. Brzezinski, 1970, pp. 3, 8.
80. Estimates vary depending upon the criteria used. See, among others, Willetts, 1997, p. 288; Enriquez, 1999; and the Union of International Association's annual inventory of IGOs and NGOs in the *Yearbook of International Organizations*.
81. Young, 1972, p. 136.
82. Keohane and Nye, 1977, p. 26.
83. Mansbach, Ferguson, and Lampert, 1976, p. 25.
84. Rosenau, 1990.
85. Modelski, 1972, p. 274.
86. See Callaghy, 1997.
87. Strictly speaking, the terms "world society" and "global society" more accurately convey our meaning. While acknowledging the continued importance of the sovereign territorial state, this broader understanding of society provides conceptual space for examining how entities other than the Westphalian territorial state affect world order.

Chapter 7

1. Hoffmann, 1998, p. 60.
2. Starr, 2001, p. 221; also see Smith, 1999, p. 113; and Giddens, 1990, p. 178.
3. UN High Commissioner for Refugees, as reported in Brown et al., 1999; for trends in the annual flows of refugees and displaced people between 1960 and 2000, see Kegley and Wittkopf, 2001, p. 344.
4. See Rubin, 2000, p. A7.
5. For a survey of the most significant global conditions at the start of the twenty-first century, see Halliday, 2001.
6. Although the Cold War did not involve a war *between* the great powers, the period was fraught with tension and littered with chronic disputes that could have escalated to war at any moment. As discussed in the previous chapters, following World War II a highly unstable tier of Third World countries emerged alongside a stable great-power one. Overemphasis on the absence of great-power war since 1945 ignores proxy wars between their client states in the Third World, wars in which only one major power fought, great-power interventions, and repeated crises that at least on one occasion brought Moscow and Washington to the brink of nuclear holocaust. It also overlooks the rate at which civil wars have grown since 1989, during which, according to the Stockholm International Peace Research Insti-

tute (SIPRI, 2000), and Wallensteen and Sollenberg, 2000, pp. 635–640, more than 100 internal wars within states have occurred; less than ten between states erupted in the same 1989–1999 period.

7. See especially Kaplan and Katzenbach, 1961; also Hoffmann, 1971.
8. See Waltz, 2000.
9. Fuller, 1932, p. 153.
10. Glennon, 1999, p. 6.
11. Eyffinger, 1998, p. 183; also Lesaffer, 1997; for a dissenting view, see Duchhardt, 1989.
12. Wilkinson, 1999, p. 142. Some analysts view Bourbon France between 1661 and 1713 as Europe's only great power (see Layne, 1993, p. 17). While France was Europe's richest state, with a culture that was emulated across the continent, it lacked the overwhelming preponderance and power projection capabilities that would qualify it as a superpower. Rather than holding a position comparable to the United States after the Cold War, it was simply the strongest of several great powers, which included England, the Austrian Hapsburgs, the Netherlands, the Ottoman Empire, Spain, and Sweden (see Levy, 1983, p. 47). Had Louis XIV acquired the entire Spanish empire following the death of Carlos II, a nonhegemonic unipolar system might have emerged.
13. Brzezinski, 1997, p. 24.
14. Rothkopf, 1997, p. 43.
15. Huntington, 1988–1989, p. 91.
16. Nordlinger, 1995, p. 90.
17. Layne, 1993, p. 32.
18. As Johnson, 2000, p. 4, points out, if one includes every type of military installation that contains any representative of the U.S. military, the number would climb to over eight hundred.
19. Hyland, 1993, p. 27. The characterization of the United States as an indispensable nation comes from Secretary of State Madeleine Albright as reported in the *New Republic*, May 25, 1998, p. 20.
20. Nye, 1992, p. 88.
21. Krauthammer, 1991, pp. 23–24.
22. For more detail on our conceptualization of polarity and polarization, see Kegley and Raymond, 1994, pp. 53–57; for a recent argument on behalf of the abiding relevance of structural realism as the best model of the global future, see Waltz, 2000.
23. Castells, 1996.
24. Appadurai, 1996., p. 23. Robert Jackson, 1990, uses the term *quasi-states* to refer to political entities that are legally independent but materially dependent on others for their welfare. Many of them are hardly viable: 87 have fewer than 5 million inhabitants, 55 have less than 2.5 million, and 35 fewer than 500,000. The sovereign state of Nauru, for instance, "is a Pacific atoll of eight square miles, with 8,000 inhabitants, many of whom are rich from the sale of phosphates. When the atoll gets washed away or runs out of phosphates, that will be the last of Nauru," note Ferguson and Mansbach, 1999, pp. 91–92.
25. Deibert, 2000, p. 205.
26. For a discussion of the concept of "international norm" and how norms fit together in a normative order, see Raymond, 1997; for an interpretation stressing how established norms influence the behavior of states whose self-interests require

them to equate a reputation for normcompliance with prestige and power, see Kaplan and Katzenbach, 1961.

27. Philpott, 2000, pp. 222–223.
28. Philpott, 2000, p. 212.
29. Hinsley, 1986, p. 71.
30. Forsyth, 1992, p. 28.
31. Gottfried Wilhelm Leibniz. as cited in Herz, 1976, p. 107.
32. A. Rivier, as cited in Fenwick, 1965, p. 254.
33. Akehurst, 1987, p. 258.
34. Mayall, 1978, p. 124; Gong, 1984, pp. 3–4.
35. Hardin, 1995, pp. 72–106.
36. For a comprehensive analysis of the role of commitment norms in world politics, see Kegley and Raymond, 1990.
37. One of the areas experiencing significant change since the Peace of Westphalia pertains to the use of force for self-preservation. Although scholars like Hall, 1924, p. 322, maintain that "almost the whole of the duties of states are subordinated to the right of self-preservation," many others agree with Schwarzenberger, 1956, p. 346, that "the mischievous notion of 'self-preservation' is overdue for elimination from the vocabulary of the international lawyer." For them, self-preservation is not an essential, absolute right that permits each state to decide for itself when forcible measures of self-help are warranted. For a concise summary of the growth of international legal norms within the Westphalian order, see Fitzmaurice, 1958.
38. Gross, 1968, p. 53.
39. Falk, 1998, pp. 26, 28, 33–34. An early criticism of the state-centric conception of the international legal order can be found in the work of C.W. Jenks, cited in Weston et al., 1980, p. 9. "International law," Jenks originally wrote in the late 1950s, "can no longer be adequately or reasonably be defined or described as the law governing the mutual relations of States . . . it represents the common law of mankind in an early stage of development, of which the law governing the relations between States is one, but only one, major division."
40. See Falk, 1997, 1985a; Gross, 1969.
41. Nye, 2001, p. 106.
42. Higgins, 1990, p. 205.
43. Crossette, 2000, p. A1.
44. Joffe, 1990, p. 35.
45. See Wright, 2000a, for a penetrating analysis of how and why a non-zero-sum norm of cooperation has paradoxically developed from the zero-sum competition of states engaged in preparations to wage a Hobbesian "war of all against all."
46. On the realism of idealism in an age when the demise of the territorial state was first becoming seen as a possibility, see Herz, 1976.
47. Cited in Kegley, 1992a, p. 28.
48. Grotius, 1949, p. 263, writing in 1625.
49. Brierly, 1963, p. 398.
50. Clive Parry, 1968, as cited in Kegley and Wittkopf, 2001, p. 599.
51. Gidon Gottlieb, 1982, as cited in Kegley and Wittkopf, 2001, p. 600.
52. Other major post-World War II legal instruments that advance the cause of human rights include: the Convention on the Prevention and Punishment of the Crime of Genocide (1951), the Convention Relating to the Status of Refugees (1951), the

Convention on the Elimination of All Forms of Racial Discrimination (1969), the Convention on the Elimination of All Forms of Discrimination Against Women (1981), the Convention Against Torture and Other Cruel, Inhuman or Degrading Treatment or Punishment (1987), and the Convention Concerning Indigenous and Tribal Peoples in Independent Countries (1991).

53. Arend and Beck, 1993, p. 4.
54. Gross, 1968, p. 46, emphasis added.
55. Claude, 1988, as cited in Kegley and Wittkopf, 2001, p. 608.
56. Cohen, 1987, pp. 15–17.
57. "The one trend that is sure to dominate the coming . . . quarter-century," observes Fareed Zakaria, 1999, p. 99, "is the decline of the power of the state."
58. Vincent, 1986, p. 151.
59. Van Creveld, 2000.
60. Guéhenno, 1997.
61. See Dehio, 1962, and Gulick, 1955.
62. Nye, 2001, p. 99.
63. Kauffman, 1995, p. 299.
64. Brown and Alexander, 1994, p. 273.
65. Mazarr, 1999, p. 192.
66. Butterfield, 1962, p. 81.
67. Axelrod, 1984, p. 174; Baier, 1986, p. 232.
68. Rengger, 1997, p. 472. Lesaffer, 1997, p. 87, makes the worthwhile argument that although Westphalia engendered a "culture of mistrust," the parties to the settlement were acutely aware that a presumption of trust was lacking, and it needed to be restored if international cooperation was to develop.
69. Fukuyama, 1995.
70. In making this argument on behalf of a post-Westphalian world order built around an ethic of social trust, the astute reader will readily identify our sub-text: In thinking about the place of ethics in statecraft in the new global order, we contend that it would be mistaken to endorse a purely instrumental pragmatism that evaluates alternative courses of action exclusively by "rational" cost-benefit analyses of their relative merit. Nihilism is not an approach that can serve national interests in the twenty-first century. We should not defend this extreme amoral version of realism, but bury it, because, we believe, an ethical consensus *is* needed more than ever to promote justice and seek security in a new world order that is not really new, and certainly not orderly. We purposely reject the postmodern thesis of deconstructionists that all ethical positions are equally valid or useful because faith in faith and reason are unjustified and nothing can be known with confidence. We would be terribly mistaken if we were to ascribe to an undifferentiated ethical relativism and/or nihilism in an effort to preserve that flexibility of response which Westphalian realists regarded as a supreme value; if there are no immutable moral truths independent of human authority, and every rule of right and wrong is presumed to be circumstantial, then all action becomes permissible. A blind relativism comes dangerously close to condoning any self-serving action and opens the door to pure expediency unrestrained by moral limits. There *are*, we submit, eternal classical ethical precepts (such as the principles of proportionality and discrimination within the Christian just-war tradition) that speak to the morality of alternate responses to the outbreak of aggression. We would

be remiss in our moral duties if we fail to clarify our values by evaluating the relevance of such percepts to today's circumstances.

Chapter 8

1. Landy, 1992, p. 8.
2. Speech to the United Nations, December 7, 1988. Trust greatly facilitates cooperation and is a prerequisite for its deepest, most robust forms. Nevertheless, trust is not absolutely necessary for minimal levels of collaboration. Zbigniew Brzezinski once noted this in his comments on arms control negotiations with the Soviet Union. When asked whether the United States could trust the Soviet leadership, he responded: "The point is not to trust them; it's to find an agreement that is self-reinforcing" (cited in Hawthorn, 1988, p. 115). Yet, as Gorbachev counters, "difficult issues are far more easily and quickly resolved if there is trust between political leaders." Cited in Forsberg, 1999, pp. 617–618.
3. Lesaffer, 1997, p. 92.
4. Richelieu, 1961, pp. 81–82, writing in the first half of the seventeenth century.
5. See Waltz, 2000, p. 8.
6. Lewis and Weigert, 1985, p. 969.
7. Deutsch, 1958, p. 265.
8. Baier, 1986. For recent attempts at developing a more clear, coherent understanding of trust, see Gambetta, 1988; Hollis, 1998; Lane and Bachmann, 1998; Lazaric, 1998; Seligman, 1997; Dunn, 1996; Misztal, 1996; and Fukuyama, 1995.
9. Jones, 1996, p. 14.
10. Mishra, 1996, pp. 264–269.
11. Gambetta, 1988, p.218.
12. Humphrey and Schmitz, 1998, pp. 40–41.
13. Kegley, 1976.
14. Keohane, 1986.
15. See Laughlin and Willis, 1903; Culbertson, 1937; Thibaut and Kelly, 1959; Gouldner, 1960; Homans, 1961; and Blau, 1964.
16. See Jensen, 1963; Gameson and Modigliani, 1971; Phillips and Crain, 1974; Raymond and Skinner, 1978; Richardson, Kegley, and Agnew, 1981; Thompson and Rapkin, 1982; Dixon, 1986; Raymond, 1987; Goldstein and Freeman, 1990; Leng, 1993.
17. Patchen, 1998, pp. 187–188.
18. Druckman, 1990.
19. Kramer, 1994, p. 349. As expressed by one of the early critics of the atomized utilitarian models emanating from rational choice theory: "Actors do not behave or decide as atoms outside a social context. . . . Their attempts at purposive action are instead embedded in concrete, ongoing systems of social relations." Granovetter, 1985, p. 487; compare Wrong, 1961.
20. See Rengger, 1997, p. 483.
21. Hoover, 1997, pp. 19–27.
22. Tajfel, 1982; Turner, 1987.
23. Lewicki and Bunker, 1996, pp. 119–125.
24. Becker, 1996, p. 50.
25. Kramer, Brewer, and Hanna, 1996, pp. 372–373.

26. Lewis and Weigert, 1985, p. 976.
27. Hwang and Burgers, 1999, p. 118.
28. Komorita and Parks, 1996.
29. Cited in Wilson, 1998, p. 9.
30. Jervis, 1997, p. 132.
31. Vasquez, 1998, p. 369; Wayman and Diehl, 1994, p. 262; Cusack and Stoll, 1990, p. 190.
32. Kegley and Raymond, 1990, pp. 250–255.
33. Leng, 1983.
34. Gochman and Leng, 1983; Leng and Gochman, 1982.
35. Mansbach and Vasquez, 1981.
36. Midlarsky, 1984.
37. Wallace, 1972.
38. Sample, 1997; Diehl and Crescenzi, 1998, pp. 113–114.
39. Siverson and King, 1979.
40. Geller and Singer, 1998, p. 138; Wayman, 1984; Wallace, 1973.
41. Leng and Goodsell, 1974, p. 194.
42. Bremer, 1993, p. 18.
43. For a discussion of the concept of "wars of rivalry," see Vasquez, 1993, pp. 64–75.
44. Vasquez, 1993, p. 261.
45. In fact, sometimes trust has the opposite effect, encouraging inflexible aspirations and contentious tactics. The key variable is the perceived resistance of an adversary to yielding. A trusted opponent with a history of accommodation may be expected to give in to the demands of others whenever his or her position does not seem firm. Pruitt and Rubin, 1986, p. 38.
46. Hwang and Burgers, p. 126.
47. Larson, 1997, p. 704.
48. Shakelford and Buss, 1996, p. 1162.
49. Luhmann, 1979, p. 45.
50. Kelley, 1973.
51. Our description of this strategy draws from the work of Leng, 1993, Patchen, 1988, Axelrod, 1984, and Osgood, 1962.
52. Lindskold, Walters, and Koutsourais, 1983; Lindskold, 1978; Pilisuk and Skolnick, 1968.
53. Goldstein and Freeman, 1990; Leng and Wheeler, 1979; Etzioni, 1967.
54. Kaplowitz, 1984.
55. Fisher and Ury, 1981, p. 27.
56. Bixenstine and Gaebelein, 1971.
57. Gruder and Duslak, 1973.
58. Shriver, 1995, pp. 6–9.
59. Tavuchis, 1991, p. 31.
60. Scheff, 1994, p. 135.
61. Goffman, 1971, p. 113.
62. Braithwaite, 1989.
63. There is some evidence that overresponding may be an impediment to eliciting cooperation and building trust. People who bestow favors upon others that are so great that the recipient cannot ever hope to repay often are looked on as unfavorably as those who give things contingent on burdensome terms of repayment.

For an analysis of the role of reassurance in building reciprocity-based trust, see Kydd, 2000.

64. Kriesberg, 1998b, p. 184.
65. Kriesberg, 1998b, p. 192.
66. Fisher and Ury, p. 38.
67. Cited in Fry and Raymond, 1983, pp. 236–237.
68. Cited in Pickles, 1974, p. 215.
69. Cited in Hanrieder and Auton, 1980, pp. 99–100.
70. Ackermann, 1994, pp. 241–242.
71. Robert Picht, as cited in Ackermann, p. 240.
72. Calleo, 1967, p. 48.
73. Scheingold, 1971, p. 378.
74. Pinson, 1966, p. 567.
75. Hanrieder and Auton, 1980, p. 119.
76. Cited in Craig, 1982, p. 46.
77. Haas, 1971, p. 39. Social learning was not confined to the upper echelons of the French and German governments. At almost every stage "the decisions of the Community involved not just technicians and bureaucrats, but political parties and interest groups." Pentland, 1973, p. 94.
78. Compared to Germany, France enjoyed considerable freedom of action. As Franz-Joseph Strauss once quipped: "Look at France. What can't the French do? They can get away with anything. They could almost hang four or five cardinals without troubling their relations with the Holy See." Cited in Barzini, 1983, p. 105.
79. Ackermann, p. 237. Decades after the creation of the E.C.S.C., the development of a new European identity was neither complete nor guaranteed to replace older national loyalties. According to recent public opinion polls, nearly half of all Europeans do not feel any sense of European identity. *The Wall Street Journal* (October 18, 1998), p. 1.
80. Keohane, 1984, p. 88.
81. *New York Times* (September 3, 2000), p. 4, emphasis added.
82. Recognizing this problem, United Nations Secretary-General Kofi Annan has proposed a "Global Compact" with multinational firms and business associations to promote good corporate citizenship in host countries. See the report of the High-Level Meeting on the Global Compact, held on July 26, 2000 at UN Headquarters in New York City. <http://www.un.org/partners/business/gcevent/press/summary.htm>.
83. Rengger, 1997, p. 472.
84. Thomson, Meyer, and Briggs, 1945, p. 128.
85. Thomson, Meyer, and Briggs, p. 129.
86. Morgenthau, 1985, p. 360.
87. Zacher, 1992, p. 62.
88. Marks, 2000.
89. Marks, 2000.
90. Ferguson and Mansbach, 1999, p. 230.
91. Rosenau, 1999, p. 293.
92. Van Creveld, 2000, p. 39.
93. "The Treaty of Westphalia Remains Relevant Today," *The Times* (London), December 30, 1999 <http://news.beograd.co>.

94. Falk, 1997; Murumba, 1993.
95. Lugo, 1996.
96. Mathews, 2000, p. 64.
97. Axtmann and Grant, 2000, p. 45. For a discussion of the concept of global governance and how it differs from a world government, see Commission on Global Governance, 1995. Other important works include Desai and Redfern, 1995; Murphy, 1994; Simai, 1994; and Sakamoto, 1994. While some scholars predict that global governance will eventually evolve into a set of legislative, executive, and judicial structures that are linked to their institutional counterparts at the national level (see Dorn, 1999, p. 132), others express strong reservations about the very notion of global governance. Cf. Dorn, 1999; Finkelstein, 1995.
98. Newman, 1987, p. 25.
99. This discussion draws from Brown, 1992.
100. Strange, 1999, p. 345.
101. Soros, 2000, p. 52.
102. Krasner, 1997, p. 651.
103. Krasner, 1999, p.69.
104. Waltz, 2000.
105. Lipschutz, 1992.
106. Bull, 1977, p. 264.
107. See Chisholm, 1989; Väyrynen, 1999.
108. Rengger, 1997, p. 479.
109. Strange, 1999, p. 345.
110. Annan, 2000.
111. Grotius, 1949, pp. 262, 442, writing in 1625.

References

Abu-Lughod, Janet L. *Before European Hegemony: The World System A. D. 1250–1350.* New York: Oxford University Press, 1989.

Ackermann, Alice. "Reconciliation as a Peace-Building Process in Postwar Europe," *Peace & Change* 19 (July 1994): 229–250.

Acta Pacis Westphalicae: Im Auftrage der Vereiningung zur Erforschung der Neueren Geschichte Hrsg. Münster: Aschendorff, 1962.

Ajami, Fouad. "The New Faith," *Foreign Policy* 119 (Summer 2000): 30–34.

Akehurst, Michael. *A Modern Introduction to International Law,* 6th ed. London: Unwin Hyman, 1987.

Albrecht-Carrié, René. *Europe 1500–1848.* Paterson, NJ: Littlefield, Adams, 1964 and 1953.

Annan, Kofi. *We the Peoples: The Role of the United Nations in the 21st Century,* Millennium Report of the United Nations Secretary General, 2000. http://www. un. org/ millennium/sg/report/ch. 1/htm.

Appadurai, Arjun. *Modernity at Large: Cultural Dimensions of Globalization.* Minneapolis: University of Minnesota Press, 1996.

Applbaum, Arthus Isak. *Ethics for Adversaries: The Morality of Roles in Public and Professional Life.* Princeton, NJ: Princeton University Press, 1999.

Appleby, R. Scott. *The Ambivalence of the Sacred: Religion, Violence, and Reconciliation.* Lanham, MD: Rowman & Littlefield, 2000.

———. "The Evolution of the Sacred: From Religious Militance to Peace-Building," *The Joan B. Kroc Institute for Peace Studies Report* 11 (Fall 1996): 1–4.

Arend, Anthony Clark, and Robert J. Beck. *International Law and the Use of Force.* London: Routledge, 1993.

Aron, Raymond. *Peace and War: A Theory of International Relations.* Translated by Richard Howard, and Annette Baker Fox. New York: Praeger, 1968a.

————. *Progress and Disillusion: The Dialectics of Modern Society*. New York: New American Library, Mentor Books, 1968b.

Asch, Ronald. *The Thirty Years' War: The Holy Roman Empire and Europe, 1618–48*. New York: St. Martin's Press, 1997.

Axelrod, Robert. *The Evolution of Cooperation*. New York: Basic Books, 1984.

Axtmann, Roland, and Robert Grant. "Living in a Global World: Globalization and the Future of Politics," pp. 25–54 in *Issues in International Relations*, edited by Trevor C. Salmon. London: Routledge, 2000.

Baier, Annette. "Trust and Antitrust," *Ethics* 96 (No. 2, 1986): 231–260.

Bailey, Thomas A. *The Art of Diplomacy*. New York: Appleton-Century-Crofts, 1968.

Barkun, Michall. *Law Without Sanctions*, New Haven, CT: Yale University Press, 1968.

Bar, Max. *Die Politik Pommerns Wahrend des Dreissigjahrigen Krieges*. Osnabrück: Zeller, 1966.

Barber, Benjamin R. *Jihad vs. McWorld*. New York: Random House, 1995.

Barber, Bernard. *The Logic and Limits of Trust*. New Brunswick, NJ: Rutgers University Press, 1983.

Barnet, Richard J. *The Lean Years: Politics in an Age of Scarcity*. New York: Simon and Schuster, 1980.

Barker, T. Mack. *The Military Intellectual and Battle: Raimondo Montecuccoli and the Thirty Years' War*. Albany: State University of New York Press, 1975.

Barkun, Michael. *Law Without Sanctions*. New Haven, CT: Yale University Press, 1968.

Barraclough, Geoffrey. *The Origins of Modern Germany*. Oxford: Basil Blackwell, 1946.

Barudio, Gunter. *Der Deutsche Krieg, 1618–1648*. Frankfurt am Main: S. Fischer, 1985.

Barzini, Luigi. *The Europeans*. New York: Simon and Schuster, 1983.

Barzun, Jacques. *From Dawn to Decadence: 500 years of Western Cultural Life, 1500 to the Present*. New York: HarperCollins, 2000.

Becker, Lawrence C. "Trust as Noncognitive Security about Motives," *Ethics* 107 (October 1996): 43–61.

Beller, Elmer A. *Propaganda in Germany during the Thirty Years' War*. Princeton, NJ: Princeton University Press, 1940.

Bennett, D. Scott. "Security, Bargaining, and the End of Interstate Rivalry," *International Studies Quarterly* 40 (June 1996): 157–184.

Beveridge, William. *The Price of Peace*. New York: Norton, 1945.

Bireley, Robert. *Religion and Politics in the Age of Counterreformation: Emperor Ferdinand II, William Lamormaini, S. J., and the Formation of Imperial Policy*. Chapel Hill: University of North Carolina Press, 1981.

Bixenstine, V. E., and J. Gaebelein. "Strategies of 'Real' Opponents in Eliciting Cooperative Choice in a Prisoner's Dilemma Game," *Journal of Conflict Resolution* 15 (No. 2, 1971): 157–166.

Blaney, David L., and Naeem Inayatullah. "The Westphalian Deferral," *International Studies Review* 2 (Summer 2000): 29–64.

Blau, Peter M. *Exchange and Power in Social Life*. New York: Wiley and Sons, 1964.

Blum, Jerome, Rondo Cameron, and Thomas G. Barnes. *The Emergence of the European World*, 2nd ed. Boston: Little, Brown, 1970.

Bosbach, Franz. *Die Kosten des Westfalischen Friedenkongreses: Eine Strukturgeschichtliche Untersuchung*. Münster: Aschendorff, 1984.

Bostdorff, Denise M. *The Presidency and the Rhetoric of Foreign Crisis*. Columbia: University of South Carolina Press, 1993.

Bougeant, G. *Histoire des Guerres et des Negociations Qui Precederent le Traite de Westphalie, Sous le Regne de Louis XIII.* Paris: Musier & Durand, 1767.

Bowle, John. *The Unity of European History.* London: Jonathan Cape, 1948.

Bozeman, Adda B. *Politics and Culture in International History.* Princeton, NJ: Princeton University Press, 1960.

Braithwaite, John. *Crime, Shame and Reintegration.* Cambridge: Cambridge University Press, 1989.

Brecher, Michael, and Jonathan Wilkenfeld. "International Crises and Global Instability," pp. 85–104 in *The Long Postwar Peace,* edited by Charles W. Kegley, Jr. New York: HarperCollins, 1991.

Brecke, Peter. "The Characteristics of Violent Conflict since 1400 A. D. " Paper presented at the Annual Meeting of the International Studies Association, Washington, DC, February 17–20.

Bremer, Stuart A. "Advancing the Scientific Study of War," *International Interactions* 19 (Nos. 1–2, 1993): 1–26.

Brierly, J. L. *The Law of Nations,* 6th ed. Oxford: Oxford University Press, 1963.

Britt, Albert Sidney III, Jerome A. O'Connell, Dave Richard Palmer, and Gerald P. Stadler, *The Dawn of Modern Warfare.* Wayne, NJ: Avery Publishing, 1984.

Brooke, James. "Clinton's Unity Call Stuns Canada," *International Herald Tribune* (October 11, 1999): 4.

Brown, Chris. *International Relations Theory: New Normative Approaches.* New York: Columbia University Press, 1992.

Brown, Lester et al. *The State of the World.* New York: W. W. Norton, 1998.

Brown, Lester R., Michael Renner, and Brian Halweil, eds. *Vital Signs 1999.* New York: Norton, 1999.

Brown, Robert, and Michael Alexander. "Sovereignty in the Modern Age," *Canada-United States Law Journal* 20 (1994): 273–281.

Bruun, Geoffrey, and Wallace K. Ferguson. *A Survey of European Civilization.* New York: Houghton Mifflin, 1969.

Brzezinski, Zbigniew. *The Grand Chessboard: American Foreign Policy and Its Geostrategic Imperatives.* New York: Basic Books, 1997.

———. *Between Two Ages: America's Role in the Techtronic Era.* New York: Viking, 1970.

Bueno de Mesquita, Bruce. "Popes, Kings, and Endogenous Institutions: The Concordat of Worms and the Origins of Sovereignty," *International Studies Review* 2 (Summer 2000): 93–118.

Bull, Hedley. *The Anarchical Society: A Study of Order in World Politics.* New York: Columbia University Press, 1977.

———. "The Grotian Conception of International Society," pp. 50–73 in *Diplomatic Investigations,* edited by Herbert Butterfield and Martin Wight. Cambridge, MA: Harvard University Press, 1968a.

———. "Society and Anarchy in International Relations," pp. 34–49 in *Diplomatic Investigations,* edited by Herbert Butterfield and Martin Wight. Cambridge, MA: Harvard University Press, 1968b.

Burch, Kurt. "Changing the Rules: Reconceiving Change in the Westphalian System," *International Studies Review* 2 (Summer 2000): 181–210.

Butterfield, Herbert. "The Balance of Power," pp. 132–175 in *Diplomatic Investigations: Essays in the Theory of International Politics,* edited by Herbert Butterfield and Martin Wight. Cambridge, MA: Harvard University Press, 1968.

——. *The Statecraft of Machiavelli.* New York: Collier, 1962

Callaghy, Thomas M. "Globalization and Marginalization: Debt and the Underclass,"*Current History* (November 1997): 392–396.

Calleo, David P. *Europe's Future: The Grand Alternatives.* New York: W. W. Norton, 1967.

Camilleri, J. A., and Richard A. Falk. *The End of Sovereignty: The Politics of a Shrinking and Fragmenting World.* Cheltenham: Edward Elgar, 1993.

Caporaso, James A. "Changes in the Westphalian Order: Territory, Public Authority, and Sovereignty," *International Studies Review* 2 (Summer 2000): 1–28.

Carr, E. H. *The Twenty-Years' Crisis, 1919–1939: An Introduction to the Study of International Relations.* London: Macmillan, 1939.

——. *International Relations since the Peace Treaties.* London: Macmillan, 1937.

Castells, Manuel. *The Rise of the Network Society.* Oxford: Basil Blackwell, 1996.

Cavendish, Richard. "The Treaty of Westphalia. " *History Today* 48 (November 1988): 50–52.

Center for World Indigenous Peoples. *The State of Indigenous Peoples.* Olympia, WA: Center for World Indigenous Peoples, 2000.

Chan, Steve. "In Search of Democratic Peace: Problems and Promise," *Mershon International Studies Review* 41, Supplement 1 (May 1997): 59–91.

Chandler, David G. *Atlas of Military Strategy: The Art, Theory and Practice of War, 1618–1878.* New York: Sterling, 1998.

Chisholm, Donald. *Coordination Without Hierarchy: Informal Structures in Multiorganizational Systems.* Berkeley: University of California Press, 1989.

Church, William F. *Richelieu and Reason of State.* Princeton, NJ: Princeton University Press, 1972.

Clark, George. *War and Society in the Seventeenth Century.* Cambridge: Cambridge University Press, 1958.

Claude, Inis L., Jr. "Preface," pp. ix–x in *Law, Power, and the Sovereign State,* edited by Michael Ross Fowler and Julie Marie Bunck. University Park: The Pennsylvania State University Press, 1995.

——. "The Balance of Power Revisited," *Review of International Studies* 15 (January 1989): 77–85.

——. *Swords into Plowshares: The Problems and Progress of International Organization.* New York: Random House, 1964.

——. *Power and International Relations.* New York: Random House, 1962.

Clodfelter, Michael. *Warfare and Armed Conflicts,* Vol. 1. London: McFarland, 1992.

Coffman, Peter. "Obligations Erga Omnes and the Absent Third State," *German Yearbook of International Law,* Vol. 39. Berlin: Duncker and Humblot, 1997.

Cogswell, Thomas. *The Blessed Revolution: English Politics and the Coming of War, 1621–1624.* New York: Cambridge University Press, 1989.

Cohen, Marshall. "Moral Skepticism and International Relations," pp. 15–34 in *Political Realism and International Morality,* edited by Kenneth Kipnis and Diana T. Meyers. Boulder, CO: Westview, 1987.

Collection of Treaties of Peace and Commerce. London: J. Backer, 1714.

Combes, Francois. *Histoire de la formation de l'équilibre européen par les Traités de Westphalie et des Pyrénées.* Paris: E. Dentu, 1854.

Commission on Global Governance. *Our Global Neighborhood.* New York: Oxford University Press, 1995.

Conner, Walker. "Ethnonationalism," pp. 196–220 in *Understanding Political Development,* edited by Myron Weiner and Samuel P. Huntington. Boston: Little Brown, 1987.

Cooper, Robert. "The Post-Modern State and World Order," *New Perspectives Quarterly*, Special Issue (Summer 1997): 48–55.

Cox, Robert. *Production, Power and World Order: Social Forces in the Making of History*. New York: Columbia University Press, 1987.

Craig, Gordon A. *The Germans*. New York: New American Library, 1982.

Craig, Gordon A., and Alexander L. George. *Force and Statecraft*, 2nd ed. New York: Oxford Univeresity Press, 1990.

Crossette, Barbara. "World Leaders Set Lofty Goal for Future," *The State* (Columbia, SC) (September 9, 2000): A1, A5.

Culbertson, W. *Reciprocity: A National Policy for Foreign Trade*. New York: McGraw-Hill, 1937.

Cusack, Thomas R., and Richard J. Stoll, eds. *Exploring Realpolitik*. Boulder, CO: Lynne Rienner, 1990.

D'Amato, Anthony. *International Law: Process and Prospect*. Irvington, NY: Transnational Publishers, 1995.

Davies, Norman. *Europe: A History*. Oxford: Oxford University Press, 1996.

Davis, Wade. "Vanishing Cultures," *National Geographic* (August 1999): 62–89.

Dawson, Doyne. *The Origins of Western Warfare*. Boulder, CO: Westview, 1996.

Dehio, Ludwig. *The Precarious Balance: Four Centuries of European Power Struggle*. Translated by Charles Fullman. New York: Alfred A. Knopf, 1962.

Deibert, Ronald J. "Network Power," pp. 198–207 in *Political Economy and the Changing Global Order*, 2nd ed., edited by Richard Stubbs and Geoffrey R. D. Underhill. Don Mills, Ontario: Oxford University Press, 2000.

Desai, Meghnad, and Paul Redfern, eds. *Global Governance: Ethics and Economics of the World Order*. London: Pinter, 1995.

Deudney, Daniel. "Global Village Sovereignty," pp. 299–325 in *The Global Environment*, edited by Norman J. Vig and Regina S. Axelrod. Washington, DC: Congressional Quarterly Press, 1999.

Deutsch, Morton. "Trust and Suspicion," *Journal of Conflict Resolution* 2 (December 1958): 265–279.

Diehl, Paul F., and Mark J. C. Crescenzi. "Reconfiguring the Arms Race-War Debate," *Journal of Peace Research* 35 (January 1998): 111–118.

Dixon, William J. "Reciprocity in United States-Soviet Relations: Multiple Symmetry or Issue Linkage?" *American Journal of Political Science* 30 (No. 2, 1986): 421–445.

Doran, Charles F. *The Politics of Assimilation: Hegemony and Its Aftermath*. Baltimore and London: The Johns Hopkins Press, 1971.

Dorn, A. Walter. "The United Nations in the Twenty-First Century: A Vision for an Evolving World Order," pp. 118–135 in *World Order for a New Millennium*, edited by A. Walter Dorn. New York: St. Martin's Press, 1999.

Doyle, Michael W. *Ways of War and Peace*. New York: W. W. Norton, 1998.

Druckman, Daniel. "The Social Psychology of Arms Control and Reciprocation," *Political Psychology* 11 (No. 4, 1990): 553–581.

Dunan, Marcel. *Larousse Encyclopedia of Modern History: From 1500 to the Present Day*. New York: Harper & Row, 1964.

Duchardt, Heinz. "Westfälischer Friede und Internationale Beziehungen im Ancien Régime," *Historische Zeitschrift* 249 (1989): 533–539.

Dunn, John. *The History of Political Theory and Other Essays*. Cambridge: Cambridge University Press, 1996.

Ellerman, Christine. "Command of Sovereignty Gives Way to Concern for Humanity," *Vanderbilt Journal of Transnational Law* 26 (May 1993): 341–371.

Elster, Jon. "Norms of Revenge," *Ethics* 100 (July 1990): 862–885.

Enriquez, Juan. "Too Many Flags?" *Foreign Policy* 116 (Fall 1999): 30–50.

Epstein, John. *The Catholic Tradition of the Law of Nations*. 1935.

Etzioni, Amitai. "The Kennedy Experiment," *Western Political Science Quarterly* 20 (June 1967): 316–380.

Eyffinger, Arthur. "Europe in the Balance: An Appraisal of the Westphalian System," *Netherlands International Law Review* 45 (1998): 161–187.

Falk, Richard A. *Law in an Emerging Global Village: A Post-Westphalian Perspective*. Ardsley, NY: Transnational Publishers, 1998.

———. "The Grotian Moment: Unfulfilled Promise, Harmless Fantasy, Missed Opportunity?" *International Insights* 13 (Fall 1997): 3–34.

———. "Sovereignty," pp. 851–853 in *The Oxford Companion to Politics of the World*, edited by Joel Krieger. New York: Oxford University Press, 1993.

———. "The Grotian Quest," pp. 36–42 in *International Law*, edited by Richard Falk, Friedrich Kratochwil, and Saul H. Mendlovitz. Boulder, CO: Westview, 1985a.

———. "The Interplay of Westphalia and Charter Conceptions of International Legal Order," pp. 116–142 in *International Law*, edited by Richard Falk, Friedrich Kratochwil, and Saul H. Medlovitz. Boulder, CO: Westview, 1985b.

———. *A Study of Future Worlds*. New York: Free Press, 1975.

Fenwick, Charles G. *International Law*, 4th ed. New York: Appleton-Century Crofts, 1965.

Ferguson, Yale H., and Richard W. Mansbach. "Global Politics at the Turn of the Millennium: Changing Bases of 'Us' and 'Them'," *International Studies Review* 1 (Summer 1999): 77–107.

———. "History's Revenge and Future Shock," pp. 197–238 in *Approaches to Global Governance Theory*, edited by Martin Hewson and Timothy J. Sinclair. Albany: State University of New York Press, 1999.

Fields, Lanny B., Russell J. Barber, and Cheryl A. Riggs. *The Global Past*. Boston: Bedford, 1998.

Finkelstein, Lawrence S. "What Is Global Governance?" *Global Governance* 1 (September 1995): 367–372.

Fisher, Roger, and William Ury. *Getting to Yes*. Boston: Houghton Mifflin, 1981.

Fitzmaurice, Gerald. "The General Principles of International Law, Considered From the Standpoint of the Rule of Law," *Recueil des Cours*, Vol. 2. Leyden: A. W. Sijthoff, 1958.

Fletcher, C. R. Leslie. *Gustavus Adolphus and the Thirty Years' War*. New York: Capricorn Books, 1963.

Ford, Christopher A. " Preaching Propriety to Princes: Grotius Lipsius and Neo-Stoic International Law," *Case-Western Reserve Journal of International Law* 28 (Spring 1996): 313–366.

Forsberg, Thomas. "Power, Interests and Trust: Explaining Gorbachev's Choices at the End of the Cold War," *Review of International Affairs* 25 (October 1999): 603–621.

Forsyth, Murray. "The Tradition of International Law," pp. 23–41 in *Traditions of International Ethics*, edited by Terry Nardin and David Mapel. Cambridge: Cambridge University Press, 1992.

Frederick, Howard H. *Global Communication and International Relations*. Belmont, CA: Wadsworth, 1993.

Friedman, Thomas C. "DOScapital," *Foreign Policy* 116 (Fall 1999): 110–116.

Fromkin, David. *The Independence of Nations*. New York: Praeger, 1981.

Fry, Earl H., and Gregory A. Raymond. *The Other Western Europe: A Political Analysis of the Smaller Democracies*, 2nd ed. Santa Barbara, CA: Clio Press, 1983.

Fukuyama, Francis. "Second Thoughts: The Last Man in a Bottle," *The National Interest* 56 (Summer 1999): 16–33.

———. *Trust: The Social Virtues and the Creation of Prosperity*. New York: Free Press, 1995.

———. *The End of History and the Last Man*. New York: Free Press, 1992.

Fuller, J. F. C. *The Dragon's Teeth: A Study of War and Peace*. London: Constable, 1932.

Gaddis, John Lewis. *The Long Peace: Inquiries into the History of the Cold War*. New York: Oxford University Press, 1987.

Gambetta, Diego. "Can We Trust?" pp. 213–237 in *Trust: Making and Breaking Co-Operative Relations*, edited by Diego Gambetta. Oxford: Basil Blackwell, 1988.

Gameson, William, and Andre Modigliani. *Untangling the Cold War*. Boston: Little, Brown, 1971.

Gardiner, S. Rawson. *Epochs of History: The Era of the Thirty Years' War, 1618–1648*. New York: Charles Scribner's Sons, 1895 and 1900.

———. *Letters and Other Documents Illustrating the Relations between England and Germany at the Commencement of the Thirty Years' War*. London: Westminster, 1865–1868.

Gardner, Richard N. "The Role of the UN in Environmental Problems," pp. 69–86 in *World Eco-Crisis: International Organizations in Response*, edited by David A. Kay and Eugene B. Skolnikoff. Madison: University of Wisconsin Press, 1972.

Gay, Peter, and R. K. Webb. *Modern Europe to 1815*. New York: Harper & Row, 1973.

Geller, Daniel S., and J. David Singer. *Nations at War: A Scientific Study of International Conflict*. Cambridge: Cambridge University Press, 1998.

Giddens, Anthony. *The Consequences of Modernity*. Stanford, CA: Stanford University Press, 1990.

Gilchrist, J. *The Church and Economic Activity in the Middle Ages*. New York: Macmillan, 1969.

Gilpin, Robert. *The Challenge of Global Capitalization*. Princeton, NJ: Princeton University Press, 2000.

———. *War and Change in World Politics*. Cambridge: Cambridge University Press, 1981.

Giraud, Charles. *Le Traité d'Utrecht*. Paris: Plon Fréres, 1847.

Gleditsch, Nils Petter. "Democracy and Peace," *Journal of Peace Research* 29 (November 1992): 369–376.

Glennon, Michael J. "The New Interventionism: The Search for a Just International Law," *Foreign Affairs* 78 (May/June 1999): 2–7.

Gochman, Charles S., and Russell J. Leng. "Realpolitik and the Road to War," *International Studies Quarterly* 27 (March 1983): 97–120.

Goffman, E. *Relations in Public*. New York: Harper, 1971.

Golding, Martin P. *Philosophy of Law*. Upper Saddle River, NJ: Prentice-Hall, 1975.

Goldsborough, James. "Out-of-Control Immigration," *Foreign Affairs* 79 (No. 5, 2000): 89–101.

Goldstein, Joshua, and John R. Freeman. *Three-Way Street: Strategic Reciprocity and World Politics*. Chicago: University of Chicago Press, 1990.

Gong, Gerrit W. *The Standards of "Civilization" in International Society*. Oxford: Clarendon Press, 1984.

Gottlieb, Gidon. "Global Bargaining: The Legal and Diplomatic Framework," pp. 109–130 in *Law Making in the Global Community*, edited by Nicholas Greenwood Onuf. Durham, NC: Carolina Academic Press, 1982.

Gouldner, Alvin W. "The Norm of Reciprocity: A Preliminary Statement," *American Sociological Review* 25 (April 1960): 161–178.

Govier, Trudy. *Social Trust and Human Communities*. Montreal: McGill-Queen's University Press, 1997.

Granovetter, Mark. "Economic Action and Social Structure: The Problem of Embeddedness," *American Journal of Sociology* 91 (November 1985): 481–510.

Gross, Leo. "The Peace of Westphalia, 1648–1948," pp. 25–46 in *International Law in the Twentieth Century*, edited by Leo Gross. New York: Appleton-Century-Crofts, 1969. Also printed pp. 45–67 in *International Law and Organization*, edited by Richard A. Falk and Wolfram F. Hanreider. Philadelphia, PA: Lippincott, 1968.

Grotius, Hugo. *The Law of War and Peace*, translated by Louise R. Loomis. New York: Walter J. Black, 1949. Originally published in 1625.

Gruber, Lloyd. *Ruling the World: Power Politics and the Rise of Supranational Institutions*. Princeton, NJ: Princeton University Press, 2000.

Gruder, Charles L., and Robert J. Dulak. "Elicitation of Cooperation by Retaliatory and Nonretaliatory Strategies in a Mixed-Motive Game," *Journal of Conflict Resolution* 17 (No. 1, 1973): 162–174.

Guéhenno, Jean-Marie. "The Typology of Sovereignty." Paper presented at the United States Institute of Peace Conference on Virtual Diplomacy, 1997.

———. *The End of the Nation-State*. Minneapolis: University of Minnesota Press, 1995.

Gulick, Edward Vose. *Europe's Classical Balance of Power*. Ithaca, NY: Cornell University Press, 1955.

Gurr, Ted Robert. "Managing Conflict in Ethnically Divided Societies: A New Regime Emerges," pp. 173–186 in *The Global Agenda*, 6th ed., edited by Charles W. Kegley, Jr. and Eugene R. Wittkopf. Boston: McGraw-Hill, 2001.

Gurr, Ted Robert, and Barbara Harff. *Ethnic Conflict in World Politics*. Boulder, CO: Westview, 1994.

Gutman, Myron P. "The Origins of the Thirty Years' War," *Journal of Interdisciplinary History* 18 (Spring 1988): 749–770.

Haas, Ernst B. "The Study of Regional Integration: Reflections on the Joy and Anguish of Pretheorizing," pp. 3–42 in *Regional Integration: Theory and Research*, edited by Leon N. Lindberg and Stuart A. Scheingold. Cambridge, MA: Harvard University Press, 1971.

Hackman, George G., Charles W. Kegley, and Viktjok Nikander. *Religion in Modern Life*. New York: Mcmillan, 1957.

Hall, William Edward. *A Treatise on International Law*. Oxford: Clarendon, 1924.

Halliday, Fred. *The World at 2000*. London: Macmillan, 2001.

Hanrieder, Wolfram F., and Graeme P. Auton. *The Foreign Policies of West Germany, France, and Britain*. Upper Saddle River, NJ: Prentice-Hall, 1980.

Harbour, Francis V. *Thinking about International Ethics*. Boulder, CO: Westview, 1999.

Hardin, Russell. *One for All: The Logic of Group Conflict*. Princeton, NJ: Princeton University Press, 1995.

Hardt, Michael, and Antonio Negri. *Empire*. Cambridge, MA: Harvard University Press, 2000.

Hatch, Nathan O. *The Democratization of American Christianity*. New Haven, CT: Yale University Press, 1989.

Hausser, Ludwig. *The Period of Reformation, 1516 to 1648*. London: Strahan, 1873.

Hawthorn, Geoffrey. "Three Ironies in Trust," pp. 111–126 in *Trust: Making and Breaking Co-Operative Relations*, edited by Diego Gambetta. Oxford: Basil Blackwell, 1988.

Heckel, Martin. *Deutschland im konfesionellen Zeitalter.* Gottingen: Vandenhoeck & Ruprecht, 1983.

Held, David, Anthony McGrew, David Goldblatt, and Jonathon Perraton. "Managing the Challenge of Globalization and Institutionalizing Cooperation Through Global Governance," pp. 134–146 in *The Global Agenda,* 6th ed., edited by Charles W. Kegley, Jr. and Eugene R. Wittkopf. Boston: McGraw-Hill, 2001.

———. *Global Transformations: Politics, Economics and Culture.* Cambridge: Polity Press, 1999.

Hemleben, John. *Plans for World Peace through Six Centuries.* Chicago: University of Chicago Press, 1943.

Henkin, Ascher. *Must We Have War?* Boston: Bruce Humphries, 1934.

Hermann, Margaret G., and Charles W. Kegley, Jr. "Democracies and Intervention," *Journal of Peace Research* 38 (No. 2, 2001): 237–245.

———"Ballots, A Barrier Against the Use of Bullets and Bombs: Democratization and Military Intervention," *Journal of Conflict Resolution* 40 (September 1996): 436–460.

———. "Rethinking Democracy and International Peace," *International Studies Quarterly* 39 (December 1995): 511–533.

Herz, John H. *The Nation-State and the Crisis of World Politics.* New York: David McKay, 1976.

Higgins, Ronald. *Plotting Peace.* London: Brassey's, 1990.

Hinsley, F. H. *Sovereignty,* 2nd ed. Cambridge: Cambridge University Press, 1986.

Hirst, P. "The Global Economy: Myths and Realities," *International Affairs* 73 (No. 3, 1997): 409–425.

Hoagland, Jim. "Team Europe's New Lineup," *Washington Post National Weekly Edition* (October 18, 1999): 5.

Hobsbawm, Eric J. *Nations and Nationalism Since 1780.* Cambridge: Cambridge University Press, 1990.

Hoffmann, Stanley. *World Disorders: Troubled Peace in the Post-Cold War Era.* New York: Rowman & Littlefield, 1998.

———. "International Law and the Control of Force," pp. 34–66 in *The Relevance of International Law,* edited by Karl Deutsch and Stanley Hoffmann. Garden City, NY: Doubleday-Anchor, 1971.

Hollingshead, James R. *The Household of Caesar and the Body of Christ.* New York: University Press of America, 1998.

Hollis, Martin. *Trust Within Reason.* Cambridge: Cambridge University Press, 1998.

Holm, Hans-Henrik, and Georg Sørensen. "What Has Changed?" pp. 1–17 in *Whose World Order? Uneven Globalization and the End of the Cold War,* edited by Hans-Henrick Holm and Georg Sørensen. Boulder, CO: Westview, 1995.

Holsti, Kalevi J. *Peace and War: Armed Conflicts and International Order 1648–1989.* Cambridge: Cambridge University Press, 1991.

Homans, George. *Social Behavior.* New York: Harcourt, Brace and World, 1961.

Homer-Dixon, Thomas E. "Environmental Scarcities and Violent Conflict," *International Security* 19 (Summer 1994): 5–40.

Hoover, Kenneth, with James Marcia and Kristen Paris. *The Power of Identity.* Chatham, NJ: Chatham House, 1997.

Hopkins, Terrence K., Immanuel Wallerstein, and Associates. "Cyclical Rhythms and Secular Trends of the Capitalist World Economy: Some Premises, Hypotheses, and Questions," pp. 124–170 in *World-System Analysis: Theory and Methodology,* edited by Terrence K. Hopkins, Immanuel Wallerstein, and Associates, Beverly Hills, CA: Sage, 1992.

Howard, Michael. *War in European History.* Oxford: Oxford University Press, 1986.

Hsiung, James C. *Anarchy and Order: The Interplay of Politics and Law in International Relations.* Boulder, CO: Lynne Rienner, 1997.

Humphrey, John, and Hubert Schmitz. "Trust and Inter-Firm Relations in Developing and Transition Economies," *Journal of Development Studies* 34 (April 1998): 32–61.

Huntington, Samuel P. *The Clash of Civilizations and the Remaking of World Order.* New York: Simon and Schuster, 1996.

———. *The Third Wave: Democratization in the Late Twentieth Century.* Norman: University of Oklahoma Press, 1991.

———. "The U. S.—Decline or Renewal?" *Foreign Affairs* 67 (Winter 1988–1989): 76–96.

Husain, Mir Zohair. *Global Islamic Politics.* New York: HarperCollins, 1995.

Hwang, Peter, and Willem P. Burgers. "Apprehension and Temptation: The Forces Against Cooperation," *Journal of Conflict Resolution* 43 (February 1999): 117–130.

Hyland, William G. *Reexamining National Strategy.* Carlisle Barracks, PA: Strategic Studies Institute, U. S. Army War College, 1993.

Ikenberry, G. John. "The Spread of Norms in the International System. " Paper presented at the Annual Meeting of the American Political Science Association, Washington, DC, 1987.

Jackson, Robert H. *Quasi-States: Sovereignty, International Relations and the Third World.* Cambridge: Cambridge University Press, 1990.

Jacoby, Susan. *Wild Justice: The Evolution of Revenge.* New York: Harper and Row, 1983.

James, Alan. *Sovereign Statehood: The Basis of International Society.* London: Allen and Unwin, 1986.

Janis, Mark W. "Sovereignty and International Law: Hobbes and Grotius," pp. 390–400 in *Essays in Honour of Wang Tieya,* edited by R. St. J. Macdonald. The Hague: Kluwer Academic Publishers, 1993.

Jensen, Lloyd. "Soviet-American Bargaining Behavior in the Post-War Disarmament Negotiations," *Journal of Conflict Resolution* 9 (September 1963): 522–541.

Jervis, Robert. *System Effects: Complexity in Political and Social Life.* Princeton, NJ: Princeton University Press, 1997.

Joffe, Josef. "Entangled Forever," *The National Interest* 21 (Fall 1990): 35–40.

Johnson, Chalmers. *Blowback: The Costs and Consequences of American Empire.* New York: Henry Holt, 2000.

Johnson, James Turner. *Morality and Contemporary Warfare.* New Haven, CT: Yale University Press, 1999.

———. "Onward, Christian Soldiers?" *First Things* 88 (December 1998): 45–48.

———. "Grotius' Use of History and Charity in the Modern Transformation of the Just War Idea," *Grotiana* 4 (1983): 21–34.

Johnson, Laurie M. *Thucydides, Hobbes and the Interpretation of Realism.* De Kalb: Northern Illinois University Press, 1993.

Jones, Dorothy. *Code of Peace: Ethics and Security in the World of Warlord States.* Chicago: University of Chicago Press, 1992.

Jones, Karen. "Trust as an Affective Attitude," *Ethics* 107 (October 1996): 4–25.

Juergensmeyer, Mark. *The New Cold War? Religious Nationalism Confronts the Secular State.* Berkeley: University of California Press, 1993.

Kainz, Howard P. *Philosophical Perspectives on Peace.* Athens: Ohio University Press, 1987.

Kaiser, David. *Politics and War. European Conflict from Philip II to Hitler.* Cambridge, MA: Harvard University Press, 1990.

Kamen, Henry. *Philip of Spain.* New Haven, CT: Yale University Press, 1998.

Kaplan, Morton A. *System and Process in International Politics.* New York: Wiley, 1957.

Kaplan, Morton A., and Nicholas de B. Katzenbach. *The Political Foundations of International Law.* New York: John Wiley and Sons, 1961.

Kaplan, Robert D. *The Coming Anarchy.* New York. Random House, 2000.

———. "The Coming Anarchy," *The Atlantic* (February 1994): 44–76.

———. *Balkan Ghosts: A Journey Through History.* New York: St. Martin's Press, 1993.

Kaplowitz, N. "Psychopolitical Dimensions of International Relations: The Reciprocal Effects of Conflict Strategies," *International Studies Quarterly* 28 (No. 4, 1984): 373–406.

Kauffman, Stuart. *At Home in the Universe? The Search for Laws of Self-Organization and Complexity.* New York: Oxford University Press, 1995.

Kauppi, Mark V., and Paul Viotti. *The Global Philosophers.* New York: Lexington Books, 1992.

Kegley, Charles W. *Politics, Religion and Modern Man.* Quezon City: University of the Philippines Press, 1969.

Kegley, Charles W. Jr., ed. *Controversies in International Relations Theory: Realism and the Neoliberal Challenge.* New York: St. Martin's, 1995.

———. "The New Global Order: The Power of Principle in a Pluralistic World," *Ethics and International Affairs* 6 (1992a): 21–40.

———. "The Long Post War Peace During the Cold War: Some New Conventional Wisdoms Reconsidered," *Jerusalem Journal of International Relations* 14 (December 1992b): 1–18.

———. ed. *The Long Postwar Peace: Contending Explanations and Projections.* New York: HarperCollins, 1991.

———. "Selective Attention: A General Characteristic of the Interactive Behavior of Nations," *International Interactions* 2 (June 1976): 101–104.

Kegley, Charles W. Jr., and Margaret G. Hermann. "A Peace Dividend? Democracies' Military Interventions and Their External Political Consequences," *Cooperation and Conflict* 32 (December 1997): 339–369.

Kegley, Charles W. Jr., and Gregory A. Raymond. *From War to Peace.* Boston, MA: Bedford, 2002.

———. *How Nations Make Peace.* New York: Bedford/St. Martin's, 1999.

———. *A Multipolar Peace? Great-Power Politics in the Twenty-First Century.* New York: St. Martin's Press, 1994.

———. *When Trust Breaks Down: Alliance Norms and World Politics.* Columbia: University of South Carolina Press, 1990.

Kegley, Charles W., Jr., Gregory A. Raymond, and Margaret G. Hermann. "The Rise and Fall of the Nonintervention Norm," *Fletcher Forum of World Affairs* 22 (Winter/Spring 1998): 81–101.

Kegley, Charles W., Jr., Gregory A. Raymond, Richard A. Skimmer, and Robert M. Rood, eds. *International Events and the Comparative Analysis of Foreign Policy.* Columbia: University of South Carolina Press, 1975.

Kegley, Charles W., Jr., and Eugene R. Wittkopf, *World Politics.* 8th ed. Boston: Bedford/St. Martin's, 2001.

———. *World Politics,* 7th ed. New York: St Martin's/WORTH, 1999.

Kelley, Harold. "The Process of Causal Attribution," *American Psychologist* 28 (No. 1, 1973): 107–128.

Kennedy, Paul. *The Rise and Fall of the Great Powers.* New York: Random House, 1987.

Keohane, Robert O. "Reciprocity in International Relations," *International Organization* 40 (Winter 1986): 1–27.

———. *After Hegemony: Cooperation and Discord in the World Political Economy.* Princeton, NJ: Princeton University Press, 1984.

Keohane, Robert O., and Joseph S. Nye, Jr. "Power and Interdependence in the Information Age," pp. 26–36 in *The Global Agenda*, 2nd ed., edited by Charles W. Kegley, Jr. and Eugene Wittkopf. Boston. McGraw-Hill, 2001.

———. "Globalization: What's New? What's Not? (And So What?)," *Foreign Policy* 118 (Spring 2000): 104–119.

———. "Complex Interdependence, Transnational Relations, and Realism: Alternative Perspectives on World Politics," pp. 257–271 in *The Global Agenda*, 2nd ed., edited by Charles W. Kegley, Jr. and Eugene R. Wittkopf. New York: Random House. 1988.

———. *Power and Interdependence*, 2nd ed. Glenview, IL: Scott, Foresman/Little, Brown, 1989 and Boston: Little, Brown, 1977.

Kissinger, Henry A. *Diplomacy.* New York: Simon and Schuster, 1994.

Kobrin, Stephen J. "Back to the Future: Neomedievalism and the Postmodern Digital World Economy," *Journal of International Affairs* 51 (Spring 1998): 361–386.

———. "Electronic Cash and the End of National Markets," *Foreign Policy* 107 (Summer 1997): 65–77.

Komorita, Samuel S., and Craig D. Parks. *Social Dilemmas.* Boulder, CO: Westview, 1996.

Kramer, Roderick M. "Integrative Complexity and Conflict Theory: Evidence of an Emerging Paradigm," *Negotiation Journal* 10 (October 1994): 347–357.

Kramer, Roderick M., Marilynn B. Brewer, and Benjamin A. Hanna. "Collective Trust and Collective Action: The Decision to Trust as a Social Decision," pp. 357–389 in *Trust in Organizations: Frontiers of Theory and Research*, edited by Roderick M. Kramer and Tom R. Tyler. London: Sage, 1996.

Krasner, Stephen D. *Sovereignty: Organized Hypocrisy.* Princeton, NJ: Princeton University Press, 1999.

———. "Pervasive Not Perverse: Semi-Sovereigns as the Global Norm," *Cornell International Law Journal* 30 (No. 3, 1997): 651–680.

———. "Compromising Westphalia," *International Security* 20 (1995/1996): 115–151.

———. "Sovereignty and Intervention," pp. 228–249 in *Beyond Westphalia?* edited by Gene M. Lyons and Michael Mastanduno. Baltimore, MD: The Johns Hopkins University Press, 1995.

———. "Westphalia and All That," pp. 235–263 in *Ideas and Foreign Policy*, edited by Judith Goldstein and Robert O. Keohane. Ithaca, NY: Cornell University Press, 1993.

Krauthammer, Charles. "The Unipolar Moment," *Foreign Affairs* 70 (No. 1, 1991): 23–33.

Kriesberg, Louis. *Constructive Conflicts: From Escalation to Resolution.* Lanham, MD: Rowman & Littlefield, 1998a.

———. "Coexistence and the Reconciliation of Communal Conflicts," pp. 183–198 in *The Handbook of Interethnic Coexistence*, edited by Eugene Weiner. New York: Continuum, 1998b.

Kudrle, Robert T. "Three Types of Globalization: Communication, Market, and Direct," pp. 3–23 in *Globalization and Global Governance*, edited by Raimo Väyrynen. Lanham, MD: Rowman & Littlefield, 1999.

Kuhn, Joseph. "Globalization Sparks Another Anarchist Revival," *International Herald Tribune*, (August 7, 2000): 2.

Kydd, Andrew. "Trust, Reassurance, and Cooperation," *International Organization* 54 (Spring 2000): 325–357.

Landy, Joanne. "Peace from Below," *Boston Review* 17 (November/December 1992): 8–9.

Lane, Christel, and Reinhard Bachmann, eds. *Trust Within and Between Organizations: Conceptual Issues and Empirical Applications*. Oxford: Oxford University Press, 1998.

Lang, Anthony F., Jr., and James N. Lang. "Between Theory and History," *PS* 31 (June 1998): 209–215.

Langer, Herbert. *The Thirty Years' War*. New York: Hippocrene Books, 1980.

Larson, Deborah Welch. "Trust and Missed Opportunities in International Relations," *Political Psychology* 18 (No. 3, 1997): 701–734.

Laughlin, J. L., and H. P. Willis. *Reciprocity*. New York: Baker & Taylor, 1903.

Lauterpacht, Hersch. "The Grotian Tradition in International Law," pp. 10–36 in *International Law*, edited by Richard Falk, Friedrich Kratochvil, and Saul H. Mendlovitz. Boulder, CO: Westview, 1985.

———. *International Law*, Vol. 2. Cambridge: Cambridge University Press, 1975.

Layne, Christopher. "The Uniploar Illusion: Why New Great Powers Will Rise," *International Security* 17 (Spring 1993): 5–51.

Lazaric, Nathalie. *Trust and Economic Learning*. Cheltenham, U. K.: Edward Elgar, 1998.

Lee, Stephen J. *Aspects of European History 1494–1789*, 2nd ed. London: Routledge, 1986.

Leng, Russell J. *Interstate Crisis Behavior, 1816–1980: Realism versus Reciprocity*. Cambridge: Cambridge University Press, 1993.

———. "When Will They Ever Learn? Coercive Bargaining in Recurrent Crises," *Journal of Conflict Resolution* 27 (September 1983): 379–419.

Leng, Russell J., and Charles S. Gochman. "Dangerous Disputes: A Study of Conflict Behavior and War," *American Journal of Political Science* 26 (No. 4, 1982): 664–687.

Leng, Russell J., and Goodsell, R. "Behavioral Indicators of War Proneness in Bilateral Conflicts," *Sage International Yearbook of Foreign Policy Studies*, Vol. 2, edited by Patrick J. McGraw. Beverly Hills: Sage, 1974.

Leng, Russell J., and Hugh B. Wheeler. "Influence Strategies, Success, and War," *Journal of Conflict Resolution* 23 (December 1979): 655–684.

Lesaffer, Randall. "The Westphalian Peace Treaties and the Development of the Tradition of Great European Peace Settlements Prior to 1948," *Grotiana* 18 (1997): 71–95.

Levy, Jack S. "The Rise and Decline of the Anglo-Dutch Rivalry, 1609–1689," pp. 172–200 in *Great Power Rivalries*, edited by William R. Thomson. Columbia, SC: University of South Carolina Press, 1999.

———. "An Introduction to Prospect Theory," *Political Psychology* 13 (June 1992): 171–186.

———. *War in the Modern Great Power System, 1495–1975*. Lexington: University of Kentucky Press, 1983.

Lewicki, Roy J., and Barbara Benedict Bunker. "Developing and Maintaining Trust in Work Relationships," pp. 114–139 in *Trust in Organizations: Frontiers of Theory and Research*, edited by Roderick M. Kramer and Tom R. Tyler. London: Sage, 1996.

Lewis, J. David, and Andrew Weigert. "Trust as a Social Reality," *Social Forces* 63 (June 1985): 967–985.

Lieberman, Bernhardt. "I-Trust: A Notion of Trust in Three-Person Games and International Affairs," pp. 359–371 in *Social Processes in International Relations*, edited by Louis Kriesberg. New York: John Wiley & Sons, 1968.

Limm, Peter. *The Thirty Years' War.* New York: Longman, 1984.

Lindskold, Svenn. "Trust Development, the GRIT Proposal, and the Effects of Conciliatory Acts on Conflict and Cooperation," *Psychological Bulletin* 85 (July 1978): 772–793.

Lindskold, Svenn, P. Walters, and H. Koutsourais. "Cooperators, Competitors, and Responses to GRIT," *Journal of Conflict Resolution* 27 (No. 3, 1983): 521–532.

Lipschutz, Ronnie D. *After Authority: War, Peace, and Global Politics in the 21st Century.* Albany: State University of New York, 2000.

———. "Reconstructing World Politics: The Emergence of Global Civil Society," *Millennium* 21 (No. 3, 1992): 389–420.

Litfin, Karen T. "Environment, Wealth, and Authority: Global Climate Change and Emerging Modes of Legitimation," *International Studies Review* 2 (Summer 2000): 119–148.

Lockhart, P. Douglass. *Denmark in the Thirty Years' War, 1618–1648: King Christian IV and the Decline of the Oldenburg State.* Cranbury, NJ: Associated University Presses, 1996.

Louis XIV, "The State's Need for Military Triumphs," pp. 158–162 in *Basic Texts in International Relations,* edited by Evan Luard. New York: St. Martin's Press, 1992.

Luard, Evan. *Conflict and Peace in the Modern International System.* Albany: State University of New York Press, 1986.

———. *War in International Society.* New Haven, CT: Yale University Press, 1986.

———. *Types of International Society.* New York: Free Press, 1976.

———. *Conflict and Peace in the Modern International System.* Boston: Little, Brown, 1968.

Lugo, Luis E., ed. *Sovereignty at the Crossroads?* Lanham, MD: Rowman & Littlefield, 1996.

Luhmann, Niklas. *Trust and Power.* New York: Chichester, 1979.

Lyons, Gene M., and Michael Mastanduno, eds. *Beyond Westphalia: State Sovereignty and International Intervention.* Baltimore: The Johns Hopkins University Press, 1995.

Maine, Henry Sumner. *Ancient Law.* Boston: Beacon Press, 1861.

Maland, David. *Europe at War 1600–1650.* Totowa, NJ: Rowman and Littlefield, 1980.

Mansbach, Richard W., and John A. Vasquez. *In Search of Theory: A New Paradigm for Global Politics.* New York: Columbia University Press, 1981.

Mansbach, Richard W., Yale H. Ferguson, and Donald E. Lampert. *The Web of World Politics: Nonstate Actors in the Global System.* Upper Saddle River, NJ: Prentice-Hall, 1976.

Maoz, Zeev. "Realist and Cultural Critiques of the Democratic Peace: A Theoretical and Empirical Re-Assessment," *International Interactions* 24 (No. 1, 1998): 3–89.

Maoz, Zeev, and Bruce Russett. "Normative and Structural Causes of Democratic Peace, 1946–1986," *American Political Science Review* 87 (September 1993): 624–638.

Marks, Edward D. "From Post-Cold War to Post-Westphalia," *American Diplomacy* 1 (Winter 2000) <http://www. unc. edu/depts/diplomat/amdipl_14/marks_westph .html>.

Martin, David. *Does Christianity Cause War?* New York: Oxford University Press, 1998.

Massoud, Tansa George. "War Termination," *Journal of Peace Research* 33 (November 1996): 491–496.

Mathews, Jessica T. "The Information Revolution," *Foreign Policy* 119 (Summer 2000): 63–65.

———. "Are Networks Better Than Nations," pp. 8–11 in *Perspectives: Global Issues,* edited by James M. Lindsay. Boulder, CO: Coursewise Publishing, 1998.

Mattingly, Garrett. *Renaissance Diplomacy.* Boston: Houghton Mifflin, 1971.

Mattli, Walter. "Sovereignty Bargains in Regional Integration," *International Studies Review* 2 (Summer 2000): 149–180.

Mayall, James. "International Society and International Theory, " pp. 122–141 in *The Reason of States*, edited by Michael Donelan. London: George Allen & Unwin, 1978.

Mazarr, Michael. *Global Trends 2005*. New York: St. Martin's Press, 1999.

McCormick, John. "The Role of Environmental NGOs in International Regimes," pp. 52–71 in *The Global Environment*, edited by Norman J. Vig and Regina S. Axelrod. Washington, DC: Congressional Quarterly Press, 1999.

McKay, John P., Bennett D. Hill, and John Buckler. *A History of Western Society*, 4th ed. Boston: Houghton Mifflin, 1991.

Meinecke, Friedrich. *Machiavellism: The Doctrine of Raison d'Etat and Its Place in Modern History*. New Haven, CT: Yale University Press, 1957.

Melloan, George. "Political Baggage Burdens a Summit," *The Wall Street Journal* (August 29, 2000): A27.

Meyjes, G. H. M. "Hugo Grotius as an Irenicist," pp. 43–64 in *The World of Hugo Grotius*, edited by The Grotius Committee of the Royal Netherlands Academy of Arts and Sciences. Amsterdam: APA-Holland University Press, 1984.

Micklethwait, John, and Adrian Wooldridge. *A Future Perfect: The Challenge and Hidden Promise of Globalization*. New York: Crown, 2000.

Midlarsky, Manus I. "Preventing Systemic War," *Journal of Conflict Resolution* 28 (December 1984): 563–584.

Miller, Lynn. *Global Order: Values and Power in International Politics*. Boulder, CO: Westview, 1985 and 1990.

Mishra, Aneil K. "Organizational Responses to Crises: The Centrality of Trust," pp. 261–287 in *Trust in Organizations: Frontiers of Theory and Research*, edited by Roderick M. Kramer and Tom R. Tyler. London: Sage, 1996.

Misztal, Barbara A. *Trust in Modern Societies: The Search for the Bases of Social Order*. Oxford: Polity Press, 1996.

Modelski, George. *Principles of World Politics*, New York: Free Press, 1972.

Modelski, George, and William R. Thompson. *Leading Sectors and World Powers*. Columbia: University of South Carolina Press, 1996.

———. *Seapower in Global Politics, 1494–1993*. Seattle: University of Washington Press, 1988.

Moore, Rebecca R. "Globalization and the Future of U. S. Human Rights Policy," *The Washington Quarterly* 21 (Autumn 1998): 193–212.

Morgenthau, Hans J. *Politics Among Nations: The Struggle for Power and Peace*, 6th ed., rev. by Kenneth W. Thompson. New York: Alfred A. Knopf, 1985.

Mowat, R. B. *A History of European Diplomacy, 1451–1789*. London: Edward Arnold, 1928.

Murphy, Cornelius F., Jr. *The Search for World Order*. Dordrecht: Martinus Nijhoff, 1985.

———. "The Grotian Vision of World Order," *American Journal of International Law* 76 (July 1982): 477–498.

Murphy, Craig N. *International Organization and Industrial Change: Global Governance Since 1850*. New York: Oxford University Press, 1994.

Murumba, Samuel K. "Grappling With A Grotian Moment: Sovereignty and the Quest for a Normative World Order," *Brooklyn Journal of International Law* 19 (No. 3, 1993): 829–869.

Nagel, Thomas. *Moral Questions*. Cambridge: Cambridge University Press, 1979.

Naylor, F. Hare. *The Civil and Military History of Germany, from the Landing of Gustavus to the Conclusion of the Treaty of Westphalia.* London: J. Murray, 1816.

Neustadt, Richard E., and Ernest R. May. *Thinking in Time: The Use of History for Decision Makers.* New York: Free Press, 1986.

Newman, Charles. "What's Left Out of Literature," *New York Times Book Review* (July 7, 1987): 1, 24–25.

Niebuhr, Reinhold. *The Structure of Nations and Empires.* New York: Charles Scribner's Sons, 1959.

———. *Moral Man and Immoral Society: A Study of Ethics and Politics.* New York: Charles Scribner's Sons, 1932.

Nordlinger, Eric A. *Isolationism Reconfigured: American Foreign Policy for a New Century.* Princeton, NJ: Princeton University Press, 1995.

Northrop, F. S. C. *The Taming of The Nations: A Study of the Cultural Bases of International Policy.* New York: Macmillan, 1954.

Numelin, Ragnar. *The Beginning of Diplomacy.* London: Oxford University Press, 1950.

Nye, Joseph S., Jr. "The Changing Nature of World Power," pp. 94–106 in *The Global Agenda,* 6th ed, edited by Charles W. Kegley, Jr. and Eugene R. Wittkopt. Boston: McGraw-Hill, 2001.

———. "Redefining NATO's Mission in the Information Age," *NATO Review* 47 (Winter 1999): 12–15.

———. "What New World Order?" *Foreign Affairs* 71 (Spring 1992): 83–96.

———. *Bound To Lead: The Changing Nature of American Power.* New York: Basic Books, 1990.

Ogg, David. *Europe in the Seventeenth Century.* London: Adam and Charles Black, 1948; and New York: Collier Books, 1960.

Ogier, François. *Journal du Congrès de Munster.* Paris: Librairie Plon, 1893.

Ogilvie, Sheilagh C. "Germany and the Seventeenth Century Crisis," *The Historical Journal* 35 (No. 2, 1992): 417–441.

Organski, A. F. K. *World Politics.* New York: Knopf, 1968.

Osgood, Charles E. *An Alternative to War or Surrender.* Urbana: University of Illinois Press, 1962.

Osiander, Andreas. *The States System of Europe, 1640–1990.* New York: Oxford University Press, 1994.

Pages, Georges. *The Thirty Years' War.* London: Adam and Charles Black, 1970.

Palmer, R. R., and Joel Colton. *A History of the Modern World,* 7th ed. New York: Knopf, 1984.

Pangle, Thomas L., and Peter J. Ahrensdorf. *Justice Among Nations: On the Moral Basis of Power and Peace.* Lawrence: University Press of Kansas, 1999.

Parker, Geoffrey. ed. *The Thirty Years' War.* New York: Rutledge, 1998a.

———. *The World Is Not Enough: The Grand Strategy of Philip II.* New Haven, CT: Yale University Press, 1998b.

———. *The Thirty Years' War.* London: Routledge & Kegan Paul, 1984.

———. "The Thirty Years' War," *History Today* 32 (August 1982): 50–51.

Parks, Craig D., and Samuel S. Komorita. "Reciprocity Research and Its Implications for the Negotiation Process," *International Negotiation* 3 (No. 2, 1998): 151–169.

Parry, Clive. "The Function of Law in the International Community," pp. 1–54 in *Manual of Public International Law,* edited by Max Sørensen. New York: St. Martin's, 1968.

Paskins, Barrie. "Obligation and the Understanding of International Relations," pp.

153–170 in *The Reason of States: A Study of International Political Theory*, edited by Michael Donelan. London: Allen & Unwin, 1978.

Patchen, Martin. "When Does Reciprocity in the Actions of Nations Occur?" *International Negotiation* 3 (No. 2, 1998): 171–196.

———. *Resolving Disputes Between Nations: Coercion or Conciliation?* Durham: Duke University Press, 1988.

Paul, Darel E. "Sovereignty, Survival and the Westphalian Blind Alley in International Relations," *Review of International Studies* 25 (No. 2, 1999): 217–231.

Pelton, Joseph N. "Telecommunication for the 21st Century," *Scientific American* 278 (April 1998): 80–85.

Pentland, Charles. *International Theory and European Integration*. New York: Free Press, 1973.

Peterson, Donald K. "Globalization and Telecommunications Leadership: The Future Ain't What It Used to Be," *Vital Speeches of the Day* 56 (June 15, 1990): 529.

Petrie, Charles. *Earlier Diplomatic History, 1492–1713*. London: Hollis and Carter, 1949.

Phillimore, Walter Frank George. *Three Centuries of Treaties of Peace*. London: John Murray, 1917.

Phillips, Warren R., and Robert C. Crain. "Dynamic Foreign Policy Interactions: Reciprocity and Uncertainty in Foreign Policy," pp. 227–266 in *Sage International Yearbook of Foreign Policy Studies*, Vol. 2, edited by Patrick J. McGowan. Beverly Hills: Sage, 1974.

Philpott, Daniel. "The Religious Roots of Modern International Relations," *World Politics* 52 (January 2000): 206–245.

———. "Sovereignty: An Introduction and Brief History," *Journal of International Affairs* 48 (Winter 1995): 353–368.

Pickles, Dorothy. "France: Tradition and Change," pp. 203–236 in *The Foreign Policies of the Powers*, edited by F. S. Northedge. New York: Free Press, 1974.

Pilisuk, M., and P. Skolnick. "Inducing Trust: A Test of the Osgood Proposal," *Journal of Personality and Social Psychology* 20 (No. 1, 1968): 122–133.

Pillar, Paul R. *Negotiating Peace: War Termination as a Bargaining Process*. Princeton, NJ: Princeton University Press, 1983.

Pinson, Koppel S. *Modern Germany*. New York: Macmillan, 1966.

Pirages, Dennis. *Global Technopolitics: The International Politics of Technology and Resources*. Belmont, CA: Brooks/Cole, 1989.

Polisensky, Joseph. *War and Society in Europe, 1618–1648*. New York: Cambridge University Press, 1978.

Porshnev, F. Boris. *Muscovy and Sweden in the Thirty Years' War*. New York: Cambridge University Press, 1995.

Porter, Bruce D. *War and the Rise of the State*. New York: Free Press, 1994.

Preece, Jennifer Jackson. "Minority Rights in Europe: From Westphalia to Helsinki," *Review of International Studies* 23 (No. 1, 1997): 75–92.

Pruitt, Dean G., and Jeffrey Z. Rubin. *Social Conflict: Escalation, Stalemate, and Settlement*. New York: Random House, 1986.

Quinton, Anthony. "Political Philosophy," pp. 274–362 in *The Oxford History of Western Philosophy*, edited by Anthony Kenny. Oxford: Oxford University Press, 1994.

Rabb, Theodore. *The Thirty Years' War. Problems of Motive, Extent, and Effect*. Boston: Heath, 1964.

Randle, Robert F. *The Origins of Peace*. New York: Free Press, 1973.

Ray, James Lee. *Democracy and International Conflict: An Evaluation of the Democratic Peace Proposition.* Columbia, University of South Carolina Press, 1995.

Raymond, Gregory A. "Necessity in Foreign Policy," *Political Science Quarterly* 113 (No. 4, 1998–1999): 673–688.

———. "Problems and Prospects in the Study of International Norms," *Mershon International Studies Review* 41 (November 1997): 205–245.

———. "Demosthenes and Democracies: Regime-Types and Arbitration Outcomes," *International Interactions* 22 (No. 1, 1991a): 1–20.

———. "The Use of Ethotic Argument in Foreign Policy," pp. 1036–1040 in *Proceedings of the Second International Conference of Argumentation,* edited by Frans H. Van Eemeren et al. Amsterdam: Strichting Internationaal Centrum voor de Studie van Argumentatie en Taalbeheersing, 1991b.

———. "Canada Between the Superpowers: Reciprocity and Conformity in Foreign Policy," *American Review of Canadian Studies* 17 (Summer 1987): 221–236.

Raymond, Gregory A., and Richard A. Skinner. "An Extension and Replication of Findings on the Role of Third Parties in the Middle East," *International Interactions* 4 (No. 2, 1978): 155–176.

Reade, H. G. Revell. *Sidelights on the Thirty Years' War.* London: K. Paul, Trench, Trubner, 1924.

Reddaway, William F. *A History of Europe: From 1610 to 1715.* London: Methvuen, 1948.

Regan, Patrick M. *Civil Wars and Foreign Powers: Outside Intervention in Intrastate Conflict.* Ann Arbor: University of Michigan Press, 2000.

Reinicke, Wolfgang H. "Global Public Policy," *Foreign Affairs* 76 (November-December 1997): 127–138.

Rempel, Gerhard. *The Thirty Years' War.* Available from Internet, 1998. http://mars.acnet .wnec.edu/~grempel/courses/wc2/lectures/30yearswar/html.

Rengger, Nicholas. "The Ethics of Trust in World Politics," *International Affairs* 73 (No. 3, 1997): 469–487.

Reynolds, David. *One World Divisible.* New York: W. W. Norton, 2000.

Richardson, Neil, Charles W. Kegley, Jr., and Ann Agnew. "Symmetry and Reciprocity as Characteristics of Dyadic Foreign Policy Behavior," *Social Science Quarterly* 62 (March 1981): 128–138.

Richelieu, Cardinal (Armand Jean du Plessis). *The Political Testament of Cardinal Richelieu.* Translated by Henry Bertram Hill. Madison: University of Wisconsin Press, 1961.

Riker, Thad W. *A History of Modern Europe.* New York: Knopf, 1949.

Ringmar, Erik. *Identity, Interest and Action: A Cultural Explanation of Sweden's Intervention in the Thirty Years' War.* New York: Cambridge University Press, 1996.

Roberts, Adam. "Grotius," pp. 368–369 in *The Oxford Companion to Politics of the World,* edited by Joel Krieger. New York: Oxford University Press, 1993.

Roberts, Michael. *Essays in Swedish History.* London: Weidenfeld & Nicolson, 1967.

———. *Gustavus Adolphus: A History of Sweden 1611–1632.* 2 vols. London: Longmans, Green, 1958.

Rocca, Francis X. "High Art, Humble Origins," *Wall Street Journal* (August 23, 2000): A20.

Rochester, J. Martin. *Between Two Epochs: What's Ahead for America, the World, and Global Politics in the Twenty-First Century?* Upper Saddle River, NJ: Prentice Hall, 2002.

Roelofs, H. Mark. "Comment on Michael C. Munger's 'Political Science and Fundamental Research,'" *PS* 33 (September 2000): 517–519.

Roelofsen, Cornelis. "Grotius and the Development of International Relations Theory," *Grotiana* 18 (1997): 97–120.

Rosecrance, Richard. *The Rise of the Virtual State.* New York: Basic Books, 1999.

———. *The Rise of the Trading State: Commerce and Conquest in the Modern World.* New York: Basic Books, 1986.

Rosenau, James N. "Stability, Stasis, and Security: Reflections on Superpower Leadership," *Global Forum* 1 (June 2000): 1–65

———. "Toward an Ontology for Global Governance," pp. 287–301 in *Approaches to Global Governance Theory,* edited by Martin Hewson and Timothy J. Sinclair. Albany: State University of New York Press, 1999.

———. *Turbulence in World Politics: A Theory of Change and Continuity.* Princeton, NJ: Princeton University Press, 1990.

Rosenthal, Joel H. "From Victory to Peace," *Mershon International Studies Review* 42 (December 1998): 363–365.

———. *Righteous Realists.* Baton Rouge: Louisiana State University Press, 1991.

Rothkopf, David. "Cyberpolitik: The Changing Nature of Power in the Information Age," *Journal of International Affairs* 51 (Spring 1998): 325–359.

———. "In Praise of Cultural Imperialism?" *Foreign Policy* 107 (Summer 1997): 38–53.

Royal, Robert. "Columbus and The Beginnings of the World," *First Things* 93 (May 1999): 32–38.

Rubin, Trudy. "Dangerous Doctrine," *The State* (Columbia, SC) (September 5, 2000): A7.

Russell, William. *The History of Modern Europe.* Philadelphia: A. Small, 1802.

Russett, Bruce. *Grasping the Democratic Peace: Principles for a Post-Cold War World.* Princeton, NJ: Princeton University Press, 1993.

Said, Abdul A., and Luiz R. Simmons, eds. *Ethnicity in an International Context.* New Brunswick, NJ: Transaction Books, 1976.

Sakamoto, Yoshikazu, ed. *Global Transformation: Challenges to the State System.* Tokyo: United Nations Press, 1994.

Sample, Susan G. "Arms Races and Dispute Escalation: Resolving the Debate?" *Journal of Peace Research* 34 (February 1997): 7–22.

Sassen, Saskia. *Losing Control? Sovereignty in an Age of Globalization.* New York: Columbia University Press, 1996.

Scheff, Thomas J. *Bloody Revenge: Emotions, Nationalism, and War.* Boulder, CO: Westview, 1994

Scheingold, Stuart A. "Domestic and International Consequences of Regional Integration," pp. 374–398 in *Regional Integration: Theory and Research,* edited by Leon N. Lindberg and Stuart A. Scheingold. Cambridge: Harvard University Press, 1971.

Schiller, Friedrich von. *History of the Thirty Years' War.* New York: Harper & Brothers, 1864.

———. *The History of the Thirty Years' War in Germany.* Translated by Captain Blaquiere. London: 1799.

Schumpeter, Joseph A. "The Sociology of Imperialisms," pp. 3–130 in *Imperialism and Social Classes,* translated by Heinz Norden. New York: Meridian Books, 1955.

Schwarzenberger, Georg. "The Fundamental Principles of International Law," pp. 195–383 in *Recueil des Cours,* Vol. 1. Leyden: A. W. Sijthoff, 1956.

Seligman, Adam B. *The Problem of Trust.* Princeton, NJ: Princeton University Press, 1997.

Senn, Frank C. *Christian Liturgy: Catholic and Evangelical.* Minneapolis, MN: Fortress Press, 1997.

Setton, K. Meyer. *Venice, Austria, and the Turks in the Seventeenth Century.* Philadelphia: American Philosophical Society, 1991.

Shakelford, Todd K., and David M. Buss. "Betrayal in Mates, Friendships, and Coalitions," *Personality and Social Psychology Bulletin* 22 (November 1996): 1151–1164.

Shriver, Donald W., Jr. *An Ethic for Enemies: Forgiveness in Politics.* New York: Oxford University Press, 1995.

Simai, Mihaly. *The Future of Global Governance: Managing Risk and Change in the International System.* Washington, DC: United States Institute of Peace Press, 1994.

Singer, J. David. "Peace in the Global System: Displacement, Interregnum, or Transformation?" pp. 56–84 in *The Long Postwar Peace,* edited by Charles W. Kegley, Jr. New York: HarperCollins, 1991.

Singer, Max, and Aaron Wildavsky. *The Real World Order.* Chatham, NJ: Chatham House, 1993.

Siverson, Randolph M., and Joel King. "Alliances and the Extension of War," pp. 37–49 in *To Auger Well,* edited by J. David Singer and Michael Wallace. Beverly Hills: Sage, 1979.

Smith, Anthony D. *Myths and Memories of the Nation,* New York: Oxford University Press, 1999.

Smith, Steve. "Is the Truth Out There? Eight Questions About International Order," pp. 99–110 in *International Order and the Future of World Politics,* edited by T. V. Paul and John A. Hall. Cambridge: Cambridge University Press, 1999.

Sørensen, Max. *Manuel of Public International Law.* New York: St. Martin's, 1968.

Sorokin, Pitirim. *Modern Historical and Social Philosophies.* New York: Dover, 1963.

Soroos, Marvin S. "Global Institutions and the Environment: An Evolutionary Perspective," pp. 27–51 in *The Global Environment,* edited by Norman J. Vig and Regina S. Axelrod. Washington, DC: Congressional Quarterly Press, 1999.

Soros, George. "The Age of Open Society," *Foreign Policy* 119 (Summer 2000): 52–53.

Sporschill, Johann. *Der Dreissigjahrige Krieg.* New York: G. &B. Westermann, 1848.

Spruyt, Hendrik. "The End of Empire and the Extension of the Westphalian System: The Normative Basis of the Modern State Order," *International Studies Review* 2 (Summer 2000): 65–92.

———. *The Sovereign State and Its Competitors.* Princeton, NJ: Princeton University Press, 1994.

Starr, Harvey. "The Institutional Maintenance of Twenty-First Century World Order," pp. 216–229 in *The Global Agenda,* edited by Charles W. Kegley, Jr. and Eugene Wittkopf. New York: McGraw-Hill, 2001.

———. *Anarchy, Order, and Integration: How To Manage Interdependence.* Ann Arbor: University of Michigan Press, 1997.

Stein, Janice Gross, and Louis W. Pauly. *Choosing to Cooperate: How States Avoid Loss.* Baltimore: The Johns Hopkins University Press, 1993.

Steinbruner, John. D. *Principles of Global Security.* Washington, DC: Brookings Institution, 2000.

Stockholm International Peace Research Institute (SIPRI) *SIPRI Yearbook 2000.* Stockholm: International Peace Research Institute, 2000.

Strange, Susan. "The Westfailure System," *Review of International Studies* 25 (No. 3, 1999): 345–354.

———. *The Retreat of the State: The Diffusion of Power in the World Economy.* Cambridge: Cambridge University Press, 1996.

Strong, C. F. *Dynamic Europe: A Background of Ferment and Change.* London: University of London Press, 1945.

Swift, Adam. *Global Political Ecology.* London: Pluto Press, 1993.

Tajfel, H. *Social Identity and Intergroup Relations.* Cambridge: Cambridge University Press, 1982.

Tallett, Frank. *War and Society in Early-Modern Europe 1495–1715.* New York: Routledge, 1992.

Tavuchis, N. *Mea Culpa: A Sociology of Apology and Reconciliation.* Stanford, CA: Stanford University Press, 1991.

Tesón, Fernando R. *Humanitarian Intervention: An Inquiry into Law and Morality.* Dobbs Ferry, NY: Transnational Publishers, 1988.

The History of Treaties. London: J. Baker, 1712.

Thibaut, John W., and Harold H. Kelly. *The Social Psychology of Groups.* New York: John Wiley, 1959.

Thompson, Kenneth W. *Fathers of International Thought,* Baton Rouge: Louisiana State University Press, 1994.

Thompson, William R., ed. *Great Power Rivalries.* Columbia: University of South Carolina Press, 1999.

———. "Dehio, Long Cycles, and the Geohistorical Context of Structural Transition," *World Politics* 45 (October 1992): 127–152.

———. "The World-Economy, The Long Cycle, and the Question of World-System Time," pp. 35–62 in *Foreign Policy and the Modern World System,* edited by Pat McGowan and Charles W. Kegley, Jr. Beverly Hills, CA: Sage, 1983.

Thompson, William R., and David Rapkin. "Conflict, Inertia, and Reciprocity: Coping with the Western Bloc," in pp. 241–265 *Foreign Policy: USA/USSR,* edited by Charles W. Kegley, Jr. and Pat McGowan. Beverly Hills: Sage, 1982.

———. "Collaboration, Consensus, and Détente: The External Threat-Bloc Cohesion Hypothesis," *Journal of Conflict Resolution* 25 (December 1981): 615–637.

Thomson, David, E. Meyer, and A. Briggs. *Patterns of Peacemaking.* London: Kegan, Paul and Trench, 1945.

Tikkanen, Henrik. *The Thirty Years' War.* Lincoln: University of Nebraska Press, 1987.

Toulmin, Stephen. *Cosmopolis: The Hidden Agenda of Modernity.* Chicago: University of Chicago Press, 1990.

Toynbee, Arnold J. *A Study of History,* Vol. 9. London: Oxford University Press, 1984.

Trachman, Joel. "Reflections on the Nature of the State: Sovereignty, Power and Responsibility," *Canada-United States Law Journal* 20 (1994): 399–415.

Tuchman, Barbara W. *The March of Folly: From Troy to Vietnam.* New York: Ballantine Books, 1984.

Turner, J. C. *Rediscovering the Social Group: A Self-Categorization Theory.* Oxford: Basil Blackwell, 1987.

Union of International Associations. *Yearbook of International Organizations.* Munich: K. G. Sauer, 2000.

United Nations Development Programme. *Human Development Report.* New York: Oxford University Press, 1999.

Valentin, Veit. *The German People.* New York: Alfred A. Knopf, 1946.

Van Creveld, Martin. "The New Middle Ages," *Foreign Policy* 119 (Summer 2000): 38–40.

Van Dervort, Thomas R. *International Law and Organization.* London: Sage, 1998.

Vasquez, John. *The Power of Power Politics.* Cambridge: Cambridge University Press, 1998.

———. *The War Puzzle.* Cambridge: Cambridge University Press, 1993.

Väyrynen, Raimo. "Norms, Compliance, and Enforcement in Global Governance," pp. 25–46 in *Globalization and Global Governance,* edited by Raimo Väyrynen. Lanham, MD: Rowman & Littlefield, 1999.

Viault, Birdsall S. *Modern European History*. New York: McGraw Hill, 1990.

Vincent, R. J. *Human Rights and International Relations*. New York: Cambridge University Press, 1986.

Vinogradoff, Paul. *Outline of Historical Jurisprudence*. London and New York: Oxford University Press, 1920.

Walker, R. B. J. *Inside/Outside: International Relations as Political Theory*. Cambridge: Cambridge University Press, 1993.

Wallace, Michael. "Alliance Polarization, Cross-Cutting, and International War, 1815–1964: A Measurement Procedure and Some Preliminary Evidence," *Journal of Conflict Resolution* 17 (December 1973): 575–604.

———. "Status, Formal Organization, and Arms Levels as Factors Leading to the Onset of War, 1820–1964," pp. 49–69 in *Peace, War, and Numbers*, edited by Bruce M. Russett. Beverly Hills: Sage, 1972.

Wallensteen, Peter, and Margareta Sollenberg. "Armed Conflict, 1989–99," *Journal of Peace Research* 37 (September 2000), 635–649.

Wallerstein, Immanuel. *The Politics of the World-Economy*. Cambridge: Cambridge University Press, 1984.

Waltz, Kenneth N. "Structural Realism After the Cold War," *International Security* 25 (Summer 2000): 5–41.

Walzer, Michael. *Just and Unjust Wars*. New York: Basic Books, 1977.

Ward, A. W. "The Peace of Westphalia," pp. 395–433 in *The Cambridge Modern History*, Vol. 4, *The Thirty Years' War*. Cambridge: Cambridge University Press, 1966.

Ward, Robert Plummer. *An Enquiry into the Foundation and History of the Law of Nations in Europe*, Vol. 1. London: J. Butterworth, 1795.

Watson, Adam. *The Evolution of International Society*. London: Routledge, 1992.

Watson, Francis. *Wallenstein, Soldier Under Saturn: a Biography*. New York: Appleton-Century-Crofts, 1938.

Wayman, Frank W. "Bipolarity and War: The Role of Capability Concentration and Alliance Patterns Among Major Powers, 1816–1965," *Journal of Peace Research* 21 (No. 1, 1984): 61–77.

Wayman, Frank W., and Paul F. Diehl, eds. *Reconstructing Realpolitik*. Ann Arbor: University of Michigan Press, 1994.

Wechsler, Herbert. "The Issue of the Nuremberg Trial," pp. 125–136 in *From Nuremberg to My Lai*, edited by Jay W. Baird. Lexington, MA: D. C. Heath, 1972.

Wedgwood, C. Veronica. *Der Dreissigjahrige Krieg*. Munchen: Pl List, 1967.

———. *The Thirty Years' War*. London: Jonathan Cape, 1944; and London: Lowe & Breydone, 1938.

Weede, Erich. "Democracy and War Involvement," *Journal of Conflict Resolution* 20 (September 1984): 395–411.

Weiss, Linda. *The Myth of the Powerless State*. Ithaca, NY: Cornell University Press, 1998.

Welch, David A. *Justice and the Genesis of War*. Cambridge: Cambridge University Press, 1993.

Weston, Burns H., Richard A. Falk, and Anthony A. D'Amato. *International Law and World Order*. St. Paul: West, 1980.

Wight, Martin. *Systems of States*. Leicester: University of Leicester Press, 1977.

———. "The Balance of Power," pp. 148–175, in *Diplomatic Investigations*, edited by Herbert Butterfield and Martin Wight. Cambridge, MA: Harvard University Press, 1968a.

————. "Western Values in International Relations," pp. 89–131 in *Diplomatic Investigations*, edited by Herbert Butterfield and Martin Wight. Cambridge, MA: Harvard University Press, 1968b.

Wilkinson, David. "Unipolarity Without Hegemony," *International Studies Review* 1 (Summer 1999): 141–172.

Willetts, Peter. "Transnational Actors and International Organizations in Global Politics," pp. 287–310 in *The Globalization of World Politics*, edited by John Baylis and Steve Smith. Oxford: Oxford University Press, 1997.

Wilson, Peter H. "War in German Thought from the Peace of Westphalia to Napoleon," *European History Quarterly* 28 (No. 1, 1998): 5–50.

Wolgast, Elizabeth. *The Grammar of Justice*. Ithaca, NY: Cornell University Press. 1987.

Wright, Quincy. "How Hostilities Have Ended: Peace Treaties and Alternatives," *The Annals* 392 (November 1970): 51–61.

————. "The Outlawry of War and the Law of War," *American Journal of International Law* 47 (July 1953): 365–376.

————. *A Study of War.* Chicago: University of Chicago Press, 1942.

Wright, Robert. *Non Zero: The Logic of Human Destiny.* New York: Random House, 2000a.

————. "Pax Kapital," *Foreign Policy* 119 (Summer 2000b): 67–68.

Wriston, Walter B. *The Twilight of Sovereignty: How the Information Revolution Is Transforming Our World.* New York: Scribner's, 1992.

Wrong, Dennis. "The Oversocialized Conception of Man in Modern Sociology," *American Sociological Review* 26 (No. 2, 1961): 183–193.

Young, Oran R. "The Actors in World Politics," pp. 125–144 in *The Analysis of International Politics,* edited by James N. Rosenau, Vincent Davis, and Maurice A. East. New York: Free Press, 1972.

Zacher, Mark W. "The Decaying Pillars of the Westphalian Temple: Implications for International Order and Governance," pp. 58–101 in *Governance Without Government: Order and Change in World Politics,* edited by James N. Rosenau and Ernst-Otto Czempiel. Cambridge: Cambridge University Press, 1992.

Zakaria, Fareed. "The Empire Strikes Out: The Unholy Emergence of the Nation-State," *New York Times Magazine* (April 18, 1999): 99.

Zeller, Gaston. *Les Temps Modernes,* Vol. II: *De Christophe Colombe á Cromwell;* Vol. III: *De Louis XIV á 1789.* Paris: Hachette, 1955.

Photo Credits

Index

and trust, 215
tolerance. *See also* intolerance
  in Bohemia, 56
  in France, 46
  and Thirty Years' War, 96
  and Westphalia, 137
Torstensson, Lennart, 76, 81, 83
trade
  maritime, 140–143, 146
  and national borders, 161–162
  and Netherlands, 140–142
  post World War II, 160
  and sovereignty, 225
  and Thirty Years' War, 95–96
transparency, 202, 215
Transylvania, 59
Trauttmansdorff, Maximilian Graf, 110
treaties. *See also specific treaties*
  binding nature, 191–192
  Grotian view, 121, 191
  post-Westphalian, 141 (graph)
  and war spirit, 12, 103
trends. *See also* globalization
  civil society, 165–166
  democratization, 164–165
  failed states, 168–170
  humanitarian intervention, 166–168
  organizing principle, 152–153
  parochialism, 172
trust. *See also* credibility; mistrust
  versus accomodation, 215
  building, 213–221
  concept, 206–207
  and globalization, 203, 220–221
  identity-based, 209–210, 216–221
  and *laissez faire,* 152–153
  reciprocity-based, 208–209, 214–216, 225
  and shared goals, 216
  types, 207–210
Tuchman, Barbara, 28–29, 30–31
Turner, J. C., 209
twenty-first century
  parallels with seventeenth, 2–3, 17–19, 149–151, 180–185
  peace plans, 155
  U.S. role, 186

U

unilateralism, 155, 200
Union of Utrecht, 231 n.86
United Nations. *See also* Annan, Kofi

and force, 197–198
and human rights, 167–168, 197–198, 223
Millenium Summit, 173–174, 194–196
peacekeeping function, 181
and sovereignty, 223
Stockholm Declaration, 163
and Westphalia, 107
United Provinces. *See* Netherlands
United States
  and elections, 165
  twenty-first century role, 185–188
Universal Declaration of Human Rights, 167
universalism, 135, 151. *See also* cosmopolitanism
Urban VIII, 61, 82, 115
Ursulines, 34
Ury, William, 215, 217
Utrecht, Treaty of, 125, 145, 147, 179

V

Valentin, Veit, 99, 109, 111, 127
Valtellina, 59, 61–62, 80
values
  and globalization, 173
  Machiavellian, 22–23
  of Richelieu, 72
  and Thirty Years' War, 93
  and trust, 209–210
  Western, 171
Van Creveld, Martin, 199, 223
Vasquez, John, 212, 214
Väyrynen, Raimo, 255 n.107
Venezuela, 193
vengeance, 73
Versailles, Congress of, 125
Viault, Birdsall S., 46
Vienna, Congress of, 125
Vincent, R. J., 199
Viotti, Paul, 72, 118, 119
virtualization, 160–161
Volmar, Isaac, 110
Von Hutton, Ulrich, 32
Von Mansfeld, Albert, 66
Von Sickingen, Franz, 32

W

Wallenstein (Waldstein, Albrecht Wenceslas von), 64
  dismissal, 53, 68